SOCIAL DIAGNOSIS

BY

MARY E. RICHMOND

DIRECTOR CHARITY ORGANIZATION DEPARTMENT
RUSSELL SAGE FOUNDATION
AUTHOR OF
"THE GOOD NEIGHBOR," ETC.

NEW YORK
RUSSELL SAGE FOUNDATION
1917

Printed May, 1917
Reprinted June, 1917
Reprinted October, 1917
Reprinted April, 1918
Reprinted October, 1918
Reprinted October, 1919
Reprinted July, 1921
Reprinted June, 1923
Reprinted December, 1925
Reprinted July, 1928
Reprinted August, 1930
Reprinted June, 1932
Reprinted June, 1934
Reprinted February, 1935
Reprinted April, 1936
Reprinted November, 1940
Reprinted November, 1945
Reprinted April, 1955
Reprinted January, 1964

WM. F. FELL CO · PRINTERS
PHILADELPHIA

TO

ZILPHA DREW SMITH

WHOSE STEADY FAITH IN THE POSSIBILITIES OF SOCIAL CASE WORK HAS BEEN THE INSPIRATION OF THIS BOOK AND OF ITS AUTHOR

One of the most striking facts with regard to the conscious life of any human being is that it is interwoven with the lives of others. It is in each man's social relations that his mental history is mainly written, and it is in his social relations likewise that the causes of the disorders that threaten his happiness and his effectiveness and the means for securing his recovery are to be mainly sought.

—*DR. JAMES JACKSON PUTNAM*

No matter how mean or hideous a man's life is, the first thing is to understand him; to make out just how it is that our common human nature has come to work out in this way. This method calls for patience, insight, firmness, and confidence in men, leaving little room for the denunciatory egotism of a certain kind of reformers. It is more and more coming to be used in dealing with intemperance, crime, greed, and in fact all those matters in which we try to make ourselves and our neighbors better.

—*CHARLES HORTON COOLEY*

Only the sham knows everything; the trained man understands how little the mind of any individual may grasp, and how many must co-operate in order to explain the very simplest things.

—*HANS GROSS*

PREFACE

FIFTEEN years ago, I began to take notes, gather illustrations, and even draft a few chapters for a book on Social Work in Families. In it I hoped to pass on to the younger people coming into the charity organization field an explanation of the methods that their seniors had found useful. It soon became apparent, however, that no methods or aims were peculiarly and solely adapted to the treatment of the families that found their way to a charity organization society; that, in essentials, the methods and aims of social case work were or should be the same in every type of service, whether the subject was a homeless paralytic, the neglected boy of drunken parents, or the widowed mother of small children. Some procedures, of course, were peculiar to one group of cases and some to another, according to the special social disability under treatment. But the things that most needed to be said about case work were the things that were common to all. The division of social work into departments and specialties was both a convenience and a necessity; fundamental resemblances remained, however.

With other practitioners—with physicians and lawyers, for example—there was always a basis of knowledge held in common. If a neurologist had occasion to confer with a surgeon, each could assume in the other a mastery of the elements of a whole group of basic sciences and of the formulated and transmitted experience of his own guild besides. But what common knowledge could social workers assume in like case? This was my query of fifteen years ago. It seemed to me then, and it is still my opinion, that the elements of social diagnosis, if formulated, should constitute a part of the ground which all social case workers could occupy in common, and that it should become possible in time to take for granted, in every social practitioner, a knowledge and mastery of those elements, and of the modifications in them which each decade of practice would surely bring.

This narrowed my proposed topic to the beginning processes of case work, but at the same time widened it enormously in demanding for its treatment an experience of all the various types of such work. As the executive head, in those days, of a large family agency, I had little time for study, so the task was set aside for nearly nine years.

More than six years ago, however, after I had become a member of the staff of the Russell Sage Foundation, it was again taken up.

Meanwhile, the wider usefulness of social evidence, social diagnosis, and social treatment, both in their own special field and in the other professions, even when these latter dealt with people who were neither dependent nor delinquent, had begun to dawn upon me. It was evident that social case work could supplement the work of justice, of healing, and of teaching. Groups of workers in some of our American cities, moreover, were doing notable things in the regular social agencies; they were developing quietly a diagnostic skill in dealing with the difficulties of human beings which should be given ample opportunity, especially in its formative period, to grow to the full stature of social technique, untrammeled by long established professional traditions, whether of courts, hospitals, or schools.

I turned to this task in the winter of 1910–11 for the second time, therefore, with a quite different outlook from that of earlier days and with the determination to push my inquiries as far beyond the limits of my own personal experience as possible. Mr. Francis H. McLean, who was my colleague in the Foundation at the time of this second beginning and who has rendered invaluable assistance throughout the undertaking, had already invited a group of social case workers (most of them but not all connected with charity organization societies) to prepare short papers describing informally their methods and experiences in taking the steps which, in their work, preceded the development of a plan of treatment. This group was added to later, and some of their papers—on such subjects, for instance, as present neighborhood sources of information, relations with employers in the study of a work record, methods of conducting a first interview, etc.—were privately printed and given a limited circulation among their fellow workers in charity organization. This was done partly for the purpose of getting the benefit of criticisms. The papers were too experimental for publication. They contained passages of great value, however, of which free use has been made, with credit given, in Part II of this book.

The next step was to engage two case workers of experience—one in family and one in medical-social work—to study original case records for a year. Their case reading was done in five different cities. No attempt was made to arrive at an average of the case work in these cities. On the contrary, our aim was to bring to light the best social work practice that could be found, provided it was actually in use and not altogether exceptional in character. In addition these case readers held many interviews with case workers, all of which were carefully reported. As my own experience had been so largely in the charity organization field, especial pains was taken to center most of this case reading and interviewing in the child-helping and the medical-social agencies. A large part of the illustrative material used so freely in Part II is drawn from the much larger stock of case notes and of reports of interviews prepared by these two case readers, though use has also been made of notes from my own case reading and of the field memoranda of my colleagues in the Charity Organization Department of the Foundation.

As this Department had been interested from the time of its organization in the teaching of case work in the various schools for social workers, it began to edit a group of original records, most of them current cases, to be used in the class room. These were printed in full with all their sins upon their heads (bad work is almost as instructive as good) and were used in class conferences by a small, accredited group of teachers of case work. Criticisms and comments based upon certain of these records were also gathered from a number of specialists. As noted elsewhere, the experiment of printing the records of cases could not be a public one, because their subjects were real people whose confidences had to be respected. Even when all names had been changed, there were few things more identifiable, we found, than a full social case record. The experiment, limited though it had to be, has brought to light many valuable suggestions which are used in these pages.

For the most part the subject of social diagnosis defies statistical treatment, though as a means of getting started and to arrive at a rough quantitative measure of the relative frequency with which the various outside sources of information and co-operation were consulted, a brief statistical study was made. Fifty-six social agencies engaged in a number of different forms of social case work in three cities were persuaded to let us list the outside sources consulted by each in fifty cases. The results of this study are given in Part II and in one of the Appendices.

One of the minor methods of study adopted was to correspond with or interview social case workers who had changed from one type of case work to another—from work with families to child protection, from settlement work to probation or medical-social service—in order to learn the changes of method and the shiftings of emphasis made necessary by their change of task.

The foregoing methods supplied the data for Part II; and the sifting of these data and the interpretation of what was significant in them have been the work of such portions of several years as could be spared for the task. The errors that were found have been frankly commented upon in this book. Since methods in case work are rapidly improving, these may now belong to the past in the particular places in which we found them. Nevertheless there is always a chance that they are surviving somewhere else.

For the variations in the processes leading to diagnosis, still another method of gathering data was tried. How could these variations, many of them made necessary by the different types of social disability, be indicated comprehensively enough and compactly enough to be of daily service for reference? The plan was hit upon of gathering in from many specialists suggestions for a series of type questionnaires—not to consist of questions to be asked the case worker's client, not schedules to be filled out, but lists of suggestive queries which, at some time in his inquiry, the case worker might find it worth while to ask of himself. Such a battery of interrogations as is presented in Part III is sure to be misunderstood by somebody; it is confessedly a clumsy device, but no other way has occurred to me or my colleagues of giving the case worker, in small compass, a bird's-eye view of the *possible* implications of a given disability. It will be seen that some questionnaires were prepared by one hand, some by another; while still others have been made by members of our departmental staff in consultation with case workers. These latter in particular must be understood to be experimental in their present form; they will have to be revised from time to time as it is possible to get further light from specialists who understand not only their own specialty but the needs of social workers.

The most difficult of all my problems has been to make a presentation of the subject of evidence in Part I which would be of practical value to the case worker. He is handling evidence all the time. How can he learn to handle it in such a way as to aid him in achieving a truly social result? When Professor Hans Gross was preparing his large handbook for the investigating officers of European law courts,[1] he planned at first to have each part written by a specialist—by a physician, an armorer, a photographer, etc. But these specialists could not, he finally decided, meet the needs of the investigating officers by sufficiently keeping in view their aims and the conditions of their work. Therefore, though Gross reflected that the various chapters of his book "would have been set out in a more scientific manner" by such a plan, he was constrained for his purpose to adopt a less ambitious one. With far less equipment than Gross, who had an encyclopedic mind, this is what I have had to do, and I could not have done it without very generous help in criticism and revision from those who knew law and history, psychology and logic, as I did not.

Both Professor J. H. Wigmore, Dean of Northwestern University Law School, and Professor Lucy Salmon, head of the department of history at Vassar, have been kind enough to make suggestions regarding individual chapters. Special acknowledgment too should be made of the invaluable service rendered by Mrs. Ada Eliot Sheffield of Cambridge, Massachusetts, who has not only read and criticised the larger part of my manuscript, but in connection with Part I has gathered some of the illustrative material and has given the whole part a thorough revision, amounting in at least two of its chapters to collaboration. Mrs. Sheffield's

[1] Criminal Investigation. A practical handbook for magistrates, police officers, and lawyers. Translated by J. Adam and J. C. Adam. Madras, A. Krishnamachari, 1906.

thorough knowledge of social case work under both state and private auspices has made her assistance doubly valuable.

Acknowledgment cannot be made individually to the several hundred case workers who have answered letters, examined questionnaires, lent case records, and helped me in a dozen other ways. They lead lives filled with demands and are accustomed to spend themselves unsparingly, so that each and all met this one more demand with prompt cheerfulness. Mention can be made, however, of those who have been associated with me in the Russell Sage Foundation in gathering data for this book or in correcting its first draft. Mr. Francis H. McLean should head this list, and the two case readers, Mrs. Hilbert F. Day and Mrs. H. S. Amsden. I am also indebted to Miss Margaret F. Byington, Miss Caroline L. Bedford, and to my present associate, Miss Mary B. Sayles. Valued help was rendered at one stage of gathering material by the departments of social investigation of the Chicago School of Civics and Philanthropy and of the Boston School for Social Workers.

In 1914, as Kennedy lecturer of the New York School of Philanthropy, I used portions of these data that I had then gathered in a course of six lectures. I had to disclaim at that time and do now any idea that one who "crams" technical discussions of method becomes thereby an efficient practitioner. Not only is practice under leadership needed in addition to book knowledge, but an attractive and forceful personality is an indispensable factor. The method that ignores or hampers the individuality of the worker stands condemned not only in social work but in teaching, in the ministry, in art, and in every form of creative endeavor. Yet in none of these disciplines have practitioners refused to profit by process studies in their own field, in none have they found ordered knowledge the enemy of inspiration. Phillips Brooks once said of a certain type of minister, "The more the empty head glows and burns, the more hollow and thin and dry it becomes." Any social worker who has had to gather up the pieces after a supposed original genius who had dispensed with precedent and technique would be at a loss to say which leaves behind him the more completely burnt out territory—the purely inspirational worker or the one who leans too heavily upon rules and formulæ.

For the benefit of those who find certain of the bibliographical references in the footnotes too scant, it should be explained that these have been deliberately cut to the briefest possible form wherever the books or articles referred to, because they bore directly upon my theme, have been included in the Bibliography at the end of the volume. Fuller details will always be found there. It should be added that, in the illustrations taken from actual cases which are given throughout the volume, names have in all instances been changed.

Finally, no one will accuse me of disloyalty to the group with which I have been identified so long because I have not hesitated to point out its present weaknesses on the diagnostic side. My task was undertaken because there were weaknesses, but it could not have been pushed forward if many social case workers had not been doing effective and original work, though often under great difficulties. If, after examining these pages, the harassed and overburdened practitioner is tempted to think their counsels impracticable under the conditions which necessarily limit his daily task, let him ask himself whether "necessarily" does not beg the question, and whether some of those conditions should not and cannot be changed. Then, if he is still sure that I am at fault, or if he finds other errors, whether of omission or of commission, let him write and tell me so. I have good reason for inviting criticism. No one knows better than I how tentative this discussion is. In the remote chance of there being another edition of this book, however, I should like to make it more useful than, with my utmost endeavors, I am now able to.

MARY E. RICHMOND.

New York, April, 1917

TABLE OF CONTENTS

PART I

SOCIAL EVIDENCE

LIST OF TABLES

PART I
SOCIAL EVIDENCE

CHAPTER I

BEGINNINGS

THOUGH the social worker has won a degree of recognition as being engaged in an occupation useful to the community, he is handicapped by the fact that his public is not alive to the difference between going through the motions of doing things and actually getting them done. "Doing good" was the old phrase for social service. It begged the question, as do also the newer terms, "social service" and "social work"—unless society is really served. We should welcome, therefore, the evident desire of social workers to abandon claims to respect based upon good intentions alone; we should meet halfway their earnest endeavors to subject the processes of their task to critical analysis; and should encourage them to measure their work by the best standards supplied by experience—standards which, imperfect now, are being advanced to a point where they can be called professional.

The social workers of the United States form a large occupational group. A majority of them are engaged in case work[1]—in work, that is, which has for its immediate aim the betterment of individuals or families, one by one, as distinguished from their betterment in the mass. Mass betterment and individual betterment are interdependent, however, social reform and social case work of necessity progressing together. This fundamental truth will appear repeatedly as the present discussion of social diagnosis advances.

[1] Thus, a study made of the social workers in New York City, which does not include those in public departments or public institutions, shows that the private agencies of New York were employing in salaried positions 3,968 social workers in 1915. Of this number, 501 were engaged in "community movements—research and propaganda." The city is headquarters for a large majority of the national social reform movements, which fact accounts for the size of this second figure; in any other city it would be a smaller proportion of the total. All the other social workers counted were dealing with individuals, but some of these—in settlements and recreational activities, for example—were giving an unknown proportion of their time to dealing with individuals in groups. Deducting these also, therefore, approximately 2,200, the number remaining, were in social agencies doing case work. See Devine, Edward T., and Van Kleeck, Mary: Positions in Social Work. Pamphlet of the New York School of Philanthropy, 1916.

Since social case work is too large a subject to be covered in one volume, its initial process alone will be the subject of this book.

When a human being, whatever his economic status, develops some marked form of social difficulty and social need, what do we have to know about him and about his difficulty (or more often difficulties) before we can arrive at a way of meeting his need?[1] The problem may be one of childhood or old age, of sickness, of exploitation, or of wasted opportunity, but in so far as it concerns some one individual in his social relationships it is not alien to social work as here understood. The effort to get the essential facts bearing upon a man's social difficulties has commonly been called "an investigation," but the term here adopted as a substitute—social diagnosis—has the advantage that from the first step it fixes the mind of the case worker upon the end in view.[2] The primary purpose of the writer, in attempting an examination of the initial process of social case work, is to make some advance toward a professional standard. The volume, then, is addressed first to social workers.

But another audience has been kept in view in its preparation. Much of the process herein described is undoubtedly applicable, with modification, to human situations which do not come within the purview of social work as now organized. The special field of social diagnosis lies in social case work. It is destined in addition to become an adjunct in the fields of medicine, education, juris-

[1] The word *social* has many meanings. Its use throughout this book assumes that wherever there are two individuals instead of one, human association or society begins. As relations among human beings become groupal, they continue to be social even in groups too large for personal contact, provided the groupal relation continues to influence the minds of the units which compose the group. The more or less arbitrary groupings of human beings in which no such influence is apparent (into dependents or delinquents, for example) are often described as social too, but they do not here concern us. When Dr. James J. Putnam said, in the passage which is one of the mottoes of this volume, "It is in each man's social relations that his mental history is mainly written, and it is in his social relations likewise that the causes of the disorders that threaten his happiness and his effectiveness and the means for securing his recovery are to be mainly sought," he was writing of the patients of a neurologist; but we may safely assume that he was thinking not only of the intimate personal relationships of these patients, but of their occupations, recreations, and total of social contacts. For there is a very real sense in which the mind of man is the sum of these contacts. Consideration of the bearing of this concept upon our subject is reserved for the end of Part II. (See Chapter XIX, The Underlying Philosophy.)

[2] See the definitions of Chapter III, and the much fuller discussion of Chapter XVIII, Comparison and Interpretation.

prudence, and industry. While knowledge from these fields is being applied to social case work, the latter has developed methods that will be useful in return.

In this new discipline, as in each of the others, discoveries that were made with pain and difficulty by the pioneers of one generation have become commonplaces of our thinking in the next. There is a half century of hard social endeavor between Edward Denison's despairing exclamation—"Every shilling I give away does fourpence worth of good by helping to keep their [his beneficiaries'] miserable bodies alive, and eightpence worth of harm by helping to destroy their miserable souls"[1]—and the request made by a physician in an American city a few years ago. This physician, who had seen in his hospital practice the excellent service given by the trained social workers of the hospital in unravelling the social complications of its patients, asked their leader to let him engage one of them to render like service to a private patient of his—a patient abundantly able to pay, and unlikely to be benefited medically without social treatment. The social service department of the hospital was unable to spare a worker from its staff, but recommended one with the requisite qualifications from the staff of a relief society.

The point to be noted is that the skilful methods which made this undertaking possible had been built up laboriously by those who had shared Denison's questionings and later by several case work groups which struggled forward independently. Important contributions have been made to social diagnosis by at least three of these groups—those identified with the charity organization, the children's court, and the medical-social movements. In the first of these movements interest in diagnosis shows two divergent impulses—one toward emphasis upon economic status to the exclusion of other equally important aspects of human affairs; the other toward a broader conception, which led its advocates from the very beginning—though without training and with few resources—to take the whole man into consideration. In the children's court movement some of the methods of experimental psychology have

[1] Quoted by Mrs. Josephine Shaw Lowell in "The Evils of Investigation and Relief," *Charities*, July, 1898, p. 9. Denison was a volunteer almoner in 1860 for the London Society for the Relief of Distress.

been adapted to the needs of social inquiry. The medical-social movement is modifying in a striking way both medical and social practice.

I. THE ECONOMIC AND THE MORE COMPREHENSIVE APPROACH

1. The Forerunners. In some ways it was unfortunate that the first attempts to introduce investigation into the charitable treatment of dependency (for it was in this field that social diagnosis had its beginnings) were made by social reformers who were primarily economists, or who took their cue from the economists. This came about from the fact that the beginnings of social diagnosis were in England, where, after the riot of sentimentality interrupted by spasms of severity which had passed for statesmanship in the treatment of distress from the time of Elizabeth, charitable reforms attempted in the first quarter of the nineteenth century gave rise to the phrase "a thorough investigation." Thomas Chalmers used it in Glasgow as early as 1823 in connection with his parish work, and later it was used by the systematizers of German poor relief at Elberfeld.[1] On the other hand, the Poor Law reformers of 1834 turned their backs upon the idea, counting upon

[1] See Charles R. Henderson's edition of The Christian and Civic Economy of Large Towns by Thomas Chalmers, p. 261, for a passage on individual inquiry. The reformers of poor relief in Elberfeld, Germany, in 1852, quoted Chalmers, but neither then nor later does his fine spirit seem to have been made manifest to them. At least, in an undated pamphlet which bears internal evidence of belonging to the early '70's, Andrew Doyle, an English Poor Law inspector, could introduce a description of the methods of inquiry in use in Elberfeld—methods which he admired—in these terms:

"It was assumed by the framers of the English Poor Law, and is still assumed by those who continue to take any interest in administering it upon the principle upon which it was founded, that no real test of destitution can be devised except the test of the workhouse. As the application of that test is as yet no part of the Elberfeld system, it will be asked—what is the substitute for it?

"In the first place the applicant for relief is subjected to an examination so close and searching, so absolutely inquisitorial, that no man who could possibly escape from it would submit to it. He is not one of several hundreds who can tell his own story to an overworked relieving officer, but one of a very few, never exceeding four—frequently the single applicant—who is bound by law to answer every one of that long string of questions that his interrogator is bound by law to put to him. One of the peculiar merits claimed, and I believe rightly claimed, for this system is that before a man can obtain relief it must be shown that he cannot exist without it."—The Poor Law System of Elberfeld, p. xv.

Doyle gives a long list of minute questions which each applicant must answer. All of these have a direct relation to economic status with the exception of "religious profession," "the state of health of each member of his family," and "whether or not the children are sent to school."

willingness to enter the workhouse as a test of destitution and upon the workhouse itself as a deterrent that would render individualized inquiry unnecessary. Often the advocates of inquiry in those earlier days had nothing but the economic aspects of a given human situation in mind, and, when called upon to explain their phrase, "a thorough investigation," emphasized no resources save those of income, no obligations save those that were liabilities of relatives for support or repayment. The treatment they contemplated, therefore, looked to the repression of unnecessary demands upon public bounty rather than to the release of energy, the regenerating of character, or the multiplication of health opportunities, opportunities for training, and the like.

No general statement such as this can be entirely fair. Chalmers himself was a man of genius and vision who saw the need of liberating the powers of self-help and mutual help within the people themselves, and who realized the part that personal service might play in this task. But he had not then at hand most of the materials out of which modern social diagnosis and social treatment are now in process of being built. For every one thing that could then be done about a man's attitude toward his life and his social relations, about his health, housing, work, and recreation, there are now a dozen things to do. The power to analyze a human situation closely, as distinguished from the old method of falling back upon a few general classifications, grows with the consciousness of power to get things done.

2. Charity Organization Beginnings. The London Charity Organization Society, heir to Chalmers' ideas and student of the Elberfeld system, included in its membership from the beginning a small group of social reformers who, while impressed with the necessity for regulating relief-giving, especially concerned themselves with efforts to place distressed people above the need of relief and, in doing this, to study and release their latent possibilities. As early as 1869, the year in which the London society was founded, Miss Octavia Hill had given, before the Social Science Association, the first description that we have been able to find of inquiry with social reinstatement as its motive and aim. It is the first passage in which the human being himself, in his social as distinguished from his economic environment, seems to emerge:

By knowledge of character more is meant than whether a man is a drunkard or a woman is dishonest; it means knowledge of the passions, hopes, and history of people; where the temptation will touch them, what is the little scheme they have made of their lives, or would make, if they had encouragement; what training long past phases of their lives may have afforded; how to move, touch, teach them. Our memories and our hopes are more truly factors of our lives than we often remember.[1]

From that day to this the struggle in the charity organization movement between what may be termed the comprehensive method of inquiry and of treatment and the exclusively economic one has gone on. Conditions in this country made it possible for Miss Hill's ideas to bear fruit here more promptly than in England. Her essays made a profound impression. In New York, the State Charities Aid Association reprinted Homes of the London Poor in 1875, while in Boston the system of "volunteer visiting" owed its impulse in large part to her writings. So lasting is the impress of beginnings that even today it is possible to recognize signs of Miss Hill's influence and of the spirit of her 1869 statement in the current case records of certain of the American charity organization societies.

In a number of the American societies, however, the economic program of inquiry was for a long time the more usual one. Some of the earlier documents actually describe investigation as repressive.[2] In fact, no one can understand the diversity in the charity organization societies of today who does not realize that in this country the early movement had several independent beginnings, and that, in one of these, Miss Hill's work in London and her occasional essays were the shaping influence, while in some of the others inquiry and treatment centered around questions of relief or no relief.

3. First Attempts to Establish Standards. It is to the credit of the societies identified with the broadest of these initial impulses that they have been dissatisfied with their own work. Although they have failed again and again to make their inquiries into individual situations skilful and effective, they have been aware of

[1] Life of Octavia Hill, C. E. Maurice, p. 258.

[2] See especially S. Humphreys Gurteen's Handbook of Charity Organization, published by the author in Buffalo in 1882. While in some passages another note is struck, on p. 146 he expressly refers to investigation as repressive. Some American leaders of the movement were doing the same as late as 1904.

such shortcomings and have applied themselves to achieving a greater measure of success. Both in England and here they have attempted to formulate experience.[1] The American leaders have protested, moreover, in no uncertain terms against regarding investigation as an end in itself, without reference to the use to which the information obtained may be put. This was notably true of Mrs. Josephine Shaw Lowell, founder of the New York society, who wrote:

> We had in New York, in the hard times of 1893 and 1894, a most painful experience in this regard. The very word "investigation" seemed then to have been made a sort of shibboleth by the newspapers, and in too many cases, by the ministers also. To every remonstrance against methods of relief-giving which were injurious to the character of those who were supposed to be helped by them, and cruel in their entire disregard of their comfort, happiness, and moral and physical well-being, it seemed to be considered a sufficient answer to say: "All the cases have been thoroughly investigated," and it was evidently thought that this answer ought to be entirely satisfactory to charity organizationists, even though the investigations were made, not for the purpose of furnishing guidance and knowledge for a long course of "treatment" by which weak wills might be strengthened, bad habits be cured, and independence developed, but in order that a ticket might be given by means of which, after a long, weary waiting in the street in the midst of a crowd of miserable people, whose poverty and beggary were published to every passerby, some old clothes or some groceries might be got.[2]

The year before this was written (1897), Edward T. Devine, secretary of the New York society, made a strong plea for improvement in the personnel of the investigators, for their training, and for a clearer definition of the end which investigation has in view. In the following year he organized[3] the summer course of training which was to develop later into the New York School of Philanthropy, the first of the training schools for social workers established in this country. The opening of these schools gave a strong impetus to developments already under way in social agencies. It became more apparent than ever, for example, that investigation was not merely a notion of the charity organization societies, that

[1] See, for example, the early English statement of C. J. Ribton-Turner: Suggestions for Systematic Inquiry, 1872; and "How to Take Down a Case" in the 1896 Occasional Papers of the London Charity Organization Society. The Boston Associated Charities has given us Miss M. L. Birtwell's all too brief "Investigation" (*Charities Review*, January, 1895, pp. 129–137).

[2] See "The Evils of Investigation and Relief" in *Charities*, June, 1898.

[3] Under the directorship of Philip W. Ayres.

this process was essential wherever the reinstatement of a human being was to be attempted. On the other hand, practical instruction in social diagnosis and treatment was made possible for the school students by the case work opportunities (analogous to the "bedside opportunities" in medical instruction) offered to them from the beginning by the charity organization societies and later by other agencies. Case work cannot be mastered from books or from class room instruction alone, though both have their place in its mastery.

If social case work is indebted to the schools and the social agencies jointly for their encouragement of a technique in common, it must look to social reform to make possible a technique that is varied and flexible. New methods of social treatment have been developed by the charity organization campaigns for better housing and for the prevention of tuberculosis; by the long struggle of another group of social reformers to secure diagnosis and care of the feeble-minded; by child labor reform, by industrial legislation, by the recreation movement, the mental hygiene movement, and a host of other social reforms. The significance of these reforms here is that, after they had achieved a measure of success, case work treatment had at its command more varied resources, adaptable to individual situations, and that therefore the diagnosis of those situations assumed fresh importance.

Summing up the main facts of the relation of charity organization to social diagnosis, it may be said, First, that the movement developed and fought for the beginnings of this process. Second, that some of its earliest leaders had grasped the idea of the sympathetic study of the individual in his social environment. Third, that this conception, imperfectly realized, was often thrust aside by belief in the commanding importance of economic data. Fourth, that progress in diagnosis necessarily awaited the development of varied methods of treatment, there being at first no accepted program of treatment other than the giving or withholding of relief.[1] Fifth, that the promotion of preventive measures which made varied treatment possible, notably of those looking to the better

[1] Here and there individuals and agencies had broader conceptions of what could be done, but in the earlier days these were carried out with difficulty against the main current of charitable activity, which ran strongly toward dole-giving.

housing and health of the people, became an important part of charity organization work.

II. THE APPROACH BY WAY OF CHILD STUDY

Movements more or less independent in origin may act and react upon one another in such a way as to make it difficult to unravel their beginnings. The idea of juvenile probation, for example, goes back to the '60's. The Boston Children's Aid Society and later (1869) a state visiting agency which was established in Massachusetts interested themselves in probation. In addition, the Boston Municipal Court began to hold separate hearings of children's cases. It was not until 1899, however, when representatives of the women's clubs, the children's agencies, and the social settlements in Chicago were able to secure the passage of a juvenile court law, combining the ideas of probation, separate hearings, and the specialized judge, that the first juvenile court was organized.

The contribution of the children's court movement to social diagnosis deserves more than passing mention. It drew upon the family agencies, and upon the children's agencies even more largely, for its technique; but it developed a point of view of its own, as is shown by the following passage in which Judge Harvey H. Baker of the Boston Juvenile Court describes the duty of the judge:

> In determining the disposition to be made of the case the procedure of the physician is very closely followed. The probation officer investigates the case and reports to the judge all available information about the family and other features of the environment of the boy, the boy's personal history at home, in school, at work, and on the street, and the circumstances attending the particular outbreak which got him into court. The boy himself is scrutinized for indications of feeble-mindedness or physical defects, such as poor eyesight, deafness, adenoids. The judge and probation officer consider together, like a physician and his junior, whether the outbreak which resulted in the arrest of the child was largely accidental, or whether it is habitual or likely to be so; whether it is due chiefly to some inherent physical or moral defect of the child, or whether some feature of his environment is an important factor; and then they address themselves to the question of how permanently to prevent the recurrence.[1]

Two years before this was written, the judge of the Chicago Juvenile Court had begun to urge the importance of procuring, in

[1] *The Survey*, February 5, 1910, p. 649.

addition to family histories, thorough physical and mental examinations for all court children.[1] This court was the first social agency to utilize to the full applied psychology—a source of insight the use of which had been developed in the psychological clinic only a few years before the Chicago court was organized.[2] A Psychopathic Institute was organized in connection with the court in 1909.

This institute has been from the first under the direction of Dr. William Healy, whose three books—The Individual Delinquent, Pathological Lying, and Honesty—embody the results of his institute studies of juvenile court children. Social case workers read these books with more interest than they do any others relating to child study. Although The Individual Delinquent is "a text-book of diagnosis and prognosis for all concerned in understanding offenders," its discussion of method contained in the first third of the book makes it a text-book for all engaged in the study of human beings. In his simpler statement, Honesty, intended for teachers and parents, Dr. Healy holds a similar point of view regarding the influences to be brought to bear upon character to that developed nearly fifty years before from a different angle and with a different equipment by Miss Octavia Hill. He believes that stealing is usually a symptom, not a disease, and that the physical, mental, and social facts behind that symptom must be grasped and interpreted if we are to effect a cure.

III. THE MEDICAL APPROACH

In the earlier days of the charity organization movement in this country, physicians used to appeal to the societies to advocate the adoption of some form of inquiry by hospitals and dispensaries to prevent the fraudulent use of free medical charities by those who could afford to pay. This is another instance of that inadequate conception, already mentioned, of a problem which presents aspects

[1] See Judge Julian W. Mack's address in Proceedings of National Conference of Charities and Correction for 1908 (Richmond, Va.). p. 374.

[2] As early as 1896 Lightner Witmer of the University of Pennsylvania had opened such a clinic and had begun to receive children for examination from schools and children's agencies; later he did examining also for the juvenile court. The examinations as now made at the University of Pennsylvania's clinic are physical and social as well as mental. Ten years later (1906) Henry H. Goddard began his work for the feeble-minded at Vineland, N. J., and developed the use of the Binet-Simon measuring scale.

of greater significance for social treatment than the exclusively economic.

Doctors and charity organization workers co-operated to better purpose when the New York Charity Organization Society began in 1902, through a special committee on tuberculosis, its first campaign for the prevention of disease. Other movements for improving public health soon followed, some initiated by the medical profession and some by social workers. Although each one of these has influenced social diagnosis, the most direct influence exerted upon this process by the medical profession comes from the medical-social service movement.

Medical-social service owes its origin to Dr. Richard C. Cabot, who in 1905 organized the first social service department in the out-patient department of the Massachusetts General Hospital. It was "conceived by a physician who, in seeking the improvement of dispensary practice, found in the social worker a potent means for more accurate diagnosis and more effective treatment."[1] What Dr. Cabot had in mind in bringing trained social workers into the dispensary and later into its separate clinics was not a mixture of medical and social work but their chemical union. The fuller development of this idea in recent years is best described in his own words:

> In our own case work in the social service department of the Massachusetts General Hospital we are accustomed to sum up our cases in monthly reports from the case records by asking about each case four questions: What is the physical state of this patient? What is the mental state of this patient? What is his physical environment? What is his mental and spiritual environment? The doctor is apt to know a good deal about the first of those four things, the physical state, and a little about the second, the mental, but about the other two almost nothing. The expert social worker comes with those four points in mind to every case. It is of interest to notice that this fourfold knowledge is not the goal of the social worker merely; it is the goal of every intelligent human being who wants to understand another human being. Suppose a man was about to be married to a member of your family and you wanted to know whether he deserved this great promotion. You would want to know just those four things the social worker needs to know . . . (a) his physical condition, (b) his character, (c) the physical condition under which he has been brought up and lives, and (d) the mental and spiritual influences under which he has grown up and now lives. It would be the same if you were studying candidates for a paying teller's position, for a governor's position,

[1] From Social Work in Hospitals, by Ida M. Cannon, p. 15 sq.

for the headship of a college, or for president of the United States. Social work, as I see it, takes no special point of view; it takes the total human point of view, and that is just what it has to teach doctors who by reason of their training are disposed to take a much narrower point of view. They can safely and profitably continue that narrow outlook only in case they have a social worker at their elbow, as they should have, to help them. Each of us has his proper field, but we should not work separately, for the human beings who are our charges cannot be cut in two.[1]

The half of the senior class of medical students at Harvard who take their clinical work at the Massachusetts General Hospital also take a course there in medical-social work under its chief of social service, and some of the medical colleges in other cities give similar instruction. Even more directly related to our subject is the systematic instruction in medical matters which this Boston medical-social department now gives to non-medical social workers. Indeed, the medical-social movement has had a marked influence upon the daily work of other social agencies by giving them a clearer notion of the bearing of health upon the social welfare of the individual.

All of these streams of experience—the judicial, the psychological, and the medical—are modifying social case work profoundly, and as indicated earlier are being modified by it in turn. A tendency to drift away from effective standards is sometimes noticeable, however, in the social work connected with court or clinic. The explanation of this lies in the fact that long established professions cast a long shadow. They have their traditions, their routine of procedure, their terminology, their sense of professional solidarity. Social work has few of these things. When, therefore, the doctor or judge receives social workers as an adjunct to his clinic or court, he may have but a dim idea of the distinctive contribution of authenticated and interpreted social fact which they should bring to his professional work. In this case, he tends to fit them into the traditions of his own calling, and to ignore the characteristics of theirs. The judge has been known to use them for detective work; the physician, accustomed to implicit obedience from nurses, may use them for errands to patients or for semi-clerical service. One unfortunate result, apart from the waste of opportunity, is that if any social observations are

[1] Proceedings of the National Conference of Charities and Correction for 1915 (Baltimore), p. 220 sq.

possible and if any social statements are taken, they are accepted at their face value by professional men who are accustomed in their own field to apply rigid tests, but who fail to recognize the need or the possibility of testing social evidence. The nature of social evidence and the tests which social experience and the principles of reasoning should enable us to apply to it will be the theme of the next four chapters.

CHAPTER II

THE NATURE AND USES OF SOCIAL EVIDENCE

THE processes which lead up to social diagnosis and thence to the shaping of a plan of social treatment may be divided into the collection of evidence and the drawing of inferences therefrom. The collection of evidence comes through the social worker's first relations (1) with his client,[1] (2) with his client's family, and (3) with sources of insight outside the family group. These stages will all be described in detail in Part II, as will also the further stage (4) of comparing the evidence gathered from these various sources (inference), and of interpreting its meaning (diagnosis).

I. SOCIAL EVIDENCE DIFFERENTIATED

From the beginning of his task the social case worker deals with testimonial evidence in a way shaped by the end for which it was obtained; namely, the social treatment of individuals. As he proceeds he often finds himself in need of more knowledge as to the weight which should be attached to the social evidence he has gathered. Are there rules of evidence, principles of choice, that can guide him in selecting from a group of unassorted observations and testimonies those which he can rely upon from those which must be accepted "with a grain of salt"? If so, are these principles peculiar to social work, so that its practitioners will be obliged to dig them out from their own experience alone, or may they hope to find them already identified in law book or laboratory?

That there are such rules to guide the social worker is intimated

[1] Those with whom social case workers are dealing are called by many names—applicants, inmates, cases, children, families, probationers, patients are only a few of them. One word will be used for all, usually, in this volume—the word "client." Its history is one of advancement from low estate to higher. First it meant "a suitor, a dependent." Later it meant "one who listens to advice," and later still "one who employs professional service of any kind." The more expert the service, the more appropriate the word, which has the advantage, moreover, of democratic implications. When a public defender in California serves defendants too poor to employ him, he still thinks of them as his clients.

by a correspondent who had gone from a charity organization society to a society to protect children from cruelty. He writes:

> As a result of my experience both with C. O. S. and with S. P. C. C. investigators, there seems to me a weakness in the training of the C. O. S. district secretary, who from the nature of her duties is constantly required to weigh evidence but who has not got clearly in mind the fundamental differences between different classes of evidence and their different values. I do not now refer to the nice discriminations; those I am content to leave to trained lawyers to squabble over. Not only would the co-operation with an S. P. C. C. be at once improved but evidence as it stands in a C. O. S. investigation would be increased in value and reduced in bulk. I confess to considerable impatience at times when I find district secretaries of some and even of great experience apparently *valuing every statement equally and then adding the items together to find a total.*

Many will share this correspondent's impatience with such arithmetic. Nevertheless, no considerable group of social case workers—whether in a society to protect children or a charity organization society or anywhere else—seem to have grasped the fact that the *reliability* of the evidence on which they base their decisions should be no less rigidly scrutinized than is that of legal evidence by opposing counsel. On the other hand, the question of admissibility, the rules for which were framed mainly to meet the average juryman's lack of skill in testing evidence, does not enter into the weighing of facts as gathered by an agency all in whose service are, or can be, trained to this special task. Skill in testing evidence, as leading to such proof as social workers need, is in no way dependent upon a knowledge of the legal rules of admissibility. Social evidence, like that sought by the scientist or historian, includes all items which, however trifling or apparently irrelevant when regarded as isolated facts, may, when taken together, throw light upon the question at issue; namely, as regards social work, the question what course of procedure will place this client in his right relation to society? Many an item, such as a child's delayed speech, for instance, may have no significance in itself, whereas when considered in connection with late dentition and walking and with convulsions it may become a significant part of evidence as to the child's mentality. Social evidence, then, has an advantage over legal evidence in that it can include facts of slight probative value. Without this advantage social case work would not be possible, since the problem of the orientation of a family or individual is far more complex than the single question as to whether or not a litigant or a defendant is to be penalized. Moreover, facts having a subjective bearing, like that of delayed speech just instanced, are especially characterized by their cumulative significance. Variations between people in mental endowment, in "personality," display themselves ordinarily not in a few conspicuous acts, but in a trend of behavior evidenced by innumerable trifling remarks or by a succession of decisions and impulses each unimportant in itself. Evidence of this cumulative sort, therefore, is essential wherever, as in social work, decisions rest upon intimate understanding of character.

In examining the reliability of evidence, social case work should make its own application of universal tests; and, coming late to the task, should be able to profit by the experiences not merely of law, but of history and of natural science. The various professions apply rules of evidence for arriving at truth, each according to its own special conditions. The scientist uses controlled experimentation because he works with material which may be brought under complete control. He may, for instance, till half of an orchard whose physical conditions, soil, grade, exposure, etc., are the same throughout. If the tilled half bears much better than the untilled, he concludes that tilling increases the product of fruit trees. When, however, the farmer in the fable digs in his orchard for buried treasure, and in place of gold finds his promised fortune in an unprecedented yield of fruit, he probably draws no causal inferences whatever.

Should a social worker have the task of showing whether the farmer's labor had paid or not, he would get the testimony of the farmer, of his family, and his neighbors as to the previous care of the trees; their evidence as to any other measures of improvement he might have taken, such as pruning, thinning out, etc.; their recollection, corroborated by governmental reports, of weather conditions, pests, etc., of preceding years. He would take account of hearsay evidence, of persistent rumors, of the general appearance of the man's farm and home. As a result, the social worker might establish or discredit the value of tillage in this instance with a fair degree of probability.

Suppose on the other hand some decision in a law court should turn on the question whether or not it was his tilling of the soil that had brought the farmer an increased yield of fruit. The court would deal in the main with the same facts as the social worker, namely, with the testimony of witnesses, with government reports, or with an inspection of the premises; the difference would be that a court would guard with scrupulous care the admission of hearsay evidence and would exclude rumors; that it would, in short, hold each witness to a responsibility for his statements, allowing him in the main to say nothing of which his own knowledge was not first-hand. This evidence might or might not satisfy the court beyond a reasonable doubt that it was justified in concluding that tillage had increased the farmer's yield. But these restrictions upon evidence are necessary in law because of the obligation the judge is under of sifting evidence for a jury who are liable to allow undue weight to items which have small value as proof.

The common difference between the point of view of social worker and court stands out in the following instance of alleged parental neglect:

SOCIAL EVIDENCE WHICH LED A CASE WORK AGENCY TO ASK COURT ACTION THROUGH A SOCIETY TO PROTECT CHILDREN

1. Three rachitic children aged seven, five, and three years; the oldest could not walk at all at four years; the second and third had bowed legs and walked with difficulty at three years old. Although the oldest child has been three and a half years in a hospital where it was sent by a social agency, the parents omitted to take the other children to the dispensary for examination and advice. The social worker made seven calls to urge them to do this. They assented each time, but were increasingly resentful at what they regarded as an intrusion into their private affairs, and did nothing. The social worker construed this as parental neglect.

REASONS WHY THE SOCIETY TO PROTECT CHILDREN BELIEVED THAT THE COURT WOULD NOT ACT

1. "No doctor has yet made a definite statement as to the serious result of failure on the parents' part to follow directions in the treatment of these children." A court would not accept a layman's judgment even on so obvious a matter as extremely bowed legs, because this might establish a precedent which in most instances would work badly. A layman's opinion in such a case as this is a less responsible one than a doctor's, since the latter's professional standing is involved in his statements. Even with a physician's statement "it is very difficult to make such neglect the basis of a case in court." The father supports his family, the mother gives good care as she understands it. The court, fearing that doctors may disagree, hesitates to

force a debatable treatment upon well-meaning, if ignorant parents. One might venture to predict that courts will more readily consider neglect of this sort as they grow inclined to take common sense risks instead of resting on the letter of precedent.

2. This family has lived for six years in two tiny rooms on the top floor. Although their tenement rooms are sunny and clean, the children do not get sufficient exercise or air. The parents refuse to move, as the rent is small.

2. The sunniness of the tenement and the fact that the mother keeps it clean would prevent a court from regarding these cramped quarters as evidence of culpable neglect. Public opinion would not uphold the court in making an issue over home conditions that were not considerably below the ideal held by social workers. The social worker often forgets this.

3. A year and a half after having been urged to have the two younger children examined, the mother took the youngest child to the hospital and promised to bring the second child. Eight months later she had not done this.

3. "While it looks as if the family had been neglected in years past either deliberately or through ignorance, or both, the situation today is not clear." The oldest child is still in the hospital, the youngest has received hospital care, and the mother has promised to take the second child to the out-patient department. With this evidence of good intentions, a doctor's statement (see 1) would be necessary to satisfy a court of present neglect.

Here was a deadlock. In asking court action on the ground of parental neglect the social worker was in effect calling upon the court to accept his interpretation of the evidence as establishing the fact of neglect, and to order the children to be submitted to physicians for treatment. The court, on the other hand, as interpreted by the society to protect children, would require the physician's testimony as a link in establishing the fact of neglect and would be unlikely to act until the social worker himself had done the thing he was asking the court to do; namely, confront the case with a doctor. It would seem to a layman as if in such a case the court might safely summon the parents and child into court, admit the child's bowed legs and the social worker's efforts to persuade the family as evidence, and put this father and mother on probation to consult any reputable doctor they chose.

It is clear, then, that whereas social evidence is distinguished from that used in natural science by an actual difference in the subject matter, it differs from legal evidence not in the sort of facts offered, but in the greater degree of probative value required by the law of each separate item. The additional testimony which the court would have asked in the instance cited was not different in kind from what the social worker already had.

In short, social evidence may be defined as consisting of any and all facts as to personal or family history which, taken together, indicate the nature of a given client's social difficulties and the means to their solution. Such facts, when duly tested in ways that fit the uses to which they are to be put, will influence, as suggested in the preceding chapter, the diagnosis of physical and mental disorders, will reveal unrecognized sources of disease, will change court procedure with reference to certain groups of defendants, and will modify methods in the school class room. To a certain extent social evidence is already exerting this influence, but the demand for such evidence is likely far to outstrip the supply during this next decade.

II. THE WIDER USE OF SOCIAL EVIDENCE

Scattered and tentative as they still are, the signs of such coming demand are nevertheless unmistakable; the uses of social evidence in the older professions are beginning to multiply, as the following illustrations will show:

A specialist in the *diagnosis of feeble-mindedness* committed two difficult girls to custodial care, largely on the facts supplied him from first-hand observations by a children's aid society as to the characteristics of these girls and of their families. The "stream pictures" furnished in summaries of two case records, covering two years in one instance and nine in the other, were his most conclusive evidence.

The nature of these stream pictures may be gathered from Dr. W. E. Fernald's discussion of the evidence needed by the psychiatrist for making a diagnosis of mental defect. Some of this evidence, although obtainable by social workers, is of course medical in character, that is, delayed dentition, late walking, delayed speech, a history of convulsions in the first few years of life, the presence of degenerative stigmata. Much of it, however, is precisely the slight but cumulative evidence which social workers habitually gather as bearing on disabilities; namely, facts of family and personal history with special reference to the period of infancy and early childhood, a relatively long continuance of untidy habits (of childhood), the public school grade in relation to age, inability on the part of the patient to apply himself continuously either in school or in any other occupation without constant supervision. In some cases with only slight intellectual defect, the inability to "make good" socially will be a deciding factor in the diagnosis.[1]

All of this information, including the medical, should be given in the history of a client which the social worker is preparing to submit to a psychiatrist.

The contributions of social work to medicine are not confined to the diagnosis of feeble-mindedness. As we have seen in the first chapter, *medical diagnosis and treatment* are beginning to show the influence of the social evidence gathered in the medical-social departments of hospitals and dispensaries.

We have also seen in the discussion of Beginnings that the children's courts of the United States owe their existence to social workers. These courts *supplement legal evidence by social.* Not only have the courts come to recognize the value of a more liberal inclusion of imperfectly relevant evidence in disposing of child offenders; they are growing to feel that even the method of gathering this evidence has an influence upon the welfare of the child. They believe that such investigation should be inspired not by the ambition to run down and convict a criminal but by a desire to learn the best way to overcome a boy's or girl's difficulties. The need of modifying in these courts the usual legal procedure is thus commented upon by Flexner and Baldwin:

> The best interests of the child make it necessary for the court to consider hearsay and other evidence of a more or less informal kind which would ordinarily under strict rules of evidence be excluded. It is of the utmost importance that the court should avail itself of just the kind of evidence that the investigator [the probation

[1] Fernald, Walter E., M. D. (Superintendent of the Massachusetts School for the Feeble-minded, Waverly, Mass.): The Imbecile with Criminal Instincts, p. 745. *American Journal of Insanity,* Vol. LXV, No. 4, April, 1909, pp. 731–749.

See also questionnaire regarding a Child Possibly Feeble-minded in this volume, Chapter XXVII.

officer] presents. If it should finally be determined that the laws as drawn do not permit the introduction of such evidence, express provision should be inserted in the statutes allowing its use.[1]

Another court having its origin in needs brought to light by social work is the court of domestic relations, which may in time be merged with the children's court. It suffers at present from inability to secure and use the necessary social evidence. This experiment, like many others, will continue to fall short of full usefulness until social workers develop the diagnostic skill that will enable them to offer to the court authenticated and pertinent information. The following is a case in point:

A court of domestic relations sentenced a man for desertion and non-support on the testimony of his wife. The wife then applied to a charity organization society for relief for herself and four children. The district secretary, assuming that on the face of it this convicted man was good-for-nothing, asked her committee to arrange for assistance to the family. It was with reluctance that the secretary at the suggestion of her committee agreed to make what she regarded as a superfluous investigation of the man's side of the story. This inquiry, however, brought statements from employers, former neighbors, relatives, etc., which showed that the trouble lay not with the man, who was a decent enough fellow, but with the woman, who was probably mentally unbalanced. Instead of voting relief, therefore, the district committee asked the judge to release the man.

In short, the secretary in question would hardly have been qualified to persuade a court of the helpfulness of social evidence, while she herself was capable of treating an inference—that as to the man's character—as if it were an evidential fact.

Many educators, even though not thinking in terms of social work, are recognizing their need of obtaining *social histories of pupils* and of giving differential treatment based upon them. The social worker's method they sometimes take over with little understanding of its details. For instance, Madame Montessori in her Pedagogical Anthropology makes a plea for differential treatment of pupils and gives a whole chapter to the question of securing the biographical history of the pupil and of his antecedents;[2] but she apparently has little conception of the varying reliability of the

[1] Flexner, Bernard, and Baldwin, Roger N.: Juvenile Courts and Probation, p. 52. New York, Century Co., 1914.

[2] Montessori, Marie: Pedagogical Anthropology (Translated from the Italian by Frederic Taber Cooper), pp. 404–453. New York, Frederick A. Stokes Co., 1913.

different sources from which such social evidence must be had, or of the tests that could be applied to assure reliability.

Stuart Courtis, of the New York Committee on School Inquiry, who starts with an effort to test, by measurements based upon arithmetic alone, the efficiency of school and children, arrives finally at two interesting conclusions: First, that life histories alone can make plain the play of those hidden forces which are constantly modifying the results of educational effort; and second, that where marked differences in the social life of the different types of children exist, those differences must be reflected in school methods. For reasoning cannot be taught from a text alone. "Reasoning is a process of adjustment to a situation, and only as children have experienced the fundamental characteristics of a situation can they intelligently make the necessary adjustments to it."[1]

The beginnings of social case work in a field closely allied to education, in *vocational guidance,* serve to illustrate how, in the enthusiasm of promoting a new discovery, the need of social evidence may be overlooked. In this line of endeavor (though not in some others, where the illustration may still serve as a warning) the oversight was only a temporary one. The first volume of advice addressed to what were to be known as "vocational counselors" gave specimen interviews for their instruction. One of these is with a lad of nineteen in Boston who comes for vocational guidance and says that he wants to be a physician.[2] The following is a part of the counselor's printed report:

> He was sickly looking, small, thin, hollow-cheeked, with listless eye and expressionless face. He did not smile once during the interview of more than an hour. He shook hands like a wet stick. His voice was husky and unpleasant, and his conversational power, aside from answering direct questions, seemed practically limited to "ss-uh," an aspirate "yes, sir," consisting of a prolonged *s* followed by a non-vocal *uh*, made by suddenly dropping the lower jaw and exploding the breath without bringing the vocal cords into action. He used this aspirate "yes-sir" constantly, to indicate assent, or that he heard what the counselor said. He had been through the grammar school and the evening high; was not good in any of his studies, nor especially interested in any. His memory was poor. He fell down on all the tests

[1] Courtis, Stuart A.: The Courtis Tests in Arithmetic (Section D of Subdivision I of Part II of the Report on Educational Aspects of the Public School Systems of the City of New York), pp. 150–155. City of New York, 1911–12.

[2] Parsons, Frank, Ph. D.: Choosing a Vocation, p. 114 sq. Boston, Houghton Mifflin and Co., 1909.

for mental power. He had read practically nothing outside of school except the newspapers. He had no resources and very few friends. He was not tidy in his appearance, nor in any way attractive. He knew nothing about a doctor's life; not even that he might have to get up any time in the middle of the night, or that he had to remember books full of symptoms and remedies.

The boy had no enthusiasms, interests, or ambitions except the one consuming ambition to be something that people would respect, and he thought he could accomplish that purpose by becoming a physician more easily than in any other way.

When the study was complete, and the young man's record was before him, the counselor said:

"Now we must be very frank with each other. That is the only way such talks can be of any value. You want me to tell you the truth just as I see it, don't you? That's why you came to me, isn't it,—not for flattery, but for a frank talk to help you understand yourself and your possibilities?"

"When the study was complete!" Psychologists realize now that tests of memory, like most other mental tests, must be repeated to eliminate accidental factors; but assuming that the counselor had made the psychological tests with care, he still has ignored many factors, which though not measurable by tests would yet modify the social diagnosis. He tells the boy that he cannot be a doctor, that he might succeed in some mechanical or manufacturing industry, that he must cultivate a cordial smile by speaking before a glass, that he must read solid books, study to prepare for citizenship, and so on. Such unconstructive vocational guidance the counselor apparently supposed to be a form of social treatment. Had he used his opportunity to acquire social evidence as well as psychological, he might have instituted treatment that would have struck at the root of the boy's difficulty. Here is a boy who has been attending the evening high school for several years. Has he been employed during the day; if so, at what? Is this work of a kind that would account, in part at least, for his failure as a student? Are there removable causes not only for his lack of success but for his physical condition as well? In the case of such a boy, should not a medical diagnosis precede vocational advice? What are his home surroundings? Have his parents plans for him or aptitudes of their own that would suggest possibilities in him? Are any of his family already known to some of the hundreds of social workers in Boston?[1] If so, a summary of this social work experience might be suggestive. The book containing this illustrative

[1] For a description of the confidential exchange see p. 303 sq.

interview was written to aid vocational counselors, presumably busy men. Nevertheless the question as to what a boy is to do with his working days for years to come is too vital a one for such summary disposal. The interview here quoted, ignoring the possible aid of other specialists, professes to be complete in itself, whereas a few letters and telephone messages to employers, teachers, confidential exchange of information, and the boy's parents, together with a reference to a competent physician, would have brought to light social and physical factors which contributed to the boy's ill success, and would have indicated how to remove them.

The counselor dealt with symptoms only. He assumed that an examination of the boy as regarded his appearance, speech, and mental reactions, during that brief cross-section of time, would give all the data necessary for treatment. Only to one who was all-wise and all-knowing could a single examination have been thus fruitful.

Variations of these same ideas crop up in unexpected places. Scientific shop management has accepted the principle of studying the *personal traits of the individual workman* and of basing his advancement upon such study, but for lack of social technique its present application of the principle is often too crude and sometimes too undemocratic to illustrate our theme.

It would seem that social evidence is beginning to receive recognition. The endeavors of social workers are bringing to light ways of thinking and doing that prove useful in quite other fields. The fact that law, medicine, history, and psychology, in their effort to break new ground, have been opening the same vein of truth, shows a growing demand for the kind of data that social practitioners gather. The absence of any generally accepted tests of the reliability of such evidence, however, still keeps this new demand itself ill defined and unstandardized. Personal histories which might appear sufficiently authenticated to a shop manager might strike a neurologist as inadequate for conclusions, while they would certainly be open to objections from a court. Progress on the social side of these several fields of endeavor will be hastened as social workers subject their own experiences to a more critical and searching analysis.

It was not to be expected that industry, or education, or jurisprudence, or medical science, or preventive social legislation should wait, before they developed in harmony with the thought of today, until the arts of social diagnosis and treatment had caught up. All of these went forward in their several ways, but their very advance has emphasized the need of skill in this newer art. Technique has not occupied the attention of the social workers themselves so much as has the rapid development of new social specialties, some of them ill considered, perhaps, but all following inevitably upon that flowering of social ideals in this country which belongs to the last fifteen years. The time has now arrived to take fuller advantage of these new developments.

Attention to the details of social evidence is so new in case work that, in addition to the comparing of case work experiences attempted in Parts II and III of this book, it has seemed necessary to seek light wherever it could be found. Social work has its own approach to evidence, but wherever men of first-rate standing in other professions have discussed, in a way not too technical to be understood by the layman, this subject of evidence, it is worth our while to give attention. As will be seen from the Bibliography,[1] free use will be made in these pages of the remarkable contributions of Professor Hans Gross to criminal jurisprudence, of Professor J. H. Wigmore's Principles of Judicial Proof, and of James B. Thayer's Preliminary Treatise on Evidence at the Common Law. Dr. S. Weir Mitchell, Dr. Paul Dubois, Dr. Richard C. Cabot, and Dr. S. J. Meltzer have all written about medical diagnosis in a way which is suggestive and stimulating even to those who have had no medical training. The modern approach to the study of history is clearly set forth in a book that case workers should all read, the admirable Introduction to the Study of History by Langlois and Seignobos. Alfred Sidgwick's books on logic have also been consulted in the treatment of the subject of inferences. From applied psychology, apart from the measuring scales now in use, we are likely to receive in the future contributions which may, in many important particulars, modify the methods described in this book. Until case workers know more about psychology, however, than they now do, they will not be able even to formulate their needs in

[1] See page 483.

a way to command the psychologist's attention. There are, then, tasks of absorbing interest awaiting the social case workers of this and the next generation.

SUMMARY OF THIS CHAPTER

1. Social evidence may be defined as consisting of all facts as to personal or family history which, taken together, indicate the nature of a given client's social difficulties and the means to their solution.

2. Depending as it does less upon conspicuous acts than upon a trend of behavior, social evidence often consists of a series of facts any one of which would have slight probative value, but which, added together, have a cumulative effect.

3. Social evidence differs from legal evidence in that it is more inclusive and that the questions at issue are more complex. For these reasons, careful scrutiny of the reliability of each item of such evidence is all the more necessary.

4. The usefulness of social evidence outside of what is usually described as social work has been demonstrated in the diagnosis of physical and mental disorders, in the procedure of courts with certain groups of defendants, in the differential treatment of children in the schools and in their vocational guidance. As tests of its reliability are better formulated and more generally accepted, it will be put to still wider use.

5. Social work has its own approach to evidence, but as regards the testing of its evidential material it has much to learn from law, medicine, history, logic, and psychology.

CHAPTER III

DEFINITIONS BEARING UPON EVIDENCE

THE first interview with one needing treatment, the early contacts with his immediate family, the consultations with those outside his family who may give insight or co-operation, the examination of any documents bearing upon his problem, the later correlation of these separate items—all these processes of social case work are steps in what we hope will be a helpful course of action. They lead up through social diagnosis to a plan of treatment. The relation of diagnosis to this practical end cannot be too much insisted upon. Before turning to the discussion of this relation in present-day case work practice, however, it is necessary, even at the risk of some repetition, to prepare the way for the more concrete material which is to follow by giving at this point a few formal definitions.

I. CERTAIN TERMS FREQUENTLY USED

1. Diagnosis. The use of the word diagnosis is not restricted to medical case work; it means in zoölogy and botany, for example, "a brief, precise, and exclusively pertinent definition." In social diagnosis there is the attempt to arrive at as exact a definition as possible of the social situation and personality of a given client.[1] Investigation, or the gathering of evidence, begins the process, the critical examination and comparison of evidence follow, and last come its interpretation and the definition of the social difficulty. In common use, case workers often call all of this "an investigation," but, as their besetting sin is to slur over the processes of comparison and interpretation and to overemphasize the gathering of items of evidence, there is an educational advantage in using for the whole process the word which describes more especially the end of the process. Investigation enters into diagnosis, it enters

[1]See fuller discussion in Chapter XVIII, Comparison and Interpretation, p. 357.

into the laborious and learned seeking for truth which deserves to be termed *social research*, and it forms an important part of the many inquiries into social conditions which do not meet the exacting requirements of research, but which may properly be described as *social investigations*. While the word investigation is used in all these forms of social inquiry, the place which the process itself fills in social diagnosis, however necessary, is subordinate. An added advantage in the word diagnosis is that its use in medicine has given it the valuable connotation of a time limit. A diagnosis may be and often must be revised, of course, but a relatively inelastic time limit, together with the beneficent action always in view, constitute the controlling conditions of diagnosis in social work.

2. Witnesses. In so far as personal statements rather than documents are drawn upon by social diagnosis for its evidence, case work deals directly with *witnesses*. These must not be confused with trained *observers*. The latter word belongs to natural science; the former is primarily a law term. The observer is trained to accuracy, is on the lookout for facts tending to uphold or discredit some hypothesis; the witness reports what he has seen or heard incidentally in the course of his daily life. The observer uses controlled experimentation as his method, approaching his subject with impersonal detachment; whereas the witness has no method, is liable to personal bias, and is accurate or not according to his native powers of observation and memory. Rarely is the witness whose testimony is recorded in the interviews of social records an observer in the scientific sense.[1]

Case records sometimes ask for and set forth the statements of *references*. The word describes those who vouch for another. The slackness of its meaning is reflected in the quality of evidence secured, this frequently amounting to no more than the "vouching" of the early days of English law courts, when almost the only evidence sought was that of witnesses who swore under oath to the innocence or guilt of the defendant. Social case workers are sometimes content with equally bare testimony as to a man's sobriety and industry even from references who are presumably in command of facts which would throw light upon the cause of his need and

[1] See Chapter II, Nature and Uses of Social Evidence, p. 40.

upon possible methods of removing it. For example, a clergyman who refers a family for aid with the statement that he has known the man for some time and can vouch for him, must be in possession of some definite facts about the man in question which would prove helpful in planning treatment for the family. The initial difficulty in case work is always that of getting at facts which are ample and pertinent.

3. Fact. What do we mean by the word fact? It is not limited to the tangible, as James Bradley Thayer has pointed out.[1] Thoughts and events are facts. The question whether a thing be fact or not is the question whether or not it can be affirmed with certainty. Social workers do not always bother to ask themselves whether the statements they make can be affirmed with certainty. It is no unusual thing, for example, to read in a social case record the entry, "Gave the inquiring agency all the facts in this case," or "Asked the committee what they would advise in view of the facts in our possession," when not a single fact or only a few irrelevant ones had been obtained. Records even show instances of letters having been sent to other states or countries suggesting action on some family situation and presenting "the following facts," when the alleged facts are no more than unverified statements intermingled with the opinions and conjectures of the writer. The following is a case in point:

A case work agency wrote this answer to an agency in another state: "The Aid Society here in X has known the Y family since January, 1910, and we have consulted their record and also have looked up two references given in your letter. A year ago the Aid Society looked up Mr. Y's work references and his employers all speak ill of him. They say he was a shifty fellow who drank heavily, did unsatisfactory work, was untruthful, and has even been accused of stealing. We have heard that Mr. Y has at different times gone under assumed names. We believe that Mrs. Y is of a much better sort than her husband, though we have only her friends' word for it."

The "facts" in this case were that the Aid Society, although its acquaintance with the family began in 1910, had not kept track of them all that while, but had only the intermittent knowledge accompanying two appeals for relief. The employers who "all speak ill of him" consisted of but one employer with whom the man worked a year and whom he left of his own accord. This one employer, however, did speak of the man as shifty. The testimony as to drink came from a landlady, not an employer, while the accusation of theft was made by the woman's

[1] Preliminary Treatise on Evidence, p. 191.

brother, the theft being of clothes loaned by this brother which the man wore when he left his relative's house owing money for board. Mr. Y had used no alias but the last name of his stepfather, and the alleged reason for his doing this had not been verified. The last sentence is frankly a mere expression of opinion.

However near the truth may be the general impression conveyed by this letter, since the statements taken one by one could not be "affirmed with certainty," the agency to which this information was sent could not, on such a basis, plan treatment that would strike at the root of the trouble.

Every body of organized knowledge and skill advances in accord with its command of facts relevant to its aims. To take an instance far afield: An advertiser, writing in *Printers' Ink*, says that "Many an advertisement contains little arid spots, each of which represents a fact which the copy writer didn't know, and the lack of which had to be glossed over with language." This sentence might have been written about many a social case record, though it would have fitted the record of ten years ago still better.

The gathering of facts in any field of interest is made difficult first by faulty recollection or by inexpert or prejudiced observation on the part of persons giving testimony, and second by a confusion between the facts themselves and inferences drawn from them on the part either of witnesses or, in the special realm of our study, of social workers.

The confusion between the fact itself, even when accurately observed, and the inferences drawn by the observer is well illustrated by Dr. S. J. Meltzer:

> A physician has given . . . let us say, five grains of phenacetin to a pneumonia patient with a temperature of 105° F. on the seventh day of the disease. The temperature dropped to normal and the patient got well. The non-critical physician might record it as a fact that five grains of phenacetin reduced a temperature of 105° F. to normal and cured the patient. But this was not a fact; it was a conclusion [an inference] and a wrong one . . . ; the cure was accomplished by the crisis which accidentally set in after the giving of the phenacetin. Possibly the reduction of the fever was essentially also due to the crisis. What the physician actually observed were the three facts following one another, (1) the giving of the phenacetin, (2) the reduction of the fever, and (3) the recovery of the patient. The connecting of the three facts was . . . an act different and separate from the facts he actually observed.[1]

[1] "Ideas and Ideals in Medicine," in *Journal of the American Medical Association*, May 16, 1908, p. 1577 sq.

An American statesman who justified a public act by the assertion that he "dealt with the facts," was criticised in a leading article of the New York *Evening Post* as follows:

> The assumption is that to ascertain facts and act upon them is the easiest thing in the world. Principles may be cloudy and ideals escape us, but when you have a big, brutal set of facts before you, how can you go wrong? Everybody who stops to think, however, knows that dealing with facts is one of the most delicate operations of the human mind. There is, in the first place, the enormous difficulty of making sure that the facts are as stated to us by others. Next comes the arduous duty of avoiding that "instinctive theorizing," whence the fact looks to the eye as the eye likes the look. And in the end there is the obligation to decide what is the correct inference to be drawn from the facts, once granted that they are clearly established. To say in defence of challenged conduct, "I dealt with the facts," is no defence at all unless you are able to show that you first got your facts straight and then dealt with them properly.[1]

Thus at the threshold of our consideration of social evidence, the duty confronts us of making sure what are facts in a client's situation. Evidence which is reliable and which is sufficient in amount and cogency is the first requisite for searching diagnosis; the second is clear reasoning to inferences that shall further our purpose. The use of *inference,* then, the act of passing from some fact, belief, or judgment about a matter bearing on the client's difficulty to a further judgment, is an important part of diagnostic skill. Its risks in case work, and its relation to assumptions and hypotheses, are discussed at length in a later chapter.[2]

4. Evidence. The words evidence and proof are often confused. *Evidence* is the ultimate fact or facts offered as a basis for inference; *inference,* a part of the process of reasoning from this fact or facts to another—unknown—fact; while *proof* is the result of the reasoning. In social diagnosis, the kinds of evidence available, being largely testimonial in character, can of course never show a probative value equal to that of facts in the exact sciences. All that is possible for us is to obtain proof that amounts to a reasonable certainty. Social treatment is even more lacking in precision than the treatment of disease, of which Dr. Meltzer says that every treatment is an experiment. This is true partly because social work has as yet amassed but a small body of experience, partly because its treatment demands for success an understanding of

[1] New York *Evening Post,* August 19, 1911. [2] See Chapter V, Inferences.

"characterology," for which no satisfactory body of data yet exists, but most of all because, for the social case worker, the facts having a possible bearing upon diagnosis and treatment are so numerous that he can never be sure that some fact which he has failed to get would not alter the whole face of a situation. He can, however, partially offset these handicaps by being on the lookout for the special liability to error characteristic of each type of evidence used in his investigations.

II. TYPES OF EVIDENCE

Distinctions have been made by the law that will be of some service to us here, although it would be easy to exaggerate their value. Evidence in the law is used to ascertain the existence of a particular disputed fact; in social work, as already indicated, the problem is much less simple. Nevertheless, since case work shares with the law the risks and the advantages that come from a dependence upon testimony for the bases of action, the legal classifications of evidence should be kept in mind.[1]

The kinds of evidence presented to courts may be divided into real, testimonial, and circumstantial. There are many other classifications, but they are not of general application; they refer to some special danger or weakness of evidence as offered in courts, for the sake of which a rule of caution has been established. These three kinds of evidence differ in the ways in which we make our inferences from them; in real evidence no inference is needed; in testimonial evidence the basis of our inference is a human assertion; in circumstantial evidence the basis of an inference is anything whatever except a direct human assertion. This may not seem clear, but the explanations which follow should make it so, and the distinctions made are important enough to be studied closely.

1. Real Evidence. In real evidence the very fact at issue is presented to our senses. The classic instance in the law is that of the tailor and his customer who disagree as to the fit of a coat. The tailor sues, the customer wears the coat during the trial, and the jury sees for itself whether the coat fits or not.[2] Real evidence

[1] For suggestions and criticism in this part of the chapter the author would make grateful acknowledgment to Professor J. H. Wigmore, Dean of Northwestern University Law School.

[2] Thayer's Preliminary Treatise on Evidence, p. 263.

may become the basis of an inference and usually does. Thus, a person is seen to be of a certain size and complexion, and to have a certain cast of features. These are real evidence as to his appearance, from which we may infer that he is of a certain age.[1]

In social case work, real evidence is any item of evidence had by first-hand inspection. The appearance of a client's home is real evidence as to the conditions under which he lives; the meal on the table is real evidence that his family is not without food; and so on. When, however, the case worker who makes these inspections reports them to others—to case supervisors or committees, for example—the evidence which was "real" to him is testimonial to them, as it comes to them on the assertion of the worker.

2. Testimonial Evidence. This is the assertions of human beings. There is an important distinction here for the case worker between the testimonial evidence of one who says he saw or heard the supposed fact himself, and that of one who asserts it only from what others have told him. The latter is called *hearsay* evidence. As a statement is passed along from one to another it is very easy for error to creep in. In court, therefore, the first question is, Did you see or hear this affair yourself? And if the witness says, No, Mrs. Jones told me, then the judge says, Send for Mrs. Jones, and we will ask her to tell us whether *she* saw it; and so on, until they find some first-hand observer.

The social worker and the historian cannot and need not reject an item of hearsay evidence, as the court does; but (1) they should be cautious in relying upon it, and (2) they should, if possible, probe back until they find an original observer. Few things would strengthen social diagnosis more effectively than the habit of discovering, in interviews with witnesses, the extent to which their assertions are founded on observations or on mere rumor. "An event is attested three times by three chroniclers," says Langlois, "but these three attestations, which agree so admirably, are really only one, if it is ascertained that two of the three chroniclers copied the third, or that the three parallel accounts have been drawn from one and the same source."[2]

[1] See Wigmore, J. H.: A Treatise on the System of Evidence in Trials at Common Law, Vol. II, Sec. 1150. Boston, Little, Brown, and Co., 1904.

[2] An Introduction to the Study of History, p. 94.

The following illustrations of the risks in hearsay evidence are taken chiefly from our reading of social case records.

L. H. Levin of the Federated Jewish Charities of Baltimore tells of one case treatment in which it was necessary to consult a merchant about a former employe. The merchant answered by quoting the report of his manager that the man was listless, tardy, and inclined to shirk work. Fortunately the manager was seen for further details, and was found to base his opinion solely upon the employe's tendency to come late and leave his work early. He added that the reason given by the workman was that he must take care of his home. The social worker found that the home consisted of a sick wife and a number of helpless children, and that the husband and father felt the imperative necessity of caring for them.

[Neither manager nor merchant intended to deceive. The manager's report, however, because first-hand, showed more clearly than the merchant's what was fact and what inference, and was therefore easier to reconcile with the other evidence obtained by the social worker.]

The parents of a baby under treatment in a dispensary were boarding with a friend. A milk station nurse who was visiting this friend's family reported to the dispensary that the friend's children had syphilis, whereupon the dispensary visitor proceeded at once to advise the use of separate towels, dishes, etc. She then looked up the medical record of the boarding house keeper's children and found that the trouble was not syphilis but scabies. The milk station nurse had secured her information from the mother of these children. The original source for medical information, in other words, is the doctor or his record, and not even a layman so near to the situation as the patients' mother.

A girl was brought late at night to a hospital by a policeman. When her landlady was seen the next day by a visitor from the medical-social department of the hospital she stated that the girl had been picked up on the street in an intoxicated condition, and that the policeman who found her had said she was a "tough lot." At the police station, however, the patrolman said that he had never seen the girl until he discovered her in an unconscious condition, and that, so far as he knew, she was not intoxicated. Two physicians reported that the girl had heart attacks. The landlady was a hearsay source as to the girl's condition when picked up; the policeman a first-hand source as regards his own experiences with the girl; the doctors who had made a physical examination were the only first-hand sources as regards her physical condition.

A case worker supplies the following example of hearsay evidence from recent experience: A neighbor said of Mrs. B that she neglected her little girl and had been ordered by the school to cut off the child's hair. The inference which the investigator was intended to make and did make was—vermin. Inquiry at the school, however, showed that the child's hair had been cut off because of a rash. On another occasion the brother-in-law of this same client reported that the clinic nurse had said in a way that made it sound detrimental that she was "through with Mrs. B." Inquiry showed that this nurse, in attempting to get the little girl into a preventorium, had failed repeatedly to find Mrs. B at home (the woman was away at her work of washing and ironing), and had remarked that she would give up trying to find her.

The reporter of this case, who is a graduate of a law school, feels that many social case records show a failure to recognize the burden of proof as resting on the one who attacks a client's character, and even a tendency on the part of some case workers to accept without scrutiny any bit of unfavorable testimony that may help them to classify clients more readily. The rule of law which requires that the best evidence procurable shall be produced would, in her opinion, be a safeguard. Moreover, the social records that had come to her notice did not show that in weighing evidence allowance had been made for prejudice where it undoubtedly existed. Prejudice or bias in witnesses is one of the things for which to cultivate a keen eye, as will appear in the discussion of Testimonial Evidence in the next chapter.

3. Circumstantial Evidence. This is the catch-all; it includes everything which is not the direct assertion of a human being. By "direct assertion" is here meant one which if true would establish the point immediately at issue; whereas an indirect assertion —indirect evidence of any kind, in fact—merely asserts some other fact which, in turn, tends to establish the point at issue.

Suppose the point to be determined in a given case is whether a husband feels affection for his family—a question which is of practical importance sometimes in case decisions. If the wife states that her husband does not care for her and their children, she is giving direct testimonial evidence. She may be mistaken or she may misrepresent, but the assertion bears directly upon the issue, and the only risks involved in accepting her evidence as proof are the risks involved in judging her competence and her bias. When, however, she names certain cumulative circumstances from which might be inferred the state of the man's affections; when she says that he gives her $6.00 a week out of $22, that he spends over half of his leisure time away from home, that he is irritable when he does appear there, etc., these statements, which would be direct testimony as to his habits, are only indirect testimony as to his indifference. Now this indirect testimony is subject to the same tests of competence and bias as the wife's direct testimony, both being the assertions of a human being. But to the inferences drawn from the former additional tests must be applied; these assertions of fact, if believed, become the bases of an inference to another fact. We must ask: Do they, taken together, fairly indicate the thing inferred? Do the meager allowance, the frequent absences, and the irritability—granting all to be true—really mean what the wife asserts that they mean? Are any other explanations possible? If they are, it is the duty of the case worker to seek for them.

Note in the foregoing the cumulative effect of adding item to item of indirect evidence, each a comparatively weak basis of inference in itself, but gaining in cogency with every circumstance added. Circumstantial evidence, always indirect, is characteristically cumulative. Moreover, any fact in the material universe or in the mind of man may become the basis from which some other fact is inferred. The trustworthiness of this indirect evidence, apart from the bias and competence of the witness through whom it may have come, depends upon a set of considerations which vary with the nature of the subject matter—for example, electric wires, coal, medicine, cooking utensils, sewer gas; whereas the trustworthiness of direct evidence depends upon certain human traits possessed in varying degrees by all witnesses, such as honesty, bias, attention, memory, suggestibility, etc. The relation of these traits to evidence will be discussed in the next chapter.

Despite the difficulty of drawing correct inferences from circumstantial evidence, it has the advantage over direct testimonial evidence that the inference does not depend upon the elusive personal trustworthiness of a witness; for example, if a child's back is wounded in a certain way, the shape of the wound may be such as indicates infallibly that it was beaten with an instrument and that the father's assertion about the child's falling down stairs must be false. The case worker will have to use both kinds of testimonial evidence—direct and indirect. In using indirect evidence, moreover, he will have to adapt his tests to an infinitely varied subject matter.

Besides these cardinal distinctions of evidence, there are certain minor distinctions which may be of service to the social worker.

Oral testimony defines itself. It is the main reliance of the social diagnostician.

Documentary evidence is of many kinds, from formal documents of legal origin to the informal letters and writings of private persons. This subject of the uses of documents in case work is important enough to receive separate treatment in Chapter XIII, Documentary Sources. Suffice it to say here that it is a dangerous thing to trust to anyone's memory of a document; hence the rule of law, Always look at the document itself. If a tenant says, "The landlord sent me a notice to get out," call for the document. It may read: "*If* you do not pay your rent by next Monday, I will put you out," which is a different thing.

Expert evidence is one species of testimonial evidence. Its use signifies that the subject under consideration is one which is believed to need special skill in observing and judging. The advantage of expert testimony lies in the skill of the person giving it. A physician can tell to what extent certain children are suffering in health, whereas the social worker's opinion would be of little value. Hence, call in an expert whenever the judgment to be made is one that should not be based on ordinary experience. The disadvantage of expert testimony lies in the bias which specialists are apt to develop. A policeman is a specialist in crime; looking for the same thing always, his bias may become in time a marked tendency to expect to find it on every hand.

Character evidence needs no defining. Since the social worker seeks to discover the possibilities of bettering a client's situation, he naturally must look for those traits in the client and his family which may further or obstruct his purpose.

Years ago, when it often happened that the choice of treatment hardly went further than between the giving or refusing of coal and groceries, character evidence in social work was, as in the law courts, a mere generalized estimate, favorable or unfavorable, of an individual's characteristics. He was either worthy of relief or unworthy. The social worker's preoccupation, like the lawyer's, was with desert. Since on that basis the case worker's decision against any client's application for aid became invidious, the presumption, as a matter of justice, had to be in the client's favor. The burden of proof rested with those who gave evidence as to unworthiness. One still sometimes finds this point of view in private agencies and public departments. As a rule, however, the case worker's interest is approaching an impartial study of personality, such as concerns itself not with the meting out of punishment or reward (the offering of almshouse or outdoor relief, for example) but with the determining of all traits, whether in their good or their bad aspects, as they affect the possibility and the method of social reconstruction. The successful outcome of case work is nowhere more dependent upon flexibility of method than in the study of personal traits. The choice of method being wide, and there being, generally speaking, no presumption in favor of one diagnosis rather than another, the social case worker, like the physician, has little call to consider the "burden of proof." Nevertheless, since the worker in his effort to arrive at an understanding of a client's personality must be free to take into account not only hearsay evidence but, with due precautions, even rumor, he may find it sometimes necessary to guard against his own infirmities of judgment by placing, as already suggested, the burden of proof with regard to his client's less admirable traits upon those who give this unfavorable testimony.

The relative importance of the distinctions made in this chapter is in many ways greater to the lawyer, historian, or scientist, than to the social worker. The conspicuous thing which the social case worker can learn from the lawyer is the risks involved in the various types of evidence, while from the historian he can learn the importance of a rigorous examination of sources of information as to their trustworthiness. From physician and psychologist social work has more to learn than from either lawyer or historian, inasmuch as science, unlike law or history, can throw direct light on the social needs and possibilities of the case worker's clients.

SUMMARY OF THIS CHAPTER

1. Social diagnosis is the attempt to arrive at as exact a definition as possible of the social situation and personality of a given client. The gathering of evidence, or investigation, begins the process, the critical examination and comparison of evidence follows, and last come its interpretation and the definition of the social difficulty. Where one word must describe the whole process, *diagnosis* is a better word than *investigation*, though in strict use the former belongs to the end of the process.

2. A controlling condition in social diagnosis is its relatively inelastic time limit —as compared, that is, with other forms of social inquiry. This does not mean that a social diagnosis cannot be revised; often it must be. Another controlling condition is the beneficent action always in view.

3. The word *fact* is not limited to the tangible. Thoughts and events are facts. The question whether a thing be fact or not is the question whether or not it can be affirmed with certainty. The gathering of facts is made difficult by faulty observation, faulty recollection, and by a confusion between the facts themselves and the inferences drawn from them.

4. *Real* evidence is the very fact at issue presented to our senses. *Testimonial* evidence is the assertions of human beings. *Circumstantial* evidence is the catch-all; it includes everything which is not the direct assertion of a human being—the assertion, that is, which if true would establish the point at issue.

5. The three classes of evidence which are of general application may be distinguished by the way in which we make inferences from them. In real evidence no inference is needed; in testimonial evidence the basis of our inference is a human assertion; in circumstantial evidence the basis of our inference may be anything at all.

6. There is an important distinction in testimonial evidence between the evidence of one who says he saw or heard the supposed fact himself, and that of one who asserts it only from what others have told him. The latter is *hearsay* evidence. It should be relied on with caution, and a very necessary practice in interviewing witnesses is to discover the extent to which their assertions are founded on observations or on mere rumor.

7. There is another important distinction in evidence between direct and indirect evidence. Circumstantial evidence is always indirect and characteristically cumulative. In direct evidence, the only tests of trustworthiness needed are those usually applied to human traits, such as honesty, bias, attention, memory, suggestibility, etc.

CHAPTER IV

TESTIMONIAL EVIDENCE

AFTER an historian has established the genuineness and authorship of a document, his next care is to discover the competence and bias of the man who made it; to go back, in short, to the testimonial evidence, the human assertions, on which the document is based. The following passage summarizes many of the queries suggested by Langlois and Seignobos[1] in their discussion of the tests of an author's good faith and accuracy. Questions of legal competency aside, it will be seen that, with slight variations, these tests would apply to the competence and bias of any witness. They are most suggestive in the field of social work and deserve the case worker's careful consideration.

Good Faith. Were there any practical advantages to be gained by the witness who made the statement in its present form? Had he an interest in deceiving? What interest did he think he had? (We must look for the answer in *his* tastes and ideals, not in our own.) If there was no individual interest to serve, was there a collective interest, such as that of a family, a religious denomination, a political party, etc.? Was he so placed that he was compelled to tell an untruth? Was some rule or custom, some sympathy or antipathy, dominating him? Was personal or collective vanity involved? Did his ideas of etiquette, of what politeness demanded, run counter to making a perfectly truthful statement? [We do not know a man at all until we understand the conventions that form so large a part of the moral atmosphere which he breathes.] Or again, has he been betrayed into telling a good story, because it made an appeal to the artistic sense latent somewhere in all of us?

Accuracy. Was the statement an answer to a question or a series of questions? (It is necessary to apply a special criticism to every statement obtained by interrogation.) What was the question put, and what are the preoccupations to which it may have given rise in the mind of the person interrogated? Was the observer well situated for observing? Was he possessed of the special experience or general intelligence necessary for understanding the facts? How long before he recorded what he observed? Or did he record it, like some newspaper accounts of meetings, before it happened? Finally, was the fact stated of such a nature that it could not have been learned by observation alone?

[1] Introduction to the Study of History, p. 165–176.

Like the historian, the case worker must have for the weighing of the evidence with which he deals a clear understanding of the two factors which condition the value of testimony; namely, (1) the witness's opportunity to know the facts and the way in which he has used this opportunity—his competence, in short; and (2) those ideas or emotions of the witness which may prejudice his judgment—his bias.

I. THE COMPETENCE OF THE WITNESS

Case workers heed the competence of a witness only in an unavowed and hit-or-miss fashion. Their daily experience it is true teaches them to take roughly into account the witness's opportunity to know the facts. For instance, they frequently find that the person referring a client for care thinks he has had ample opportunity to know the client's affairs when the reverse is the case.

A charitable woman asked relief for a capable widow whom she said she had known well for years. It appeared, however, that she did not know how many children were at home, whether the oldest son was working, what were the woman's habits as to drink, what the family income was, or whether, in fact, they needed aid at all. She had not been to the home of this family for several years, and had taken the statement of need as the widow gave it to her one day in church. The charitable woman was quite surprised, as her conversation with the secretary of the agency proceeded, to discover how superficial was her knowledge of any of the real circumstances of the widow's family life.

The social worker has to be on guard against this same risk in consulting the relatives of a client. Some relatives know a great deal, and others, who think they know everything, really know very little.

An agency tried to interest fairly well-to-do relatives in the needs of a delicate man with a wife and several children. They were not responsive. They claimed they had already helped more or less, that they had burdens of their own, and that he was a loafer, a "poor shrimp," as one of the kin described him. It turned out that the man had locomotor ataxia, the result of syphilis. With this medical diagnosis, which explained to a considerable extent the man's ill success, the worker again appealed to the relatives, this time with good results.

This man's brothers and cousins had had no opportunity to learn the crucial point in his situation, and were therefore not competent witnesses as to his character for industry.

Ordinarily employers would not be competent witnesses as to a man's home conditions; social acquaintances as to his industrial capacity; nor a social agency that trusted to intuitions as to his personal repute. These would be facts concerning which the groups named could have had no knowledge.

The use which a witness has made of his opportunity to know the facts is a subject which social workers have hardly begun to consider; it therefore does not admit of adequate discussion at present. Inasmuch as this use depends upon the witness's powers of attention and memory, upon his suggestibility, etc., any searching inquiry into the relation of these factors to a witness's competence must come from the psychologists. To case workers, however, will have to be entrusted the application of the elements of psychology to testimonial evidence in their own field.

1. Attention. The closeness of attention on the part of any witness to an incident in his own or another's situation[1] depends upon the importance which at the time he attaches to it, or, it may be, upon the existence of a similarity between some part of that incident and something which he has experienced before—upon his "funded thought."[2] This "funded thought" is his material for

[1] In one of the short, unpublished papers referred to in the Preface, Mr. Julian Codman, writing on "Evidence in its Relation to Social Service," gives the following instance of inattention:

One day Mr. P, a lifelong resident of Nahant, a man of high cultivation and exceptional ability, and an enthusiastic golfer, came to the chairman of the green committee of the Golf Club and told him that he thought part of the course was unsafe for passers-by. This was a place where the county road crossed the course. He said that he thought a notice should be put up warning all players to look and see that the road was clear of foot-passengers and carriages before playing a ball from the teeing ground. The chairman suggested a notice as follows, and asked if that would be sufficient:

"DANGER: All persons before driving from this tee are cautioned to see that no one is passing in the road."

Mr. P said that he thought such a sign would be just the thing.

"Well," said the chairman, "a sign in exactly those words in letters three inches long in black paint on a white ground has been in front of your eyes every time you have driven off that tee during the last six years."

Have you any doubt that, if Mr. P had been called on the witness-stand to testify as to the presence or absence of a sign in that particular tee, he would have taken his oath that no such sign existed? And he would have so sworn with the utmost confidence in his correctness. [The explanation for this gentleman's apparent inattention may have been that for six years he had heeded the warning given by the sign board automatically, and that therefore its importance for himself had long disappeared.]

[2] "I remember vividly a case of jealous murder in which the most important witness was the victim's brother, an honest, simple woodsman, brought up in the wilderness, and in every sense far-removed from idiocy. His testimony was brief,

thinking, the sum total of ideas which his traditions, education, and experience have made an integral part of his mind. New experience which is entirely strange, which he can relate to nothing in his past thinking, he will not heed.

A woman whose husband showed signs of mental disturbance consented to his being observed with a view to commitment for hospital care. She did this, however, merely because she was desperate at what she considered his incorrigible laziness, and because she knew she would be better off without him. The social worker interested could neither make her see that he was other than normal mentally, nor give her a conception of what it meant to be insane without violent mania. His occasional abuse of his wife, his desire to keep her in the house so that she should not talk with neighbors, his ungrounded suspicions of her fidelity and of his son's honesty, she apparently took for granted as "crankiness—the way he was made." His incompetence even in the least skilled work she of course accounted for as wilful indolence.

This woman was familiar with the idea of the unreasonable and lazy husband, and totally unfamiliar with the idea of an early stage of insanity. This last idea therefore could not command her attention and credence as an explanation of her troubles. A case worker who wants to get evidence throwing light on mental abnormalities from uneducated people is likely to have better success by leading them to talk not about "peculiarities" but about temper, laziness, etc.—familiar domestic phenomena. The social worker, then, in weighing evidence, must take account of differences in the funded thought of witnesses, in so far as this is likely to affect the objects or incidents to which a particular witness will give attention.

The influence of the social worker's own funded thought upon his success in collecting evidence shows in the following instance, supplied by one who was training young case workers:

decided, and intelligent. When the motive for the murder, in this case most important, came under discussion, he shrugged his shoulders and answered my question—whether it was not committed on account of a girl—with 'Yes, so they say.' On further examination I reached the astonishing discovery that not only the word 'jealousy' but the very notion and comprehension of it were totally foreign to the man. The single girl he at one time had thought of had been won away from him without making him quarrelsome, nobody had ever told him of the pangs and passions of other people, he had had no occasions to consider the theoretic possibility of such a thing, and so 'jealousy' remained utterly foreign to him. It is clear that his hearing now took quite another turn. All I thought I heard from him was essentially wrong; his 'funded thought' concerning a very important, in this case a regulative, concept, had been too poor."—Gross, Criminal Psychology, p. 21–22.

A post-graduate student in sociology had been sent, after careful directions, to visit a family, but apparently there had been no hooks in his mind on which to hang his instructions. He could not tell, when he returned to the office, whether the wife and mother seemed in good health or bad, he had no idea of the woman's approximate age, or of the number of her children (there were a lot, he thought), of the number and size of the rooms, or of their condition. But he did learn that the husband and father was working and that he was a member of a union. As the young man was writing a thesis upon Trade Unionism, the inference is obvious. He saw what he knew enough to notice.

2. Memory. Social case records are "a series of miniature biographies," says Professor J. M. Vincent, "the materials for which are gathered while the subject is still living. In part these are autobiographical and have both the strength and weaknesses of personal memoirs."[1] The weakness of personal memoirs is the misleading impression that they give of being contemporary testimony when they are not; in reality they are memory material;[2] the most significant things that they narrate may have happened months or years before.

It is characteristic of the uneducated narrator with whom the social worker frequently has to deal that he must often arrive indirectly at the time which has elapsed since any given event. He remembers by associating this event with certain others, the dates of which are wellknown, such as a public calamity (a war, earthquake, or fire); a national or civic landmark (a holiday, an election); a family event which is on record (a birth, marriage, or death); a natural phenomenon (the seasons, the tides, the weather).[3]

What appears a defect in memory may sometimes be the inexpressiveness often met in ignorant people, an inability to find or to arrange in cogent order the words needed to describe a past experience.[4] The silence of the peasant has probably a different

[1] From one of the short, unpublished papers referred to in the Preface.

[2] See Langlois and Seignobos, An Introduction to the Study of History, p. 175.

[3] The distance in time between two events both of which are in question is arrived at in the same way. "If anybody says that event A occurred four or five days before event B, we may believe him, if, e. g., he adds, 'For when A occurred we began to cut corn, and when B occurred we harvested it. And between these two events there were four or five days.' "—Gross, Criminal Psychology, p. 384.

[4] "In other words, discrepancies or inadequacies may appear in reports, which are due, not only to misdirected attention, malobservation, and errors of memory, but also to lack of caution or of zeal for accurate statement, to scanty vocabulary, to injudicious phraseology, or, of course, to deliberate intent to mislead."—Guy M. Whipple, reprinted by Wigmore in Principles of Judicial Proof, p. 576.

source. One worker of considerable experience with Lithuanian peasants attributes it to their doubt as to what is going on in the stranger's mind, and whether the latter thinks in the same way as do their own people. As they find common intellectual ground, they drop their reticence. It takes no small skill on the part of an interviewer, however, to start the train of ideas which will induce frank communication from such people.

Memory material is liable to two changes in repeated reporting.

Whipple calls attention to the fact that repetition "tends in part to establish in mind the items reported, whether they be true or false, and . . . tends also to induce some departure in the later reports, because these are based more upon the memory of the verbal statements of the earlier reports than upon the original experience itself."[1]

In social case work the first, unrehearsed statement of a client or of those who know him is likely to be the fullest and most reliable. Competent workers dread the client who has told his story to several different social agencies. Becoming tired of repeating his account of his situation, he leaves out essential parts, or else, having found that certain incidents had a desired influence upon his hearers, he emphasizes them and perhaps slights others quite as significant.

3. Suggestibility. A third factor which affects a person's competence as a witness is his suggestibility. By that we mean an over-readiness to yield assent to and to reproduce the assertions of other people. A witness may confuse observations made by others with his own; he may give a facile acceptance to what he reads[2] as well as to what he hears. Dr. Frankwood E. Williams,[3] when secretary of the Massachusetts Society for Mental Hygiene and member of the Prison Board in that state, noted as one of the most conspicuous factors in the misdoings of boys at the State

[1] Whipple, reprinted by Wigmore in Principles of Judicial Proof, p. 580.

[2] "A first and natural impulse leads us to accept as true every statement contained in a document, which is equivalent to assuming that no author ever lied or was deceived; and this spontaneous credulity seems to possess a high degree of vitality, for it persists in spite of the innumerable instances of error and mendacity which daily experience brings before us."—Langlois and Seignobos, Introduction to the Study of History, p. 155.

[3] In 1917, Associate Medical Director, National Committee for Mental Hygiene.

Industrial School at Shirley their ready suggestibility for either good or evil.[1]

A children's agency had a discouraging struggle with an unusually bright girl in her early teens. She came under the influence of two older girls of low character and did just what they proposed, which was to go on the street. On the other hand, when under the influence of the agency's visitor, she conducted herself properly and showed an ambition to make something of herself. In company with respectable, intelligent people, she rose to their level, but would drop back again the moment she chanced upon evil counsels. She would be as absorbed in a revival meeting as in some sailor whom she happened upon afterwards. This girl, although aware of her suggestibility and of just how it might affect her prospects, apparently could not control it.

The following illustration, although of an adult, shows the same weakness:

A man who was a good workman, married, with several children, lost two successive positions on the ground of his dishonesty. The second time the charge was that of receiving stolen goods, the theft itself having been committed by two other employes. Between his arrest and trial he got work as a chauffeur, and used his employer's car without permission until he ran into a telegraph pole and damaged the machine. He was placed on probation for a year. After a few months of temporary jobs, his probation officer got him steady work. From then on he improved, receiving an advance in wage and then the promise of a foremanship. To the delight of his wife, his interest in his children awakened. The man himself said he owed all to the probation officer, who, as he observed, was wonderful in his understanding of men. Unfortunately for this fellow, probation terms end. At last accounts he had disappeared, leaving his children to be supported by charity. While under the supervision of a man of good standards this man could keep straight. Without that brace he went to pieces.

The case worker must bear in mind that suggestibility may influence not only the client's conduct, but also his thinking and his standards. The girl just cited, in the presence of a refined, earnest woman worker, would rise above the coarse speech and free demeanor which she finds an asset among low companions. A kindly bias common to social workers leads them, in the case of any client who interests them, especially a young one, to try to get at those traits that give most promise of amended conduct. Roused by this bias, the girl's suggestibility, taken together with

[1] "The one factor that more than any other is responsible for the poor reports of children is their excessive suggestibility, especially in the years before puberty." (Whipple, reprinted by Wigmore in Principles of Judicial Proof, p. 580.) This is strikingly illustrated in Whipple's report of a Belgian murder trial, reprinted by Wigmore. (The Puyenbroeck Case, Principles of Judicial Proof, p. 521.)

her desire to please, may make her not only seem but be so different a person while in the presence of the social worker that the latter forms a mistaken estimate of her character as a whole. What is true of such a girl as the one referred to, is true to a lesser extent of the man who was influenced by the probation officer.

Suggestibility may even reach the extent of leading to mistaken confessions:

A judge was about to sentence to prison a woman who had been arrested for disorderly conduct and for attracting a crowd on the street. Although she made a long and circumstantial confession of immorality, her apathetic manner awakened doubt in the mind of a social worker present. This worker, having secured a suspension of sentence, traced the woman's husband and relatives to another city and found that her claim to have been long leading a prostitute's life was without foundation. The prisoner's "disorderly conduct" was due to an epileptic seizure. Her confession showed the need, not of a prison sentence, but of observation in a psychopathic hospital.

This woman, arrested for disorderly conduct, was undoubtedly assumed by the police to be of low character and probably put in jail among women of this sort. May the layman venture to surmise that the frank talk about unsavory experiences to which such women are prone, and to which she would have been a listener, may have suggested to her enfeebled mind the story she told the court?

4. Leading Questions. Closely related to the suggestibility of witnesses is the response which they may make to "leading questions." The social case worker must be on guard against getting back as alleged fact some mere conjecture of his own which he has implicitly expressed by his wording, or by the inflection of his voice. A case worker with little faith may ask, "You have no relatives who would take in the baby while you go to the hospital, have you?"; whereas the worker who gets results would put the question, "Which of your sisters could best take the baby?"

A worker in training reported to the district secretary under whom she was visiting that one of her clients had misrepresented her daughter's wages. The secretary asked, "Did Mrs. B actually say that Bertha was earning $5.00 a week?" After thinking a moment, the worker replied, "Why no, but when I said, 'Bertha is earning $5.00 a week, is she not?' she said 'Yes.'"

The permissibility of leading questions[1] in social work is solely

[1] In courts of law those leading questions are objectionable in direct examinations (1) which embody a material fact and suggest a desired "yes" or "no" in

a matter of adapting the means in a given case to the end in view. This end, the social readjustment of the client and of his affairs, may be defeated by a detective manner or by a shrewd framing of questions such as places the subject at a disadvantage. The stage of social inquiry in which case investigators prided themselves upon an ability to catch people tripping, to surprise an admission, has given way to a diagnostic method which, shunning small subterfuges such as raise barriers between worker and client, establishes the latter's confidence by a direct approach and by putting aside, to be sought elsewhere, questions that can be answered equally well from another source.

"In my early experience," writes Miss Zilpha D. Smith, "I was apt, in interviews, to make, out loud, deductions from what had been told me, and then ask if my conclusion was right. I learned to check myself in doing this, for it invited untrue statements."

It is, however, not always possible to avoid leading questions. Some minds are so sluggish, others so unwilling or unable to recollect a series of events until a starting point has been supplied, that the common rule against leading questions in case work, like the similar rule in law, must be "understood in a reasonable sense."[1] Some forms of the leading question remove the temptation to be untruthful, as in the following example:

A medical-social worker was talking with a patient about whom there was a perceptible odor of strong drink. She began, "What kind of liquor do you ordinarily drink and how much?" Then, not waiting for an answer, continued, "With the disease which you have and the kind of medicine you are taking, all liquor is bad, and certain kinds are very dangerous." The man told her that he took gin and how much. She feels that had she asked, "Do you drink?" he would have denied it.

The question "Do you drink?" is often taken to mean "Do you drink to excess?" "Are you a drunkard?" and is of course offensive. The worker framed her question in a way dictated as much by politeness as by investigating skill.

It cannot be claimed that framing such questions as will elicit the truth is always easy, nor will there be unanimity of opinion as

reply; (2) which contain assumptions that facts are known that are not known, or that answers have been given that have not been given; (3) which constitute an argumentative series. See Greenleaf on Evidence, p. 538 sq., for exceptions to these rules.

[1] Greenleaf on Evidence, p. 537.

to what is and what is not permissible on ethical grounds. Take, for illustration, a statement in Mrs. Solenberger's book on Homeless Men.[1] To a homeless man of over thirty, applying for relief and guidance, she was accustomed to say in her first interview not "Are you married?" but "Where is your wife?"; not "Have you a family?" but "How much of a family have you?" Some students of social work have objected to this as a form of deception, advocating "Are you married?" as the more honest question. Experience has shown, however, that "Are you married?" usually leads to the answer "No," while "Where is your wife?" usually reveals the existence of a wife.

A doctor once gave an amusing example of how to avoid the leading question. He found that when he asked his patients whether they were better they said "Yes," and when he asked them whether they were worse, they also said "Yes," so that he had learned to force from them an original opinion by framing his inquiry: "Well, are you worse or better, or *how* are you this morning?" Questions can often be avoided by the use of circumstantial evidence. A probation officer need not say "Do you smoke cigarettes?" but "Let me look at your hands."

To sum up, leading questions may suggest to the client answers which are not true, or they may prevent the establishment of confidence between worker and client. When used at all, it should be with an awareness of these dangers on the part of the social worker.

II. THE BIAS OF THE WITNESS

1. Racial or National. The risk of bias in testimony is so obvious that social workers become alive to it in a general way. In the industrial centers of the United States bias arising from race must be constantly allowed for. One of the social worker's difficulties with foreigners is that he does not understand their conventions any more than they do his; a knowledge of their history and of their old world environment is indispensable to the most helpful relations with them. In a paper on a group of South Italians[2] known to her as a social worker, Miss Ida Hull names, among other

[1] Solenberger, Alice Willard: One Thousand Homeless Men. A Study of Original Records, p. 22. Russell Sage Foundation Publication. New York, Charities Publication Committee, 1911.

[2] One of the short, unpublished papers referred to in the Preface.

things to be kept in mind, the fact that they have tilled the soil of their primitive communities according to Virgilian methods, that they have lived where parish jealousies were strong, where the machinery of government—of the courts, for instance—was distrusted; that they are intensely proud of their race and their language, and resentful, therefore, of any assumption of superiority in others; that they act from emotional rather than from reasoned motives; and that they prefer the leisurely and indirect approach.

Letting fly the question direct means receiving in return evasions, prompted by a repugnance for what seems intruding brusqueness. Hurry is absolutely fatal to a successful interview. Social amenities must have their place, and the conversation must proceed in such fashion that the important point seems to come in rather incidentally, or to be suggested by the family itself.

The perplexing experience of a young worker bears this out. She was an enthusiastic and capable college graduate who belonged to the Society of Friends and had been trained to the habit of telling the unflinching truth. Whenever she visited a family in "little Italy" who were bred in the tradition that the courteous thing to do was to say whatever a guest seemed to desire said, there was a clash of standards which finally brought about her assignment to a district less alien to her traditions.

Social workers will sometimes meet a class bias in peasants from the old world. The case worker is more likely to assume humility in a peasant than to recognize his family pride and the grounds for it. For example,

A young peasant girl expressed astonishment that an older woman, who had been adopted from an institution in childhood, had been able to get a good husband. She wondered that such a man would take a woman when he could not know from what sort of people she came. She herself was expecting to marry a man the character of whose forebears she knew as well as she knew her own.

Such a girl would be likely to give biased evidence about one who was without established family respectability. Miss Emily G. Balch describes the peasant attitude as follows:

A peasant is thus something quite distinct from anything that we know in America. On the one hand, he is a link in a chain of family inheritance and tradition that may run back for centuries, with a name, a reputation, and a posterity. On the other hand, he is confessedly and consciously an inferior.

And of racial bias among the various Slavic nationalities, she says,

> In American communities they have different churches, societies, newspapers, and a separate social life. Too often the lines of cleavage are marked by antipathies and old animosities. The Pole wastes no love on the Russian, nor the Ruthenian on the Pole, and a person who acts in ignorance of these facts . . . may find himself in the position of a host who should innocently invite a Fenian from County Cork to hobnob with an Ulster Orangeman on the ground that both were Irish.[1]

One in receipt of unfavorable evidence from a Pole about a Russian, therefore, would have to allow not so much for personal as for racial bias.

The use of interpreters also presents difficulties. When people who do not speak English have to be interviewed through one, the results are the reverse of satisfactory. As one worker put it, if an interpreter can fulfill his part in an honest, unbiased, and intelligent way, he had better be turned into a social worker and do the case work needed himself. Such interpreters are almost non-existent.

> A Polish interpreter, either through a misunderstanding or from self-interest, told a deserted wife with three children that she was to be deported by the state. She ran off, leaving the children to public care. It took two months to find her and reunite her and the children, and three years for the state visitor to gain her confidence. Her bias naturally inclined her to trust the statement of one of her own race and language.[2]

2. Environmental. Bias also accompanies standards of conduct springing from this or that kind of education or environment.

> An ex-probation officer states that the police officers other than the one making the arrest in the criminal courts where he served would never give him unfavorable information about a prisoner before sentence. They would allow him to spend several hours running down previous arrests, etc., or would be silent while the court gave him some old jailbird as a probationer for a first offense, rather than be guilty of the meanness, as they thought it, of hitting a man who was down.[3] After the case was settled they would tell what they knew, showing respect for the probation officer's acuteness if he had not been fooled and some good-natured contempt for him if he had. It never occurred to them that to succeed in eluding justice might have a bad effect upon the prisoner's character.

[1] Our Slavic Fellow Citizens, p. 42 and p. 8.

[2] See also reference to interpreters in Chapter VI, The First Interview, p. 118 sq.

[3] The need of better court records, which would have saved the probation officer and his client from some of these mistakes, is discussed in Chapter XIII, Documentary Sources.

One meets this personal as contrasted with a social standard of ethics frequently in people of fine character and of otherwise good intelligence. Mayors, clergymen, teachers, employers may suppress the truth where they think this would help someone for whom they are sorry. They want to give him "another chance," often regardless of the chances he may have already wasted, and of the treatment best calculated to make him a useful citizen.

A woman whose maid had caused her great annoyance by staying out till the small hours night after night, and had later left because pregnant, told none of this to another mistress who inquired about the girl some months later. She said she did not want to be the one to do it.

This woman thought she was being kind. Again, as in the case of the police, it never occurred to her that this might be a poor way to get the girl started right. She did not know how to take active steps to help her maid, and so did the one passively kind thing that presented itself.

A medical-social worker had occasion to consult a former employer of one of her patients about the patient's insurance. The employer denied any knowledge of it, though the insurance records showed his signature to payments. Here was an honorable man making a false statement. He explained later that he had promised his employe not to tell about the insurance. The denial was due to what he regarded as the demands of loyalty.

Of course, the social worker cannot ask that witnesses violate their own standards of ethics. These instances show a kindheartedness that no one would wish less. In the last illustration, however, what was presumably good nature led the employer to make a promise which was obviously futile.

3. The Bias of Self-interest. This form of bias is of course universal. When, therefore, a witness testifies reluctantly and apparently against his interest, his testimony has special weight.

A charity organization secretary was interested in a family consisting of a widower and four children under fifteen. These children came to the office one day, saying that their father when drunk had turned them out of doors, and that they had spent the night with a cousin. The secretary called at once on this cousin, finding his wife at home and himself in bed in the next room. The wife said nothing except that the children had been there as they said. The next day the secretary called again and found the woman alone. This time she said she had not dared to talk openly on the previous day, because her husband would not approve of her saying things about his uncle. The uncle, the children's father, was drunk most of the time. Although the children should be taken away, she could not go to court about it. Her husband, too, drank and often beat her. She did not dare complain about this even to her own relatives, because her husband had said that he would kill her father and brother if she did.

This evidence, given under circumstances that warrant one's believing that the woman had nothing to gain and possibly much to lose by telling it, carries a strong presumption of truth.

The suppression of facts from a desire to escape work and receive assistance instead is a fairly obvious form of self-interest. The following is the only illustration of this particular fault that need be given:

An Italian girl of thirteen was referred to a medical-social department for general hygiene. There were two younger children, the mother was dead, the father out of work, the home wretched. A young man living there was said by the patient to be her cousin. The relationship was so described by the public relief officials, the school teacher, and the Italian society—all of which seemed to be confirmatory evidence. But a priest who was seen thought that the young man was a brother, and, as a matter of fact, he was. All of the other agencies had taken the statement from the family—a first-hand source but not a disinterested one. Relatives not living with the family group told the truth, and proof of the brother's responsibility for support was taken into court, with the result that both father and son were induced to go to work.

A less evident form of self-interest, or of what the witness thinks is such, is the impulse to gratify some strong emotion. For instance, a young unmarried mother with an unfortunate past wrongfully accused a former lover of being the father of her child, because she wanted to pay him back for an old score. Again, an exasperated mother applied to an agency to get them to make her stubborn, lazy daughter work and be obedient. She said she could do nothing with the girl. It turned out that the mother drank, had always abused her daughter, and was herself immoral. The likelihood seemed to be that she made the complaint partly because she wanted the girl to support her and thought to get this through the society's supervision, and partly because she feared that, once the daughter was no longer as amenable to authority as when a child, her younger attractions might alienate the affection of a man who had been living with the mother.

Self-interested bias also shows itself in another form, in individual or collective self-esteem. An ex-probation officer states that when she has asked girl shoplifters from respectable families how they happened to do such a thing, again and again she has met the reply, " I don't know what got into me." Her acquaintance with such girls satisfied her that they had not thought of shoplifting as a serious offense against the law. It had seemed to them a peccadillo, something rather smart to put through without detection, like stealing a car ride. When they found themselves behind prison bars, they were shocked to see themselves without illusion as thieves, under disgrace. They had never intended to be that; they had thought of themselves as being far-removed from the criminal class. After release, their rallying self-esteem led them to the half-expressed feeling that it was not their real self that had committed a crime.

Collective self-esteem appears frequently as family pride.

The secretary of a charity organization society interviewed the brother and sister-in-law of a deserted wife who was asking relief for herself and children. The brother blamed his sister's husband for being "no good," and for not supporting his family, but could offer no suggestions as to future plans. His wife, however, advised boarding the children out on the ground that their mother could not go out to work and at the same time care for them.

A former landlord also condemned the husband, saying that while the deserted wife lived in his house she had taken excellent care of it and paid her rent regularly. He did not consider it her fault that the man deserted. Although this landlord had heard that she went to town with men, he did not regard her as vicious. She undoubtedly needed the money, since she never seemed strong enough for work.

With further inquiry, more evidence came to light of this mother's wrong-doing. The secretary then went again to the sister-in-law who, finding the woman's character known, testified that the husband had been away many years, that the last two children were not his, but were the offspring of two different men, the last of whom was paying the woman an allowance and still living with her from time to time. The court removed these three children from the mother.

The family pride which led the brother and sister-in-law in this case to withhold the truth in the first place was of course a feeling one must respect, however disastrous its possible results to the children involved or however annoying it may be to a busy worker. They had never seen the worker before and perhaps could not judge how carefully he would guard confidences or how much power or interest he might have in remedying a bad situation. The landlord's bias was twofold. His standards of conduct were evidently easy, inclining him to be tolerant beyond reason, and his interests as a landlord prejudiced him in favor of a good tenant.

There is a bias of self-esteem to which social workers, especially the clever or informed ones, may themselves become liable. A desire to be thought penetrating may lead them to interpret facts of conduct with over-subtlety, to see a certain motive where it does not exist. To such over-subtlety the social worker is tempted in dealing with a case of the following type: She learns that a man's relatives have habitually characterized his marriage as a very good match on his wife's part. Learning further that the husband has never told his family of his wife's capability as a manager, she interprets these facts to mean that the man has not wanted to modify his family's flattering partiality of judgment towards himself. This inference on the worker's part might easily spring from vanity at her astuteness, rather than from unbiased reasoning. As is true of all prejudice, the cure of this bias lies in becoming aware of it.

Finally, this discussion of testimonial evidence should not close without the further warning that there is always danger—though the danger here is greatest for the beginner in social work—in the attempt to substitute the results of formulated experience for our own unguided impulses. We may easily become, for a time at least, hypercritical. The new worker, while throwing himself with enthusiasm into the task of mastering a new discipline, may lose his perspective. "The extreme of distrust in these matters," says Langlois, "is almost as mischievous as the extreme of credulity." The case worker's best safeguard against formalism and skepticism is a concern for the interests of his client.

SUMMARY OF THIS CHAPTER

1. The two factors which condition the value of a witness's testimony are his competence and his bias. Competence includes both the witness's opportunity to know the facts and the way in which he has used this opportunity. Bias includes those ideas and emotions of the witness which may prejudice his judgment.

2. A witness frequently thinks he has had ample opportunity to know the facts when the reverse is the case. The use which a witness has made of his opportunity to know the facts is conditioned by his powers of attention and memory, and by his suggestibility.

3. Closeness of attention to an incident depends in part upon the importance attached to it at the time, and in part upon the stock of ideas or "funded thought" of the observer.

4. The time at which an event took place is often recalled by associating it with some other event the date of which is already known. It is characteristic of memory material that it deteriorates with repetition. The first, unrehearsed statement of a witness is often the most trustworthy.

5. An over-readiness to yield assent to or reproduce the assertions of others often impairs the value of a witness's testimony. Such suggestibility may even lead to mistaken confessions.

6. Closely related to this characteristic of suggestibility is the danger involved in asking "leading questions." It is not always possible to avoid them, but the case worker can at least cultivate a watchful eye for their use, so that he shall not be betrayed into accepting back as fact what he has himself suggested by the form of his query.

7. The commonest forms of bias encountered in social work are racial or national and environmental bias, and the bias of self-interest. Collective self-esteem, one form of which is family pride, may be classified under this last-named head.

CHAPTER V

INFERENCES

FORMAL treatment of the processes of reasoning is not within the scope of this book. The application of those processes to social diagnosis, however, will appear in brief illustrations of ways in which a case worker's inferences (justifiable or not), his conscious or unconscious assumptions, and his predispositions help or hinder his diagnosis of a client's situation. An understanding of a client's difficulties, like any advance in knowledge, comes from the interplay of two methods; namely, that of direct testimony to facts in his life—treated in the two preceding chapters—and that of inference from these facts to others that are unknown.

I. HOW INFERENCE IS MADE

Inference, then, a passing from known to unknown facts, is the reasoning process—most familiar when it takes the form of drawing a conclusion from the relation existing between a general truth and a particular instance. It may, however, proceed from many particular cases to a general rule, as well as from a rule to some new fact about a particular case. Reasoning from particular cases to the general rule is shown in the following brief passages taken from The Charity Visitor:[1]

A knowledge of the number of rooms occupied is necessary in order to determine whether the family is living under dangerously overcrowded conditions, either from a physical or from a moral standpoint.

The constantly shifting family is certainly in need of some kind of assistance. . . . Also the fact of a change of residence suggests some reason for change, which is often a salient factor, particularly when the change is from one section of the city to another or from one city to another.

The membership of a man in a labor union is in itself an indication that he is a workman and associates with workmen; if his "card is clear," that is, if he is in good standing and his dues are paid up, there is further assurance of his reliability.

[1] The Charity Visitor, Amelia Sears, pp. 23, 26–27, 35.

Here are three general rules familiar to the case worker which are inferences from a large number of instances (1) of the effect of an insufficient number of rooms, (2) of the significance of a family's constantly shifting, and (3) of a man's membership in a union. The validity of each of these rules depends upon the accuracy with which the particular instances from which the rule was inferred were noted, upon the number and essential similarity of these instances, and upon the absence of exceptions.

Reasoning from a rule to some new fact about a particular case is illustrated by this item taken from our case reading:

> A man with a record of drink owed a bill to a hospital. Its social worker learned from the cashier at the patient's place of business that he had recently received a considerable sum of money for accident insurance. The inference drawn was that he could pay his hospital bill.

The implied general truth of which this case appeared to be an instance is that "People who have money enough on hand can pay their debts." It is obvious that without this general truth in the background of one's mind the above inference could not be drawn and the man's having or not having received money would bear no meaning for us. On the other hand, how did we get our dictum that people who have money can pay their debts? This rule is an inference drawn from innumerable particular cases to this effect that have occurred within everyone's experience.

It is evident, then, that in reasoning one must be prepared to support the conclusion by reassuring a doubter at either or both of two points. The doubter may challenge it by asking either. (1) Is the rule appealed to strictly true? or (2) Is the given instance really a particular case of that rule?

> A critic of a case record writes, "I infer that there must be some resource not discovered, as a family of seven could hardly have subsisted for three months on those grocery orders from the city only, even if the milk mentioned May 7 continued. I conclude it did not, since there is a new application for it in August."

The general rule implied in the first inference in this case is stated here, namely, that a family of seven cannot live on the usual public relief order. The rule implied in the second inference is that people do not apply for the same aid from the same source while they are already receiving it. As was true in the preceding case, both these rules are in turn inferences drawn from many particular instances in the past (1) of the minimum diet which can sustain life, and (2) of the habits of rational beings.

A child had been returned to its home from a hospital, and it had become necessary to learn whether malnutrition was due to unwise diet in the home or to the straitened circumstances of the family. The record of the medical-social department making the inquiry reads: "Family have two extra rooms which they are not trying to rent to lodgers. If in straitened circumstances this would not be the case."

Is the general rule sound on which the inference in this case is based; namely, that families in straitened circumstances rent their extra rooms? That depends, as before stated, upon how many instances of this have been observed, and upon the accuracy of the observation.

In the process of our investigation of a case, an inference may pass through various stages of certainty. Its first stage is often tentative. It is a *hypothesis*, a possibility to be proved or disproved by further evidence. In a first interview, for instance, the skilful worker forms many hypotheses, holding some for the confirmation of further evidence, accepting a few as proven by the evidence before him, and discarding others as the interview proceeds.

To illustrate this a case worker recommends trying the experiment of removing the "face card" (sheet of information in tabular form at the beginning of a case record) from the unread history sheets and drawing from the card alone—see the one for the Ames family reproduced on the following page—a series of inferences. This worker regards such an exercise as good drill for a beginner, since it approximates the mental processes he should go through in making an investigation. From the fact given on the Ames face card that this family of five lived in six rooms at a rental equal to their highest weekly wage, the worker in question inferred that they had a fairly high home standard. Had she made this inference in the course of her interview with the family, she would have gone on to confirm it by inquiring whether they had had or expected to have lodgers or whether they had taken the house merely through inertia because it was the first decent one they had lighted on, etc. If the family's statement barred out these other explanations and fell in with her inference, she would accept the latter as a fact. Again, the worker learned from the face card that four

FACE CARD

Surname AMES *Date* 5–10–09

Date	*Address*	*Rent per Mo.*	*Rms.*
5–10–09	1906 Rodman St.	$12	6

First Name	*Age*	*Date of Birth*	*Occ. or School*	*Phys. Defects*
Man's				
1 Thomas	38		Hatter	Tuberculosis
Woman's Maiden				
2 Jane	28			
Children				
3 Alice		2–1903	McArthur Sch.	
4 Susan		6–1907		

Others in Family	*Kinship*	*To No.*	*Bdr. or Ldgr.*
5 Mrs. Maxwell	Mother	2	50c. wk. for rm.

Birthplace	*Nationality*	*Religion*	*Benefit Socy.*
1 Eng.	Eng.	Bapt.	
2 U. S.	Scotch	"	Benefit Order

Relatives not Living in Family	*Address*	*Kinship*	*To No.*
Joseph Ames	16 Carpenter St.	bro.	1
Clara Ames	1408 Coxton St.	sis.	1
Abel Ames	1408 Coxton St.	bro.	1
Mrs. Abington	311 2d St.	sis.	1
Mrs. Arthur Brown	1705 Alden St.	sis.	2
Mrs. Freeman	901 First St.	sis.	2

Churches Interested	*Medical Agencies Interested*	*In No.*
Tenth Bapt. Church,	Dr. Johnson, 300 Webster Ave.	1, 2
Rev. Mr. Gleason,	N. W. Tbc. Dispensary	1
7301 Clark St.	State Sanatorium	1
	Dr. Lane, 65 Dean St.	3, 4

Of No.	*Employers*	*Position*	*When*	*Weekly Earnings*
1	Caldwell's hat factory	Work on furs	1901–09	$12–$8
5	Boxton Hotel			
1	Moran's Installment House	Canvassing	3–1910	
1	Caldwell's hat factory	Doorman	4–1910	

Date	*Referred by*	*Address*
5–10–09	Miss Delancey	1616 Upton St.

Friendly Visitor	*Address*
Miss Delancey	1616 Upton St.

years elapsed between the births of Mrs. Ames' two children. This may mean miscarriages or the death of infants, either of which may have been the cause or the result of low vitality in the mother. Putting such an inference together with the fact of the man's being tuberculous (experience with the reluctance of workingmen to yield to sickness warrants the hypothesis that this man's condition is fairly advanced) and of physicians' having been consulted for both the wife and the children, the investigator makes the hypothesis that the family health is poor. If she were interviewing these people she would at once try to get at a few simple medical facts, such as an intelligent layman can ascertain and such as would indicate whether she should ask medical advice. The use of the hypothesis to the social worker in the case is to stimulate his collection not only of the medical facts indicated but of relevant social evidence as well; namely, the ventilation and heating of the family's rooms, the warmth of their clothing, their exercise, their diet, including the wife's ability as a cook. In this instance, it would be the physician and not the social worker who would establish or disprove the hypothesis of delicate health in the family. Many other inferences occur to one from this face card; namely, that the man came to this country before marriage, that he was probably married in 1901 or 1902, that his work was unskilled although he must have been acceptable to his employer, and so on. His coming to this country before marriage might perhaps be considered a safe enough inference without more evidence; the two latter inferences call for confirmation.

II. HOW INFERENCE IS CORROBORATED

In the illustration on p. 83, the inference that the family is not in straitened circumstances because no effort is being made to rent extra rooms, resting as it does on a rule open to occasional exception, should in justice to the family in question be subjected to the test of further evidence. A woman whose husband was sick and away was found to have allowed a man lodger to give her a black eye without any resentment on her part. The inference—or hypothesis—drawn from this fact as to the undue intimacy of their relations was confirmed by further evidence.

Confirming evidence may be gathered deliberately for the purpose of confirmation or it may be evidence lying in our past experience. The professional experience of social workers makes them recognize a recurring relation between the number of rooms occupied and the health and decency of the occupants; between a man's trade union record and his record as a worker; between the size of a family and the minimum amount of food they can live on; or between a family's income and their having extra rooms unrented, etc. Although none of these relations are fixed for all time, the richer the experience of the worker in supplying him with such fairly constant rules, the greater is the variety of hypotheses to which such experience can give rise, and therefore the more likely is he to light upon the hypothesis which will prove correct.

What workers sometimes complacently term their *intuitions* are often merely rapid inferences based on experience. A case in point is the following:

> A medical-social worker was explaining that she had learned to trust her intuitions. When asked for instances of what she meant by intuitions she replied, "A man was referred to me not long ago whom I classified as a jailbird at once, and sure enough I found that he had a long record at our county prison." Further questioning revealed this process of reasoning: "The man was an Irishman and had been in this country twenty-two years, but had never been naturalized, which struck me as shiftless for a man of his nationality. That made me sure that he had some reason for not wanting to vote or that he was prevented from doing so by a criminal history."

The intuition was an inference, a hypothesis which the worker's experience suggested and which served to lead her to a search for confirming evidence in the public records. It is of course possible that the man's appearance played an unrecognized part in the forming of this hypothesis.

Occasionally, because of gaps in evidence, confirmation of a hypothesis has to be sought through experiment. Such evidence is, for the purposes of social case work, far from satisfactory, because in dealing with human material experiment is controlled with difficulty. If we send to the charity woodyard an Italian whose work references are inaccessible and he leaves the work after a short stay, is he lazy, or is he incapable of adapting himself quickly to the changed conditions of work with a foreman who does not understand Italians, and with fellow workmen who do not speak his language, etc.? "The one great difficulty," says Alfred

Sidgwick,[1] "is that of making sure that when we introduce A [laziness] into a given set of circumstances nothing else comes in along with it, or directly after it, or is already there unknown to us. For if another detail, Z, [the difficulty of getting on with an American foreman, among other things] has crept in thus insidiously, the experiment fails to show that it is A rather than Z to which the effect is due."

There is a satisfaction beyond the establishing of a certain number of required facts for those who have or acquire the insight to make such tentative inference. These inferences are a means of leading us from the comparatively few known facts about any client to some of the many unknown ones which a personal social problem always contains, as well as a means of guiding our investigation into fruitful channels. Evidence gathered to corroborate or disprove a theory, to combine new facts with those previously known, thus becomes a creative thing; whereas facts collected mechanically item by item to fill out a schedule or meet a minimum requirement of some sort lack the interrelation that would give them significance. They give but a sketchy outline of a client's needs. When evidence is meager, ingenuity in the making of one working hypothesis and then another and patience in trying them out by experiment may be the only way of arriving at the truth. As we proceed with our inquiry and get, from the accumulating facts and from the use of these in testing our successive hypotheses and inferences, the evidential material for accurate diagnosis, reasoned knowledge gradually takes the place of hypothesis.

In making an advance in knowledge, whether in law, science, or social work, certain risks are involved. Those contained in erroneous testimony have been discussed in the preceding chapter. Assuming then that our testimony is reliable, there are still risks that arise (1) from the process of thinking, or (2) from the thinker's state of mind.

III. THE RISKS INVOLVED IN THINKING

The risks in the process of thinking may occur in four ways; we may have a mistaken general rule, a mistaken particular case, a mistaken analogy, or a mistaken causal relation.

[1] Application of Logic, p. 91.

1. Mistaken General Rule. Suppose that in the case cited on p. 86 we infer that the Italian in question is lazy. We thereby imply that as a general rule needy men who refuse to work at the charity woodyard are lazy. There are, however, frequent exceptions to this rule, other explanations of a man's refusing such work. Therefore the general rule is open to question, and the inference in the particular case is, as a consequence, of doubtful validity.

Again take the case of James Smith, who withholds the name of his present employer. May we say "as a general rule, the man who puts obstacles in the way of consulting his employer is a man with a poor work record" and draw the inference that James Smith wants to conceal his inefficiency? Hardly. Here too there are so many possible reasons besides the one given for such an unwillingness on the part of employes that we must apply this general rule only with great caution.

> Couples who are married have neither embarrassment nor hesitancy in giving this information [*i. e.*, date and place of marriage] unless they are purposely withholding facts of early life.[1]
>
> "It is quite conceivable," writes a critic of this statement, "that the question might have been asked as if it were an accusation that the couple interviewed were not married, or that it might have been so taken by a hypersensitive person. Such an apparent attitude of suspicion does not always bring, in return, the proof wanted and producible; it sometimes brings instead a stubborn refusal, or else the information is given with real embarrassment. Also (2) clients may honestly not remember the date and the year, or (3) they may consider it unimportant and not germane to their present situation." [2]

Therefore this general rule is untrustworthy and reasoning which depended upon it would be invalid. In the case of the Browns, who hesitated when asked for the information, you could not infer such concealment with any certainty.

[1] The Charity Visitor, p. 21. Some excellent examples of sound inference have already been given from Miss Sears' pamphlet. In the attempt, however, to formulate generalized statements applicable to given combinations of case work circumstance, there is always the danger—a danger which the present volume illustrates too, probably—of assuming that in no case can the outer fringe of circumstance not specifically included in the combination make another conclusion necessary. The inference quoted above and a few others that follow, taken from The Charity Visitor, illustrate this risk.

[2] For some of the comments quoted in this part of the chapter, the author is indebted to a group of former students, especially to Miss Marion Bosworth and Miss Ruth Cutler.

A definite statement of the floor and the part of the house in which the family lives . . . indicates . . . economic status, the probable sanitary condition of the home, and, taken in comparison with the part of the house at a previous address, the advancement or deterioration of the family fortunes.[1]

Has it been the common experience of social workers that knowledge of the floor and the part of the house in which a family lives indicates these three distinct conditions?

A case worker suggests the following exceptions: A family may have risen economically above its rooms or neighborhood but be held there by some tie of kinship, nationality, sentiment, or by accustomedness and inertia. Or a family's idea of thrift may lead them to deprive themselves and their children of what we consider necessities in order to keep a bank account intact. Or again, inconvenient rooms may be in an exceptionally favorable location, near the work of some member of the family, near a church, a settlement, a day nursery, etc. As regards the relation suggested between "floor" and "sanitary conditions" experience does not bear it out. The comparison suggested with a "previous address" might mean nothing, but on the other hand comparison with a series of such addresses would probably have significance.

In short, this rule is subject to so many exceptions or qualifications that we can but regard it as mistaken. When, then, we find a family living in a third floor back on Y Street we cannot from that infer their income and the sanitation of their home.

The following rule is evidently of doubtful validity, since it holds good only with certain exceptions:

Information concerning the school opportunities of any illiterate person should be most carefully gathered and, unless the history shows a gross exploitation of the individual that more than accounts for his illiteracy, it is advisable to have the mental ability of the illiterate person tested.[2]

As regards those who come from states where there is or has been no compulsory education law and as regards foreigners this rule should be more tentatively stated. Lack of opportunity and lack of compulsion have made illiteracy common among some of them —among the Galician farmers, for instance.

The mere statement of the age and the grade of the child is of value in showing whether or not he is a retarded child. If he is below his grade, a special effort must be made to ascertain whether he is backward merely as a result of bad environment, neglect, physical condition, or irregularity of attendance, or whether he is a mental defective.[3]

[1] The Charity Visitor, p. 23.

[2] The Charity Visitor, pp. 34–35.

[3] The Charity Visitor, p. 32.

Here the various possibilities are indicated, thus safeguarding the statement adequately.

The social worker must bear in mind that the "general rules" that enter into reasoning in the field of human conduct can never be of universal application; that is, they will all be liable to many exceptions. This, however, does not disqualify them from serving to advance knowledge about particular cases. For instance, if 75 per cent of the couples who hesitate to give information about their marriage do so with the motive of concealing discreditable facts, the worker cannot, it is true, from such a rule deduce with any assurance the conclusion that a given reticent couple has a scandal to conceal. But he can make such an approximately general rule the basis of a tentative inference, a hypothesis, which will serve as a guide to his inquiry into the past life of a given couple. The hypothesis may be disproved by further evidence, the couple in question turning out to have an honorable reason for reticence. Nevertheless, it is the worker's merely tentative inference, based on a rule of only partial application, which will have been the first step in bringing the truth to light.

2. Mistaken Particular Case. Since an inference is drawn not from a general rule standing by itself, but from such a rule as it is applied to a particular case, it follows that, however unimpeachable the rule, the particular case may not come under it. The rule that "the constantly shifting family is certainly in need of some kind of assistance"[1] may be accepted by all social workers. If, however, the breadwinner is an exhibitor of trained dogs who takes his wife and children on business tours, this is not a shifting family in the sense intended in the rule. The term *shifting family* at once becomes ambiguous for this particular case.

Take again the case cited on p. 82 of the patient who was inferred to have been able to pay his hospital bill because he had recently received an accident insurance. The rule back of the inference was that people who have money enough on hand can pay their debts—a sound enough dictum. The first assumption was that this particular patient's case came under the rule. But how did it turn out? The man on being questioned produced a receipt for the board of his children which had just been paid. The sum

[1] The Charity Visitor, p. 26.

amounted to almost the total of his insurance. The particular case, then, was different from what it was first supposed to be. This man was not a person with money on hand. The case did not fit the rule.

Again we may have the rule "first offenders are hopeful subjects for probation." In a given instance, however, the offender may have been a boy who had been pilfering undetected for years or a girl who had had sexual relations with boys and men since childhood, although only now brought to court. In the sense intended by the general rule neither of these is a first offender.

3. Mistaken Analogy. Inference is often drawn by what appears to be an analogy between some one case under consideration and another which, in those respects that are of importance for the purpose in hand, closely resembles it. For instance, if a worker, knowing of a number of cases of tuberculosis among hatters who had worked in the same factory with Ames,[1] conceived the purpose of attempting to render more sanitary the processes of the hat trade, he would look for a probable analogy between the facts of these several cases and of men in other hat factories as to working conditions, incidence of the disease, etc.; whereas if his purpose were to get Ames himself well and self-supporting, he would look for a different set of analogies in making his diagnosis and would emphasize many things in which Ames and his family differed from the other cases of tuberculosis in hat factories.

Again, suppose that Mrs. X's explanation, that the beer seen going into her tenement was left there temporarily for a neighbor, proved to be a falsehood. A worker hearing the same explanation offered under apparently similar circumstances by Mrs. Y might reason by analogy that this was the same old excuse and that Mrs. Y like Mrs. X was a drinking woman. Whereas, if he inquired further he might find that Mrs. Y's neighbor, who was not a teetotaler, had been so kind to Mrs. Y during her children's sickness that Mrs. Y could not refuse her the small favor of taking in her kettle of beer. The analogy, therefore, would prove a mistaken one. The two cases would have had only a superficial similarity as to the points under consideration. This is the danger in reasoning by analogy, and is one into which we all of us fall. We know the frequency with which relief officers reason that since

[1] See face card on p. 84.

salt cod and beans are acceptable diet for family A, they must be equally so for family B. The first family may be composed of a sturdy mother with big husky boys, while the second may be a tuberculous woman with tiny children. Both are widows with children, and beyond that the analogy does not hold.

Our tendency to assume more similarity than exists between the circumstances of an old case and of a new one, and hence apply our experience with the one to the other, often checks the acquisition of new knowledge. This tendency may be neutralized in the discussions of any representative case committee—one made up, let us say, of a few professional and business men, of several housewives, a neighborhood tradesman, a nurse, a trade unionist, and of some of the social workers in the various special agencies. Unless an opinion is imposed upon all by someone whom they respect as an authority, each one present will at once draw inferences from the outline of the case presented. A large majority of these inferences will have been shaped by analogy with the different experiences of these people of varying occupations and background. Where discussion is free, the diversities of view tend to offset each other and to bring out facts showing which analogy holds good and which is unwarranted.

4. Mistaken Causal Relation. One fact shown on the face card given on p. 84 is that Mrs. Ames' mother lives with her, although Mr. Ames is ill and the family in need of aid. Suppose one infers as the cause of this situation that the old lady has less pleasant relations with her other daughters and their husbands than with the Ameses. Would this cause operate by itself or would it be likely to act along with other causes to produce the given effect? The common inclination is to seek for one cause. Social workers, however, need to bear in mind that where cause must be sought in human motives, as is apt to be the case in their work, they must expect to find not that it is a single simple cause, but that it is complex and multiple. In the case of Mrs. Ames' mother, should it turn out that the cause after all was simple, the social worker can test first the adequacy of this alleged causal relation. Having accepted the mother's liking for Mrs. Ames as adequate cause, the worker must now ask whether the operation of this cause is thwarted by any circumstance. The mother may prefer

Mrs. Ames' companionship only when she has her to herself. When the husband is at home, jealousy or lack of sympathy with him may seriously mar her pleasure. In this case the preference for Mrs. Ames, although in itself an adequate cause, would be thwarted in its action. Whether this is the case or not the worker must apply the third test of causal relations and inquire whether there may be some other cause for the mother's living with the Ameses. The next alleged cause the worker must examine by the same method as this.

Again, we see on the face card that Ames worked at canvassing for only a month, when he returned to his old employer as doorman. What can we infer as a reason? Either he was not efficient at the canvassing or was not physically equal to it or he preferred a steady job with definite wage in a place he knew. Any one of these causes would have been adequate, none of them is thwarted by any other cause, but all three are equally possible. We can therefore make but a tentative inference.

The facts that the first work Ames sought after leaving the tuberculosis sanatorium was canvassing, and that this was not his usual occupation, suggest that he had received medical advice to get outdoor work. This inference answers all three tests. While this may not be the only conceivable reason for his doing this work, it is certainly the most probable one. In reasoning on people's behavior, one would seldom arrive at more than a strong probability of truth.

Mrs. F, a mother of growing girls, insists on keeping a man lodger and living in a wretched tenement over a saloon, in spite of generous offers from relatives of better living conditions. Shall we infer lax standards of living? This cause is adequate, it is thwarted by no other circumstance, but is it the only possible cause of her apparent stubbornness? She says herself that the objectionable tenement is near the children's school and that the landlord has been good to her. It is also conceivable that she is not eager to move near her relatives. Our inference, therefore, as to her standards is not justified except as a hypothesis to be confirmed by more evidence.

IV. THE RISKS ARISING FROM THE THINKER'S STATE OF MIND

1. Predispositions. Besides the risks involved in thinking as such, there are risks arising from the thinker's state of mind. The social worker, like all others, has certain personal and professional predispositions against which he needs to be on guard. What do we mean by predispositions? For our present purpose we may stretch the application of the word somewhat to include the sum of all those personal and professional habits of thinking and all those feelings and inclinations with which we approach each new problem. Our predispositions are both equipment and handicap. They are an equipment in that they are essential to individuality; they are a handicap in that they limit knowledge in one direction or another. For instance, when social case work agencies first became aware that their records showed a confusion between fact and opinion, they tried to meet the difficulty by instructing their workers to omit impressions, opinions, and inferences of their own, and to enter upon case records "nothing but the facts," reporting each of these colorlessly, "as it happened." Workers who attempted to follow this rule produced records which have been likened to unstrung beads; in the attempt to eliminate all prejudice, they eliminated the judgment and discernment which would have given to the whole investigation unity and significance.[1]

Predispositions may obscure for us the significance of one set of facts by leading us to exaggerate the importance of another set, while at the same time they are so much a part of us that we may easily be unaware of their existence and consequently of their danger. Such an effort to disregard the fact of our having predispositions as that shown by the case work agencies who wanted "nothing but the facts" from their visitors is likely to hamper investigation by deceiving the mind into a belief in its own impartiality. It is the worker's very *awareness* of his special predisposition on which depends the reliability of his observation and judgment. Once he brings a prejudice into the light of day, he can offset its influence on his thinking.

[1] A critic of these pages, who has examined many case records of late in many different parts of the United States, adds: "Not only 'unstrung beads' but all about the same size. Wherever the 'only the facts' rule applies, the tendency is for every fact, big and little, to occupy about the same space in the record. Everything is brought to a dead level."

2. Assumptions. As professional workers become experienced they are apt to gather a set of salted-down rules, or more correctly assumptions, which they thereafter apply as needing no further proof. Some of these assumptions are warranted, others are not. In dealing with cripples, for example, social workers may adopt unhesitatingly the assumption that physical handicap is the cause of unemployment. Closer acquaintance with cripples would show that many do well in employment, and that of those who do not, some fail through temperament, some through the limitations of their earlier industrial experience, and some through one or another physical cause unrelated to the handicap in question. In fact, the common assumption that the cripple's industrial difficulties are insurmountable is his most serious handicap.

Again, there is an assumption among not a few workers that laziness is within a man's control, whereas, while we may not be able to say it is never so, we know that it often is not.

A few years ago it was assumed among social workers in some communities that a girl with a second illegitimate child was hopelessly degraded and that therefore no private agency should attempt to cope with the problem; public authorities should give the necessary care. Indeed this feeling was so strong that private rescue homes receiving these girls were thereby somewhat discredited. Today courageous intensive endeavor has shown that some of the most successful work of reconstruction can be done with the unmarried mother of two children.

The reason assumptions such as these persist is that they are not examined; they are taken on faith. If, however, a worker knows his assumption to be what it is—unproven—he may venture to act upon it. He may know, for instance, that a given man's laziness may conceivably be a manifestation of disease, yet, barring any other indication of illness, he may think best to assum the fellow's culpability and push him to get work.

In any profession one acquires certain predispositions, or habits of thought, from the conditions of one's allotted task and particular occupational environment. A worker in a child-helping or a family rehabilitation agency in a large American city, working among recently arrived foreigners who have become dependent, may regard immigration as a menace, unless his own racial prejudices happen to offset this idea. The child-placing agent sometimes assumes that a family home is the best place for every child, and the institution worker may lean too far the other way. The charity organization worker easily takes economic independence and family solidarity as being invariably the first considerations, while the health worker readily slights both. Each specialist, therefore, should ask himself to what particular overemphasis he is rendered liable by the nature of his task, and at that particular point he should be at especial pains to collect with impartiality the evidence on which he bases decisions.

3. Some Other Habits of Thought. There are, besides untested assumptions, other habits of thought that case workers of any kind are liable to fall into. We found that, until our case reading revealed the fact, some workers were unaware that they consulted the same favorite sources of information habitually, to the exclusion of other sources equally good or better, or that they co-operated heartily with only a certain few agencies—usually with those most accessible. Such methods mean a narrowed resourcefulness, with a few favorite remedies applied, a few combinations of stops pulled out, no matter what the demands of the situation or the resources available. Moreover, in changing from one city to another or from one field of social work to another, a worker must guard against holding fast to habits which may have been time-saving originally but which are useless under changed conditions.[1] If a municipality's department of health or of correction has been unco-operative, one who faces a new administration or who leaves that community for another must be ready to drop the habit of doing without this help from public officials and must welcome a changed situation.

Again, the trend of modern social ideals often confirms in the more sophisticated case worker a habit of thinking in averages. Sometimes a case worker tends to become overabsorbed in the individual case, but a commoner failing of the modern type of

[1] "When at shearings or markings they run the yearlings through a gate for counting, the rate of going accelerates until the sheep pass too rapidly for numbering. Then the shepherd thrusts his staff across the opening, forcing the next sheep to jump, and the next, and the next, until, Jump! says the flock-mind. Then he withdraws the staff, and the sheep go on jumping until the impulse dies as the dying peal of the bells." Austin, Mary: The Flock, p. 114. Boston, Houghton, Mifflin, and Co., 1906.

worker is that, oppressed by the condition of the mass, he misses a clear conception of the one client's needs. He thinks of him as one of a class. No client will meet with successful social treatment if so regarded, because it is usually his particular situation and not that part of his circumstances which he shares with others that is the immediate point at issue. Sidgwick has this general truth in mind when he says, "In forming a careful conclusion about a particular case, no one with any sense will use the method of probabilities if he has an opportunity of getting behind it and understanding the causes at work in the special case."[1] Sidgwick means by his warning about the "method of probabilities" that, though a certain manifestation may have been proved statistically to have one significance in ninety-seven instances out of a hundred, and a quite different significance in the three others, this ratio, useful for action affecting a hundred in the mass, has a different sort of value in dealing with a single case about which more intimate knowledge is available. The value of such a ratio for the single case is that it necessarily gives rise to a hypothesis that the case in question is one of the ninety-seven. This hypothesis is useful in that it guides the inquiry which may or may not show the single case to be one of the majority. An assumption to this effect, however, where more knowledge is available about a particular case, the ratio does not justify. Were the case worker himself one of the three, would he care to be treated by a social practitioner whose habit it was to assume his client to be one of the ninety-seven? At the same time it would hardly be an intelligent practitioner who did not under these circumstances look upon it beforehand as probable that the client would turn out to be one of the ninety-seven.

There is always a risk that one's personal likes and dislikes may influence judgment. Take, for example, the prejudices and special tendencies that belong to the various racial and social groupings. Even those comparatively rare persons whose knowledge of the characteristics of many different social groupings of people is broad enough to have overcome mere class prejudice in themselves still belong to a certain habit-group and are attracted or repelled by like or unlike customs and manners in others. People of narrower

[1] The Application of Logic, p. 69.

opportunity are almost without exception warped in their judgment by one class or racial prejudice or another, while at the same time they assume that social bias exists only in the other fellow. As such personal predispositions, when allowed swing, hinder his work, the social case worker needs to learn to set them aside.

Besides the risk in drawing inferences which arises from personal and professional predispositions, there is a risk that springs from the thinker's own desire in the particular instance, (1) to see his hypothesis confirmed, and (2) to secure prompt action. Such a hypothesis, for instance, as that about the Irishman with the prison record[1] becomes, because of its very ingenuity, the favorite child of our brain. In this case, it is true, the worker sought corroborating evidence. Nevertheless, the danger that commonly besets case workers is that of becoming so fond of some particular hypothesis that it will seem in no need of proof. This tendency may have especially serious consequences in the case of a first hypothesis that we have to make in a more or less obscure case in order to get started. The whole diagnosis may be vitiated by an unwarranted assumption at the beginning.

The worker's own desire to secure prompt action in a particular instance is also often responsible for invalid inference. In the case cited on p. 350, Chapter XVIII, in spite of contradictions in the evidence, the worker in his hurry to get an answer to the district attorney drew inferences in favor of the wife; whereas, had he stopped to test these inferences, he would have been led to get at once the additional facts that showed the husband to be the better of the two.

If we may count, as two essentials of the social diagnostician's equipment, his ability to weigh the risks involved in the types of evidence described in the chapter on Definitions, and his ability to measure and allow for the characteristics of human beings as witnesses—a topic which has also received attention—there is still the third essential; namely, the ability to discriminate between fact and inference and, through inference, to deduce new facts. Then, when the items of evidence in a case seem to be at hand, there comes a time for considering them *as a whole*. The same reasoning and testing that has been applied to its separate items

[1] See p. 86 of this chapter.

must be applied deliberately to the evidential mass. We shall return to this later in Chapter XVIII, in considering the comparison of part with part, as well as the final act of interpretation, the act of social diagnosis itself.

When we face each situation of our work with a mind alert to receive and follow suggestions, alert to utilize experience, and to make, try, and test one hypothesis after another; when we start out with entire willingness to prove or disprove our every inference, then the well tested inference reveals new fact, and new fact suggests new inference until gradually our case work acquires a strong, closely woven texture and our case histories become documents that will well repay study. It is upon such case history study, in fact, that social case work will have to depend, in large measure, for advancing standards and new discovery. Before turning to the practical details to which so large a part of the remaining chapters of this book will be devoted, it should be said with emphasis that there can be no good case work without clear thinking; that in social diagnosis sound reasoning is fundamental.

SUMMARY OF THIS CHAPTER

1. Inference is the reasoning process by which we pass from known fact to fact that is unknown. From many particular cases we may infer a general truth, or, as happens more often in case work, from a general truth we may infer some new fact about a particular case.

2. A first-stage or tentative inference is called a hypothesis. Resourcefulness in making and patience in testing hypotheses are fundamental to success in case work.

3. Corroboration of a tentative inference may have to be gathered deliberately or it may lie in our past experience. Past experience may also suggest a variety of hypotheses—the richer the experience the greater the variety, and the greater also the likelihood of discovering the particular one which will prove to be correct.

4. Gaps in evidence may make it necessary to seek confirmation of a hypothesis through experiment, though the conditions of controlled experiment are achieved with difficulty in social work.

5. In addition to the risks involved in testimony which may be incompetent or biased, there are risks in the process of reasoning from testimony even when it is known to be reliable, including risks in the reasoner's own state of mind.

6. The risks involved in the reasoning process may occur in four ways: we may have a mistaken general rule, a mistaken particular case, a mistaken analogy, or a mistaken causal relation.

7. General rules that apply to human conduct are never of universal application. Often also the particular case assumed to come under a given general rule is different from what it is supposed to be, and therefore does not come under the rule in question.

8. Resemblances between two cases may exist, but *at the points under consideration* the resemblance may be only superficial. This is the danger in reasoning by analogy.

9. The common inclination is to seek for one cause. Where cause must be sought in human motives, however, we must expect to find that it is not a single simple cause but complex and multiple.

10. The chief risks arising from the case worker's own state of mind are found in his personal and professional predispositions and in his assumptions—in the salted-down rules, that is, which are the product of his experience.

11. The best safeguard against predispositions is to be aware of them. Once a personal prejudice, for example, is brought into the light of day, its influence upon thinking can be offset.

12. In the same way, if a worker knows his assumption to be what it is—unproven—he may venture to act upon it in the absence (after search) of evidence proving it to be unwarranted. Unwarranted case work assumptions persist because they are not examined and are taken on faith.

13. Other ways of thinking against which case workers may be warned are the habitual use of a few favorite sources of insight or co-operation, the continued disuse under changed circumstances of a source which was formerly not available, the habit of thinking in averages, and the habit of regarding with especial favor a first or an ingenious hypothesis.

PART II

THE PROCESSES LEADING TO DIAGNOSIS

CHAPTER VI

THE FIRST INTERVIEW

WE TURN now to the details of social case work method. It will be necessary to remember that in any art the description of its processes is necessarily far more clumsy than are the processes themselves. In the last analysis moreover, the practitioner of an art must discover the heart of the whole matter for himself—it is of the essence of art that he shall win his way to this personal revelation; but an intimate knowledge of the successes and failures, the experiences and points of view of his fellow practitioners will be found to be essential too. The thirteen chapters that follow attempt to analyze the experiences of case workers in their daily use of the four processes which lead to social diagnosis.

These four processes are (1) the first full interview with a client, (2) the early contacts with his immediate family, (3) the search for further insight and for sources of needed co-operation outside his immediate family, (4) the careful weighing in their relation to one another of the separate items of evidence thus gathered and their interpretation. By interpretation is meant the attempt to derive from all the evidence as exact a definition as possible of the client's social difficulties—the act of interpretation is the act of diagnosis.

It cannot be assumed that any one of these processes is always completed before another begins. When the First Interview is held in the client's home, contacts with the family often overlap our first contact with the client. As soon as we have two statements instead of one, whether these come from the family or from outside sources, we begin to reason about them, to compare them, and to draw certain tentative inferences from them. Nevertheless there are these four processes, distinguishable despite their interplay.

Many social workers are of the opinion that the most difficult and important is the first—the initial interview. Probably this is the part of the diagnostician's task in which personality, as contrasted with technique, counts for the most, for here he should establish some basis of mutual understanding and get some clues to the evidence which will shape his judgment later. "I am more and more convinced," wrote the secretary of a large family agency years ago in a personal letter, "that the finished skill of a good social worker is most shown in this first visit or interview. No knowledge of general principles, no cleverness in gaining co-operation, no virtues in the worker, and no committee, however wise, can make up for want of skill in gaining quickly the confidence of the family, and getting the foundation for all good work to follow." Though this emphasis is usually justified, it has two possible dangers: It may discourage us, when ground has been lost in the First Interview or not gained, from pushing forward to win the needed understanding later. It may betray us, on the other hand, into resting back upon the outcome of an apparently satisfactory first statement and failing to put forth our best endeavors in the further necessary steps.

I. MODIFYING CIRCUMSTANCES

Among the circumstances which must modify everything said about First Interviews, four groups are important enough to be kept always in mind: these are circumstances relating to (1) the nature of the task, (2) the origin of the application, (3) the place of the interview, and (4) the recorded experience available as a starting point. To clear the ground for consideration of scope and method these must take precedence.

1. The Nature of the Task. The form of service to be undertaken can be interpreted narrowly or broadly, of course, but in either case a number of variations of method are traceable to the nature of the particular case worker's task. If an agent of a society to protect children from cruelty knows that he may be cross-examined by the lawyer for the defense as to what took place in his First Interview with the defendant, inevitably this will modify his mode of approach, for he must be able to testify, upon occasion, to the exact form of his questions. Or if, to take another kind of service, a probation officer is known to come from the court and to represent it, certain conditions, favorable and the reverse, are created by this fact; the officer has more authority but less freedom than a social worker who lacks the court background. He often finds it difficult to lead the minds of those directly concerned in a court case away from the immediate to the wider issues.[1] A worker who was formerly with a charity organization society and then became the agent of a state department for the care of children found it much harder to get information in her second capacity than in her first. People applied to her for a perfectly definite object, namely, to have their children taken by the public; they were tremendously on their guard against giving information that would be likely to interfere with that object. On the other hand, the agent of a private charity known to control a large relief fund finds his interviews hampered by this fact at every turn. The immediate material benefit looms large; the other beneficent functions of the organization and the steps taken to carry them out are little understood or are even thrust aside with impatience.[2]

The hospital and the school furnish admirable means of approach for social work; people like to talk about their ailments and about their children. Both have this disadvantage, however, that the

[1] A former probation officer writes, "Conversation that had to do with the offender was easy; talk that would go deeper into the family situation taxed ingenuity and tact."

[2] "On my first movements through the poorest parish in Glasgow, I was thronged by urgencies innumerable, because of my official connexion with the secular charities of the place, and which did invest me with the character of an almoner in the eyes of the general population. . . . What I judged and apprehended as the consequence of this was, that it would neutralise the influence which I wanted to have as a Christian minister. I saw that this would vitiate my influence among them. I felt that it would never do if I were to go among them, first as a dispenser of temporal good things, and then as urging upon them the things which make for their everlasting peace. I felt the want of compatibility between the two objects, and, rather than defeat my primary object, I determined to cut my connexion with the city charities . . . and I will not forget the instant effect of this proceeding when it came to be understood—the complete exemption which it gave me from the claims and competitions of a whole host of aspirants who crowded around me for a share in the dispensations of some one or other benevolent trust or endowment of other days; and yet the cordial welcomes I continued to meet with when, after I had shaken loose of all these, I was received and recognised by the people on the simple footing of their Christian friend, who took cognisance of their souls, and gave himself chiefly to do with the scholarship of their young, and the religious state of their sick, and their aged and their dying."—Chalmers on Charity, p. 154 sq.

task which is easily understood and easily explained tends to become limited in scope—to ignore the relation, for instance, between health questions and economic questions, between questions of child welfare and those of family responsibility. Short tasks of any kind seem, on their face, to make thorough diagnosis an unnecessary preliminary. Much of our social work is so cut up and subdivided at present that it drifts into rapid-fire, hit-or-miss forms of treatment. If the nature of a particular form of service makes a careful definition of the client's social difficulties seem impertinent, there is always a chance that the details of its program are in need of revision, that it should operate in a smaller territory or attempt to benefit fewer people and really cover the ground.[1]

2. The Origin of the Application. (a) The client comes in person to the social agency of his own initiative; (b) or with a letter of reference from some individual or organization, or with an oral statement that he has been so referred; (c) someone acting in his individual capacity or as representative of an organization comes personally, instead, in the client's interest; (d) or sends his request through the mail or by telephone. Thus we find our First Interview modified at the very start not only by the nature of our own interest but by the way in which it is evoked. If the client visits us, whether of his own initiative or otherwise, our program varies somewhat from that following a request to visit him. If individual citizens or organizations in some way concerned for his welfare make the request, we have one advantage in that a possible outside source of insight and co-operation is available from the very beginning.

3. The Place of the Interview. The place in which the First Interview is held depends in part upon the nature of the task and its origin, but not wholly upon these. Societies dealing with questions of family relief and, in these later days, with family rebuilding have changed their policy several times with regard to the place of the interview. Following the line of least resistance, the older type of worker usually conducted First Interviews at his office desk, with record form before him and pen in hand. He asked each question in the order indicated by the items on the form, and

[1] Another excuse often given for hasty preliminary inquiry is the probability that the case will be transferred to another social agency for treatment. See Chapter XVI, Social Agencies as Sources, on the advisability of thorough diagnosis before transfer, p. 313.

filled in a short summary of the perfunctory reply before going on to the next: Assistance asked? "Coal and groceries." Cause of need? "Out of work." Any relatives able to assist? "No."

As a reaction against this stupid compiling of misleading items, many American case workers have abandoned the office interview, except in emergencies and in dealing with the homeless. It is their practice to take only time enough, when application is made at the office, to assure themselves that treatment is probably needed, and then promptly to make a visit to the home, where, in an unhurried talk, the basis is laid for further acquaintance.

The arguments in favor of holding the First Interview in the home instead of in the office are, in family work, (a) Its challenge to the case worker at the outset to establish a human relation, at the risk, if he fail, of coming away without the simplest and most elementary data. In the office, clients are on the defensive and justify their visits by their replies. In the home, the social worker is on the defensive; the host and hostess are at their ease. (b) Its avoidance of the need of so many questions, some of which are answered unasked by the communicative hostess and by her surroundings. To the quiet observer the photographs on the wall, the framed certificates of membership in fraternal orders, the pensioner's war relics, the Sunday school books, the household arrangements are all eloquent. And far more revealing than these material items are the apparent relations of the members of the household to one another—the whole atmosphere of the home. (c) Its provision of natural openings for a frank exchange of experiences. "The great facts of birth and death alone are sufficient to make the whole world kin," and these and the universally interesting comparison of diseases form a good basis for that kind of informal intercourse which belongs to the fireside. Then, if some of the children are present for a part of the time at least, there is a good chance for comparing notes about brothers and sisters, their ages, names, namesakes, etc.[1] (d) Its further emphasis upon the personal side when there has been no visit by the client to an office, but when his situation has been reported there instead by others; its relegation of official paraphernalia and attitudes, in such instances at least, to the rear.

[1] See Miss M. L. Birtwell's pamphlet on Investigation.

A few years ago these arguments in favor of the home interview would have been regarded as inadequately offset by the counter-arguments of greater convenience, accuracy, and saving of time in the office interview. But now a certain number of social workers, even some of those specializing in family work, are beginning to feel that there is much to be said in favor of the office interview, if properly conducted. They assume that the one who conducts it will later visit the home, that there will be no lesion at this important point through a division of the task between two workers. The return to the older method is a return with a difference—a return with office equipment which assures entire and uninterrupted privacy, ample time, no herding of waiting clients, and no record form or other bit of officialism in the foreground.[1]

Inquiry as to current practice in other forms of social work shows interesting variations. The general secretary of a society to protect children from cruelty feels that it is most important to see the home environment before making any inquiries outside. The agent of a public department for dependent children finds that clients come to the office of the department braced and tense. She urges that only a clerk see them, and that the First Interview be held in their own surroundings. On the other hand, a charity organization worker tells of stolid Bohemian housewives who pay little attention to visitors at their homes, continuing their housework so unconcernedly during an entire interview that it is impossible to make any real progress. The strongest evidence in favor of the office interview comes from the medical-social group. One of these, who was formerly a district secretary of a charity organization society, furnishes the following memorandum:

The hospital social worker always has a good straightforward introduction to the patient in the perfectly definite request or inquiry made by the doctor: "In-

[1] "We have found," Mrs. Chesley of the Paine Fund writes in the *Survey* for May 22, 1909, "that the best place to obtain this knowledge [of the client's point of view] has been in the privacy and seclusion of the little room of the Parish House which the committee uses for an office. Of course, applicants are seen in their homes, often many times, but people are much more self-conscious in their homes, especially if we go as strangers and our visit is unexpected. In the majority of homes we are never free from interruptions from children or neighbors, and we can never be quite sure that there is not someone in the next room listening to all we say."

The statement as to self-consciousness may be open to question, but the lack of privacy in many crowded city neighborhoods is undoubtedly a real difficulty.

struction in hygiene," "sanitarium care," "light work," "medicines don't help what is the trouble at home?" "help in buying brace, $9," etc. The patient can almost without exception see the connection between the worker's questions and this definite object. Hence he is not suspicious or puzzled, and you are freed from any temptation to indirectness, subterfuge, concealment or ambiguity, into which you might drift in spite of yourself while striving to help a poor person referred by somebody "who does not wish his name used," or who thinks the poor family "so proud and sensitive that they must never know the associated charities is called in," or by that wealthy relative who would like to help but "does not wish the poor cousins to know where the money comes from." Such situations seem to me to involve positive deception. I know they have entangled more than one C. O. S. worker, and it seems to me that a definite stand should be taken and a way out found, as the final results of such work can only be an injury to all concerned.

In the hospital no such situation can possibly arise—you can proceed by the shortest and most direct route to the matter in hand. The air is clear, and you can look your patient straight in the eyes and say, perhaps, "The doctor naturally can't stop to discuss with you how you are going to get this expensive brace, but if you will explain to me just how you are situated, we will talk over possible plans." This leads quite naturally to a businesslike discussion of income and expenses and resources of all kinds, without any "fishing for facts." As a result, (a) the first interview takes place at the hospital; (b) the introduction is easy and the approach to the immediate problem direct and businesslike; (c) extended explanation is sometimes needed to make the patient see the relation of the interview to his recovery—this is done frankly and seldom fails. (I recall only two cases of failure in the year and a half I have been at the hospital.) (d) The co-operation of the patient in revealing his story is pretty sure.

Two medical-social workers suggest one exception in favor of the home interview. Deaf patients often come to the social service department from the clinical examination too sick and tired to stand another long interview. If questioned at all, they must be questioned so loudly that they become conscious of being overheard and are too embarrassed by this to talk freely. In such cases only those statements are taken which are needed to identify the patient in the confidential or social service exchange,[1] and the First Interview is held in the home.

Some interviews are best held on neutral ground, as at a settlement or some other neighborhood center. A children's worker describes a painful interview with a domestic who had applied to have her child boarded out, held in the front room of the house in which she was at service. It happened to be a doctor's office, and she was so fearful of the return of the doctor that it was im-

[1] For description see Chapter XVI, Social Agencies as Sources, p. 303 sq.

possible to get her to talk freely. The interview should have been postponed to some other time and place.

It would seem, to sum up, that wherever the sense of strangeness may be worn away most quickly, wherever a good understanding with our client may be established most easily, is the right place for the first long talk; and whether this place be the home or the office must depend upon conditions which vary with locality, with the nature of the work to be undertaken, and with the temperament and equipment of the worker. The preoccupation of the client with the immediate crisis is one of the things to be avoided in the choice of a place; no conditions should interfere with our efforts to lead his mind back to the events that will reveal the deeper-seated difficulties of his life, and forward to the possible ways out. In so far as the home and its familiar objects suggest the more normal aspects of his life, they are a great help. Some places in their very nature emphasize the crisis—a court room does, or the waiting room of a busy relief bureau. This emphasis is a barrier between case worker and client.

4. The Recorded Experience Available as a Starting Point. It will save the client's time and assure him better service to discover at once whether he has ever before been a client of the social agency now about to take up his application. For a dozen reasons—the fact that the agency has offices in different parts of the city, has removed its offices, has changed its workers, or is one of a number of organizations doing similar work—he will not always be able to answer this question correctly; sometimes he may not wish to do so; but data enough to settle whether he or other members of his immediate family are already known should be procured before the full interview with him gets under way. Action can be taken more promptly and intelligently and many preliminaries be dispensed with, if the earlier record, should there be one, is consulted without a moment's delay.

If the client makes his application in person, this is easily done. At the very beginning of talk with him, first names of his immediate family, ages of children, present address, and former addresses (if the last removal was recent) can be had, and these will enable a clerk to find the previous record, if any, in the office files. It would seem unnecessary to mention this, if some social agencies were not known to be very careless in the matter.

Wherever a confidential or social service exchange has been established among the social agencies of a community, the clerk can take the further step, at the same time, of telephoning to the exchange. In the absence of an exchange, other social agencies which have been mentioned by the client or which are likely to be interested can be inquired of, but the service that an exchange can render, as developed fully in a later chapter, becomes a great protection to everyone concerned, most of all to the client himself.[1]

When the exchange reports, in reply to inquiry, that certain other agencies which it names have also inquired about the client on such and such dates, their experience should be had before our first visit to his home, and preferably before our first full interview. The details of these consultations are also described under the heading of the Confidential Exchange; they need not detain us here, except to add that, where the data first given reveal no record and fuller data—names of relatives, etc.—are at hand a little later, after the fuller interview, there should be a second inquiry of the exchange, and a second search, of course, of the agency's own files.

II. SCOPE

It might be said that the circumstances which modify a First Interview most of all are the case worker's own knowledge of social disabilities, and his conception of the possibilities of social treatment. But these are something more than circumstance; they are the medium, the surrounding atmosphere of all his endeavor. His attitude toward social disabilities and their treatment, plus his native instinct for the facts and values of human nature, are an important part of his social philosophy. Every item in the processes leading to diagnosis, from the first moment of the First Interview, through the unwinding of the last clue, to the final step of defining in as specific terms as possible the client's actual social situation, will be shaped by this knowledge and by this philosophy or will be marred by their lack. Formative in its influence also is

[1] See section, the Confidential Exchange, in Chapter XVI, Social Agencies as Sources.

the clear determination to make the treatment of which diagnosis is only a first step helpful.

Starting with these assumptions, what should be, in general, the objects and scope of a First Interview?

The establishment of a good understanding at this point has seemed to some workers so important and they have so overrated its difficulty that they have advocated confining the First Interview to expressions of friendly interest and sympathy, in the hope that the clues upon which outside inquiries depend may be gradually elicited later. But dodging the difficulty makes more difficulty. If a good understanding were our goal, this might be the way in which to begin; but our purpose is to get something done, and usually the saving of time is a most important part of getting that something effectively accomplished. The social diagnosis that is not made with a reasonable degree of promptness may be made too late. This view is emphasized by a case worker of long experience in a letter written to one of comparatively short experience, who, working in a family agency, advocated delay because clients so often in their first contacts with him seemed to have "framed up" their story. The adviser wrote:

> Is not the made-up story you hear usually focussed upon today's situation, and is not a part of it really true? There are a few deliberate frauds who are clever enough to make up a long tale and have it hang together, but most people, well-to-do or poor, are not quick-witted enough for this. A kindly listener who hears what the applicant has made up his mind to say, and sympathetically draws him on to talk of other things, getting a story which runs back through all his life and looks forward to the future, has got something of which the made-up story forms a very small part. If the mind of the person in distress is all on the present, one may say, "Well, suppose I am able to arrange just what you ask, what about next week or month or year?" One secretary likes, when she can, to say to a man, "Now suppose you could arrange life just as you wanted it, what work would you really like to be doing?"—thus getting at a man's ideals and encouraging him by letting his mind dwell on them for a moment. Sometimes she is able to turn things that way or to some task more congenial than the old one. That for the future. As to the past, one of my friends has learned that the question addressed to a husband or wife of "How did you two happen to get acquainted?" will often lighten present distress by a memory of happier times, and also bring a flood of information as to the relatives on both sides, former home and occupation, the standard of living to which they were then accustomed, and so on.
>
> From points which do not seem to them essential, and would not to the investigator but that earlier omissions have proved them so, one gets clues not only to

possible inquiry from others, but to the character and psychology of the family itself. Afterward what proves to be untrue may be ignored, and between the family and the investigator a common knowledge of what is true may be taken for granted.

Are you quite sure that your own attitude—the feeling that what the applicant is going to tell you when he first appears "is a story well framed up"—one that will "not hold good upon investigation"—is as free from the suspicion that you deprecate as is the method I advocate? Guiding the conversation does not mean questioning, necessarily. . .

You remember I pointed out in the M—— record that you had to go twice to the hospital and doctor because you had not got in the first interview with either of them all they were willing to tell. The same waste of time and energy is avoided by a full first interview with the family, and it is sometimes not so easy to get information in the second interview with a family—they believing that they have told before all that is necessary—as it is from a hospital or a doctor to whom one can more easily explain.

As to the family's attitude, it is often like that of a patient who for the first time finds a doctor who really gets to the bottom of his trouble, taking in not merely obvious present symptoms but showing unexpected insight into matters of whose relation to the trouble the patient has been unconscious. The patient goes away with new hope and fresh resolves to do his full part. Of course, not everything is gained in one interview. That is to be supplemented by outside inquiries, and when one can arrange for continued personal relationships, by the gradual unfolding that comes in these. Sometimes later interviews prove of equal value. But without exception in my experience, investigators who have taken your view as to the first interview have been the least successful in the *average* outcome as to their families.

Here, then, we have the attitude: a cheerful willingness to listen to the present symptoms which seem so important to the one interviewed, but a quiet determination to get below this to a broader basis of knowledge, by carrying the client's mind forward to hopes and possibilities ahead, and backward to the happier, more normal relations of the past.[1] And since, if we would help him, we must break through the narrow circle of our client's own view and get into the wider one of those who know and understand him, we must depend upon the First Interview for those clues which are most likely to supplement and round out his story. "I never mean to leave a family," says a case worker of long experience, "until I have some clue or other for obtaining outside information, no matter how long it takes me to get it."

[1] Emergency interviews may seem to present an exception to this general statement. They are discussed later, p. 131.

It would appear, then, that the objects of a First Interview are fourfold:

1. To give the client a fair and patient hearing.

2. To establish, if possible, a sympathetic mutual understanding—a good basis, that is, for further intercourse.

3. To secure clues to whatever other sources of information will give a deeper insight into the difficulties of his situation and their possible solutions.

4. To begin even at this early stage the slow process of developing self-help and self-reliance, though only by the tonic influence which an understanding spirit always exerts, and with the realization that later the client's own level of endeavor will have to be sought, found, and respected.[1]

These apparently separate and sometimes apparently conflicting tasks are four parts of one purpose. We wish to serve, and we desire to influence in order to serve, but influence exerted in a mistaken direction would be worse than futile; we wish to serve, and we desire to know in order to serve, but knowledge is an impotent thing in the hands of one who has lost, through impatience, the chance to use it. Consideration of this aspect emphasizes the difficulty. The way out of the difficulty is to see clearly that frank and informal talk can be a help both in winning a common understanding and in securing clues to the coadjutors who can help us to understand still better. How soon the ground already won can be lost without their co-operation any candid examination of social case records would prove only too conclusively. Social work is team work. It must be conceded that good will and patience will not always bring the needed data; it is possible to waste time by pushing stubbornly and immediately for every available clue. In a small minority of interviews, it is better to trust to finding more clues outside in the course of following up the few that are grudgingly

[1] "The study of defectives and failures brings home to us most forcibly a fundamental fact of economics,—that certain persons are adequately endowed for small demands, but are bound to fail under an excessive demand. There would be far more happiness and real success in mental hygiene, if more people would realize that at every step, every person can do *something* well and take a satisfaction in doing it, and that this satisfaction in something *done* is to be valued as ten times greater than the satisfaction taken in mere thought or imagination, however lofty." —Adolf Meyer: What Do Histories of Cases of Insanity Teach Us Concerning Preventive Mental Hygiene During the Years of School Life?

revealed; and, with a still smaller remnant, treatment has to begin in an experimental way before any evidence can be brought to light upon which a plan of treatment can be solidly based.

III. METHOD

1. The Approach. As often happens, the best description of method comes to us from practitioners in other fields. Dr. Adolf Meyer in an unpublished document instructs the psychiatrists who are his students as follows:

> For any examination, the *mode of approach* is absolutely decisive of the result. The reserve of the patient is usually a factor to be reckoned with, or, if not the reserve, at least the unwillingness to show a clear picture of decidedly peculiar experiences. It is, therefore, necessary to gain the confidence by treating the patient "as a sensible man or woman," and, wherever the patient does not speak freely, to begin with questions about whether they have all they need for their comfort, to pass to some of the least irritating topics, such as will most likely elicit a pleasant answer and create a congenial starting point. In perfect privacy and, as Head says, with the choice of a quiet confidential hour and the precaution of changing the subject when irritation begins to adulterate the account, and before the patient has been exposed to the influences of the ever present blasé fellow patient, the statements can usually be obtained quite fully, often with a feeling of relief in the patient, and a distinct gain in the relation between physician and patient. That any chances for self-humiliation must be eased with verbal suggestion and that any appearance of obnoxious ridicule or dictation or correction and unnecessary argument must be avoided, should not require special insistence. It certainly requires a great deal of knowledge of man to choose the right moments and it is to such an extent a matter of inborn tact, that it is doubtful whether any written rules can do more than bring out in a more definite order that which one has already.

Privacy, absence of hurry, frequent change of topic, with some deliberate padding to ease the strain, particularly "when irritation begins to adulterate the account," and yet through all a clear conception on the part of the interviewer that a certain goal must if possible be reached, and a slow, steady, gentle pressure toward that goal—this, in brief, is our program. Giving the client all the time he wants often leads to that fuller self-revelation which saves our time and his in the long run. Pressure of work! Lack of time! How many failures in treatment are excused by these two phrases! But, wherever else the plea of lack of time may be valid, it is peculiarly inappropriate at this first stage, for no worker ever has leisure enough in which to retrieve the blunders that result inevitably from a bad beginning.[1] Save time, if need be, at some stage of treatment, but not at the First Interview. "The physician who comes in like a gust of wind," says Dr. Paul Dubois, "looks at his watch, and speaks of his many engagements, is not cut out to practice this psychotherapy. It is necessary, on the contrary, that the patient should have the impression that he is the only person in whom the physician is interested, so that he may feel encouraged to give him all his confidences in peace." And again, "Let your patient talk; do not interrupt him even when he becomes prolix and diffuse. It is to your interest as well as his to study his psychology and to lay bare his mental defects. Help him, however, to get on the right road, and to give correct expression to his thoughts."[2] "A great many witnesses," says Gross, "are accustomed to say much and redundantly, and again, most criminal justices are accustomed to try to shut them off and to require brief statements. That is silly."[3] This ability to feel and to show concentrated interest in a client's individual problem is a fundamental condition of good social case work.

The following illustrations gathered from case workers may contain some suggestions as to method of approach, though the beginner who attempted to copy them instead of trying to understand the spirit behind them would be making a mistake. Further illustrations will be found in the reports of First Interviews in Appendix I.

An agent for a state department for dependent children says that it is impossible to "frame up" any introductory speech. She never knows what she is going to say until she sees her client face to face. She was sent to visit a woman who had lost sight of her eight-year-old illegitimate child for a long time. Through relatives the agent had been able to trace the mother, who had married and now had a young baby. She found the woman in a neat flat, and said at once, "I have come on a most unfortunate errand and I wish that it had not been necessary for me to come; won't you let me come in, please, for I feel sure that you would rather that we were not overheard." When she went into the kitchen where the little baby was in a cradle, she spoke to the child and talked to the mother about it until the mother was more at her ease; then she told the object of her visit. The mother at first tried to deny the relationship, but finally, when she realized that the agent was sure

[1] For a fuller discussion of the time element in diagnosis see Chapter XVIII, Comparison and Interpretation, p. 361.

[2] Psychic Treatment of Nervous Disorders, pp. 242–3.

[3] Criminal Psychology, p. 18.

of her position, she acknowledged the child and promised to pay regularly for its care.

A district secretary of an associated charities in her First Interview with Mrs. G. found her "very melancholy and at first reserved and silent." The six-year-old little girl who was present was wearing spectacles. Pleased at the perfectly natural interest shown in Bessie, in her attempts at writing, in the history of her eyes, etc., the mother soon thawed out, and began to tell her story.

An associated charities worker who had learned to be leisurely and had also learned to avoid points of irritation tells of an old woman who entered her office with the exclamation, "Now, ma'am, don't begin by telling me to go to the almshouse, because that's just what I don't want to do." There was a circus parade going by, and the secretary said, "Well, anyway, let's go and see the parade." After watching the parade about half an hour, they started back to the office, and the woman, catching hold of her sleeve, said, "Now, I just want to say I am willing to go to the almshouse if *you* think it best."

An S. P. C. C. worker who has much to do with wayward girls gets them seated in the best chair and "mentally comfortable" through friendly chatter before she begins to talk to them about the painful happenings that have brought them to her desk.

There entered a charity organization society's office one day a woman soon to become a mother who demanded a warrant for the arrest of her husband instanter. She had no time to waste; the children would be coming home from school and must have their luncheon. The secretary looked at her watch and said quietly, "School is not dismissed before twelve o'clock. You have a whole hour and a quarter before your children can possibly get home. Do sit down and make yourself comfortable." Then, seizing the natural opening, "Where do the children go to school?" This led on naturally to a great deal of talk about the children, before the irritating behavior of her husband was allowed a full half-hour's elucidation.

Dr. William Healy says of his interviews with the parents of juvenile delinquents: "The opening of the interview with some such friendly and reasonable statement as the following has been found in itself to have a rationalizing effect. One may say: 'Well, you people do seem to have a difficult affair on your hands with this boy. Let's sit down and talk it all over, and study it out together—how it all began and what's going to happen. I'm at your service. Did you ever think it all out carefully?' . . . The response is nearly always gratifying. The attitude of all concerned becomes much the same as when the family physician makes a complete study and inquiry into the possible causes for an obscure ailment or defect. We get accounts of characteristics, and environments, and forebears, and other antecedents, and even histories of offenses unknown to the authorities, that throw often a great, new light on what should be done with and for the offender. Just this alone shows how vastly necessary it is to have, as in any other business like endeavor, the attitude that wins success."[1]

With regard to interviews with people not born in this country, some workers,

[1] The Individual Delinquent, p. 35.

who happen to have many applications from immigrants coming from one part of Europe, provide their offices with maps of that region. A large map of Ireland showing the smaller places, hangs in a certain district office. Often the district secretary and an exiled Irishman pore over it together to find the mark which indicates the whereabouts of his native hamlet. In one of the district offices of another charity organization society—an office in the Italian quarter—clients who came originally from the vicinity of Rome and those from small villages in the south of Italy are often reminded of the old life and started talking about it by two pictures on the wall, one Roman and one a country scene.

Where interviewer and interviewed cannot speak the same language the approach is doubly difficult. The objections to making it through the English-speaking small children of the family are obvious enough, though this is often done. Some large organizations employ case workers of the several nationalities from which they have the largest number of non-English-speaking clients. Where these workers know more about the foreign language than they do about the special problems of the immigrant or about social work, the results are not happy, but it is becoming increasingly possible to find case workers with the double equipment. The use of interpreters is an expedient which is full of difficulty.

"He is, of course, a necessary evil," says Miss Ida Hull of the interpreter in a paper on South Italians already quoted, "unless the social worker himself speaks Italian and understands the dialects. The professional interpreter is ubiquitous. Since he usually represents himself as the friend of the family it is not always easy to determine just what his standing in the case really is. Appearances are often deceptive, as he may live in the neighborhood and may respond when the family calls from the window. Such professional interpreters are retained by their clients, not to translate the family's statement, but to achieve some desired end. They soon come to know about what sort of story will win attention, and to act accordingly. They receive from fifty cents to five dollars a trip, or sometimes a lump sum for a certain result, be it easy or difficult to attain. One such interpreter, in a burst of indignation against a client 'friend' who had not paid, spoke of a widower who had been a 'perfect gentleman' and had at once handed over the ten dollars which she had asked for inducing the city to take charge of his children. (And the Associated Charities thought it had been responsible for that!) Since these professionals 'repeat' they gradually become known for what they are,—sometimes fairly honest and sometimes utterly unreliable; but always, of course, in the work as a business proposition.

"The interpreter who may be considered a prominent citizen, and who goes out to interpret only when he has a personal end to gain, is a more perplexing factor. His connection with the problem is doubly difficult to discover when he adds the role of interpreter. One such man, of good business reputation, came to ask the assistance of the Associated Charities for a young woman in trouble, who had been given his address in another city and who was then stranded and alone except for the shelter which he was forced to give temporarily. He stated the case briefly, and a call was promised and planned for an hour when it was hoped that he would be out. He was on hand, however. To the first question, 'How long has she been in this country?' the girl replied in Italian 'three months.' Her business manager turned to the investigator and translated 'one year.' When the investigator replied 'but *tre mesi* does not mean one year,' and added that she understood Italian, the interview was really over though it took a half hour of polite interchange before it appeared to be terminated; and then this prominent citizen had decided to assume all responsibility himself.

"Many investigators try to secure as interpreter an Italian connected with some sort of social work. This seems the easiest way at the outset, but there are disadvantages. Such an interpreter is almost certain to explain rather than to translate. While much explanation may be necessary, all investigators will certainly want to know just what the family said as well as what they meant by what they said. Then it may very well happen, that, in proportion as the interpreter can speak authoritatively, the conduct of the case falls into his hands. A first investigation can hardly be conducted as a partnership enterprise. An instance of the failure of such an attempt concerns a most competent and co-operative Italian social worker who acted as interpreter in the case of a deserted wife. This wife, when asked if she had men lodgers, replied in the negative, and then the investigator begged for further questions as to the owners of three coats, all in the same stage of decay, which were hanging in a bedroom. Instead of pursuing that subject, however, the interpreter stopped to explain in detail that a Sicilian wife could not keep men boarders in the absence of her husband, as such a course would be regarded as highly improper. The interpreter regarded further questions along that line as insulting and the investigator could not courteously press the point. The information given as to Sicilian etiquette was unimpeachable; but, alas! later developments showed that this particular Sicilian woman had done many things which could not be sanctioned even by less rigid codes of conduct.

"Picking up an interpreter at random is a dangerous expedient. The difference in dialects may make it impossible for the family and interpreter to understand each other well. Then the family may object for a variety of reasons to telling their troubles to that particular person. The chance interpreter may be a gossip in whom the family cannot safely confide; she may be a creditor; she may seem their social inferior because of having been born a few miles too far south.

"Perhaps on the whole the best way to arrange for the first interview is for the investigator to go to the house and to look so brim full of interesting things to say that the family will seek the interpreter they prefer. The one they choose is likely to be in sympathy with their point of view and to try to present it. If the first interpreter proves inadequate, others may be sought for later interviews. Checking one by another is a way of correcting interpreters in their mistakes, both intentional and unintentional, but the most successful way of treating the interpreter problem is to learn the language and so either to eliminate or to control them."

2. Clues and Questions. A number of case workers have been asked to write as careful an analysis as possible of the process of some of their own recently held First Interviews, stating the physical and social conditions under which the interview took place; the first five minutes of getting under way; the direction taken by the first full flood of talk; any efforts made to direct the stream; the obstacles encountered and how overcome; the distinct points of illumination and insight, and how these were led up to; the clues to the experience and points of view of others interested in their client, and how these clues were secured; impatient pressure, if any, for premature action, and how it was set aside; possible centers of soreness and how they were avoided; and what understanding about the next meeting, if any. As might have been anticipated, some of the best interviewers proved to be the worst possible analyzers of the process, but a few of the analyses secured are given in Appendix I.

These analyses were not needed to prove, though they do prove, that the worker must at once begin, as soon as the interview opens, to draw certain tentative conclusions—they are little better than conjectures at this stage—and must also be prepared to abandon these as the interview and the later story develop. Take, for instance, one of the analyses at hand in which a man, out of work for several months, applies to a family agency in a city to which he had just come with his wife and child. In answer to the first comment of the interviewer that she understands he is a locomotive engineer, he volunteers the statement that he was disqualified by "nervous trouble" in November and has not worked since. At once there comes to mind some outline of the things that the vague phrase "nervous trouble" might cover. Is the disease physical? Mental? A result of some habit, of alcoholism or drug-taking? The very first line of questioning takes the direction of finding out what kind of medical care the man has had. This brings the name and address of a doctor in another town, whose advice can be sought later. But the possibilities further suggested by "nervous trouble"—such as drug habits, etc.—lead the worker somewhat later to cover carefully the man's whereabouts since his discharge, his means of maintaining his family, his reasons for leaving his farmer father with whom he and his family have been staying, etc. At any moment, either during the interview or later, information obtained may show that some one or more of the hypotheses that prompted the questions asked are untenable. They must never be clung to obstinately. This warning has been given in earlier chapters, but it will bear repetition.

In the interview with a deserted wife, given in Appendix I, this same process appears again and again. Husband and wife got on well when they were in another city, the client says. Though the man may not return and though further inquiry may easily prove that the statement is a mistaken one, still make a mental note of it. It may have a bearing upon diagnosis; it may have a bearing upon treatment. If the man "got her into trouble" before they were married, as the wife states, this suggests complications with relatives on both sides of the house, and a forced marriage, perhaps, in which there was little affection. The very next questions follow this line of thought, making allowance, however, for the chance that after the children came the father's sense of family responsibility developed. This wife comes to the associated charities office homeless, after a violent quarrel with her mother. But has she no other place to go? Yes, there are relatives and some of them can be and are communicated with by telephone. The fact that they have telephones is in itself an indication of certain material resources, at least, and so on.

These processes of reasoning, of inference, of making a first hypothesis as a tentative starting point, have been considered in Part I, and, following the gathering of evidence, its correlation, as discussed much later, involves a reweighing of inferences already drawn; but any interview in which the social worker was not using his reasoning faculties in this way every moment would be lifeless and useless. The habit of weighing, comparing, considering must be understood to belong to all the processes described in every part.

It would seem, from the analyses received, that interviewers may be divided into those who follow a fairly fixed order of procedure, and those who begin wherever the situation suggests a natural opening and let the interview develop as it will, bringing it back from time to time to cover some absolutely essential point, but checking off mentally the unasked questions as they happen to be answered. Under some conditions, when conducting an interview through an interpreter for instance, direct queries are unavoidable. Both of these groups recognize the disadvantages of rapid-fire questioning, however, and realize that the more clearly an investigator has in mind the things that he ought to know, the more completely can he avoid the manner of the official examiner; they differ in that the one holds a loose rein and the other a tight one.

One interviewer in the "fixed order" group tries if possible to get the person interviewed to begin with his birthday and develop his story in chronological order. Another, though not holding herself strictly to any established order, strives usually to get the "family make-up" first, including names, ages, and birthplaces of the father, mother, and each child, and of any other members of the family group. Birthplaces suggest previous residences. She then tries to muster in her own mind what she calls the "physical and industrial resources," the transition from the first to the second grouping being easily made by some such remark as, "Well, this certainly is a big family. How do you manage? What is your husband doing?" This leads on to earnings, employers, physical condition, etc. The beginner is often even more precise than this. Not only does he memorize what is known as the face card of the case record that he will later have to fill in, but he makes the mistake too often of allowing his interview to be shaped by the accidents of the size and arrangement of the card.[1]

There is no one way of conducting a First Interview, and it may be that upon occasion any one of the foregoing methods might have to be resorted to, but the more flexible method of the worker who keeps his mind open to all natural avenues of approach and utilizes them to the full is likely to yield better results in the long run and in the majority of cases. An interviewer who is an advocate of the freer method writes that she lets the story go on as it will, beginning anywhere that may suggest itself by accident or by the situation at the time of her arrival, but adds that she has trained

[1] "To those of us who began without a face card," writes a case worker, "and made one for our convenience, the beginners who allow themselves to be tied down by it seem tragic objects. Anything we can do to disabuse their minds of the idea that they get information in order to fill out the card will be well worth while."

herself to put the facts as she gets them in a chronological scheme, and to keep in mind gaps that must be filled—dates, addresses, specific names, numbers, etc.—as the opportunity arrives. In one hospital social service department, two workers specializing in nervous diseases use different methods. One keeps quite closely to a carefully prepared outline; the other starts with the problem because of which the patient is referred. If her department has been asked to help in finding more suitable employment, for instance, she takes employment for her first line of questioning and leads the patient into other avenues through this natural approach. She prefers direct questions to subtler methods, stopping to explain the reason for each question whenever this is necessary.

Everything that has been said in earlier chapters about methods of questioning, and more especially about leading questions,[1] applies especially to the First Interview. Not only should we frame our questions in such a way as to bring truthful replies, but we should put aside, to be sought elsewhere, all information that can be secured just as well or better from an outside source. Employers and fellow workmen are better witnesses as to a man's habits than he or his immediate family. Ages and property—things about which all sorts and conditions of men are secretive—are often matters of public record.[2] Economy of means marks the skilled worker; he asks no useless questions, he gets fewer misleading replies. Misleading replies are never just that; they are barriers between ourselves and those whom we would help, which is the best of all reasons for aiding our clients to bear truthful witness.

Certain questions must be asked, of course, but it is important to bring them forward at the right time. When we ask the head of the family seeking material assistance whether there are any relatives able to assist, he will almost invariably say "no," because his mind is bent upon securing other help.[3] Note the mis-

[1] See p. 71 sq.

[2] "I remember an instance of an agent's getting first one story, then another, and then another, about the property left and the guardianship of the children, when a visit to the probate court in the first instance would have saved a great deal of trouble and made the matter clear." —*From a private letter.*

See upon this point Chapter XIII, Documentary Sources.

[3] Sometimes clients are quite sincere in saying that their relatives will not or cannot help or advise and yet they are mistaken. "An old man assured a worker

take traceable to this cause made in the interview reported in Appendix I,[1] and how quickly the ground lost was recovered.

All of our clues are best won as "by-products of cordial intercourse," but a few of them are too important to be omitted. Those that are most frequently needed from the initial interview are (a) relatives, (b) doctors and health agencies, (c) schools, (d) employers, past and present, and (e) previous residences and neighborhoods.

(a) By far the most difficult clues to secure usually are the names and whereabouts of relatives, but for reasons explained in the chapter on Relatives as Sources these are, outside the immediate family, often our most important sources of information.[2] The questioning which associates relatives and the idea of assistance is, as just noted, psychologically unsound, but the formal question, "Have you any relatives in this city or elsewhere?" may also bring vague information about one or two and nothing about the most important ones, namely, those that are the most intelligent sources of information. Clients sometimes develop no small degree of ingenuity in keeping the social workers who are interested in them and their relatives far apart. After all plans of treatment have failed, it is too late to begin looking up the only people who can fill in gaps in previous history.

Information about relatives comes most easily in the discussion of earlier and happier times, in the talk about the normal rather than the abnormal periods of the family history. After making mental note of them during this part of the interview, it is com-

that he had absolutely no one who could help him; he had lived a solitary life, collecting natural-history specimens for a livelihood and studying the Bible and preaching in all his leisure hours, until he could neither collect more insects nor sell those he had accumulated. After much persuasion he was induced to bring the address of some relations in Canada of whom he had long lost sight, but he only did it because he thought the lady had taken a kindly interest in him and that he might as well satisfy her whims—just as in the same grateful spirit he brought her some pretty green beetles as a gift. The dreamy, gentle old man was perfectly honest in thinking this inquiry useless; but by return of post there came £10 from Canada, and news that the applicant was entitled to a sum of money under a will, which sum had been waiting for him until he could be found."—Lawrence, Miss K. L., in the London *Charity Organization Review* for March, 1912, p. 121.

[1] See p. 464 sq.

[2] The term "relatives" as used throughout these chapters applies to those kindred and connections by marriage who do not now form a part of the client's immediate family group, or share his family table.

paratively easy later on to go back and say, "Where are your brothers and sisters now?" checking them off mentally as deceased, as in the old country, as in this country, etc.[1]

"Years ago," said an experienced case worker at a charity organization meeting, "before this society was founded, I became interested in a young girl of seventeen. She appealed to me greatly. She had no mother, and claimed that her father was not good to her, and her brother and sister far away. She was attractive and much alone. I knew no one who knew more of her than I did myself, and was often puzzled how to advise her. She was anxious to take a vacant position in a family known to me, and after some consultation she went. It was the mistake of a lifetime. I see her now from time to time and never without realizing the mistake I made in permitting her to enter that family. If an agent's investigation could have preceded my first visit, the agent would have made a chance to see the father, would have learned the fact that the brother and sister were less than a mile away, that the girl had made so much trouble in the household that she was forbidden the house, and that the father was greatly puzzled to know what to do with her. With this knowledge, how much more wisely I could have advised her!"

There are exceptional circumstances in which the looking up of relatives may do more harm than good. It is usually possible to learn from some unbiased source whether the circumstances are as exceptional as they appear to be.

One case record examined contains the formal vote of an associated charities district conference that a certain woman "is too sick to be urged to give the addresses of the relatives in Seattle at present." Later they were secured without difficulty.

A woman's relatives were not seen by the agent of a charity organization society because, according to her, they had disapproved of her marriage and she would not for the world have them know that her husband was out of work and applying for aid. After persistent effort a good job was found for him. Four months later his wife applied because he had deserted her and her two small children for the *third time*, going off this time with another woman. The wife had been terrorized by him into refusing, at the time of the first application, to give her mother's name and address. A visit to the mother revealed a long history of cruelty and abuse from the man. In other words, four months had been wasted in securing adequate protection for this family—the real clients from a social work point of view—because the diagnosis that should have read, "Wife and children in need of protection from a vagabond husband and father," read instead, "Hard-working head of family out of work." The former employers seen had shielded him; his mother-in-law would not have done so.

(b) Doctors and health agencies (Chapter X) come naturally

[1] As noted elsewhere, relatives often appear at times of sickness or of death. The doctor and nurse may be able to name relatives that they have seen at such times.

and without difficulty, usually, in the unfailingly interesting details of sickness.

(c) Schools and teachers (Chapter XI) are seldom withheld when there is any talk whatever about the children.

(d) Employers, past and present (Chapter XII), come readily enough usually, especially when there is any question of securing more work or of accounting for a decrease of income. Former employers that are not mentioned, however, are even more important than those that are, if an all-round view is to be had. It must be remembered that the workmen of a large concern are often known by number instead of name, and that for purposes of identification it is necessary further to have the name of the particular shop and of its foreman.

(e) Previous residences and neighborhoods (Chapter XIV) come most easily in the discussion of present rent, etc. The family has been in the present house or apartment so many months, and before that they lived at such a place, but the addresses of the previous residences are often not specific and it is important to note them as accurately as possible. Sometimes the vagueness can be remedied by the use of the city directory and by inquiry of outside sources.[1]

We must not be so bent upon getting clues to outside information that we miss our way to the even more important inside truths of personality—to our client's hopes, fears, plans, and earlier story. In family work, we must have sooner or later a pretty clear idea not only of the main biographical outlines of the two heads of the house and of the older children, but some conception of their attitude toward life. This is far more important than any single item in their story. Families have their own plans and their own ideals—more definite ones than the social worker realizes. These must be understood and taken into account from the beginning. All our plans otherwise will surely come to grief.

3. Taking Notes. The psychological effect of a blank space after a printed question is to suggest the prompt filling in of an answer, whether the writer knows the answer or not. When in-

[1] The city directory for earlier years can often be consulted for previous residences with profit before the first visit. For use of directory see Chapter XIII, Documentary Sources, p. 265 sq.

vestigation was first attempted in connection with the earlier forms of charitable service, the filling in of a blank was very nearly the whole of the process. Sometimes the applicant (the suppliant almost) stood *behind* the investigator sitting at his desk, and the latter delivered the questions over his shoulder and wrote down the answers quite perfunctorily. The natural reaction from all this—a reaction carried farthest by the charity organization societies in their earlier days—led to the definite instruction, "Take no notes in the presence of the poor." In so far as this instruction has forced upon a large group of social workers a much more severe drill in keeping clearly in mind a mass of details without the help of pen and paper, it has been a good thing. The attitude of the average citizen toward the big corporation and its representatives has a quite close parallel in the attitude of the average patient or applicant toward social agencies. They seem powerful, impersonal things, prone to ignore the differences of which the individual is so keenly conscious, and his code for governing his relations with them is a modified, a less loyal code, than that which shapes his relations with his fellows. One of the most important results of a successful First Interview is the substitution of a personal relation and sense of loyalty for the client's standard of behavior toward impersonal institutions and agencies. In so far as note-taking emphasizes the impersonal side, it is wiser to take no notes in the presence of the client that would not appear to him at once as the obvious and courteous thing to do. No rule can be laid down, however. The nature of the task and the conditions under which the interview is held must modify our method. The worker who can forget his pencil, visit a family for the first time, conduct a First Interview full of names, addresses, ages and family details, and then come back to his office and dictate a clear and accurate statement, has at his command a better technique than one who is the slave of a schedule or blank form. Beginners often exclaim that this achievement is for them impossible; their memory is too poor and the mere effort to remember destroys all spontaneity of intercourse. Almost anyone can learn to do it, however, and it demands not half the self-discipline that dozens of processes in the other arts demand. If we take our professional work seriously enough, we shall overcome this obstacle without delay. We shall fail the first time that we try, and in successive trials, but gradually, either through visualizing our information or in some other way that comes more natural to us, the memorizing will become easy. The ability to refrain from note-taking does not mean, however, that we should invariably do so. Both methods have their place. When note-taking during the interview has seemed unwise, many workers make rough notes of names, addresses, and main heads as soon as it is closed. If they are going on from one visit to another, they often stop in the nearest drug store, or do this in the trolley car, unburdening the memory of troublesome details before beginning the next interview.

Three medical-social workers questioned on this point give the following variations of method: The first feels that filling out the face card of her record in the presence of a patient is a distinct advantage, in that the patient passes from the medical clinic into the social clinic to find very much the same routine followed in both. The simple questions and answers, moreover, come as a relief after the physical examination of the clinic. She pursues this method even when the patient challenges her reasons for so doing, on the ground that, as she believes it to be reasonable, she should be able to explain it to another. In certain cases, though these are the exception, she has to stop and explain why after almost every question.[1]

The second worker agrees with the foregoing as to routine questions of name, address, age, etc., but when the history becomes more personal in its nature, she is in the habit of dropping pen and pencil and all that would tend to interfere with spontaneity of intercourse.

The third worker cannot imagine continuing the use of the blank form where irritation appears, and believes that the question of writing or no writing ought to be settled with each patient separately. "If, when the doctor brings a patient to my office, he or she seems to be unwilling and hangs back, I try not to have him even see the pen and ink on my desk. At another time the patient may seem responsive up to the time that the blank and pen are produced; in that event they

[1] Le Play says in La Methode Sociale, 1879, p. 222, as quoted by Chapin in The Standard of Living (p. 8), that he always had the good will, even affection, of families investigated, and thinks that it was due to his method; he observed the following expedients for gaining the good will of the families:

"Not to be abrupt in pushing inquiries—an introduction from a well-chosen source helps in abridging the preliminaries; to secure the confidence and sympathy of the family by explaining the public utility of the inquiry, and the disinterestedness of the observer; to sustain the attention of the people by interesting conversation; to indemnify them in money for time taken by the investigation; to praise with discrimination the good qualities of different members; to make judicious distribution of little gifts to all."

This is taken from a description of a research investigation in which no treatment is to follow; it is not wholly applicable here, therefore, but is at least suggestive. The "judicious distribution" is open to question.

are left untouched. Many times, however, my patients take the written blank as a matter of course, and when they do, I do. Aside from the question of idiosyncrasy the 'reason for referring' should modify our method, I believe. The man or woman who wishes to pay for orthopedic plates a little at a time takes it as a matter of course that you should make out a record that includes references, etc. On the other hand, the unmarried girl who has learned for the first time that she has syphilis or is pregnant is filled with apprehension lest her misfortune become known. It does not seem possible to me to lay down any rule in our work for so delicate a relation as the approach to the patient in a medical-social department."

An S. P. C. C. agent confirms the experience of this third worker. Sometimes she goes into a family and tells them that she is going to write down everything they say, and that they will get into trouble if she finds that they have not told the truth. At other times she will not use a paper and pencil even for the dates of birth of the children, necessary though these are, getting the names and the approximate ages of the children and then going to the city registry of births for the accurate dates. She never knows until she actually sees the people which method she is going to use. It is not a question of nationality or of the circumstances of the family, but something more subtle that influences her choice.

Of the unusually full and almost verbatim records needed of office interviews with delinquents who are possibly defective, Dr. Healy writes, "It has been suggested by some observers, e. g., Binet, that a stenographer should be present to take down the subject's remarks during his work with tests. We should not at all agree to this at any stage. There should be no onlooker or any third person even surreptitiously taking notes when one is dealing with a delinquent. We have come to feel that even the Binet tests are given much more freely when the psychologist is alone with the examinee. To a considerable extent the same question comes up when the interviewer himself takes the words in shorthand. People all look askance when they know what they are saying is being taken down word for word. . . . We have tried several methods, and are convinced that by far the best scheme is to make little jottings of words and phrases and facts in an apparently careless and irregular fashion while sitting at one's desk, and then immediately after the interview to dictate as nearly as possible the actual words used. After a little practice one uses all sorts of abbreviations that really make up an individual shorthand system, and from these one can later dictate accurately the essence of interviews lasting an hour or more. This scheme works very well with us, and rarely arouses any comment from the interviewed." [1]

4. Premature Advice and Promises. Some years ago the writer, in trying to train a new worker, did not discover that this novice's First Interviews were crowded with gratuitous advice and moral instruction, until, going unexpectedly to her office one day and finding her alone, she said, "Come, I am an applicant. Interview me." The case worker is indeed fortunate whose records of

[1] The Individual Delinquent, p. 48 sq.

First Interviews, when read a few months after they have been held, reveal no plans and suggestions that are made to seem absurd in the light of further knowledge.

The First Interview with a mother who was seeking help for herself and her two children reads in part as follows: "She was advised to make a charge against her husband for non-support at once. Says her relatives do not wish her to. . . . Advised with woman regarding a position at service with the baby and commitment of the older one. Says she would not like this arrangement, is sure that she can care for the children as soon as she finds a good position." It developed later that the man and woman were not married to one another.

"We have found that it is usually unwise to give much advice in a first interview, because the patient needs to know us better that our advice may come with added force from his appreciation of the friendliness of our motive. Also we need to know the patient better in order to use his suggestibility, which is often extreme, to his best advantage." Third annual report of the Massachusetts General Hospital Social Service Department, sub-report on Psychiatric Work, 1907–08, p. 46.

Another snare for the feet of the beginner is the pressure brought by the interviewed for premature action or for definite promises of action. Any one way of setting this pressure aside is as much to be avoided as any one way of conducting the rest of the interview. A favorite device is, "My committee must be consulted," but it should be possible to give a more specific reason. The more completely we treat our clients as reasonable beings the better.

5. Bringing the Interview to a Close. The test of a successful interview, we should remember, is twofold. We must have succeeded in getting enough of the client's story and of the clues to other insights to build our treatment solidly upon fact; and we must have achieved this, if possible, without damage to our future relations, and with a good beginning made in the direction of mutual understanding. Interviews that have covered every item of past history and present situation with accuracy and care can be total failures. Interviews that have led to an enthusiastic acceptance on the part of the client of the social worker's point of view, and a lively anticipation of much benefit from future intercourse, can also be failures, though failure of the second kind need not be so fatal and complete as that of the first. We are not investigating for the sake of investigating, but for the sake of getting something done that will be permanently helpful.

In our effort to build a solid foundation we may have had to ask some embarrassing questions and touch a nerve that is sore. It is most important, where this has been the case, that in the last five or ten minutes of the interview we dwell upon hopeful and cheerful things, and leave in the mind of the client an impression not only of friendly interest but of a new and energizing force, a clear mind and a willing hand at his service. Dr. Meyer is quite right. If we know how to do it, the patient's statements can usually be obtained not only fully but with an actual feeling of relief on his part,[1] and a distinct gain in the relation between client and worker.

6. Emergency Interviews. There are cases of severe illness or other emergency in which action is too urgently necessary or the conditions are too unfavorable to admit of more than a hasty First Interview. Two of these are described by Miss Helen B. Pendleton:[2]

You cannot stop to find out whether the young Slav lying ill with typhoid in the filthy lodging house came over in the North German Lloyd or the Red Star Line, or whether he embarked from Trieste or Hamburg. Uncle Sam must get along without this particular bit of information,[3] but while you are making things happen, do not forget your clues. You must know if Peter Novak has any relatives here or whether he belongs to any church or fraternal order. And once poor Peter is provided for today, in a hospital if he will go or at home if he will not—he is too ill to be argued with—and you have these clues for the work that ought to be done on the case tomorrow, you will be justified in going on to your next interview.

Another story illustrates this matter of clues. . . . The police had telephoned a case of destitution. Police cases are always said to be destitute, but as soon as the street and number were given the district worker knew that she should find some sickening form of human suffering. The house was a rear tenement containing three apartments of two rooms each. One of the three she knew as a disreputable resort; in another three children had been ill with diphtheria the summer before; and in the third two consumptives had lived and died in succession. In these rooms she found a young man, scarcely more than a boy, in the last stages of consumption. He was in a sullen state of despair and weakness and would not talk. He had no people, he said—a brother somewhere but he did not know where he was. He had no friends and no one to care about him. He had made his bed and would lie in it.

Just here nine charity workers out of ten, perhaps, would have hurried away, after seeing that food was provided for the present need, to send a doctor and the district nurse, and to order milk and eggs to be sent to the poor fellow every day

[1] See p. 115.

[2] In one of the short, unpublished papers referred to in the Preface.

[3] This refers to the preparation of schedules for a Federal Immigration Commission.

until he died. This particular charity worker did nothing of the kind. It was growing late and she had several other visits to make, but how could she leave this poor fellow with no knowledge of him but his terrible present? Even in the midst of filth and the ravages of disease she could discern that somewhere in the past which he refused to disclose he had known the comforts of a good home. This was a case for slow persistence and searching question; the social surgeon must not falter. At last the name of a former employer slipped out. The young man learned his trade there. Good! That former employer carried on a wellknown business and would know the youth without doubt. Forty-eight hours after that interview, the sick boy was under his father's roof. His parents were respectable, well-to-do people, who had tried to bring up their son in the right way. He had fallen into bad company and evil ways, and two years before had left home in a violent passion after some of his wrong-doing had been discovered. Lately, his people had heard a vague rumor that he was ill and had telephoned to the different hospitals in the city, but had given him up for lost. When last seen by his interviewer, he had been given the best room in his father's house, a room with the sun in it all day; his people were giving him all the milk and eggs that he needed and would be glad to have the nurse call. Surely it was worth while to take time for such a result. . . . These instances are mentioned because emergency interviews are the ones which we are most apt to bungle—as *interviews*. We do the right thing for the emergency, but too frequently we do not discover the clue that will lead to our case's becoming something more than an emergency case.

An agent of an S. P. C. C. describes a visit to a home for the purpose of conducting a First Interview with the mother of the family. When she arrived at the house there was no one to be seen, but hearing voices, she walked through the kitchen to the door of the next room, where she saw two women caring for a young girl sick in bed. She asked, "Is someone sick here?" The mother replied, "Yes, Alice." Without another question, and behaving as though she had known Alice all her life, the agent soon had a physician in to examine the girl, an ambulance there to take her to the hospital, and an operation performed for appendicitis—all this without a word of protest from the mother or a single inquiry as to who she was or how she had come.

SUMMARY OF THIS CHAPTER

1. There are many circumstances that may modify the method of a First Interview. Among these are

(a) The nature of the task about to be undertaken, whether probation work, family work, protection from cruelty, etc.

(b) The origin of the application or request for service; whether from an agency or individual already interested, or from an applicant on his own behalf.

(c) The place of the interview, whether in the client's own home or at the social agency's office.

(d) The recorded experience available. Any possible previous record in the agency's files concerning either the person applying or others of his family. (Search should be made for such a record before the First Interview and again after its close.)

Any possible previous records of other social organizations that show relations with the person applying. (Where there is a confidential exchange, it should be consulted for this information both before the First Interview and after.)

2. The First Interview should (a) give a fair and patient hearing; (b) seek to establish a good mutual understanding; (c) aim to secure clues to further sources of insight and co-operation; (d) develop self-help and self-reliance within the client's range of endeavor.

The interview must not be hurried, therefore; it must be held in privacy, and with every consideration for the feelings of the one interviewed, though always with a definite goal in view.

3. Many questions have been answered before they are asked; these need not be asked by a good listener. Necessary questions should be so framed as to make truth-telling easy. Questions that can be better answered by someone else are not necessary ones.

4. The clues most frequently needed from the initial interview are (a) relatives (b) doctors and health agencies, (c) schools, (d) employers, past and present, (e) previous residences and neighborhoods.

5. The client's own hopes, plans, and attitude toward life are more important than any single item of information.

6. Note-taking during the interview is often not wise, though this depends upon the nature of the request and upon the place of the interview.

7. Advice and promises should be given sparingly until there has been time to know more and to plan more thoughtfully.

8. The last five or ten minutes of the interview should emphasize the interviewer's desire to be helpful, and prepare the way still further for future intercourse.

9. Emergency interviews call for special skill, because, though time presses, certain essential clues are more important than usual.

CHAPTER VII

THE FAMILY GROUP

A DISCUSSION of theories of society and of the organization of the family is no part of the plan of this book. The social worker's convictions about the family, even when they are those of the extreme feminist Left or of the extreme reactionary Right, will be clarified and to some extent modified, however, by a type of case work which follows wherever the facts and the best interests of his clients lead. It is true that his theories will influence his work, but more and more, if he is in earnest, will his work influence his theories. Our only concern here is with family life as a present-day fact.

It is a sobering thought that the social worker's power of influence may extend, through his daily acts, to many whom he has never seen and never, even for a moment, had in mind. This is peculiarly true of all the members who are unknown to him in the Family Groups[1] of his clients. For better or worse he influences them and they, in turn, help or hinder the achievement of the ends that he has in view.

As society is now organized, we can neither doctor people nor educate them, launch them into industry nor rescue them from long dependence, and do these things in a truly social way without taking their families into account. Even if our measure were the welfare of the individual solely, we should find that the good results of individual treatment crumble away, often, because the case worker has been ignorant of his client's family history. Suddenly and usually too late, the social practitioner is made aware of this, when tendencies that have long been hidden become operative. The following statement illustrates the diagnostic importance of family background. It appears in a singularly frank and

[1] The term Family Group as used in this chapter and later includes all who share a common table, though the parents and children—usually the most important members of the group—will receive most attention here.

intelligent study of a child-placing agency's work, made by the agency itself:

On the reception-inquiry side we found that we had accepted children in very critical need of special kinds of care without knowing the particular defects in heredity which made certain of our treatments unwise or dangerous. For example, we had one exceedingly nervous girl in charge for several years before we discovered that she had an insane grandmother; that her father and mother had both died insane, and that this strain of insanity explained certain characteristics which we had most incorrectly interpreted. We also discovered during the study that another none too robust girl suffering with congenital syphilis had three generations of ancestors with almshouse records, a grandmother who was insane and at one time a state ward, and a mother who was both epileptic and an imbecile. The need of a most protective kind of care, expressed in quietness, careful medical supervision, and freedom from strain were indicated as clear essentials; yet in one instance we were planning to put the child under very great discipline because she seemed stubborn.

After giving a number of instances, of the same general tenor, the agency adds: In no instance would it have been easy for us to have secured all this information when the children were first received; but that we learned much of it years afterwards is proof that in some cases we could, and should, have had it from the start.[1]

The foregoing experience was that of a placing-out agency; lest it be inferred that institutional work for children can more safely ignore home conditions than can placing-out, the story of Pittsburgh's institutions, as told by Miss Florence L. Lattimore, should be noted also. In her recapitulation she says:

Every time an institution had allowed a family to break up or sink, without seeing that intelligent effort was made to save it (if it were not already too late), and every time it had returned a child to a home that was unfit, it had strengthened the forces that had created the application. Every time it had placed out a child without adequate home study of the family to which he went and without adequately supervising him after placement, it had run the risk of canceling all its previous efforts to help him. Many of the children were like dropped stitches in a knitted garment, and the whole family was likely to unravel unless the trouble was caught up at the start. It was often a children's institution which received the first hint of a situation which, if unheeded, later on involved several households.[2]

A report from a hospital social service department describes a first interview held with a sickly wife at work over the washtub. She explains that her husband has been living with his mother ever since he lost his work, and the interviewer at once promises to secure extra milk for wife and children, without attempting to see the

[1] Ruth W. Lawton and J. Prentice Murphy in National Conference of Charities and Correction Proceedings for 1915 (Baltimore), p. 167.

[2] "Pittsburgh as a Foster Mother" in The Pittsburgh District, p. 427.

man. As health workers carry their services of many kinds more and more into the home, it becomes increasingly important that they learn to think of the family as a whole. Unless they do, their service will be short-circuited—an unrelated and unrelatable specialty.[1]

The need of keeping the family in mind extends beyond the period of diagnosis, of course. "I will return," says Dubois, "to this necessity of not confining one's therapeutic effort to the patients alone, but extending it to those who live with them. This is often the one way to obtain complete and lasting results."[2]

As stated in the preceding chapter, the first interview is often held in the client's home and with members of his family present. To this extent the two separate processes of making our first contacts with the client and with his family can and often do overlap. It is impossible to lay down any hard and fast rule about their combination or separation. For the highly individualized diagnosis and treatment needed for a delinquent, however, it is evident that such conditions of privacy as Dr. Healy describes[3] are necessary in the first interview. No third person must be present, nothing must distract the client's attention or interrupt the development of his story. Even then, not all will be revealed at this one time or in this one way, as Dr. Healy recognizes more fully than anyone who has yet written upon his subject.[4] "It is in each man's social relations that his mental history is mainly written"[5]

[1] "To keep a promising boy at school after the legal working age, to provide costly treatment for a sick girl, to force a well-to-do relative to support his kinsfolk, to punish a deserting husband, to withdraw wage-earners from unwholesome work—may each represent to some specialist the supreme duty of organized social work in one family where each of these needs is apparent. It may not be possible to meet them all at once, and it may be that some cannot be met at all without sacrificing other important factors in the family welfare. It is just as true in the economy of the family as it is in the economy of society at large that the interests of the individual—for his own good or for society's—must be adjusted to the interests of the whole. The recognition of this by specialists is necessary if we are to avoid danger in social treatment. Here evidently clear thinking and honest discussion are called for. This conflict can only be avoided if we are willing to study the whole problem of family responsibility. Prejudice in favor of one's own specialty must be abandoned and the matter decided in each individual case disinterestedly by the agencies concerned, on the basis of all the facts obtainable."—Porter R. Lee, in Proceedings of National Conference of Charities and Correction for 1914 (Memphis), p. 97.

[2] Psychic Treatment of Nervous Disorders, p. 44.

[3] Quoted on p. 129.

[4] "We have been surprised to find that one of the most particular portions of the work was the interviewing of the relatives."—The Individual Delinquent, p. 46.

[5] Dr. James Jackson Putnam. See motto of this volume.

and no attempt to help a human being which involves influencing his mind in any degree whatsoever is likely to succeed without a knowledge of the Family Group of which he is a part, or without definite co-operation with that group. In some forms of social work, notably family rebuilding, a client's social relations are so likely to be all important that family case workers welcome the opportunity to see at the very beginning of intercourse several of the members of the family assembled in their own home environment, acting and reacting upon one another, each taking a share in the development of the client's story, each revealing in ways other than words social facts of real significance. As regards group versus individual, home versus office interviews, the tendency has been for each form of social work to establish one unvarying procedure. Better results could be had, probably, from a discriminating use of all the different methods of approach.

In any case, it is evident that the relation a diagnostician has with his client's immediate Family Group is somewhat different from his relation with the sources of evidence and service which lie outside the family. A former creditor or the custodian of a medical or a birth record may give him information of the first importance, and never reappear thereafter in the treatment which is to follow; whereas the co-operation of the immediate family may have to be sought again and again at successive stages of the treatment, even when the social problem revealed is an individual one. For instance, take the peculiarly individual problem presented by pathological lying, a disease in which the affected person has "very little sympathy for the concern of others, and, indeed, remarkably little apperception of the opinions of others." Yet Dr. Healy emphasizes for its treatment the need of adequate co-operation in the home or from someone outside with influence over the individual.[1]

I. THE FAMILY AS A WHOLE

The remaining pages of this chapter must be taken as belonging with certain of the questionnaires in Part III and with several of the chapters on outside sources. The health of the family, its educational opportunities, the occupations of its members,

[1] Pathological Lying, Accusation, and Swindling, pp. 253 and 272.

are all matters of fundamental importance, but it has seemed more convenient to treat each of them in a separate chapter in connection with sources.[1] As regards the relation of the family make-up to certain outstanding social disabilities, such as recent immigration, desertion, widowhood, inebriety, and child neglect, these matters are emphasized in the questionnaires in Part III devoted to the particular disabilities named. The less formal discussion here of the family as a whole, of the husband and father, wife and mother, children, and other members of the household, may be taken as introductory to the questions relating to the family in these questionnaires.

1. The Main Drift of the Family Life. One who has learned, in the details of a first interview, to keep the "combined physical and moral qualities," the whole man, in view, will appreciate the importance of applying this same view to the family. The family life has a history of its own. It is not what it happens to be at some particular moment or "in reference to some particular act," but it is what it is "on the whole."[2] What will help to reveal this trend? What external circumstances over which the family had no apparent control, and what characteristics of its members—physical, mental, temperamental—seem to have determined the main drift?

Revealing things are any signs of affection and consideration in the relations of its members to one another. Again, what does the family admire? What are its hopes and ambitions? Has it shown initiative at any time? What part has religion in the home life? What ability has the home developed in its members to resist temptation? What do they do with their leisure time? Do they seek amusement together or apart? What were the two homes like from which the parents came to make this third one? A visit or two will not answer all these questions; the answer to some will come from outside sources and to others only gradually, but the worker who ignores these aspects and is entirely preoccupied with names and ages, number of rooms occupied, sanitation, in-

[1] See Chapters X, Medical Sources, XI, Schools as Sources, and XII, Employers and Other Work Sources.

[2] Jowett, Benjamin: Sermons, Biographical and Miscellaneous, p. 80. Ed. by W. H. Fremantle. New York, E. P. Dutton and Co., 1899.

come and outgo, school attendance, etc., will never win lasting results in social case work.

Nothing can interfere more effectually with a large and well balanced view than preoccupation with some picturesque minor incident. The writer remembers a family history of years ago which was made more painful than it need have been by a series of social treatments which lost all grasp of the main issues involved. These failures were due to the striking circumstance that the father of the family, which lived in great squalor, had named his youngest child Thomas Carlyle. The literary members of several charities were unduly impressed by this interesting incident in the life of a gambler.

2. The United and the Unstable Family. There is a distinction, made first by Le Play, which will help us to a better conception of the family as a whole. With reference to their power of cohesion, we shall find that families range themselves along a scale, with the degenerate family at one end and the best type of united family at the other. Whatever eccentricities a family may develop, the trait of family solidarity, of hanging together through thick and thin, is an asset for the social worker, and one that he should use to the uttermost. "It is not merely a question," says Mrs. Bosanquet (whose book, The Family, more especially Part II, should be known to every case worker), "of how long the members of a family continue to live together in one house; superficially the two types may be much alike in this respect. It is one of the proofs of the strength of the modern family that it is able to send its sons and daughters far over the face of the earth without in the least impairing the bond which unites them; while it is one of the proofs of the weakness of the degenerate family that there is no bond to hold them together at all, or a bond so slender that removal into the next street is enough to sever it. The real nature of the distinction can only become clear as we study the characteristics of the modern family at its best."[1] These characteristics are admirably developed in the second half of Mrs. Bosanquet's book, but American readers will have to bear in mind that it records the traits of a homogeneous population, of one that has been exposed to no sudden changes of environment, and no over-

[1] The Family, p. 193.

whelming temptation of newly found freedom. We find in this country many signs of disintegration due to these surface causes, even in families in which there is, at bottom, strong family feeling, and we cannot understand the evils that beset them unless we are at some pains to study the racial and national traditions that cling so tenaciously around certain of the foreign Family Groups exposed to American ideas, and that crumble away too quickly from certain others.[1]

Whenever serious estrangement occurs between husband and wife, or parent and child, the first thing to study is the differences, if any, in racial, national, and community background, with the resulting differences of custom, convention, religion, and education. Next to disparity of age, to marriage or remarriage for economic reasons, and the interference of relatives, differences of nationality, race, or religion are the most fruitful causes of trouble between man and wife, and varying degrees of adjustment to the new world environment are fruitful causes of trouble between parent and child.

It is difficult to illustrate briefly what is meant by dealing with the family as a whole with a clear conception of the main drift of the family life always in mind, but the following criticism of a case record of a deserter and his family will give some conception of the point of view:

The record comes from a charity organization society, and describes the efforts of the society to find Mr. Angus Doyle, a Scotch ship fitter who had left his Scotch-American wife, Kate, and four children, the oldest a girl of fifteen, going off this time, as was usual with him, when another baby was expected. He was a good workman, but a hard drinker and abusive. By energetic correspondence and the aid of a similar society in another state, Doyle was found, his employers were interested, and the man was induced to send $7.00 a week regularly to his family. After the fifth child was born, he came home and was overheard telling one of his mates that it made no difference where a man went in this country now, he was found out and made to support his family.

So far so good, and the critic of the record comments upon the good work of both societies in influencing the man through his employer. Sometimes such an approach simply means that the man drops his work and goes elsewhere; but there are not many shipyards in the United States, the wife was in no physical condition at the time to push through a court prosecution, and the societies probably reasoned that their best chance was to see the man in the presence of his superintendent, and appeal to him to make weekly payments.

[1] Some of these traditions are suggested in the introduction to the Immigrant Family Questionnaire, p. 384.

Returning to the family history (the criticism continues), we find three generations on the mother's side in one city neighborhood—a neighborhood of varied industrial opportunities evidently. We have the chance therefore, if we choose to take it, though the record does not help us very much, to fill in a background for Mrs. Doyle's mother, Mrs. Clayton, for Mrs. Doyle herself, and for her fifteen-year-old daughter, Margaret Doyle.

I am trying to suggest many of the possibilities instead of just a few of them, but it will be evident that some, at least, have a direct bearing upon further treatment, if there is to be any. What sort of homemaker was Mrs. Clayton? According to a physician who "knows the whole family connection," she is a "rum soak"; according to Doyle's sister (who herself "has an attractive home" and "seems very placid and sensible") she "is not the right kind of woman and easily leads Kate [Mrs. Doyle] astray." This same sister relates that the Doyles married when Kate was sixteen and Angus eighteen and that "they have never agreed"; that Mrs. Doyle is a good mother, manages her children well, and is very clean, but that on the other hand, while she is not a drunkard, she sometimes drinks—a statement corroborated, as to the past, by the physician already quoted regarding Mrs. Clayton. The sister's further statement that Mrs. Doyle had "deviled" her husband into leaving and that if she would "hold her tongue" she ought to be able to "jolly him along" and keep a nice home has little evidential value, but does suggest that Mrs. Doyle may be ill tempered or given to nagging. Altogether, there would seem to be some fault on both sides, though scant basis is revealed for Angus Doyle's statement that "his wife drank, neglected her home, their children, and his meals"; according to the visitor, the "home is neatly and attractively kept, children well mannered, woman certainly not drinking now."

As to the husband, we have little evidence that is favorable. His employers had put up with his "periodical sprees" because he was an excellent mechanic; and, knowing nothing to the contrary, his fellow workers believed his statement that he "had a dreadful life with his wife." According to the physician already quoted, he is "utterly worthless; undoubtedly a good worker, but drinks hard and cares for no one but himself." His sister did not shield him as to the drink; apparently the only virtue that she imputed to him was that he was "not lazy."

Here, then, is a situation in which there are elements, behind the obvious fact of desertion and non-support, which render the return of the deserter far from a final solution of the difficulty. He has learned a lesson, doubtless, from his latest experience; perhaps it may restrain him when next the impulse to shake off family responsibilities seizes him, though of this we can be by no means sure; but so long as he continues to be a periodic drinker and abusive, so long as he and his wife are unable to live in peace, it can hardly be said that the family problem is satisfactorily solved.

With the scanty array of facts at our disposal it is impossible to say what the next move should have been, after the deserter had been found and a regular income from him insured. It would seem that at this point time might have been taken to build in a background—to learn something of Doyle's boyhood, his home training, schooling, early work history. Inquiry of the sister might reveal, for example, that he had been a trial from his earliest years to devoted parents who had set him an excellent example—an habitual truant and runaway, let us say, who later had refused to turn in his earnings. Or again, it might appear that his record as school boy, son, and young worker had been excellent, and that his delinquencies had not begun till some years after his marriage. It is evident that there would be greater hope in the latter case than in the former of studying out, with Mrs. Doyle's aid, the underlying causes of the difficulty and finding a remedy. In the same way, coming to more recent history, it might be useful to know the effect of dull times in the shipbuilding trade upon Doyle's habits and movements. Was he at home or away, drinking or sober, during the panic of 1907–08? Is his work seasonal? What is his state of health? Has he ever been arrested? Is there any court record? Are the children fond of him?

On the industrial side, had Mrs. Doyle, who worked as a buffer in the metal works, been so engaged when her husband was at home and working, or had she worked in his absence only? In either case, what effect had her ability to earn and to support the family had upon him? But for her condition, she would have been earning $2.25 a day at the buffing wheels when the society visited her. Is this healthful work for the mother of a family? Is it related in any way to the fact of her drinking? How did the children fare under Mrs. Clayton's care in their mother's absence? What about Margaret's work in the hosiery mill—are conditions favorable to health and future prospects fair?

The society was quite right to concentrate, as regards treatment, upon the desertion issue first; to find the man, that is, and put upon him the financial burden of his family. But, having gained an excellent footing with Kate Doyle by so doing, and the whole social and industrial environment that had been too much for the family in the past remaining what it had been, was the chance to readjust their relation taken full advantage of? Their earnings were larger than usual upon the last visit—a fact which should have made constructive work easier—and the drink, the instability, the likelihood of another family breakdown should have been dealt with one by one.

Perhaps my criticism may seem to overemphasize a string of items, but all of them lead to one point; namely, that to organize the social services of a community in any vital sense, we must all be working out, in at least a minority of the families that come under our care, the *synthetic relation* of the industrial, physical, moral, and social facts which affect their welfare. In other words, what might have been a good beginning with the Doyles was mistaken for a good ending. From the very first interview with Mrs. Doyle the possibility of this wider program might have been kept in view and might have shaped the diagnosis.

Even where background is not kept in mind from the beginning, it is possible to recover the ground that has been lost and achieve synthetic results later on, though it is not so easy to do so. The Braucher case, a summary of which is given in Chapter IX, Relatives as Sources,[1] illustrates this possibility.

[1] See p. 188 sq.

II. THE HUSBAND AND FATHER

1. The Man Should Be Seen. Husband and wife are not of the same blood, be it remembered. They have a past in common, but each has had an earlier past apart, and, since in many forms of social work we see much of the wife and children and little or nothing of the husband and father, it is necessary deliberately to keep him in mind. Faulty methods of social work may have led him to think that his wife should do all the applying and explaining, but an understanding of the plans and purposes of the man of the family—his ambitions for his children and for himself—cannot be had without early personal contact with him. It is safer and it is fairer so, and our later planning and conferring should include him. "It is our business to see the man in this case," writes a critic of a family record. "He is probably all he is painted to be, but he has a right to a hearing."

At one charity office, the man of the family apologized for not sending his wife, explaining that she was too sick to come that day, or else she would have applied. He was told that the secretary much preferred to confer with him about his family's distress, because it was his affair, as the breadwinner, even more than his wife's.

As plans for various forms of child welfare multiply it is more easy than ever to overlook the man of the family. "Many probation officers fail to make the acquaintance of the fathers of the children in their care during the whole period of probation," write Flexner and Baldwin.[1] "It is generally a little difficult to get in touch with a father, but he is often the key to the whole problem. Probation officers should make an effort to have at least an acquaintance with the father of every child in their care, whether or not that acquaintance can be carefully followed up by close co-operation with him."

An S. P. C. C. worker in a small town says that she tries to get all possible information from the family direct, seeking first the man's story, then the woman's, then bringing them together, if possible, and getting, in this joint interview, a good deal of new light. She appeals to them to be frank with her in order to avoid gossip, adding, "You know how the people around here like to talk, and it will be far better for us to settle this thing ourselves if we can."

2. Place of Interview. It is often better to see the two heads of the family separately, making a special evening appointment at the case worker's office or at some other convenient place in order to do this. There may be substantial like-mindedness between husband and wife and no domestic misunderstandings, but,

[1] Juvenile Courts and Probation, p. 136.

in the joint interview, one naturally leads and the other follows, so that it is difficult to get acquainted with both.

To attempt to see the man of the family at his work place, especially if this happens to be a large concern, is unwise, though it is sometimes possible to see him there at the noon hour. His employer objects to having him called away from his work, and he is not at his ease, moreover. One social worker who attempted such an interview with a man who ran an elevator found every few sentences interrupted by the elevator bell.

The head of a department for mothers and infants in a children's organization, recognizing that it would be a mistake to communicate with a father through the unmarried mother of his child, always writes to the man, instead of sending him a message. She includes in her letter the statement that so-and-so has been to see her and told her something of their situation; that, before making any plan, she wants to talk the matter over with him; ending by saying that she will gladly meet him at her office at any hour that suits his convenience. This worker believes that men prefer to discuss all matters of business away from their own homes. In a given twelve months she wrote 25 such letters to the fathers of illegitimate children. Ten called at her office in response; seven responded by letter and four of these were seen later, though not at the office; the remaining eight did not reply.

3. The Unmarried Father. Efforts, such as the foregoing, to deal in illegitimacy cases with the father quite as directly as with the mother and child, and to do this out of court in the first instance, are further illustrated by the following case notes:

A children's society was puzzled as to whether it should urge marriage between the father and mother of a small baby. A clergyman and other references thought the young fellow careless and self-indulgent, and all the evidence seemed to be against the marriage. Not quite satisfied, however, the children's worker decided to try the experiment of having the man confronted with his own child. He proved to be one of the few fathers of illegitimate children who had, in her experience, shown an interest in their babies. His was at once an almost maternal devotion. So marked was this feeling that she encouraged the marriage. The home was happy and prosperous.

A girl with a young baby applied to this same children's society to secure support from her deserting husband. The man's relatives claimed that he had not seen his wife for three years and was not the father of her baby. The evidence narrowed down to the conflicting statements of the two sets of relatives (his and hers) and both were of unestablished reliability. Finally a meeting was arranged between man and wife in the presence of the agent, and he acknowledged his parenthood.

A charity organization society was asked by a hospital to befriend an unmarried mother of twenty with a two-weeks-old baby. She named, as father of the child, a young fellow who had come from a refined home. He was not in the city and wrote to his mother denying everything. An interview arranged between the mother and the young girl convinced the older woman that the girl was telling the truth. This did not lead to marriage, but to weekly payments toward the support of the child. From the community's standpoint it is quite as important to deal with the unmarried father as with the unmarried mother.

4. The Young Couple. That the wife and one or two babies of a young, able-bodied man should, in ordinary times, need any social service that involves material relief also is a situation which demands the closest scrutiny. To discover all the reasons for the trouble, if possible, and deal with them one by one is more difficult than to give temporary help, but an irresponsible interference with their affairs is worse than none. Notes on the recorded treatment of two young couples by a charity organization society are as follows:

Italian couple, both twenty-three, with children four, two, and one just born. Non-supporting. The first interview and succeeding investigations do not bring out clearly when the man began to be neglectful; whether he had exhibited the same traits before marriage; if they first appeared after marriage, under what circumstances; and what or who was the exciting cause. There should have been a much more searching inquiry among other relatives and old employers, and possibly friends of both before their marriage. Here is a pauper family in the making. It is either hopeful or otherwise. We do not know the woman's real character at all. We do not know how far back the man's present slackness goes. If everything points to absolute degeneracy on his part, far greater influence (through relatives and others) should be used to break up the family. If not, then the case is still left in the air, because no further treatment has been provided.

This is the case of a deserter from the Navy with a young wife (epileptic) and a two-and-a-half-year-old child. A quite compact, satisfactory investigation, with a good chronologically arranged first statement. A very satisfactory use of six sources of information, though there are reasons why the second relative should have been seen also. But with the return of the man in February, the summary closing of the case on February 15 was not wise. The man is inclined to be lazy, he has a very loving wife who is liable to "baby" him a good deal on account of what she will consider the hard time that he has been through. The wife has been put into a janitress's position (only rent free and $1.00). The wisdom of having her start in again to do work outside her own home is very doubtful. It will be necessary to keep in constant touch with this man by volunteer aid or long reach from the office—letters and sometimes calls. There are all the tendencies present for a complicated problem five years hence. Deal with them now!

5. Desertion and Inebriety. These two disabilities, which are treated more fully in two of the questionnaires, illustrate the controlling influence upon diagnosis of a program of social treatment. In the days when no distinction was made between the social treatment of the wife and children of a deserter and that of a widow's family there was little reason for mastering the history of the desertion or desertions and the characteristics of the deserter. But with the development of a new sense of social responsibility for the deserter's movements and relations to his wife and children, with provisions for his extradition, release on probation, payments to family through the court, etc., has come a new reason for differential treatment based upon differential diagnosis. Is he really a deserter, or are there reasons to believe that he is in communication with his family and still in their immediate neighborhood? The history of former desertions, if any, may throw light upon the reasons for this one and upon the man's probable movements. Even if not in communication with his own family, more often than not he will have continued to keep up relations with someone—with his own relatives, with former shop mates, or with old cronies. Are his relatives inclined to shield him or are they harboring him perhaps? If there is any chance of taking court action, proof of his marriage may be necessary. Not all deserters are equally culpable. An understanding of their difficulties and their points of view makes it clear that, given the right impetus, many of them are far from hopeless as family men. It is more important to understand the main drift of their lives than the one incident which brings them to our attention, whether this is an isolated one or the climax in a series of mistaken choices. The foundations of such an understanding are best laid in our early contacts with the Family Group.

Alcoholism is a disability which presents quite as great a variety of possibilities as desertion. In fact, there is no social disability in the treatment of which more use can be made of such indices to personality as will power, sociability, capacity for affection, and susceptibility to religious influence.[1] The problem has its medical aspects; the man's bodily and mental condition and the habits and mentality of his forebears are often the most important factors, but the social side is important too. Such environmental factors as the temperament of his wife, the comfort of his home, the family cooking, the conditions and nature of his daily employment, the character of his companions, need only to be mentioned to suggest a possible relation to his drink habits. These habits themselves vary in different men. Some are accidental drunkards; some free drinkers who occasionally get drunk; some are unable to touch alcohol without being overcome by it; some always drink with others; some are solitary drinkers; some are using drugs also or have substituted alcohol for a drug. "The treatment of the inebriate can best be expressed," says Dr. Neff, "in the word 'individualization,'"[2] and the foundations of individualized social treatment are best laid in early contacts with and observations of the Family Group.

III. THE WIFE AND MOTHER

The household speaks for the wife, answering unasked questions about her as it does not about the husband. The wife's maiden name will aid in identifying her kindred and will enable references who knew her only before her marriage to place her. (In Italian families she is still often known by her name instead of her husband's.) Her maiden name may also aid in bringing to light the records of related families under treatment. She remembers birthdays and ages and church connections better than the man does, and is the first-hand authority on the family budget, more especially the outgo. Her schooling and her work and wages before marriage help to place her, as does also her account of how

[1] "There is a passage in one of Miss Octavia Hill's essays that throws a flood of light on this question. She says that the love of adventure, the restlessness so characteristic of the Anglo-Saxon, makes him, under certain conditions, the greatest of explorers and colonizers, and that this same energy, under other conditions, helps to brutalize him. Dissatisfied with the dull round of duties that poverty enforces upon him, he seeks artificial excitement in the saloon and the gambling den. It is useless to preach contentment to such a man. We must substitute healthier excitements, other and better wants, or society will fail to reform him."—Friendly Visiting among the Poor by M. E. Richmond, p. 128.

[2] See Proceedings of National Conference of Charities and Correction for 1911 (Boston), p. 135.

she and her husband first met, and of their pre-matrimonial acquaintance. Details of her work since marriage, of its relation to her health, to care of home and children, to her husband's exertions, and the attitude of her family and friends toward her work are all of them important.

If, in tracing the main current of the family life, it becomes evident that there have been marked changes in home standards, what has been the wife's share in these changes? If her home standard was fair at one time and now is low, what factors have entered in—extreme poverty, too many children, overwork, her own or other family illnesses? In estimating the physical influence of childbearing, the children who have died and any miscarriages must also be included. Not only her husband's habits but her own must be known and understood. If, for example, she is a gossip who neglects her household duties and spends much time away from home, what poverty of opportunity and of interests, what recreational need that can possibly be met is behind this? The drink habit is not always confined to the man of the family. Even where husband and wife both drink the one habit may have two quite different histories.

1. Physical Aspects of Homemaking. A household may be in a good deal of disorder and still be essentially cleanly. The reverse is true, of course, and the distinction is worth making. Has the wife learned to sew? Does she take pleasure in making the most of the family wardrobe, or has she lost or never had this interest in clothes? What does she know about cooking? Is she a good buyer?

Upon questions of "income and outgo" the wife and mother is, as has been said, the best authority.[1] Details given under this head in the first of the questionnaires need not be repeated here, but one important point, not capable of outside verification, should be emphasized. The food habits of the family must be known in many forms of case work, because these habits are so closely related to the family's health and to its efficient use of income. The homemaker knows what food is bought and eaten, of course, but unless she keeps accounts, her estimate as to the total cost of any item of her family budget is worth very little. A case worker and

[1] The wife does not always know the earnings of her husband and older children, however.

dietitian tells of an English-speaking Polish woman with five children who, when asked how much per week was needed to buy food for her family, said, with a manner that indicated the amount might seem excessive to her visitor, "I think I must have $2.00."

No mere account of food purchases and prices, moreover, can give all the data needed, for details of choice, preparation, and consumption are half the story. And any inferences drawn from these details must take into account not only such obvious factors as the size of the family, and the ages and occupations of its members, but those conditions of health and those national and religious characteristics which have a marked influence upon food consumption. Even so definite a matter as the size of the family is complicated, in some immigrant households, by the presence of boarders for whom the housewife cooks food provided separately by each boarder.[1]

Another modifying factor is the amount of time and skill that the housewife has to devote to homekeeping. Most economies in money call for an increased outlay of work and skill. In fact, the housewife's skill is "an asset which must be included in the family resources."[2]

Any study of food questions has a very stimulating effect upon the homemaker when she shares in the whole process. She needs some such stimulation of interest, for her devotion to a difficult round of tasks is often taken entirely for granted.

When we confine our attention to the strictly diagnostic aspects of the food question, the greatest difficulty encountered will be with the housewife who cannot keep good accounts or any. This handicap means more frequent visits, some of them at meal times perhaps. As the housewife knows what she has just bought, a start in getting the rough outlines, at least, of food consumption may be had by working on a day basis and trying to discover, concerning each of the staple articles which every family is supposed to have, just what has been bought and eaten.

[1] What is left over commonly goes to the family, hence it becomes practically impossible to estimate the money expended by the family or the amount of food that they have. The visitor may judge unfairly too, when she sees the boarder's chicken cooking and assumes that it belongs to the family. On the other hand, the family may claim that its own bountiful meal belongs to the boarders.

[2] Byington, Margaret F.: Homestead, the Households of a Mill Town, p. 74. New York, Russell Sage Foundation Publication, Charities Publication Committee, 1910.

The dietitian of a public department administering mothers' pensions reports the following items of experience: "The department requires that household accounts be kept by the pensioners, and, though an untrained woman seldom keeps accurate accounts, wilful inaccuracies usually show either (1) impossible amounts of a given article, (2) costs which do not correspond with amounts purchased, or (3) monotonous repetition of the same few items. Entire absence of some essential is often an unintentional inaccuracy."

This dietitian finds that the best avenue of approach to the food question is an anemic or undersized child. The attention of the mother is called to the fact that the child does not look particularly strong, and she is asked whether he has a good appetite. What did he eat for breakfast this morning? How does this compare with what the other children ate? If, as frequently happens, the breakfast was "bread and coffee,"[1] this gives a chance for explaining the value of milk and cereals. The topic of the children's luncheon, especially that of the school children, naturally follows. Do they come home to a hot luncheon or do they buy bakery buns and cakes? Is their chief meal at noon or at night? Is it a meal at which all sit down together to eat, or do the different members of the family eat how and where they please? Is the dietary for adults and for younger children the same? When the mothers have once realized that an interest in the health of the family and not a desire to cut down monthly allowances is behind these questions, the response has usually been a cordial one.

Each visitor of this department is provided with a schedule of the normal weights of children of given ages, and secures, for the neighborhood in which she is working, a list of prices of staple foods in the stores in which prices and quality are most satisfactory.

After the actual food habits of the family have been clearly grasped—a thing that cannot usually be achieved in one or two visits—the question of finding the remedy for defects and inadequacies remains unsettled. A fair standard of food values and costs should be the basis of any budgetary estimate, but, as regards costs, the modifications necessary for each locality and each marked change in market rates should be worked out more carefully than they have been by family agencies. A unit of cost per person estimated for the whole country years ago can be very misleading. We must know also the health conditions and the family or individual idiosyncrasies that should modify our estimate. If all of the family are found to be in good physical condition on a smaller food allowance than our estimated local standard, should the standard be urged, or should this variation be ignored? All of

[1] Dr. Healy says in Honesty (p. 105) that, unexpectedly, he found the overuse of tea and coffee one of the most frequent causes of delinquency in children.

these matters are important; most of them do not belong here, however, but in a discussion of the later stages of treatment.

2. The Family Housing. The following list of the housing defects that are serious enough to arrest the attention of social workers, no matter what their errand to the home, is an amplification of one prepared by the writer in 1911.[1] Not all of these things can be covered in one visit, of course, or in two, but all are important.

a. Bad Toilet Arrangements. We visit homes frequently where there is inertia, low vitality, or even sickness without knowing definitely or taking the trouble to discover the condition of the plumbing, the trapping of the waste pipes, etc. The cleanliness of the toilets, their location and provisions for privacy, such as inside locks, have a bearing upon health and decency. An untrapped waste pipe means sewer gas, probably, and sewer gas means ill health. Where there are outside vaults a menace to health from fly infection always exists, while inconvenience of access and noisome odors combine to make the condition one of the most serious of housing evils.

b. Dampness. The condition of the cellar, the walls, and the roof, more especially of the cellar; is its floor wet or damp, has it a dirt or a cement floor, is it cluttered with rubbish or animals? Are the pipes leaking? Does the roof leak?

c. Dark Rooms. When these are used for bedrooms, the fact should be noted on our records, should be related to our family histories of disease and premature death, and should be made the subject of steady pressure upon citizens, lawbreakers, and public administrators.

d. Overcrowding. This is especially to be noted as regards sleeping accommodations. Its vital relation to health, particularly to the spread of tuberculosis, and to decency must be vividly realized and kept constantly in mind in all our plans for making people economically independent. Independence built upon a standard that ignores decency is built, of course, upon quicksand. In this connection the taking of lodgers and boarders is especially important because of the physical, moral, and social dangers involved.

e. Insufficient Water Supply. In the purity of the source and the amount are involved the condition of the cistern or tank and its care between official inspections. Is there running water and, if not, where is the nearest tap?

When we have trained ourselves to observe these things, we shall find that the unhealthful conditions discovered are some of them violations of existing statutes, others not. With regard to the first group, we should lose no time, of course, in reporting to the right place bad conditions that really are violations. The second group furnish arguments for further legislation, but they do this only when they are promptly and accurately recorded. Pending

[1] See Proceedings of National Conference of Charities and Correction for 1911 (Boston), p. 327–328.

the securing and enforcement of such legislation, it is possible to keep the worst houses and tenements empty by persuading tenants to move, and it is possible to remedy the less serious nuisances with their co-operation. It has also been found practicable sometimes to appeal directly to landlords who had been in the habit, earlier, of leaving the management of their properties to agents, and persuade them to correct the evils complained of.

IV. THE CHILDREN

Here we find blood relationship and all those undercurrents of sympathy and antagonism which it implies. Propinquity only aggravates any natural lack of sympathy. Between kindred such lacks are often fundamental. Often, however, as Mrs. Bosanquet points out, antagonism is due not so much to fundamental differences as to the assumption that there should be no difference. The implacable attitude of child toward parent, parent toward child, and of brothers and sisters toward one another is due to likenesses even more than to differences. "That a member of the family, sharing in its common nature, partaking in its impulses, instincts, sentiments, and education, can have done this thing—it is *that* which wounds deeper than all the scorn or pity from the outside, for it reveals possibilities unrealized before."[1] A probation officer tells of a girl in her care who held a grudge grimly against her mother for three years because she complained of her to the juvenile court at a critical time. So often do parents' complaints to the court cause open rebellion and permanent estrangement that this officer strives in every possible way to settle such difficulties without appearing in them.

One common cause of estrangement is the inability of children to give expression to their ambitions or to find a natural outlet for their energies. The effects of these checks are intensified in any family that is passing through a sudden change of economic status, whether that change be favorable or the reverse. The response of the different members to the outward change is a varied response; the upheaval which depresses and alienates one member acts as a stimulus to the energies and affections of another, with the result that all are thrown out of their accustomed relation

[1] The Family, p. 257.

to one another. The human situation thus created has been a favorite theme of English fiction from the Vicar of Wakefield to the latest best seller.

Other causes of estrangement are the unwise reticences of parents and their failure to appreciate, at critical periods, the physical reasons for a child's lack of control. "There is the most definite necessity," says Dr. Healy,[1] "for little people telling what they have seen and what they have done. For them to bottle up within themselves affairs of importance is a dangerous proceeding. We should most earnestly counsel that children should be accustomed to go over the items of their daily life with their guardians that there may be no hidden knowledge to be dwelled on in morbid fashion. Of all forms of prevention of delinquency I know of nothing comparable to the confidences and counsels between elders and children."

It is a commonplace of child-saving, of course, that a child placed away by one or both parents loses, in large degree, the sense of family solidarity.

The mother's attitude toward her children and theirs toward her are easily observed as they come and go in the home. A medical-social worker says that if, after the immediate purpose of her visit to a home is accomplished, she has occasion to wait to make a train and busies herself with a book or some work meanwhile, the members of the family, ceasing to react to her, begin to react to one another, and she gets an impression of the home that she might miss altogether otherwise. Have the parents good control over their children? Do the latter seem afraid of either parent? Are they punished in anger, or is self-control exercised? The unfortunate practice of some teachers, nurses, and social workers of dealing with the family's affairs almost entirely through the medium of the children has a definite bearing upon the loss of respect for parents which is so marked a characteristic of the young people in certain families.

Mention has been made of the failure of many children's institutions and societies to study the family backgrounds of their wards. Quite as grave an omission is the failure in many family agencies to individualize each child in the families under their

[1] Honesty, p. 177.

care. Aside from the consultation of school records and possible court records, both of which are items to be covered outside the home, visits to the home itself should lead to inquiries as to the physical and mental condition of every child showing any variation from the normal,[1] and should also give us a clear impression of the temperament of each of the children. What are their aptitudes, their ambitions, their small achievements? The sleeping arrangements for the children, both with reference to their healthfulness and their decency, are an important point. So are their recreations. Are their small, individual possessions respected? Have they any? What opportunities have they for sharing pleasures and duties as a part of the family? Is there any indication that they are overworked at home duties? That they are doing sweatshop work at home? Are they sent to charity offices with messages which should be taken there by adults only? Are they sent out to beg? Are they illegally employed? It should be unnecessary to add that inquiries about the children, especially with regard to matters involving their conduct, should not be made in their presence.

1. The Matter of Ages. The ages of any children in the family who are still minors may become so very important at any time that the recording of them with exactness must be urged. The only way to be absolutely sure of ages is to have day, month, and year of birth in each case and to verify these from official records.[2] Their importance is shown from the following list of actions and judgments in which such dates must be used:

a. Prosecution of parent for desertion or abandonment of infant.
b. Bastardy charges.
c. Establishing legitimacy or a previous marriage.
d. Identification of a family (where names are incorrectly given).
e. Collecting insurance.
f. Choice of a guardian.
g. Prosecution of parent for cruelty or neglect.
h. Choice of institutions for temporary placing or for commitment.
i. Entering in school and requiring school attendance.
j. Establishing legal date for going to work, for engaging in street trading, etc.
k. Establishing legal hours of work.

[1] See questionnaires on the Neglected Child and on the Child Possibly Feebleminded in Part III.

[2] See p. 256 sq.

l. Protecting from certain injurious employments.
m. Deciding right of parent to collect wages of child or receive support from him.
n. Bringing suit for accident indemnity.
o. The age of consent.
p. Fixing period during which alimony is payable in cases of legal separation or divorce of parents.
q. Securing special transportation rates.
r. Establishing the legality of a minor's marriage.[1]

The secretary of the Massachusetts S. P. C. C. puts this matter more concretely as follows: One day after a child is fourteen he can nominate a guardian; one day after he is fifteen he cannot be sent to the Industrial School; one day after he is sixteen his case cannot be considered in court under the Neglect Law; one day after he is seventeen he cannot be considered a juvenile offender; one day after she is seventeen a girl cannot be committed to the Lancaster School [girls' reformatory].

Not only the month but the exact day is essential in all the foregoing. In recording the ages of parents, the year is usually sufficient, unless a parent also is a minor.

2. The Older Children. The educational side of the children's lives is discussed in Chapter XI, Schools as Sources. It need not detain us here. When the children are about to leave school, their special aptitudes and their ambitions become very important matters. Are they thrust into dead-end occupations? Are they frequently shifted about from one job to another? These are the years in a child's life when highly individualized case work is often needed to supplement whatever plans of vocational guidance have been developed in the schools.

The attitude of the wage-earning child who takes the turning over of all his earnings to his parents as a matter of course, and

[1] Miss Amelia Sears, to whom the writer is indebted for most of the items in this list, gives the following additional reasons for seeking the exact ages of children:

"If . . . there is a lapse of three or four years between the births of two children in a large family where most of the children have come close together, three possibilities occur to the experienced case worker: First, the parents may have lost a child; second, there may have been a second marriage on the part of either the father or the mother; third, the parents may have been separated for a period. The reply to a question concerning such a lapse sometimes reveals a former desertion hitherto unmentioned; sometimes the separation of the parents at the time of migration to America, when the father may have preceded the mother by several years; or occasionally, a period of incarceration of one of the parents in a penitentiary or a hospital for the insane. On the other hand, the ages of the children not infrequently conflict with statements of the parents concerning desertion, migration or imprisonment. The explanation sometimes discloses efforts at deceit in the matter of the children's ages, and sometimes the fact of promiscuous living on the part of the parents."—The Charity Visitor, p. 29.

whose parents have always so taken it, may lead to insubordination later on. A natural reaction from complete subjection is pushed too far by the spirit of his new associates and by the invitations of his enlarged world. From the very beginning, the social worker must keep these future dangers in mind and seek a better adjustment.

Separate interviews with the grown sons and daughters of a household, especially with those who are wage-earners, are often necessary.

A woman of sixty-four had been known to a charitable society for many years, but her six children, of ages ranging from thirty-two to eighteen, had not been consulted about her unexplained habit of writing begging letters continually. A critic of the record writes: "My belief is that, in order to know the real inwardness, each and every son and daughter should be seen *away from the home*. Practically all the dealings in later years have been with the woman. I observe that the last record of any one of them being seen was made six years ago. Even then it was purely incidental. What manner of people are these sons and daughters now? How do they feel about these constant appeals? What influence are they bringing to bear upon their mother? Do they countenance the habit?"

V. OTHER MEMBERS

Relatives of the husband or of the wife often form a part of the Family Group, whether with a clearly defined share of family responsibility or with none. Sometimes they carry far more than their share of the family burden; sometimes their influence is so disturbing as to disrupt the home—a mischief often wrought by relatives who live elsewhere, but more completely achieved by those under the same roof. Records studied for this book seem to show an undue share of undesirable relatives in widow's families, where there is no man to send them packing.

In one case, a drunken father left the home of his more well-to-do children to live with his widowed daughter and her small brood just as soon as a regular allowance from a social agency had been organized for them. The widow was an easy-going person, for later she married a man that was more of a vagabond than her father even. The givers of the allowance conditioned its continuance, up to the time of the second marriage, upon the father's withdrawal.

In another widow record, the woman's brother was boarding with her. His influence upon the growing boys was found to be bad, and further aid was made conditional upon his leaving.

We must not lose sight of the strong relatives who sometimes as part of the Family Group, carry more than their share of its burdens; nor of those no longer able to earn who to that extent are a charge, yet who may be holding the group closer together and making a very definite contribution to the family life in their ability to give and to evoke real affection. There can be a natural comradeship between grandparents and the younger grandchildren, for instance, which, where it exists, is an invaluable part of the home environment of a child.

In cases of desertion it is often necessary to consider not only the influence of relatives who are or have been members of the household, but that of any lodgers or boarders who are not kindred. Their relations with the husband or with the wife sometimes help to explain marital differences. In any case, their habits have a direct influence upon the children, and the amount and regularity of their payments are an important item in figuring the budget.

If, in the foregoing discussion of earlier visits to the home, more emphasis seems to have been put upon getting an idea of its background and its trend than upon the separate items of fact needed for the face cards of case records, it must not be inferred that inexact and general impressions are in any wise recommended as substitutes for definiteness and concreteness. But a fact, however exactly stated, has little significance until it has been intelligently related to some other fact or facts, so that skill is shown, not so much in the ability to accumulate a mass of data as in the development of a sort of sixth sense for the significant facts in their true relation to one another. It is believed that a grasp of the idea of the main drift of the family life will keep the mind of the worker from staggering about among a multitude of miscellaneous particulars, will help it to discriminate between the significant and the insignificant, and will lead to a clearer diagnosis.

Another idea that will help is the concept of assets for reconstruction. The power of family cohesion already mentioned is one of the greatest of these. Somewhat different and equally valuable is their capacity for affection. Other assets are capacity for admiration, for further training, for more energetic endeavor, for enjoyment, and for all-round social development. Nothing, however small, that might serve as an asset in the course of treatment and help to carry our plans toward a successful issue can possibly be insignificant. Whether this be an affection for a small dog, an ambition to play the accordion, or a lost or mislaid loyalty, the social physician must be able to use, and he must be able to recognize in order to use, such tools as these which lie ready to his hand.

SUMMARY OF THIS CHAPTER

1. The good results of individual treatment crumble away often because the case worker has remained ignorant of his client's family history, and has been unprepared for the sudden outcropping of tendencies long hidden.

2. Early contacts with members of the Family Group are on a somewhat different plane from those with other sources of information, because the need of their co-operation in treatment is usually greater, and further contacts are more likely to follow.

3. The family has a history of its own apart from the histories of those who compose it. It follows that a conception of the main drift of the family life is very necessary in any attempt to discriminate between the significant and the insignificant in a mass of case work data.

4. Another aid to clear thinking is the habit of classifying families with reference to their power of cohesion. The united family "is able to send its sons and daughters far over the face of the earth without in the least impairing the bond which unites them." In the unstable family "removal into the next street" is enough to sever the bond.

5. This power of cohesion is only one of the assets for reconstruction in family case work. Others are capacity for affection, for admiration, for further training, for more energetic endeavor, for enjoyment, and for social development. Among the children, more especially, the smallest signs of aptitude, ambition, achievement are worth testing and developing. An ability to discover, note, and use the assets for reconstruction marks the true case worker.

6. Among the more frequent causes of estrangement between husband and wife are disparity of age, marriage or remarriage for economic reasons, interference of relatives, and differences in nationality, race, or religion.

7. Social workers often ignore the husband and father and deal exclusively with his wife and children. He should be seen and known. Especially important is this injunction when case workers are asked to aid the families of young, able-bodied men.

8. Desertion and alcoholism, like many other social disabilities, are not so much separate entities as outcroppings of more intimate aspects of the individual's personal and social life. Diagnosis must lay a solid foundation for their treatment, therefore, by pushing beyond such "presenting symptoms" to the complex of causes farther back.

9. On the home's physical side, three important aspects are income and outgo, food habits, and housing. Most difficult of these to gauge are the food habits, which often demand special study because of their direct bearing upon health and spending power.

10. The individualization of the children in the household must include the prompt noting of all variations from the normal in their physical and mental condition.

11. The exact ages of the children—day, month, year of birth—have such vital relation to their adjustment to a number of social laws and institutions that this item of fact should not be omitted.

CHAPTER VIII

OUTSIDE SOURCES IN GENERAL

REASONS for turning not only to a client's family group for insight and advice but to Outside Sources have been suggested earlier. The chief reason for seeking this further help is that, to be constructively useful, we must be able to break through the narrow circle of the client's own view of his situation, and the narrow circle also of our own prepossessions and favorite modes of procedure. We cannot afford to adopt either of these circumscribed boundaries, because none of us lives on a desert island.

Can our client's affairs ever be regarded as ready for social treatment when no Outside Sources have been consulted? Measuring by the standard of concrete result instead of preconceived theory the answer would be in the affirmative. Cases studied for this book show correct diagnoses that were arrived at without any follow-up visits to outside references, but they also show a great preponderance of failures traceable directly to this omission. The worker who uses Outside Sources freely has been so trained by the practice that he can recognize when the nature of the application and of the task undertaken makes consultation of the confidential exchange index[1] and of the impersonal public records described in the chapter on Documentary Sources the only follow-up work necessary.

Always essential, though, is the re-examination of records of the individual case, both within the agency applied to and in the agencies revealed by the exchange, where there is one. This re-examination should be made just after the first interview, and whenever later a new name comes to light, such as a name by a previous marriage.

Essential almost always is personal communication with some of those shown by the records or by the client's story to have known him at an earlier time and in quite different ways. Our relations with these Outside Sources collectively and separately will be con-

[1] See p. 303 sq.

sidered in this and the eight chapters that immediately follow. If their explanations seem endlessly detailed, it may again be urged in extenuation that this is a punishment measured out to anyone who attempts either to read about one of the practical arts or to write about it.

I. STATISTICS OF OUTSIDE SOURCES

1. A Study of the Sources Most in Use. Social workers have been so busy doing their work that they have had little time in which to formulate its processes or its results. There have been no data available as to sources of information, for instance, either as to those sources that were consulted at all, or as to the particular combinations of sources that had been found most valuable in each different form of social work. The processes in which social agencies are actually engaged, the things that they are doing, are often quite different from what they think they are doing. Accordingly, a first, very imperfect attempt has been made to get this matter of Outside Sources upon a basis of fact by asking a variety of social organizations to permit the study of 50 case records in each, taking the records chronologically. Public and private relief departments, public and private child-placing and child-caring agencies, societies to protect children from cruelty, day nurseries, home and school visiting activities, juvenile and adult probation work, charity organization societies, and medical-social service departments were among those included in this small piece of research. Information from certain of these social activities would, in some places, have had to be very fragmentary, because often scant records are kept or none at all; but three American cities were chosen, representing three different stages of development in social work for individuals, and, in so far as the condition of their social agency records would permit, the forms of work already indicated were covered in each city. It was possible to examine the records of 19 different types of social organization. Each agency seen was asked to submit to special investigators the first 50 new case records made at the beginning of its last fiscal year,[1] omitting

[1] In a few instances the beginning of the current year was substituted, and in one city the agencies filled out the schedules themselves, allowing the Russell Sage Foundation investigators to compare these, however, with the original records later.

those in which there was no treatment. A transfer of the case to another agency *after* diagnosis was counted as a form of treatment. No sources were counted unless they had been consulted before the first important decision had been made, as the purpose was to study the Outside Sources of information upon which that decision was based. "Important decision" was interpreted to mean something more than merely *ad interim* or emergent action, but was interpreted somewhat strictly, nevertheless, to avoid the kind of temporizing into which too much of our treatment drifts. If a family applied for relief and got it, or applied for institutional care of a child or adult and got it, that was an "important decision." Members of the family group, living in the same house with the client and having a common table, were not counted in this enumeration, of course, and each Outside Source, whether an individual or an agency, was counted only once in any one case. As "neighbors" are sometimes "friends" and "landlords" sometimes "employers," each was counted in the capacity in which he was the more useful. Items of information that came not directly but through another responsible social agency, either in the same city or elsewhere, were credited to their true sources instead of to the agency, but were marked as "through an intermediary." Letters, telephone messages, telegraphic dispatches, and personal visits were not differentiated.

Institutions and agencies, public and private alike, were good enough to subject themselves to the repeated visiting and questioning which even this small study entailed. Only a few of the tabulated results are germane to this chapter. Others will be referred to in the successive chapters on Outside Sources, and the more detailed tables will be found in Appendix II, together with the form of schedule used in gathering the data.

In three cities, the 56 social agencies whose records were studied consulted 10,871 Outside Sources before making their first important treatment decision in 2,800 cases (50 studied for each agency). This was an average of 3.88 Outside Sources per case, but a figure which covers such varied types of work as have already been described can mean very little.[1] It is only in comparing task with

[1] These services were, in detail, as follows: Giving material relief, making loans, procuring employment, day nursery care, other provision for dependent children,

task, source with source, and city with city that the figures have any significance, and it would be easy to exaggerate the importance of these comparisons.

There is danger in dogmatizing about the relative value of sources and about the number of sources consulted. In work with individuals averages mean very little. As one institution worker protested, "A foundling picked up on the steps of the city hall hasn't many references, you know."[1] In some cases three Outside Sources might be too many to consult, in others thirty sources might be too few; there must be wide variation, according to the nature of the task undertaken and the story developed in the first interview. But the preparation of these statistics and all the other case reading undertaken for this volume point to many more errors of omission than commission in the matter of outside inquiry. Social workers in the United States are not overinvestigating; at present they are underinvestigating, though the tables of Appendix II show that some of them have discovered and are using a wide range of sources not yet utilized by the others.

Other things being equal, the social worker who, in addition to the sources that are almost universally valuable, consults the most diverse sources of information for diverse tasks and diverse cases, is doing the best work. Such breaking through routine brings new sources to light, but a certain routine must first be mastered before it is safe or wise to attempt to be original. And after a routine has been mastered, it should be criticized and revised at frequent intervals. The schedule used in this study[2] can be turned to account in the criticism of daily procedure. Its first draft was tried out by the writer with a small group of inexperienced case workers in Philadelphia years ago. It revealed that they were neglecting "trade unions" and "fellow workmen" habitually as sources of insight and co-operation, and that they were covering the physical history of the children under their care far more completely than

advice on school matters, rescue of children from neglect, correction of juvenile delinquency, medical advice, medical care, provision for defectives, institutional care of adults, adult probation, advice on family problems.

[1] A critic informs the writer, however, that the Board of Children's Guardians in St. Louis has reduced the number of foundlings housed at city expense over half by investigations recently made. The hospital where a foundling was born has proved a good starting point for "references."

[2] See Appendix II.

their school record. In discovering our weak points, such devices have a definite use; they serve also to show how even a strong point may be overemphasized until it becomes a weak one. We become superstitious, sometimes, about a favorite source or form of inquiry.

2. Nature of Sources. A certain routine must be mastered; it will help in forming our own standard for a given form of child-saving or family or medical-social work to discover what sources are most frequently used by representative agencies in each of these classes—by agencies, that is, which appear to have a high standard of treatment; and it will even help to discover what sources are most used by those that have a low standard. All the data gathered are quantitative not qualitative, be it remembered, except in so far as the habitual use of a source discredited by the experience of good social diagnosticians—such a source as present neighbors, for instance—or the *habitual use of the same two or three sources and no more,* gives a sidelight upon quality. It was suggested that the schedule contain two additional columns—one to indicate the usefulness of the information secured, and the other to show whether the person or agency consulted had shared in the treatment later, but this seemed impracticable. In judging values as between one relative's advice and another's, we drift easily into the realm of individual opinion, but whether both relatives had been consulted at all is not a matter of opinion.

Quantitatively, then, we find that—omitting social agencies from the computation[1]—the 20 Outside Sources most used by all the agencies in each of the cities stand, in order of frequency, as shown on the opposite page.

The failure in two of the cities to consult public records of marriage, and in one city records of birth, is a sign of weakness in technique. In the first city, these stand eleventh and twelfth in the list of sources. Another indicated practice the wisdom of which has already been challenged is the frequent use of sources belonging to the present neighborhood. In the third city "present

[1] The reasons for considering social agencies separately are given in Chapter XVI, Social Agencies as Sources (p. 297). The term "social agencies" includes church sources, private agencies (family agencies, homes for adults, homes for children, S. P. C. C's, children's aid societies, day nurseries, settlements), public agencies (charities or public outdoor relief departments, adult and juvenile probation departments, municipal lodging houses, almshouses), etc.

TABLE I.—TWENTY SOURCES[a] MOST USED IN THREE CITIES, IN ORDER OF FREQUENCY OF USE

Order of frequency of use	First city (24 agencies—1,200 cases)		Second city (13 agencies—650 cases)		Third city (19 agencies—950 cases)	
	Source	Total number of consultations[b] with each source	Source	Total number of consultations[b] with each source	Source	Total number of consultations[b] with each source
1	Relatives	769	Relatives	297	Present neighbors	210
2	Physicians	564	Teachers, etc.	189	Friends	183
3	Police	358	Present neighbors	139	Physicians	171
4	Hospitals and sanatoria	357	Present landlords[c]	131	Relatives	121
5	Former employers	330	Former landlords[c]	120	Present landlords[c]	78
6	Friends	302	Friends	106	Former employers	69
7	Teachers, etc.	280	Former employers	71	Prisons or reformatories	50
8	Clergymen	264	Hospitals and sanatoria	67	Clergymen	39
9	Present neighbors	182	Physicians	65	Present employers	35
10	Present employers	147	Present employers	50	Hospitals and sanatoria	34
11	Marriage records	143	Clergymen	42	Court records	28
12	Birth records	139	Former neighbors	31	Dispensaries	24
13	Former neighbors	132	Courts	31	Fellow church members	23
14	Dispensaries	124	Dispensaries	28	Courts	22
15	Medical-social service departments	122	Medical-social service departments	24	Former neighbors	19
16	Former landlords[c]	118	Health departments	22	Former landlords[c]	18
17	Courts	107	Police	18	Teachers, etc.	16
18	Present landlords[c]	106	Birth records	14	Police	16
19	Nurses	103	Church visitors	13	Nurses	16
20	Health departments	81	Boarding homes for children	13	Present tradesmen	15[d]

[a] Exclusive of public and private charitable and social agencies.
[b] Only the first consultation with each source used was counted in any case.
[c] The term "landlord" is used to cover the owner, agent, and janitor.
[d] In the third city, district or county attorneys were consulted the same number of times as present tradesmen.

TABLE 2.—ORDER OF FREQUENCY OF CONSULTATION IN THE SEPARATE CITIES OF THE 20 SOURCES[a] MOST OFTEN USED IN THE THREE CITIES TAKEN TOGETHER[b]

Order of frequency of use in the three cities	Source	Order of frequency of consultation in the		
		First city	Second city	Third city
1	Relatives	1	1	4
2	Present neighbors	9	3	1
3	Physicians	2	9	3
4	Friends	6	6	2
5	Former employers	5	7	6
6	Hospitals and sanatoria	4	8	10
7	Teachers and principals	7	2	17[g]
8	Clergymen	8	11	8
9	Present landlords	18	4	5
10	Present employers	10	10	9
11	Former landlords	16	5	16
12	Police	3	17	18[g]
13	Dispensaries	14	14	12
14	Former neighbors	13	12[d]	15
15	Courts	17	13[d]	14
16	Nurses	19	21[e]	19[g]
17	Health departments	20	16	28[h]
18	Lawyers	21[c]	25[f]	22
19	Present tradesmen	29	24	20[i]
20	Fellow church members	22[c]	39	13

[a] Exclusive of private and public charitable and social agencies.

[b] The 20 sources most used in the three cities taken together were selected as follows: For each city all the sources were numbered in order of frequency of consultation, beginning with the source most frequently consulted. The numbers indicating the order of frequency of each source in the three cities were then added together. The 20 sources showing the smallest resulting totals are included in the table.

[c] Same number of consultations with lawyers and with fellow church members, in records of first city.

[d] Same number of consultations with former neighbors and with courts, in records of second city.

[e] Truant officers were consulted same number of times as nurses, in records of second city.

[f] Lodgers were consulted same number of times as lawyers, in records of second city.

[g] Same number of consultations with teachers, with police, and with nurses in records of third city.

[h] Former tradesmen and foreign consuls were consulted same number of times as health departments, in records of third city.

[i] District or county attorneys were consulted same number of times as present tradesmen, in records of third city.

neighbors" actually heads the list of sources, and it stands third in the second city; "present" and "former landlords" in the second city and "present landlords" in the third are also used very frequently. The significance of these differences in practice as between the first and the second and third cities, and the serious dangers involved in the use of neighborhood sources at all are brought out in the chapter on Neighborhood Sources. Another difference is in the use of "policemen," which may be accounted for by the fact that no study of probation work, either adult or juvenile, was possible in the second and third cities, while in the first city both of these and a number of other forms of work in which the evidence of the police would be important were included. The marked differences in the use of "teachers" may be accounted for by the fact that the proportion of agencies studied which dealt exclusively with children was smallest in the third city and largest in the second.

But when we consider that social case work in these many forms and these different places has not been developed out of any formulated and systematically transmitted experience, for the most part, but has felt its way quite independently, often, to processes that grew out of the necessities of the day's work, we shall find the resemblances in practice as shown in these statistics quite as striking as the differences, especially if we compare the larger groupings of sources shown in the large general Table A in Appendix II. Here the fact stands out that, with many variations within each group and variations as between groups allowed for, there still has been frequent use in all three cities of the sources classified under social agencies and churches, doctors and health agencies, former and present neighborhoods, relatives, former and present employers, schools, friends, and public records.

As to the shifting of emphasis upon one or another of these, as we change from family work to children's work, from one form of children's work to another, or from all to medical-social service, the figures show some interesting variations. Table B in Appendix II tells the story in detail. Its most important features are brought out in Tables 3 and 4 on the pages immediately following.

The first city was chosen for making this particular comparison because it was the only one of the three (at the time the study was made at least) in which the standard of treatment was quite as

TABLE 3.—TWENTY SOURCES[a] MOST USED BY AGENCIES DOING WORK WITH CHILDREN, FAMILY WORK, AND MEDICAL-SOCIAL WORK IN FIRST CITY, IN ORDER OF FREQUENCY OF USE

Order of frequency of use	Work with children (10 agencies)	Family work (5 agencies)	Medical-social work (3 agencies)
1	Relatives	Relatives	Physicians
2	Police	Hospitals and sanatoria	Hospitals and sanatoria
3	Physicians	Physicians	Relatives
4	Teachers	Former employers	Former employers
5	Former employers	Clergymen	Present neighbors
6	Clergymen	Friends	Nurses
7	Friends	Dispensaries	Teachers
8	Birth records	Teachers[d]	Clergymen
9	Present neighbors[b]	Marriage records[d]	Friends
10	Courts[b]	Fellow church members	Present landlords
11	Hospitals and sanatoria	Present employers	Medical inspectors
12	Marriage records	Present landlords	Present employers[f]
13	Former neighbors	Present neighbors	Health departments[f]
14	Former landlords	Medical-social service departments	Dispensaries
15	Present employers	Former landlords	Former neighbors[g]
16	Health departments	Former neighbors	Marriage records[g]
17	Lawyers	Nurses	Lawyers[g]
18	Present landlords[c]	Police	Medical-social service departments[h]
19	Nurses[c]	Present tradesmen	Police[h]
20	Medical-social service departments	Truant officers[e]	Birth records[i]

[a] Exclusive of public and private charitable and social agencies.

[b] Same number of consultations with courts as with present neighbors, in records of work with children.

[c] Same number of consultations with nurses as with present landlords, in records of work with children.

[d] Same number of consultations with marriage records as with teachers, in records of family work.

[e] Same number of consultations with prison and reformatory officials as with truant officers, in records of family work.

[f] Same number of consultations with health departments as with present employers, in records of medical-social work.

[g] Same number of consultations with marriage records and lawyers as with former neighbors, in records of medical-social work.

[h] Same number of consultations with police as with medical-social service departments, in records of medical-social work.

[i] Same number of consultations with a number of other sources as with birth records, in records of medical-social work.

high in children's work as in family work, and in which medical-social work could safely be compared with both. The figures for

TABLE 4.—USE OF THE 20 SOURCES[a] MOST USED IN THE FIRST CITY, BY AGENCIES DOING WORK WITH CHILDREN, FAMILY WORK, AND MEDICAL-SOCIAL WORK IN THAT CITY

Source	Number of consultations[b] with each source, per 50 cases		
	Work with children (10 agencies)	Family work (5 agencies)	Medical-social work (3 agencies)
Relatives	42.4	39.2	13.3
Physicians	18.9	20.6	53.0
Police	22.9	4.8	1.0
Hospitals and sanatoria	8.7	23.4	26.7
Former employers	13.6	18.6	5.3
Friends	12.4	13.4	3.3
Teachers, etc.	15.0	9.6	4.3
Clergymen	13.0	18.0	3.7
Present neighbors	8.9	7.0	5.0
Present employers	6.4	7.6	2.0
Marriage records	8.3	9.6	1.3
Birth records	11.6	3.6	.7
Former neighbors	8.0	5.6	1.3
Dispensaries	2.0	10.8	1.7
Medical-social service departments	3.5	6.8	1.0
Former landlords	7.1	6.4	...
Courts	8.9	1.6	.7
Present landlords	3.8	7.4	3.0
Nurses	3.8	5.4	4.7
Health departments	4.6	2.8	2.0

[a] Exclusive of social and charitable agencies, public and private.
[b] Only the first consultation with each source used was counted, in any one case.

each separate agency in the first city are given in Table B in Appendix II, thus making it possible for a student interested in forms of organization to compare the classifications in greater detail.

II. PRINCIPLES GOVERNING THE CHOICE OF SOURCES

After a social organization has abandoned the old idea that a more or less searching cross-examination of one witness (of the client, that is) is an adequate basis for action—even after it has advanced beyond this stage, its earlier adventures in social diagnosis are likely to bring endless variations on the theme of the client's present situation. It will hear this described again and again by charitable individuals and social workers, and will assume that, in listening to these detailed statements, it is gathering valuable diagnostic material. "All these people," said one critic after examining a group of case records, "seem to have been born just about two years ago. There is a great deal set down about what they and the charities have done since, but they have no past."

1. First Principle of Choice. When, the first interview over and a home visit paid, we find ourselves with a group of clues, perhaps the most important principle of action is to *strike out boldly for history* and avoid, for the time being at least, those references whose point of view is most like our own. Where there has been an investigation already, we should profit by it, of course, but where there has not, we cannot afford to lose a moment before consulting the people who knew our client at his best, if he ever had a best; who knew him at least at other times and in other relations. These can give, one from this angle, one from that, the aspects that will help us to see our subject in the round. Any notion of social efficiency that excludes the humblest sources of knowledge and help makes for inefficiency in the long run. Too often we confer with the sources that are nearest to us, and neglect those that are nearest to our client. Other things being equal, the evidence of those who knew him before the present difficulties developed is worth ten times as much as the evidence of those who have known him since. But this must not be construed as referring to *length* of acquaintance, merely. We can know people a long time and really know them very little.[1] The nature of the relation and the opportunities that it has given for self-expression are the important things.

2. Second Principle of Choice. In order that we may never have to pay two visits where one can be made to serve, a second principle will be found useful in making our choice of diagnostic sources, and in preparing, at the same time, for the co-operation which will probably be needed later in treatment. This principle is to *seek first those sources that are likely to be rich in history only and seek later those most likely to be rich also in co-operation.* It is wise to build in our background and get as clear a picture of

[1] Dr. S. Weir Mitchell says of the family doctor, who belongs to this long-acquaintance group, "He is supposed to have some mysterious knowledge of your constitution, and yet may not have asked you a medical question in months and years."—Doctor and Patient, p. 28.

our foreground as can be had before consultation is attempted with those upon whose co-operation we must depend for the success of our plan, and in part, perhaps, for its shaping. Some social workers invariably see the relatives first, others the employers, and others the doctors. Such rules save the trouble of thinking, but a more flexible method is to let the order of seeing Outside Sources grow naturally out of the individual circumstances, having in mind, however, the need of developing history first, and then, on the basis thus revealed, co-operation.

It is true that the yield in neither history nor co-operation can be accurately gauged in advance, but our conduct of the first interview should have helped us to some inferences. If we go to the people whose co-operation is likely to be valuable but whose knowledge is either biased or incomplete, at a time when we know little ourselves, we are in grave danger of launching them and of being launched upon a plan of action that must be modified almost immediately. They may easily resent any attempt at modification under such circumstances, and not only will time have been wasted for our client and ourselves, but co-operative relations will have been weakened by the false start.

One difficulty in applying this principle of choice will be with relatives, some of whom—we cannot always know which ones—may be rich in co-operation and all of whom are familiar with certain details of the early background. Though relatives are rich in history unquestionably, the fact that this is true of all of them may enable us, with the help of such hints as we get from our client's story, to apply the distinction implied in the principle; we can see first the relatives least likely to be able to co-operate actively, and later those most likely to do so. Many accidental things will probably interfere with a strict following of this principle, however. The distances to be covered, the hours at which people can be seen, the need of unusually prompt action are only a few of the conditions which will necessarily modify the order in which Outside Sources can be consulted in the daily pressure of case work.

The two principles of action here explained are well illustrated by an investigation of a widow's family, though the social worker who made it was quite unconscious, probably, of the mental processes by which she arrived at a good order of visits.

The application was made by the widow's sister—a servant whose employer wrote to a charity organization society. The first interview with the widow brought the addresses of the following: Another sister and an aunt of hers; a brother and an aunt of her husband's; the family doctor; the hospital where her husband had died; the Catholic church of the parish in which she had been living for a few months; the Catholic church of the parish in which she had lived for many years; and the Presbyterian church in this former neighborhood. Her husband had been a Protestant, and the children had attended the Presbyterian Sunday school during his lifetime.

The widow's only resources were help from the St. Vincent de Paul Council of the new parish, and from the sister who was at service. There were five children under twelve years of age to be cared for. Many workers would have gone to the present priest and to the servant girl sister at once, as the two people most practically interested. The sister knew the past history as well as any one person could know it, probably, but the worker first took the trolley car for a six-mile journey to the old neighborhood, saw the grocer with whom the family had traded before the man's death, visited the priest who had known the wife for years, the doctor who had attended them in their old home, and the principal of the school that the children formerly attended. Her next journey was to the home of the husband's brother and to his aunt, then to a politician who was said to have helped the family very lavishly, then to the Presbyterian church visitor who was reported to have been helping at the same time that the Catholic church helped. Both of these reports were disproved at once, so that they could not come up later in a way that would disturb the course of treatment. Then and only then were the widow's own relatives and her parish priest turned to—not, of course, with a view to dictating to them the plan of action that they should pursue, but with a desire to hear everything that they had to say and then, in the same interview, to confer with them as to what permanent plan could be made for the widow's benefit, and what share each could bear in its carrying out.

The new priest hardly knew the widow; the servant sister was bent upon giving her whatever character would most promptly secure material help. But earlier inquiries had reconstructed the normal life in the old neighborhood and had sifted the prejudiced gossip of the deceased husband's people, leaving, it is true, some weaknesses to be guarded against, but making it clear that here was a home worth keeping together and a plan needed that would give the mother something definite to count upon until the children were earning. The plan decided upon in the first visits to the parish priest and to the sister included a regular allowance plus half the rent from the sister at service. The church bore a share in this plan, which, with slight modifications, was continued through a series of years.

3. Third Principle of Choice. The foregoing principles may be greatly strengthened by careful observance of a third, which is that we must *seek out the witnesses who have been able to make first-hand observations in preference to those whose information is at second-hand.* In other words, we must beware of multiplying witnesses without getting new observations. This matter was touched upon in Part I, where Langlois was quoted with regard to the three chroniclers who agreed so admirably because their parallel accounts were all derived from one source;[1] but it deserves especial emphasis and further illustration in connection with this division of our subject. There are few commoner errors and few that work greater havoc in social case work than the use of items of hearsav evidence without any consciousness of their hearsay nature.

Let the treatment of one unfortunate case illustrate both the need of past history and the danger of multiplying statements without multiplying observations. A charity organization society was responsible. The head resident of a church settlement referred Mrs. O, a German widow with four children and "well known to me as a worthy, respectable woman." A first interview brought the following items: that the youngest child, a boy aged three and a half years, was blind; that the oldest girl, aged eleven, could neither read nor write, and that none of the children were going to school; that the husband had not died but had deserted, according to the wife, three years ago; that they had come to America and this particular city eleven years back; that he had no relatives living and hers were all in Germany; and that he had formerly worked at the shot works, while she had been employed by certain stores and householders. A few former addresses were given, but some of them rather indefinitely. "Left a dollar to expend on coal and food as there was almost nothing to eat. Mrs. O took it rather reluctantly. Seemed almost hurt when it was offered to her. Told her she could consider it as a loan if she wanted and pay it back when she could."

On the doorstep after the close of the interview, what clues did the social worker hold in her hand? There were three previous addresses that were indefinite but that might have been made less so with the aid of a set of city directories,[2] and a definite previous address on the waterfront where the woman had lived until a few months ago; there was a firm in town and one out of town for whom the man was said to have worked; and there were the woman's work references before her husband's departure, and the addresses of two housewives for whom she had done day's work since. The worker went first, however, to the settlement house that had referred the client for treatment. Here Mrs. O had been known for a year and a half. It was learned from another worker than the one who had written that Mr. O had deserted three years before and had not been heard from since, and that his wife was very proud, industrious, and hard-working. If the settlement workers had known Mrs. O only a year and a half, they were not competent witnesses as to the desertion, and "very proud" does not describe Mrs. O as well as would a plain statement of the acts upon which this judgment was based. The worker next visited two housewives of the neighborhood for whom Mrs. O had done day's work. Both gave much the same evidence—she was honest, industrious, hard-work-

[1] See p. 57.

[2] See Chapter XIII, Documentary Sources.

ing. Next, a letter was dispatched to Germany asking the public charities to see Mrs. O's mother, to "present to her the following facts" (namely, the desertion and the present pitiful condition), and to ask her whether she would take her daughter back and care for the children, or what she would advise. This letter brought a perfunctory reply of "not able to help" and no more. But meanwhile, without further visits to possible Outside Sources, though with repeated visits to Mrs. O herself, the society had launched out upon a plan of adequate regular allowance for the family, the girl and the other children to be sent regularly to school, the youngest child to be entered at the institute for the blind, etc.

This plan assumed the hearty co-operation of the mother, and the absence of any different and irreconcilable plans in her own mind. Little things happened that might have shaken their faith in her singleness of purpose, such as finding the girl out after dark gathering scraps of cold food, many small excuses for not keeping appointments, and removal without consultation back to the old neighborhood that had never been investigated; but the social worker was so sure of her own first impressions, re-enforced as they had been by three other impressions of the same kind, that, when it was found that a man had been boarding at Mrs. O's, her own strong protestations of innocence were treated as more than offsetting the neighborhood gossip; the man withdrew and the allowance was continued. But, as time went on, nothing happened to the children that the society intended to have happen. It had been and continued to be earnest in its efforts, but the girl was still not in school after repeated placings. (The neighborhood was a crowded one, and the school authorities had no abundance of school sittings, so that escape on the official side was easy.) The blind child had never been allowed by his mother to go to the special institution willing to receive him, or to have proper medical care outside; his condition at the end of his sixth year was so pitiable as to excite the interest of many charitable people, the children were begging frequently, and, at last, the impressionable and kindly friends of the family are found clamoring at the offices of the S. P. C. C., claiming that these children are being used to secure support for an immoral mother and must be taken immediately from a woman about whom the complainants know very little but are forced to conjecture much.

Not to judge her or condemn her, for Mrs. O's shortcomings could not have seemed so bad if her past had explained them, but just to know and help her if they could, and to protect at all hazards those four children, whose future still stretched so far ahead, the charity organization society should have had at the very beginning a clear picture of the O family at its best, before charitable ladies had made its acquaintance. There were Outside Sources of information to reveal this picture in part, and some of these would have furnished clues to others. As to the slight evidence that was gathered from the settlement and the housewives, only those to whom all statements are of equal value could have regarded this as evidence at all.

4. Fourth Principle of Choice. Another principle to bear in mind is that we must *recognize the special value of supplementary clues—of clues, that is, to sources of information not revealed in the* *first interview or in subsequent ones with the family group, but which come to light in the course of inquiry.* A source revealed casually is less likely to be prejudiced. In the protection of children from cruelty this distinction of the supplementary clue is clearly made, owing to the need of legal evidence, but it is a distinction that might have been useful in the case just cited, and that might have helped, in combination with other elements of a sound technique, to render the intervention of the society to protect children unnecessary.

5. Fifth, Sixth, and Seventh Principles of Choice. Francis H. McLean suggests three principles of choice which should be added to the four already named:

(5) We should see someone belonging to each of the groups able to view the client and the family from a different angle. Two such groups are the relatives on the husband's side and the relatives on the wife's side. If there is not time or if it seems unwise for other reasons to see all relatives, then some on each side of the house should be seen.[1] In other words, we should *think of sources in groups, and tap each group for a new set of experiences.*

(6) Some groups of sources may be called one-headed groups, in that all constituting the group are likely to see eye to eye with regard to the matter under consideration; but others are more likely to develop different points of view within the group itself. Mr. McLean places (with full recognition of the possible exceptions) schools, churches, labor unions, and benefit societies in the first class. The evidence gathered from a school principal and from his assistants will usually be in substantial agreement; the same is true of evidence from a minister and a church visitor. He places the man's relatives, those of his wife, employers, former neighbors, and tradesmen in the second class. There is always danger of not finding the truth, he thinks, unless at least two sources belonging to each of these latter groups are consulted. We should *distinguish groups all of whose members are likely to see eye to eye, and in which consultation with one source may possibly suffice, from those in which there is likely to be diverse experience within the group.*

(7) Contradictions that are apparently irreconcilable as between the evidence of one group and that of another, or as between indi-

[1] This principle is illustrated in the case cited on p. 172.

viduals in the same group, mean that further inquiry is needed to reveal motives and facts which will reconcile statements either by change or by elimination. The need of further inquiry is also indicated, usually, when the evidence all points in one direction without contradiction or inconsistency, but when also the sum of it reveals no single possible next step in treatment that promises to be useful. This arrival at no thoroughfare may be due to other causes, such as lack of imagination and resource in those responsible for taking the next step, but one cause of failure when we find ourselves at this pass is a serious and unsuspected gap in the investigation itself. We must *recognize in contradictory evidence and in a total of evidence that reveals no plan of action, the need of further inquiry.*

The foregoing seven principles of choice in deciding the order of our consultations with Outside Sources hardly deserve to be styled principles, perhaps, but from the evidence now at hand it is believed that they will have practical value for the case worker.

III. METHOD

"Just after visiting a home you come out tingling with the letters you want to write, the telephoning you want to do, the visits you wish to make to other parts of the city, but by the time you get back to the office, after making visits on one or two other cases, all this has oozed out through your fingertips, somehow. But to systematize what you got in your first visit, to conserve the feeling you had when you left the house and put it right into action, is the only way to get results." This comes from a case worker who was at the head of a busy district office in which there were often nine or ten assistants. It suggests the loss of power and of efficiency which follows a division of work at this point, especially when the division is carelessly adjusted. A new assistant in a large relief office was not a little disconcerted when he was given a memorandum of eight "references" whom he was to see about a certain client and his family, without any information as to the problem or so much as a glimpse of the case record. A division of labor is possible, even in so delicate a process as arriving at a social diagnosis, but it seldom comes without dislocation at this early stage. After the most important clues have been followed up by the one who has seen the client and his family, it is often possible to utilize assistance for visits to minor sources, though even here a full knowledge of all the preceding steps is essential before attempting to pay these additional visits.

A good deal will be said in a later chapter about communications by letter and by telephone.[1] Let it suffice here to say that evidence given face to face and eye to eye is evidence weighed and sifted by a subtle process that can never be applied to letters, blank forms, or telephone messages. The witness of application blanks is notoriously untrustworthy. An examination of the records of an orphan asylum which formerly based all its admission decisions upon the answers filled out upon such blanks reveals astonishing misstatements from presumably responsible public officials and from tradesmen, teachers, and relatives. There would seem to be something very demoralizing about a blank form.[2] Letters addressed "to whom it may concern" are almost as bad; so are letters of recommendation of all kinds. People sometimes say quite unblushingly, when asked by a social agency why they wrote this glowing letter about a certain weakling, "Well, I hoped you'd do something for him." When seen personally, they soon realize that the situation is not nearly so simple as all this, and are led on, by one who quickly grasps their point of view, to think more deeply and testify more truthfully. The personal interview, whenever it can be obtained without irritating an overbusy person, is the best method of approach.

All of our clues can be quite perfunctorily followed up, however, even when each source is personally, carefully, and exhaustively seen. The unimaginative worker, the "overworked victim of routine," can go through all the motions without achieving anything but irritation and disorganization. We must have a generous conception of what can and should be done, and some time in which to do it, before these outside informants can be made to contribute either useful information or friendly service. The worker with no such generous conceptions and purposes takes just as long to go and just as long to come back, his carfares and shoe leather

[1] Chapter XVII, Letters, Telephone Messages, etc.

[2] An exception to this is in the filling out of those public documents for misstatements in which a penalty is attached by law.

are just as expensive, and he is pretty sure to discover that nobody can do anything, that all the persons consulted know very little, and are chary of imparting that little to him. "In these records," wrote a director of one charity organization society who had been asked to criticize some of the case histories of another, "when the investigation is really begun, there seems to be a greater endeavor to get at facts than to get advice as to what to do; they give the impression of *clerical* interviews for information rather than a considering together and a securing of co-operation from all the persons interested." This result is not always due to perfunctoriness and lack of enthusiasm. It sometimes comes from an enthusiastic interest in our own plans and purposes. We are so full of them that we never give the other person a chance to help in forming them.

"One of the axioms of social diagnosis is that if a source is worth consulting at all, it is worth consulting in the right way." Many of the things that have been said about the method of a first interview apply to interviews with the family group and to these visits paid to Outside Sources also. We must give the one interviewed ample time in which to develop his point of view; must not suggest the answers to our questions; must utilize to the full all new avenues of approach and all natural openings, instead of shaping the interview to meet some preconceived idea of its content; and yet must keep the goal of a fuller knowledge and wider co-operation always in view.

We progress, in these inquiries, toward the point at which we can feel justified in assembling all our data and making a social diagnosis. Examination of our material as a whole is, in fact, the most neglected of all the diagnostic processes, but its consideration here will have to be postponed until the various groups of Outside Sources have been reviewed. Meanwhile, we must not forget that the reasoning processes come into play as soon as the first interview with a client opens[1] and are needed also in every consultation with an Outside Source. At the time of each such consultation and between the different ones, we must be comparing, reconciling, contrasting every statement with every other, and seeking to fill those gaps in the evidence which have a direct bearing upon the main

[1] See p. 120 and Chapter V, Inferences.

issue and its solution. A conception of the different kinds of evidence described in Chapter III, and of the characteristics, detailed in Chapter IV, of human beings as witnesses, should enter into and shape all these contacts with Outside Sources.

SUMMARY OF THIS CHAPTER

1. A client's social relations are not bounded by his immediate family, nor, as a rule, should our sources of insight and co-operation be so bounded.

2. A study of the Outside Sources—sources outside the immediate family group, that is—consulted in three cities by 56 social agencies of 19 different types (rendering 14 different forms of service in the cases studied) shows in 2,800 cases (50 for each agency) 10,871 consultations with such sources, counting, in any one case, only the first consultation with each source used.

3. The groups of Outside Sources frequently used, as shown in this study, are social agencies and churches, doctors and health agencies, former and present neighborhoods, relatives, former and present employers, schools, friends, and public records.

4. The following seven principles may govern choice in deciding the order in which Outside Sources should be consulted, though such accidental things as distance, accessibility, and need of unusually prompt action, will undoubtedly modify their use.

(1) Strike out boldly for history.
(2) Seek first those sources that are likely to be rich in history only, and seek later those most likely to be rich also in co-operation.
(3) Seek out the witnesses who have been able to make first-hand observations in preference to those whose information is at second-hand.
(4) Recognize the special value of supplementary clues—of clues, that is, to sources of information not revealed in the first interview or in subsequent ones with the family group, but which come to light in the course of inquiry.
(5) Think of sources in groups, and tap each group for a new set of experiences.
(6) Distinguish groups all of whose members are likely to see eye to eye, and in which consultation with one source may possibly suffice, from those in which there is likely to be diverse experience within the group.
(7) Recognize in contradictory evidence, and in a total of evidence that reveals no plan of action, the need of further inquiry.

5. Consultations with Outside Sources are best held by the one who has conducted the first interview with a client and seen his family.

6. Evidence given face to face and eye to eye is weighed and sifted by a subtle process that can never be applied to letters, blank forms, or telephone messages.

CHAPTER IX

RELATIVES AS SOURCES

AS BETWEEN the different forms of social case work, it will be seen that, in the first city (where such comparisons could be most safely made), the suburban and the city charity organization society consulted with 35 and 36 Relatives respectively in their 50 cases each, the general private relief society with 39, the public outdoor relief department with 42, the society to protect children from cruelty with 51, the city and state departments for care of children with 68 and 44 respectively, three child-placing agencies with 89, 44, and 48 respectively, a reform school with 26, a children's institution with 20, a day nursery with 29, and three hospital social service departments with 11, 6, and 23 respectively.[1] Relatives were seldom consulted by the juvenile court, but in most forms of children's work, in family work, and in medical-social work (though here in a less degree) the figures show frequent consultations.[2]

What does the reading of case records and the evidence of case workers, in so far as it has been possible to collect this in many interviews with them, show as to Relatives? Clients often do not want their Relatives seen. Why is this, and what mistakes of the social worker may justify, at least in part, this position? More and more social workers are seeking out Relatives, though more and more they are discovering their bias, and the need of sifting their evidence with great care. Just what is gained in accuracy

[1] Appendix II, Table B.

[2] It must be remembered that only the Relatives outside the immediate family group were counted in the outside sources study. The use of the word Relatives in this chapter is subject to the same limitation but to no other, for it here indicates relationship by birth, by marriage, or by descent. Brothers and sisters living at home are counted as members of the family under treatment; if living away from the family, they are classified as Relatives. A client's kindred and his wife's kindred are regarded here as his and her Relatives, though the distinction between connection by marriage and connection by descent or birth is an important one to make in our consultations.

of diagnosis and effectiveness of treatment through this source which can be had in no other way? From the data at hand, what is the case for and the case against Relatives as helps in social service, and more especially in its initial stages?

I. THE CASE AGAINST RELATIVES

To state this side of the case briefly: (1) they are partisan and prejudiced; (2) they do not know; (3) they do not understand. It may be added that they are often too overburdened to aid their kindred financially without doing themselves and their immediate families injustice. This last argument applies only indirectly to diagnosis, but, since it does apply, it will be considered in a later section of this chapter.

1. Relatives Are Partisan and Prejudiced. This is undoubtedly true, as the following instances show, but a great deal of truth may be had from a prejudiced witness, if we are careful to give his prejudice due weight and compare his statements with those of others who have not the same bias.

A widow, Mrs. D,[1] was a Catholic; her husband had been a Protestant. Before a regular allowance was organized for her and her five children, the oldest of whom was twelve, three of her Relatives and two of her deceased husband's were seen. According to his Relatives she was a spendthrift, was getting help from both Protestant and Catholic churches, had very quickly run through $300 raised for her by a local politician, had no ambition, had shown herself entirely ungrateful for the help already given by her husband's people, etc. Her own Relatives represented her as an excellent mother and homemaker, as, in short, a model person. The truth was found to be somewhere between these two extremes. The stories of the $300 and of the help from Protestant churches proved to be untrue, but some of the complaints of the husband's people were well founded, and the plan of regular assistance under personal supervision which was adopted worked all the more successfully because these contradictory statements had been sifted and to a certain extent reconciled before the plan was entered upon.

A widower with three children (man somewhat intemperate) had been referred to a children's aid society to make plans for the children's care, with the suggestion that the man's sister Jane might possibly become a homemaker for the family. The mother of the dead wife, anxious to keep the children from the father's Relatives, states that Jane is under fourteen, small for her age, and unfit to care for a home. The widower's mother, interested in securing the opportunity for her daughter, states that Jane is over sixteen, strong, large, and capable. A paternal

[1] See p. 172 for other facts concerning this same family.

aunt, not so biased as the immediate family, states that Jane is fifteen, a very wild girl and one who could not be managed even at home.

These violent prejudices as between the Relatives on one side of the house and those on the other often take the form of mischief-making between husband and wife.[1] One record studied shows

[1] "It is surprising to find in how many cases of trouble between husband and wife discord is aggravated, if not caused, by the often well intentioned interference of friends or relatives. To an outsider, even though he be a near relative, domestic conditions are apt to appear much less endurable than they actually are to the parties most concerned, and he usually makes a tolerable situation intolerable by trying to act as a *deus ex machina.*

"As to the application of the above: A girl was born in New York City of parents born in Germany. They brought German traditions with them, and trained their children to implicit obedience. The wife had been chastised by her mother even after marriage, and conceived of disobedience to parental authority as a degenerate thing. The American-born daughter, despite this rigid discipline, took a slightly modified view of her filial obligations. She had a social nature and frequently joined her young acquaintances of an evening. With the pardonable anxiety of a girl's guardians, her parents would question her very closely on her return, and, for that matter, scolded her roundly for gadding so much. A young Irishman presently figured on her horizon, an amiable, affectionate young fellow, who made much of her and grew indignant at the beratings she complained of receiving at home. The contrast between his gentleness and parental strictness overcame her compunctions, and one day they went to the church, she became a Catholic, and they were duly married. Her family were, as she expressed it, 'wild,' but the deed was done.

"In the course of time, first one child then another was born to them. The young husband did fairly well. . . . The girl's parents, however, were never reconciled to him. They couldn't overlook the difference of race, and their daughter's change of religion was a constant cross. Although she had taken two rebellious steps she was by no means free from their yoke, and not only did her duty by going to see her mother frequently, but also felt constrained to make her mother the confidante of her husband's failings—he drank occasionally. Their first prejudice fanned to fury by their daughter's complaints, the parents insisted on her bringing the delinquent into court. He was sentenced to six months' imprisonment. The wife, a mere slip of a woman, tried with what little aid her family could give her to defray her expenses by taking a janitress's place in a damp basement. The work was too much for her, and worry over her husband kept her unsettled. She got run down, and the baby began to pine. Too ignorant to perceive that there was occasion for anxiety, she called no doctor and was terrified and bewildered to wake up one morning and find the little thing had died without a sound.

"That decided her. Her husband had been writing her, begging her to take him out and promising never to drink again, yet she had hesitated. The parents threatened that if she took him back they would never lift a finger to help her no matter to what extreme of poverty or suffering she might come. She must choose once and for all between them and him. She chose . . . begged the magistrate to let her husband return to her, and said that she would move a long distance away from her parents, because she was too weak, too much under their influence to live happily with her husband if she tried to hold to them at the same time. Her request was granted, and the young couple settled in another city. He understood his wife's pliable nature well enough to forgive her entirely for having overpunished him."—Ada Eliot (now Mrs. Sheffield) in *Charities* for March 29, 1902. [Revised by the author.]

endless trouble made by the wife's sister in a family where the husband was already inclined to be jealous.

2. Relatives Do Not Know. Sometimes the most important fact in the life of our client, the one most vitally affecting his welfare, is not known to the Relatives at all. As has been said in an earlier chapter, kinship makes not only for sympathy but for antagonism. The mere closeness of the bond often leads to concealment.

3. Relatives Do Not Understand. Even where there has been no concealment, they do not understand the situation as well as they think they do; they cannot choose wisely between the effective and the ineffective plan of action; they have not themselves a sense of social values.

"I remember," writes a former district secretary of a charity organization society, "laboring with a dear old man, an elder in a Baptist church, to convince him that some radical change was needed in the manner of life of his brother's family, which consisted of a drunken father, a bedridden wife, and three daughters, on two of whom the burden of support fell. Their wages were insufficient for the family of five. All that I could get from him was that the past must be buried and that Jim must be helped now even if he had done wrong in the past. It was odd that the girls had not mentioned their distress, but he would go down there at once. That the girls should have better jobs, that the woman should have hospital care, and that the man should be supplied with light work and watched faithfully, were ideas beyond his range."

A society to protect children from cruelty in a large city finds Relatives so likely to interfere disastrously in court cases of neglect that, as a rule, where the conditions are obviously bad, it does not see the Relatives at all until after court action. The society finds that this involves less danger of making trouble in the family, and makes it easier to turn to the kindred on both sides, who are seen later of course, either for the care of one or more of the children or for active assistance in helping the family to establish a home standard that will warrant the return of the children.

One of its cases was that of a father up for neglecting to support his children. The man was sentenced to the workhouse for a year, but appealed the case. The decision was reversed in the superior court on the evidence of a brother-in-law and a sister, both of whom had been strongly urging the S. P. C. C. to do something about the wretched conditions of which they made complaint. In court they testified that the father had been doing his very best. Before taking the case into court at all the society had consulted a landlady, a previous landlord, a policeman, and three Relatives, and had itself inspected the home conditions on several occasions. In the presence of their common enemy, the court, Relatives often give directly opposite testimony from that which is secured in private interviews.

A country society to protect children reports that kindred in its rural neighborhood can be seen far more safely before a court trial than in the city, and that their co-operation, both in court and out, can be better counted upon. The work of the society seems to be better understood and to be taken more seriously. One reason for this, probably, is that public opinion, for better or worse, is more completely unified in the small place and more influential there for that reason. In the large city there are many and conflicting community standards, and the standard that has found expression in a law or a social agency may not be the one that is most compelling within a certain neighborhood group.

A public department for dependent children found it impossible to secure court action in the case of a feeble-minded woman who had given birth to her third illegitimate child and obviously needed custodial care. This was owing to the appearance of the Relatives with an offer to care for her and her children. The children were later found to be neglected, but the mother was then in Canada beyond the jurisdiction of the court. A critic of this example writes, "Could not the public department have persuaded the court to put these relatives under bond to keep the woman and children off the public? If, among them, they were able to care for a whole family—minus the man—they should have been able to give some sort of security."

A probation officer whose work shows more than the usual degree of skill states that she deems it inadvisable to see Relatives except in those cases in which it seems impossible to get at the situation without consulting them, or those that involve the taking of a boy or girl out of the family. Ordinarily she believes that seeing the Relatives "stirs up a lot of talk and leads nowhere." In many of the families known to her the family connections feel no shame whatever about a boy's being brought to court, nor does the boy himself feel any. There is little reticence about such matters, and she feels that the only way to help the family to a proper sense of shame is to say to them, "You surely do not intend to talk this thing over with your sisters' and brothers' families. If I were you I should be so ashamed of it that I should never let anyone know that it had happened."

From this same probation officer, however, comes a memorandum of a boy on probation whose mother had two married sisters and a brother just learning his trade. Through an interview with one of these sisters the officer gained sufficient confidence in the family's sense of solidarity to arrange a conference of all the Relatives, at which she succeeded in persuading them to place the boy in a Catholic college and pay his board there.[1] By way of reconciling these two entirely different modes of procedure she would only need to point out that she was dealing with two entirely different groups of people. In her first statement she was probably referring to a group that were as little attuned to legal processes as the Aran Islanders described by John Synge. The law courts, which had been superimposed upon this primitive people and were presided over by outsiders, were often used as playthings by the Islanders. A whole family connection would come down to the court and swear against all the representatives of another family connection until they became bitter enemies. "The mere fact that it is impossible to get reliable evidence in the island—not because the people are dishonest, but because they think the claim of kinship more sacred than the claims of abstract truth—turns the whole system of sworn evidence into a demoralizing farce."[2]

Without giving too much weight to any of the foregoing arguments, it may be acknowledged that social workers often show a lack of discrimination as to which Relatives to see and when. A qualitative standard is more important than a quantitative one not only in the study of sources in general, but in their daily use. If, as a story develops, the most important factor in the situation seems to be lack of employment, it is foolish to see five Relatives on one side of the house and four on the other, and then omit for lack of time all of the three previous employers. A number of the case records examined showed a rather heedless running about from one Relative to another, apparently for the sole purpose of checking their names off as "visited" upon the face card of the record.

Another mark of careless work is the tendency to turn children over to the care of Relatives simply because they *are* Relatives, when the truth of their statements, their character, habits, and

[1] For another instance of co-operation with Relatives in probation work, see p. 193.

[2] Synge, John: The Aran Islands, p. 98. Boston, Jno. W. Luce Co., 1911.

circumstances have not been inquired into at all. The practice is a common one, and will continue to be so, probably, so long as public departments and private agencies do not require and provide for individualized inquiry and treatment, or so long as their appointed agents are mentally and morally sluggish and inclined to do the thing that is easiest.

An S. P. C. C. had occasion to take up a complaint involving two small children, a boy and a girl, who were living with their grandfather. It was found that an overseer of the poor, who had been aiding the family of these children before the death of the mother, had allowed them to be taken by the Relatives without any investigation whatever. The boy, who was lame, was not receiving proper care, the girl was out of school, and the whole family were living in an old shack of one room.

An argument that can hardly be included in this case against Relatives, yet that nevertheless has some bearing, was well put to the writer by a man applying for transportation to Chicago. It transpired that he had a brother-in-law in the railroad business, and when correspondence with this Relative was suggested, the man said frankly, "No, madam, I'd rather not have him communicated with. I'd much rather have help from you, because I shall never see you again." From the client's point of view one objection to Relatives, as sources of help at least, is the sense of mutual obligation that is involved in a permanent relationship. The feeling is seldom expressed so frankly, but it is often there.

II. THE CASE FOR RELATIVES

Experience throws into bold relief the prejudice and the unwisdom of Relatives, but there is plenty of evidence on the other side which shows that in actual daily practice social workers are not only securing (1) individual and family history from kinsfolk, but are finding them a fountainhead of (2) insight (a more important matter than history), and also an effective source of (3) backing and active co-operation.

1. Individual and Family History. "Too often," writes a case worker, "we consider simply the individual family and say, 'This man drinks,' 'This woman is not a good housekeeper,' when as a matter of fact a study of the family background would give us an insight into causes. This background comes best from the relatives." Far-reaching inquiry such as eugenic studies call for is of course out of the question, but the gathering of certain facts concerning the nearer Relatives is an important part of social diagnosis because it has a direct bearing upon treatment.

In cases, for instance, where the social worker has reason to suspect the presence of mental disease, he must aim to get at facts of heredity which would assist a physician in forming an opinion of the patient's condition. The pertinent data would cover the condition of health and cause of death of parents, grandparents, brothers and sisters, uncles and aunts. The items should be especially clear and detailed whenever, in any of these Relatives, there seems to be a question of consanguineous marriage, of miscarriages, of tuberculosis, alcoholism, mental disorder, nervousness, epilepsy, cancer, deformities or abnormalities, or of any exceptional ability. Relatives often have knowledge of these things which members of the immediate family have not, and often they are less reticent. The case worker, for his part, must be familiar enough with the symptoms of the diseases mentioned to note at once any casual reference to them and then follow up the reference, making a point of getting all the facts he can about the health of the person in question.

The warning will be given elsewhere, but it should be stated here too that in recording this evidence of Relatives the social worker should mention symptoms only, excluding diagnosis except as it comes from competent medical authority. Even in so clear a case as pronounced imbecility, he should record, for example, "John's uncle says that John's sister Mary was 'not right,' that she could never learn to sew and cook," etc., including all the evidence but drawing no conclusion.

Relatives, then, are our main reliance for family history, for the story of those traits and tendencies, those resemblances and differences in a family stock which we are learning to regard as of far-reaching importance.

A large orphan asylum, which is giving a very good education to its inmates and wishes to limit its admissions to normal children, now not only depends in making its selections upon a school examination and certain mental tests, but tries to see as many Relatives on both sides of the family as possible. Especially in the cases about which there is some doubt, the asylum's investigator feels that a personal interview with each Relative is necessary. In making 55 investigations preliminary to the admissions of one month, this worker made 79 visits to Relatives, and in studying 25 other cases of children whose fitness for admission was especially in question, he saw Relatives 94 times.

2. Insight. Some items of evidence have social significance because they suggest new sources of information or possible helps in treatment later on, while others are valuable because they help us, at a time when we have felt balked and unable to decide how to proceed, to grasp at once the core of the difficulty. Relatives are not the only sources that can give these sudden insights, but they so often point the way in what have been no-thoroughfare situations, that case workers have become almost superstitious about the one Relative who has not been seen.

Even when the Relatives are unco-operative their stories are revealing. "I remember one instance," writes a worker, "where the mother flatly refused to aid the daughter's family in any way, where the brothers and sister were too self-absorbed to share with their sister even in her great distress. Yet the stand these people took, in all its ugliness, pictured the story vividly—a disobedient, ungrateful daughter and a selfish and careless sister, a woman who would, in all probability, make an indifferent wife and mother. This knowledge was of service in planning the method of attack in that particular family."

Illustrations of securing from Relatives the one essential clue—essential, that is, to any effective treatment—are so plentiful that it is difficult to choose. Take these two found in desertion cases. "We had been dealing with a desertion case quite a while," writes a district secretary of a charity organization society, "without getting anywhere. Upon visiting the wife's mother we got information that the husband was living at his own home; we went there in the evening and found him." Another charity organization society made an extensive canvass of Relatives in a desertion case, but omitted the mother of the man. After the society had assisted the family for fourteen weeks and made fruitless attempts, legal and other, to find the man, the wife had a letter from her mother-in-law inviting her to visit her, and two days later a letter from the man saying that he was at his mother's, where the woman and children joined him.

A case record that came to the attention of the writer last year covers more than a hundred pages in reporting successively the work of four different districts of one charity organization society with the Braucher family, the man an American in his late thirties with a South American wife and two small children. His story is told at some length here, because the narrative will be referred to in a later chapter on Comparison and Interpretation. In transferring the treatment of this family from the third district to the fourth, the secretary making the transfer wrote that it had been impossible to verify most of the family's statements, that Braucher had failed to follow instructions when good medical care had been procured for him, and that the family "showed industry as beggars but in no other way."

About fifty pages of the record are filled with accounts of futile attempts to get some basis of fact on which to operate, followed by attempts to befriend the family and to improve, on the very inadequate data at hand, their physical and economic condition. The man's people lived in another city, but the local charities there had given nothing more definite, in reply to inquiries, than the statement that the Relatives had been known to them and that they had "a discouraging record."

The secretary of the fourth district, taking advantage of a trip to the neighborhood of the man's early home, visited the charities formerly interested in his Relatives, read the "discouraging record," found that her client's mother was still living (he had reported her as dead, and seems to have believed that she was), looked up her address with the aid of directories, had a long talk with her and gave her the first news of her son in many years. He ran away from home when he was only sixteen, and his father, it appeared, had deserted the family before that. This personal visit to another city gave the charity organization society its first real insight into the background of its client. The mother revealed strong family feeling and she and her immediate family showed a certain degree of resourcefulness.

The secretary returned with a cordial message from her and an offer to entertain one of the little grandchildren, whose very existence had been unknown to the Relatives before. Armed with this invitation and with news of the man's people, a fresh appeal was made to him; his plans and purposes were reviewed in a long friendly talk, and, from that time, it was evident that an interest which appealed to him, a plan of life which touched his imagination, had at last been presented. His first ambition was to make a good appearance when he visited his mother, as he did soon after. His wife also began to share with him the ambition to have a better home, to which his mother could be invited on a return visit. At last there seemed to Braucher to be a good and sufficient reason for taking the few steps necessary to make medical treatment, so ineffective before, truly effective.

In less than a year's time after the discovery of these Relatives, the charity organization society was able, with the aid of the family affection and the new social interest brought into their lives, to transform these difficult clients into people who carried responsibility more cheerfully and were more interested in their little home. The steps by which this was achieved are apparent enough in the matter-of-fact pages of the record, which show that no magic was employed, and that the measure of success achieved was no accident, based, as it was, upon the insights and the interests which a group of Relatives in no sense remarkable—they had once been described as "difficult"—had been able to supply.

3. Backing and Active Co-operation. If they are close at hand, the attitude of the Relatives is seldom an entirely passive one. The illustration just given shows that not only insight but active co-operation may be won from Relatives, and emphasizes the importance of communicating with them even when they are at a distance. Still less can we afford to ignore members of the family connection who live in the same city and who often have very definite ideas with regard to our clients. If they are not with us, they may easily be against us. It is no unusual thing to find in one group of Relatives almost every variety of social and anti-social attitude, from utter indifference on the one hand to deep devotion and self-sacrifice on the other. The best of the Relatives are often as thoughtful and as eager to help as any social worker ever was. Sometimes we are dealing with situations in which the Relatives have failed—those in which they have entirely succeeded are not usually known to the social worker—but even in the history of these failures we may find that the Relatives have almost as strong a claim upon our sympathies as our clients have, and that they welcome our new, more hopeful, and more resourceful handling of an old difficulty. They have had much to bear perhaps; they have lost their influence and are glad to help through another in cases in which they despair of helping directly and effectively.

The case record of a single woman of middle age is commented upon by one of the case readers as follows: "This is one of the most real examples I have ever seen of bringing a woman up on her feet and helping her until she had confidence to stand alone. Her great happiness in at last being able to do so is pathetic and genuine." This woman was the last of her immediate family. Her father had been a hard drinker, the home had been an unhappy one, and after its breaking up her Relatives had wearied of helping one who seemed never to rise to her industrial opportunities. The charity organization society that attempted to befriend her interested a doctor, who reported that she was not mentally unbalanced, as they had suspected, but was undernourished, sensitive, and unpractical. Work was finally found for her in an office, but it took a good many months to make her self-supporting, and meanwhile a cousin, who had lost all patience, was made to understand her real situation and persuaded to aid regularly through the society.

The financial help of a well-to-do Relative is all very well as far as it goes, but the experienced social worker welcomes as his strongest ally in a difficult case the Relative who shows tact, courage, and patience. The personal and moral backing of the Relatives shown in the following instances was a great social asset.

Mrs. Chesley of the Paine Fund, Cambridge, Massachusetts, writes of a weak woman who had never been married to the deserting father of her four children, and of the way in which four Relatives, each showing a different mental attitude toward the situation, worked for the common good. "We wrote twice to the [paternal] grandfather of those children, trying to arrange an interview at his convenience, but received no replies. We wrote to the [woman's] single brother twice with the same result. The married brother worked at night. We wrote him that we would call on a certain afternoon at four o'clock. He then would have had his usual amount of sleep and be ready to see us. We found him a kindly, easy-going man with no very decided opinions. After considering the facts he thought it wise for his sister to keep the children together and for his mother to remain with them. His own financial situation was straitened. He had five children—a son, who was a widower with one child, living at home and out of work; two other sons of working age, also out of work; one girl at work and another in school. The family was held together by his small wages and what the daughter earned. He was in debt for rent and other necessities. He was willing to give his mother a home, or would contribute toward her support, and thus help his sister too. We had to show him why, under the circumstances, he was not justified in helping others. He agreed to wait until the income of the family was larger and then do what he could.

"On visiting the married sister we found that the income of her husband was sufficient only for the support of the immediate family. Again no financial aid was promised. In the sister, however, we found a strong moral character with a keen appreciation of all the difficult elements in the situation, and a realization of her duty to stand by her weaker sister and the children. Because of the lack of family resources she had urged that the children be placed in homes. She readily accepted the other plan, however, and we left her, feeling that there was at least one person on whom we could depend for the most sincere and cordial co-operation. She regretted her inability to help materially and we hope she took a little comfort from our assurance that her genuine moral interest and oversight were the indispensable elements, the real hope, of the situation. We found she was a woman very much respected in a certain circle of people among whom she had lived all her life. Her pride and self-respect were strong, and she realized that at any time her sister's real story might be known. This did not deter her—her sister was her sister through good or ill repute, and that ended the matter.

"We had now to see those two men who had not replied to our note. We called on the grandfather of the children one evening. He apologized at once for not writing, and when he explained in detail the way his time was occupied by his work and the care of an invalid wife, we did not wonder at the delay. With him we had to face a most delicate and difficult situation, one that took all our courage. Here was a quiet, dignified man who had always been fully competent to guide his own affairs. He had positively decided that his future course as to this family of his son was to treat them as though they were non-existent. He stated his reasons for such a course—good reasons, almost unanswerable from one point of view. Years before he had done all he could to prevent this union. He had seen Mrs. X, as we still call her, and told her that his son had a wife from whom he had not been divorced. His efforts were fruitless. He had, too, given much financial help during the past twelve years, and now he felt he owed all he could spare to the care of his sick wife and their approaching old age. Our sympathies were with him and we told him so, although we could not quite agree with his conclusions. We led him to consider the future of the children and his responsibility regarding them. Finally after due deliberation, he agreed to co-operate for six months by giving one dollar a week, through us, toward their support.

"We also called in the evening on the single son and brother. He boarded with a woman living on the second floor of a tenement house. The family thought this woman received most of his wages. She was certainly in his confidence, for when we inquired for him through the tube she would not give any information or open the door until the name was given. Then the man came rushing downstairs exclaiming, as soon as he opened the door, 'I have not answered your letters because I want nothing to do with my sister, and anyway I have been out of work, and I haven't any money to give her.' We said, 'Good evening,' and then he said, 'I beg your pardon,' and we began our talk on a more friendly basis, continuing the interview on the steps outside, which seemed preferable to the possibilities of the apartment upstairs. His attitude, plainly stated, was that he would not help support Mr. X's children. They might be cared for by the state or in any way the community provided for such children. We finally found ourselves discussing frankly his sister's life and character, and his own duties in relation to her. He saw that, in ways he had not realized, he had been a detrimental influence. This thought affected him more than anything else. His whole attitude changed and the result was that he promised one dollar a week and some oversight over the children, especially a troublesome nine-year-old boy. For five months he has kept his promise.

"Our next step involved an extension of the family idea. We asked a group of people who were constantly studying the best interests of children, the trustees of a home for children, if they would consider giving this mother a cash allowance so that with the other resources she might keep the family together. This they unanimously voted to do although it was the first time in the history of the institution that such a course had been taken.

"Summarizing the situation, we find:

"First, that the grandfather who felt his duty ended saw a further duty; second, that the brother who acknowledged no obligation to a weak sister saw that he had not helped her to be strong; third, that the married brother was deterred from his unwise self-sacrifice; fourth, that the sister came to realize that her strong moral support was of more value than financial aid; fifth, and lastly, that the trustees of the home took, as it seemed to us, a progressive step away from institutionalism."[1]

One record submitted for study opens with a picture of an educated man who had lost his eyesight through a drug habit, a wife also addicted to drugs, who a little later becomes insane, and their little boy, whom the mother neglects but to whom the father is so devoted that he refuses to let him be taken away. The woman's Relatives in another state did not reply to letters. The man's sister and brother, who lived still farther away, wrote that they did not wish to have anything more to do with him. A little later, however, a third member of his family, another sister, who had heard indirectly of the previous correspondence, wrote a letter full of intelligent questions: "Is it true that my brother has attempted to take his life? Will he not probably attempt to take it again? Was drink or poverty the cause? Is he in a rescue home, a hospital, or where? Is he a confirmed drunkard, and do you see any conditions that would reform him? As I under-

[1] Chesley, Annie L.: "The Responsibility of Family Life." *Survey*, May 22, 1909, p. 269.

stand, he will not be separated from the child. Is he strongly attached to his wife also?" The letter goes on to explain that the writer had not heard from her brother for more than ten years and did not even know that he was married. She is eager to do all that she can, but is a widow in delicate health and could not provide for all three of them. Then out of the depth of her interest more questions: "What caused the blindness? Is there no hope that he will ever see? It is a cruel thing to separate a family under normal conditions, but sometimes it has to be for a time at least. How old a woman might his wife be? Are you a friend, a nurse, a missionary, or a sister of charity? Excuse the inquiry. Do not lose sight of him until I can hear from you. If I should write to him, would it be wise? I have decided to help him if I can, but that will not be by sending money there. . . . I cannot think he has the thirst for drink that makes drunkards. Some strong outside influence, poverty or a weak character, must be at the bottom. Tell the particular cause of the blindness, and if there is any hope that it may not be permanent."

These questions were answered as fully as possible. Meanwhile, a further effort had been made to find the woman's Relatives. A clergyman in their town, whose name had been found in a church directory, was asked to visit them, since no charitable organization could be found to do so. His intervention brought a reply at last written by the stepmother of the woman. It was full of expressions of sorrow, and offered to give a home to the little boy, provided he could be sent at the society's expense. The next day brought a second letter withdrawing this offer, and adding that if the little boy is as unruly as his mother used to be, it would be impossible to take care of him. "You will have to get him a good home somewhere through the Children's Home, or whatever other means you have of making such arrangements. I am awfully sorry that we cannot under the circumstances do anything for him, and if he goes to the bad I would feel myself responsible."

The man's sister was made of other clay. None of her family would join her—"I stand alone as far as my family are concerned, and whatever I undertake I must try and be equal to." Nine days later (the wife had meanwhile become violent and been removed to an insane asylum) comes a third letter. "I now beg to say I have had time to think in a more collected way and come to better conclusions than when I wrote you at first." Then follow instructions as to just how to send the blind man and his little son to her home. Two weeks later the sister writes again, "I think it only courtesy on my part to write you that my brother arrived safely in due time, found some one ready to assist him in the necessary changes, and is now comfortable. The little boy is in school and seems to be rather a desirable child. . . . I would think as I observe my brother that it will be a long time before he sees, although he seems to be very hopeful. He has a good appetite, and says he rests much better here than he has for a long time."

Complaint was made to a probation department about a girl of seventeen by her mother, a widow whose record was not above reproach. The probation officer saw the paternal Relatives, and was much impressed by the two aunts, who were far more careful in their statements than "in-laws" usually are. The officer, realizing the seriousness of bringing a court complaint against the girl, felt that the case could safely be left with these Relatives, and told them so; but the aunts were rather frightened at the responsibility and said that they did not know how to talk to their niece. The officer advised them to "put it straight up to her" that they had heard she was going with a disreputable man, and to make the most of the affectionate disposition which they said she had. They succeeded in getting from her a confession and a promise to give the man up. The probation officer continues to make suggestions, but has not had to appear in the situation in any way.

With reference to several of the foreign groups, it is necessary to bear in mind that godparents hold a relation to the family quite as close as that of Relatives, and that their co-operation is invaluable. In their own country the ties of kinship—even of kindred not nearly related—are close, and it is pitiful to see the dropping away of this interest and sense of responsibility wherever America's social agencies are many and careless.[1]

4. Further Considerations. In addition to the importance of Relatives as sources of interest and backing, it may be urged that they have a moral right to be considered—the same right, whenever they have tried to do their duty, that any church or other social agency interested in a family would have in like case, only their claim is somewhat stronger because the relation is more personal.

Miss Mary I. Breed gives an instance of this:[2] "One experience came from a woman of great worth, left a widow, and doing her best to support her two boys. She was aided generously and given the friendship of a sympathetic visitor. Her family were not seen, because of her claim that they had refused all help. When she developed a mental malady her children were given into the care of the city and then an agent of the city saw the woman's brother. He was justly incensed that he had not been consulted before, as he had been both able and willing to help. His sister had been alienated from her family, and her bitterness toward them was a part of her mental disease."

Moreover, Relatives are themselves a part of the community, potentially a helpful part, and any agency interested in co-ordinating the social service of a community cannot afford to leave them out.

One interesting by-product of social work is the occasional re-establishment of family relationships and the wearing away of misunderstandings.

[1] For a discussion of the co-operation of Relatives in institutional work for children see "Pittsburgh as a Foster Mother," by Florence L. Lattimore, in The Pittsburgh District, Civic Frontage, p. 398 sq.

[2] In one of the short, unpublished papers referred to in the Preface.

Miss Breed gives an illustration of this also: "We know a Jewish widow who, after the death of her husband, had been helped most generously by her family until they lost all hope, and ceased aiding because of what seemed to them her incurable laziness. When a medical diagnosis showed that she had neurasthenia, and when a set of teeth and a long course of good food and fresh air had made her another woman, an uncle felt so contrite for his past neglect that he set her up in a small grocery shop."

An S. P. C. C. worker was applied to by a young man who had been placed out from a foundling asylum when he was three years of age. Now grown and doing well in a farming community, he wished to find his four brothers. Through correspondence with the foundling asylum and the town clerk of the community from which they originally came, their whereabouts was discovered, one of them writing, "If you wanted to see a happy young lad, you ought to have seen me. I sat down and wrote my brother a nice long letter of eight pages, and the next Monday I got an answer from him and his family's pictures. He wanted me to come right down. . . . It makes a fellow feel happy to know he is not alone in the world, and that he has some folks."

III. QUESTIONS OF SUPPORT FROM RELATIVES

Questions of support (complete or partial) from Relatives and of temporary relief to be given by them are often allowed to demoralize our diagnosis and hamper our treatment. Those who turn to Relatives for nothing but material things are unlikely to use them wisely for even this one object. The case records of public departments and of private agencies abound in such penny-wise-and-pound-foolish policies, in overemphasized legal responsibilities and underemphasized social opportunities.

Responsibility for support can be enforced by the state, which has the right of recovery from Relatives, "if of sufficient ability," in the direct line of descent. Support laws vary in the different states, but quite generally the two parents and four grandparents are responsible for the support of children, and children who have attained their majority are responsible for the support of dependent parents and grandparents.[1] Public departments and institutions receiving public subsidies are often very careless about the enforcement of these provisions. When they bestir themselves to enforce them at all, they tend to become so interested in the finan-

[1] Children are definitely held responsible in 35 states, parents in 32, grandchildren in 22, grandparents in 20, brothers in 13, and sisters in 12; in a number of these states, however, responsibility is restricted, in cases where intemperance or other bad conduct is the cause of distress, to parents and children. See Summary of State Laws relating to the Dependent Classes, United States Census, 1913. (This material has been brought up to date in Social Welfare Laws of the Forty-eight States, Wendell Huston Publishing Company, Des Moines, 1930.)

cial side of their relations with Relatives that they refuse to interview any kindred whose responsibility could not be enforced by law. They will confer with sons and daughters, parents and grandparents, that is, but not with brothers and sisters, uncles and aunts, nephews and nieces.

An associated charities record of a homeless man shows that it discovered in the first month of acquaintance with him facts that had remained unknown for sixteen years to the public insane asylums in an adjoining state. The process by which, through a slender clue, his people were found in a third state is described in another part of this volume,[1] but the point to be made here is that the failure of a state's public institutions to discover this man's family, who had been eager for news of him all these years, is not so much a failure properly to adjust a question of legal support as it is a far graver failure. It is true that the state at the present per capita cost of maintenance had expended $3,160 for his care, but it had done something more wasteful than this; it had neglected through this whole period to utilize a therapeutic agency of the first importance. The man's family proved to be sterling people, whose affection and sympathy achieved wonders for his mental health even after years of lost opportunity. The man had been a runaway from the insane hospital when he applied to the associated charities; he was discharged and living with his own people when the case record was closed.

A record from a public departmen tshows one of its agents journeying from end to end of the state to find the father of a dependent child whose mother had deserted it. The man when finally found explained that he had feared to make inquiries because of the wife's behavior. He has since been paying regularly for the child's support.

Public agencies often handle questions of support in a more perfunctory way than this, but they are not the only offenders; the financial side is too much dwelt upon by private agencies also, both in the earlier consultations with Relatives and in cooperation with them throughout the period of treatment. It is undoubtedly true that any community is appreciably poorer in which the sense of family solidarity has been weakened either through carelessness on the part of social agencies or through sentimentality among the well-to-do; but to a wooden and undiscriminating enforcement of family responsibilities may be traced a reaction in some quarters against urging any who are not comfortably off to care for their own.[2]

[1] See use of directories in Chapter XIII, Documentary Sources, p. 266 sq.

[2] See correspondence entitled "A Misplaced Burden?" in *Charities and the Commons* for Oct. 13, 1906, p. 118, in which Mrs. Simkhovitch protests against the "custom of calling upon relatives for support, or the general theory that families ought to have pride enough to look after their own. Where there is some member

Questions of relief and of support are an important but always a secondary part of treatment. The social worker whose technique has more than one dimension, who thinks constructively about the cases under his care, is not likely to overlook the social welfare of each reference visited, including that of the Relatives. In the case cited on page 190 it will be noted that Mrs. Chesley not only refused help from one Relative who offered it, but heartened another who had nothing material to give by suggesting a different and better way in which she could be helpful. The relief side is

of the family amply able to relieve the poverty of another member, it seems a natural and suitable thing to expect such care. But when, as is so often the case, a committee of some powerful charitable society with large resources to draw upon, decides in a given instance to call upon a struggling relative for aid, the decision cannot but strike one as discreditable, and from an economic point of view wasteful."

Miss Zilpha D. Smith presents the other side: "The best charity workers I know, in approaching relatives, go to ask their counsel, their co-operation, to offer an opportunity of service; and they are so frequently rewarded with as much or more than they expected, even from relatives said to be unfriendly, that they take pains never to promise not to communicate with a relative. There may be occasions when a good charity worker deems it best to delay the letter or the interview, but these grow fewer as experience teaches how to make such inquiries with sympathy and discernment—to learn much and tell little.

"The response to such an approach usually discloses the character and the resources, financial and otherwise, of the relative and his attitude toward those now in need. It may be that because pride or resentment, poverty or illiteracy made communication difficult, they have allowed the family acquaintance to weaken. Those inquirers who go, not with decision already made as to what the relative ought to do, but to talk the matter over with an open mind, do not find as Mrs. Simkhovitch implies, that family pride is the chief motive which brings help but rather affection and loyalty to one's own, the traditions and memories they have in common, enhancing ordinary human sympathy. Even if the charitable society had more ample resources than any I know, it could not afford to let these human values go to waste.

"When it is pride that offers help, should not the poor man choose whether he would rather part with his pride than his dollars? If a friendly interest in him, as well as in the person in need, continues, it will be possible later to suggest a lessening of the burden, if that is wise. A state superintendent, whose new and struggling institution had difficulty in getting sufficient appropriation, nevertheless undertook to persuade and did persuade a relative to cut down a payment of $5.00 a week to $3.50.

"Not only those in want feel the bitterness of the burden their own helplessness lays upon those who are near and dear,—many who have been ill, though with money enough for ordinary needs, have felt this deep sorrow. But there is an experience even more bitter,—when one finds himself in illness or in want and there is no one but a stranger who cares enough about him to make a sacrifice.

"I cannot believe that many charitable societies do push relatives to the wall. My observation is that they are often unwilling to take the trouble to consult relatives unless they think they are going to get a good deal of money out of them, not realizing what a great advantage, other than money, the practice of going to them brings."

often the one that seems most important to the Relative we are interviewing, and we must aim to interest him in the other aspects, to carry his mind beyond a justification of his own position, moreover, to a consideration of the other person's difficulty in and of itself. The following are examples of a less flexible method. They show some of the weaknesses of our present practice, and emphasize the importance of keeping constructive treatment always in view.

A charity organization society was asked to befriend a family in which the man was out of work and beginning to keep bad company and the woman was expecting her second child in a few weeks. Both of the man's brothers were written to in the following vein: "Your brother (giving name and address) has been out of work for a number of weeks and his family have got behind in their expenses. They owe $16 rent and a store bill of about $12. His wife is unable to help with the income owing to her present condition. She expects to be confined next month. Will it not be possible for you to help your brother and his family until he is again on his feet?" Not only the further developments in this case but the situation as revealed in the first interview pointed to the need of insight into the man's character, work relations, domestic relations, health, etc. His two brothers would also have been better witnesses than he, perhaps, to the size, whereabouts, and resources of the whole family connection, but the two letters were not answered. In all probability this lack of response was due to too early emphasis upon the matter of relief.

The subject of letters of inquiry is treated in a separate chapter,[1] but it may be well to cite here another letter which brought no reply; it was addressed to a young man's father by a charity organization society. After stating the condition of distress in which the son and his wife and his two children were found, the letter continues, "We should be glad of information in regard to man's previous record and your idea as to his ability to take care of his family. This information will be considered confidential if you desire it. Would you feel inclined to assist the family financially, provided Mr. J makes every effort to get employment?" Here the error is a double one; financial assistance is led up to as the climax; "previous record," "man," and "the family" are technical, non-human terms in what should have been a very human document.

Comment upon an Italian record submitted for study includes a reference to support questions. The man of the family had attempted to assault his own daughter at one time when he was drunk and had been shot by one of his sons, who was trying to protect the girl. The charity organization society did faithful work later to improve the broken health of the father and to befriend his better-grade wife. The two older sons entered the United States Navy and were induced by the society, in co-operation with the government, to send part of their pay home.[2]

[1] Chapter XVII, Letters, Telephone Messages, etc.

[2] A circular letter addressed by one of the United States Naval Training Stations "to the parents of apprentice seamen" reads in part: "The Commanding Officer has no authority other than to advise a man under his command as to sending money

The commentator says, "You are following the orthodox view, of course, in encouraging the United States to get half pay out of Giorgio and Giovanni. All the back family history may have had the effect of simply embittering them, though, and making them feel that this additional demand is part of the general injustice of living. Giovanni's letter gives a hint of this, and Giorgio is stationed near enough to your city for you to learn at first hand, perhaps, his theory of things. I do not mean that the payments should stop, but I wish that they might be made a part of plans worked out with these young men for saving the younger children from the awful mill that the older ones have been through."

Comment upon another Italian case record reads as follows: "One outside visit was made; namely, to the sister who had furnished transportation. It brings, for result, the one item that the 'sister can do no more,' Presumably she was asked to relieve, or this idea was allowed to get in the foreground. . . . Here was a sister able on relatively short notice to transport two adults and seven children from Italy—evidently a person of some resource. . . . I am advocating not a demand for relief from this relative, which brings almost inevitably a negative response, but an approach that would have brought out her knowledge of the old life on the other side, of the shop and the home and the daily happenings, together with the names of the other relatives that had come over from time to time. Decidedly, those who lean heavily upon the modern child welfare devices, as against the old devices of uncles and aunts and parental responsibility, make a pitiful showing sometimes—they do in this family, where, thus far, the health, the schooling, and the industrial start of these children have been hampered by the lack of history which the relatives could easily have supplied."

These criticisms of a method that thrusts relief into undue prominence must not be taken as implying that the enforcement of financial responsibility upon Relatives is foolish. Often the mere enforcement brings with it wholesome social readjustments. In cases of family desertion, for instance, the throwing of the resulting relief burden upon the man's people, when they are well able to bear it and when there is reason to believe that they know his whereabouts, has been found to hasten his return. Some social reformers have taken the position that Relatives will be more

home. Encouragement to do so, however, is given, and on simple request, provided the amount is available on the books, and the object seems worthy, the pay officer issues a check for the amount requested, and charges it to his account. Until after two months at this Station, an apprentice seaman has very little money available, hence little may be expected until after that time. Later, after transfer to a seagoing ship, any man has the privilege of alloting a part of his pay to his home; that money is drawn through the mails each month, by the person to whom it is allotted, and without regard to any further request on the part of the allotter." A letter from the commandant at this Training Station adds, in further explanation: "When we are informed that the parents of one of our young men are in needy circumstances and need the help in a financial way of the recruit, our policy is to interview the lad and endeavor to impress upon him his responsibilities in the matter."

interested in the welfare of their less fortunate kindred when the state relieves them of all sense of financial obligation. If this position prove, after experiment, to be psychologically sound, it will reverse the judgments of both educators and social workers.

IV. METHODS OF APPROACH

For merely objective matters of fact, those sources of information which are the most impersonal are the most satisfactory.[1] But Relatives are of all sources the least impersonal; and, for this reason perhaps, we find them difficult witnesses. Most social workers realize the importance of Relatives, and also the difficulty of interviewing them for the first time. Next to the first interview with the client himself, here is the greatest danger of a false start, with the added danger, moreover, of making trouble between kindred. A social worker with only one year's experience, but with a natural gift for helpful relations with people, writes in answer to a question, "In three cases in particular, I interviewed relatives when I was almost convinced myself that more harm than good would be done. Yet in two of those cases breaches of years' standing were healed, and in the other I obtained information that made all the difference in the world in dealing with that family. That harm is not more often wrought by the visits of the social worker in quest of information and co-operation seems to me to be due to the fact that, if properly approached, relatives are not apt to question her right to such a deep interest in the family, and with an almost unnatural frankness open their hearts to utter strangers. If I remember aright, I have had only one actual rebuff this winter and half an apology was afterwards made for that by another member of the family."

"If properly approached." No mere instructions can be of any value here. To be really interested, to be able to convey this fact without protestations, to be sincere and direct and open-minded—these are the best keys to fruitful intercourse. When a worker comes back again and again with the statement that the Relatives do not know or will not tell, he has probably mislaid or never had some one of these keys.

Information of how much the Relatives have done already comes

[1] This idea is developed in Chapter XIII, Documentary Sources.

with a word, and their reasons for being seriously displeased are proffered easily. It is true that too often they have been much put upon. Listen, get their point of view, remember that even the irrelevant things that they say will help you to estimate their value as witnesses, then—push beyond to the things that more immediately concern your client, being careful to seek, even here, only those items of evidence that each particular Relative seems fitted to give. Confer with them about the possibilities already in mind. "Relatives are often indignant to find we have made a pretence of consulting them merely to foist upon them our own plan." The consultation must be genuine. Sometimes their own resourcefulness puts ours to shame.

After a number of Relatives have been seen, their plans may conflict or their adherence to any one plan of action may be half-hearted. In that case it may be well to follow up the separate interviews by arranging a conference with all of them together. This makes for clearness of understanding and dignifies their part in the treatment that is to follow.

The approach to Relatives is made more difficult sometimes by the fact that the social worker is the bearer of bad news.

An S. P. C. C. was notified by a day nursery of a mother's serious neglect of her young baby. The woman was only twenty-one, had come to the city to study at a technical school, and was receiving money regularly for this purpose from her parents in another state. They knew nothing of her illegitimate child or of her marriage to its father three months after its birth. The society wrote as follows:

"We have been interested for some little time in the welfare of your daughter, Mrs. ———, and her daughter, Ethel, and, on account of the neglect of the child's parents, the Judge of the Juvenile Court has placed the child temporarily with a state agency. We might have allowed this matter to go on without bringing it to your attention, but, at the request of the Judge, who has dealt in a most kindly way with your daughter, we are asking you to come to her assistance and to save her from the degradation to which she now seems destined unless those who are most concerned about her can work vigorously for her redemption. Instead of going into the details, we should like to ask whether you or your wife or both could not come to this city and consult with us or send some one equally interested to represent you with whom the whole matter can be talked over."

Two days later the girl's father appeared and her mother soon after—simple country people and both very helpless. But another daughter of the family proved to have the necessary strength of character. She was given the legal guardianship of the child, and mother and child went back later to the country home.

The effort to get in direct communication with these particular Relatives, not trusting to letters only in so delicate a matter, was prompted by a sound instinct. Relatives are often at such a distance that personal interviews are impossible, however, and this is especially true in the United States, where frequent migrations within the large cities, and migrations from county to county or state to state make our communications with Relatives at once more difficult and more necessary.[1] Immigration is a further complication. It has been said that many of our social clues run into the Atlantic Ocean, thus compelling us to communicate indirectly through mayors, consuls, etc., in other countries.

SUMMARY OF THIS CHAPTER

1. The statements of this chapter do not apply to Relatives in the immediate family of a client, but include all others whether related by birth, by marriage, or by descent.

2. It is necessary to keep in mind in all our contacts, however, the distinction between relationship by birth or descent, and relationship by marriage, for the latter is associated, often, with a peculiar type of prejudice.

3. Discrimination must be used as to which Relatives to see and when; they should not be seen to the exclusion of other important sources. It is possible also to overestimate the claims of kindred, irrespective of character, habits, or circumstance.

4. The chief failings of Relatives as witnesses are (1) their prejudice, (2) their assumption that they know more than they really do, (3) their lack of understanding of a social situation and of social values.

5. On the other hand, differential diagnosis and treatment would be sadly impoverished without their characteristic contributions of (1) individual and family history, (2) insight, (3) backing and active co-operation.

6. Aside from their ability to serve, Relatives have a moral right (whenever they have tried to do their duty, that is) to be consulted. Our consultations with them should be genuine; they should be given a chance to aid in shaping our social policies, instead of having plans of treatment imposed upon them ready-made from without.

[1] In a study of the thirteen-year-old boys in the city schools of 78 American cities (places of between 25,000 and 200,000 inhabitants) it was found that only one in six of the fathers of these boys was living in the city of his birth, and that among the boys themselves, only a few more than half were living where they were born. Of the fathers 40 per cent, of the boys 9 per cent were foreign born; but the migration of 44 per cent of the fathers and 33 per cent of the boys was within the United States. See Some Conditions Affecting Problems of Industrial Education in Seventy-eight American School Systems, by Leonard P. Ayres. Pamphlet of the Division of Education, Russell Sage Foundation, 1914.

RELATIVES AS SOURCES

7. Responsibility for support from near Relatives can be enforced by the state. Public social agencies charged with the administration of support laws often fall into the error of ignoring the other and higher services that Relatives could render. Private agencies make a similar mistake when they approach Relatives with the sole object of procuring relief. It does not follow, however, that Relatives should be relieved of any financial responsibility that they can bear without endangering their own social welfare.

CHAPTER X

MEDICAL SOURCES

IF, ON the basis of the social case work records then available for study, this book had been written fifteen years ago, it would probably have been found that the outside source of information consulted oftener than relatives even was employers. But there has been a shifting of interest from data about earnings and occupation to data about health and disease. All of these groups of facts are closely interrelated, of course, and the change is merely one of emphasis. So marked is it, however, that there may be need later of new emphasis upon another group of sources to preserve our social center of gravity.

The lists of outside sources used by the 56 social agencies whose records were studied show that Medical Sources were consulted two and a half times as often as employers and other work sources. In 2,800 cases, to be exact, 1,828 Medical Sources were consulted and 743 work sources.[1] The multiplication in recent years of medical agencies both curative and preventive, especially in large cities like those included in our study of sources, accounts in part for this; in part, it is due to the fact that some agencies for the care of the sick now have social as well as medical records—social records that can be consulted with profit, that is. But part of it is also due to a change in the attitude of non-medical social workers toward their own task. In seeking to remedy bad social conditions they have come to recognize more fully the great handicap of bad physical conditions, and have learned to welcome, in the effort to remedy these, the aid of a newer and more constructive medical science. Their awakening is due, in part, to their own deepened experience of human need, but even more is it due to the socialized members of the medical profession, who have led the way in many departments of social endeavor—a way in which the lay social workers have been only too glad to follow.

[1] See Appendix II, Table A.

The kinds of Medical Sources most often consulted by the 56 agencies were physicians, hospitals and sanatoria, dispensaries, medical-social service departments, nurses, and public health departments. It must be conceded that social workers have been handicapped, often, in their use of these sources of information by their lack of knowledge of even the most elementary facts about disease and by their lack also of understanding of the organization and discipline necessary in a hospital or dispensary. But, as these pages are an attempt to estimate the social value of the various sources of evidence, and as the case records studied show not only the great serviceableness but the occasional failure of Medical Sources, it may be well to follow the plan already followed in the chapter on Relatives and illustrate these failures at once, even at the risk of seeming to overemphasize them. It will be evident a little later that much more can be said on the other side.

I. WHERE MEDICAL EVIDENCE SOMETIMES FAILS

Case notes under this head made in the course of our extended case reading tell their own story of (1) a non-social attitude, (2) conflicting diagnoses and prognoses, and (3) faulty medical records.

1. Non-social Attitude. Let two illustrations suffice. It may be that both show poor medical work also, but the writer makes no attempt to pass judgment upon their medical aspects:

A child-saving agency found a little girl of seven in a boarding house where she had been placed by her mother, a waitress. This mother was described as "suspicious, quarrelsome, and altogether difficult." Her child was illegitimate. The little thing's eyes were seriously inflamed, her whole face swollen, eruption behind ears and on scalp; she had been in this condition for two months, often seen by mother, but no medical care procured. The public health department had diagnosed the child's condition as syphilitic five years earlier. The mother was persuaded by the society to permit them to place the patient in a hospital, the hospital authorities agreeing to report to the society's agent a few days before discharge. Later the hospital reported that the child *had been* discharged, at the request of the mother's physician, or at the request of someone representing himself as such over the telephone. Only the last name of this physician was known at the hospital.

On complaint of a commission for the blind, a physician was prosecuted by an S. P. C. C. for failing to report a case of ophthalmia neonatorum. The eyes of a six-weeks-old baby had been irreparably injured by this disease. The physician employed was fined $50 and appealed the case. Among other witnesses for the prosecution was an eye infirmary. A copy of the prosecuted doctor's letter to the board of health was also entered in evidence against him.

None feel the results of these non-social acts or of failures to co-operate with social workers more keenly than do the more progressive of the physicians themselves. There is marked advance every year among these latter in the development of a deeper social concern.

2. Conflicting Diagnoses and Prognoses. These often delay social work very seriously, just as conflicting plans of social treatment must hamper medical work. Some of this delay is inevitable, for medicine is an experimental science, but in all probability some of it is due to unevenness in the standards of medical practitioners, and some unquestionably is due to the uneven development just referred to in the medical profession's sense of social responsibility. A society for protecting children from cruelty finds that, when it brings a physician into court to testify to certain conditions, the defendant in the case can usually find some other doctor to swear that the facts are just the reverse.

In one case, a tubercular mother had been reported to a child-saving agency because she refused to allow her six-year-old crippled son to go to a school for cripples. The boy was sleeping with his mother, and one of the physicians at a certain children's hospital said that the child could make no progress if left at home. A settlement nurse and the family physician reported that the mother was careless and was likely to infect her children. A board of health doctor objected to home surroundings and advised sending the child away. In court, however, the family was able to produce a letter from a second physician at the same children's hospital, objecting strongly to the removal of the child, as his disease was incurable, and adding, "We are willing to give the mother advice and help whenever it is necessary." This was further reinforced by another medical institution, the nurse from which reported a well-kept home.

The following memoranda summarize the various diagnoses and treatments advised in one case that was under the care of a hospital social service department: Oct. 31. Girl aged sixteen, pretubercular, needs a country home. Nov. 13. Tubercular. Too hysterical to go to a hospital; must be treated at her own home, where medical supervision will be constant and expert. Dec. 11. Operation advised for ovarian cyst. Not tubercular; hospital care. Feb. 8 of the following year. Entirely well, needs nourishing food before she commences work. Apr. 18. Tuberculosis, first stage. Sanatorium advised. Jan. 28, year succeeding. Patient quite well. Reported not to have gone to a sanatorium. Apr. 18. Major hysteria; needs long care in hospital.

The uncertainties of prognosis scarcely need illustration.

A charity organization society was caring for a wife and five children while the husband was in a hospital. On March 8, hospital reports man may have to remain two weeks longer, and that it may be a month before he is able to work. His trouble is sciatica; there is nothing that can be done for it except to see that man has absolute rest. April 12, hospital reports that man has tuberculosis of the spine; will not be able to work for at least six months, possibly more. May 8, hospital reports at present man has not tuberculosis of the spine; the trouble he is being treated for is sciatica and he seems to be responsive to treatment. If he continues to improve he will probably leave the hospital soon.

In an Italian family already mentioned in another connection[1] there were several medical diagnoses—three of the father of the family (who had had facial paralysis, apparently, after he had been shot in the jaw), one diagnosis of the son-in-law, and none, though one was needed, of the daughter, aged sixteen. A commentator adds: "I realize that delay is accounted for by the contradictory diagnoses of Mr. ——'s condition. The doctors are as fallible as we are, and we must expect to lose time while they are finding out what to do."

It should be repeated that the faults of social reports to physicians are quite as grave as any faults here noted in medical reports. "I have seen many examining physicians discouraged," writes the head of a medical-social service department, "by the poverty of social workers' reports, which are so increasingly important to a proper clinical examination and diagnosis of, for instance, a feeble-minded child."

3. Faulty Medical Records. Some conflicting diagnoses and prognoses could probably be traced to failures in the original records, or to failures in their interpretation by custodians. Dispensary records would seem, from our case reading, to be far less dependable than hospital ward records, though there are notable exceptions to this. An extreme instance of faulty method would be that of the dispensary which could never identify a patient or his record by name, age, and address, but always added, after its general disclaimer of any previous knowledge, "Tell him to come and *bring his bottle*, and then we'll know." Past medical history is often of such medical as well as social importance that dispensaries which attempt to keep records at all are surely justified in keeping them in such a way as to identify the patient recorded.

II. COMPLEMENTARY NATURE OF MEDICAL AND OF SOCIAL DATA

The discovery of the possible assistance of social history in the medical field is so relatively new that there is small wonder to find

[1] See p. 198.

it used awkwardly on both sides as yet. Two examples found in a group of hospital social service records illustrate the complementary nature of medical and of social data. Each is an instance of mistaken diagnosis in its own field, corrected by evidence from the other field later.

A physician referred a woman of twenty-six to the social service department for a pelvic disturbance needing home supervision and treatment. A home visit brought out a history of convulsions up to the age of twelve, and morning "spells" to the present time. Re-examination in the nerve clinic followed, with the result that the patient is now in an institution for epileptics.

The other side is illustrated by a diagnosis of insanity made in a dispensary.

The patient in question had been reported to an S. P. C. C. for maltreating her children when in drunken rages. Unable to discover any trace of alcoholism the society had dropped the complaint. At the dispensary, the woman confessed to the fear that, in acute attacks, she had abused her children. The S. P. C. C. could have protected the children if the mother's mental disturbance had been discovered earlier.

The complementary nature of the two fields of work is well illustrated by the difference between prescribing braces or other apparatus and securing their proper use. A critic of the case record of an Italian family referred to on the preceding page wrote to the social worker responsible for their treatment:

I distinctly question the wisdom of putting on your blank forms of inquiry addressed to doctors of dispensaries the following question: Does patient need care which dispensary cannot give? The psychological effect of blank space after a printed question is to suggest the filling in of the answer, whether the writer has one or not. This may not have been the case with Dr. ——, but his prompt filling in of the Taylor brace led to an equally prompt ordering of it without any consideration whatever of the son-in-law's willingness to wear it or ability to get any good out of it. The son-in-law got in a huff and returned the brace later,[1] which only

[1] This brings to mind a passage in Dr. Richard Cabot's address at the National Conference of Charities and Correction (Baltimore) in 1915: "In the orthopedic clinic of the Massachusetts General Hospital we treat cases of spinal curvature. They are often aided by the application of a plaster jacket which forces the deformed chest gradually back into something like correct position. It seems like a simple mechanical problem. But it isn't, for there are people who will wear a plaster jacket and there are people who won't. To make these jackets costs something; hence the social workers in that clinic are now trying to find out in advance what people will wear plaster jackets and what people won't, as it does not pay to apply plaster jackets to people who won't wear them. If there is any field for psychological study less promising than the problem of spinal curvature, I do not know it. Yet we have obtained already a rich harvest there."—Proceedings, p. 224.

shows what a child you had to deal with. The other social agencies should stand behind the medical agencies, and do their best to get people well, whether by relief or by other treatment, but the question and answer in this particular case threw the relief out of perspective. It would be interesting to trace the actual results in individual cases of a generous "handing out" of diets, appliances, etc., on the order of doctors and nurses who were given to understand that all they needed to do in order to get was to ask.

Another medical aspect of this case which seems to have been overlooked is the statement by Mrs. E that Concetta is "not quite normal." This is made in February and repeated in March in a letter to the doctor. Work had been found for Concetta previously and work was urged for her later. Her heredity and earlier history suggest the need of a most careful physical and mental examination.

It is evident that both groups of public servants—the social and the medical—will serve the public best when they have thoroughly mastered in all its details the technique of working together. The following examples of the kinds of report that have proved helpful from one group to the other may further illustrate relations between the two:

A charity organization society was interested in a family in which the father had tuberculosis, the mother was sick also, and there were two children at home. The father was sent to the country. The doctor who examined the mother made a diagnosis of umbilical hernia, from which she had been suffering for fifteen years. She was very stout, and this fact made an operation more difficult. In response to an inquiry, the doctor sent this very clear letter:

"An operation for Mrs. J is not an absolute necessity; with a carefully made belt or truss, strangulation probably will not occur, but if it should occur wearing a truss would increase the difficulties of an operation at least 50%; of course, in case of hernia, whether umbilical or otherwise, strangulation is what every surgeon fears. If the operation was done for simple umbilical hernia upon Mrs. J, I should say the chances of her getting well were between 65 and 75%; if strangulation took place, her chances of dying would be about the above. She should not be ill longer than four or five weeks and she should be able to be back at work in about eight weeks."

This statement made it possible to do two things. First, to help Mrs. J to make a deliberate choice of operation or no operation. She chose the former, and says now that she has not felt so well since she was a girl of sixteen. Second, it enabled the society to secure without difficulty the necessary relief and care for the children. The doctor underestimated the period of convalescence, but it was easy to extend a plan well started; it is going to be increasingly difficult to launch one that is vague and formless.

A doctor who had been inclined to regard social diagnoses as a fad received the following letter from a charity organization society:

"Mrs. K has promised to go to the dispensary on Monday. Mrs. K has three children, aged nine, seven, and six. She had a miscarriage between the seven and six year old. Her husband was a drinking man and very brutal to her. She was injured (lacerations, she says) when her second child was born. When the youngest was only four days old, she was up and moved, with a severe hemorrhage as a result. She left her husband several times, and finally two years ago she sent him away for good and all. Since that time she has supported herself and the children in various ways. Last fall she took the apartment where she now is, $16 a month, and worked at the —— factory days and at home nights sewing. For days at a time, she would work until 1 or 2 a. m., then get up and go to the factory at seven. She has had trouble with varicose veins, backache, and general bearing down pains. Her head and eyes have bothered her also. She has had no regular physician, but was told at the —— Hospital that she had a tumor. We are planning to pay her rent for a few months and see how she makes out on dressmaking. Her flat is pleasantly situated and seems fairly good. The kitchen is in the basement, and four rooms (one inside with double doors into the parlor) are on the first floor. They have a good bathroom."

The doctor copied most of these statements into his medical record. It should be added that the social worker who wrote the letter had had the benefit of a short period of observation in a hospital social service department, to which she had gone to study ways of strengthening the relation between her own work and that of the medical agencies.

With the new interest in public health, and the developments of public health departments of the modern type, there should be many ways in which the non-medical social agencies and these departments can be of service to one another. The New York Charity Organization Society, for example, reports service from the city's public Health Department in the following ways:

Department nurses give prenatal care to prospective mothers, and frequently persuade unco-operative mothers to take their babies to the Infants' Milk Station for examination and advice about proper feeding. Special examinations for workers in restaurants and laundries are given. In homes where there are contagious diseases, nurses visit and report needs. In the summer, when many persons, both children and adults, are sent for fresh air outings, the Health Department is depended upon by the Charity Organization Society for many of the required physical examinations. Photographic copies of records in the Bureau of Vital Statistics are frequently obtained. The Department effects forcible removal of tuberculous patients in infectious condition and forces unco-operative patients, who have been told to return sputum for examination, to do so. It maintains a special clinic for venereal disease, making blood tests whenever possible. The Board of Health maintains a special class for children having rickets, a whooping cough clinic where serum is administered, and dental clinics for school children. It reports conditions in two-family houses which do not come under the supervision of the Tenement House Department. It inspects lodging houses and attends to the segregation of tuberculous patients found in them. One of the greatest helps from the Health Department comes from the daily receipt by each district office in the Charity Organization Society of the contagious disease bulletin and also the receipt of the monthly bulletin. The Health Department is also helpful in giving information about midwives, as from this department midwives' certificates are issued. As the tuberculosis clinics connected with the Health Department use the Social Service Exchange of the Charity Organization Society, it is always possible to know when a clinic is interested in a family known to the society.

III. SOCIAL RESPONSIBILITY FOR EARLY MEDICAL DIAGNOSIS

Medical authorities are agreed that any way by which medical diagnosis could be had earlier than at present would add materially to the number of cures. It is at this point that the non-medical social worker might easily hold a strategic position, by cultivating a watchful eye for the possible indications in family and current history, in personal appearance and in mental attitude, of those physical and mental breakdowns that happen to have been preceded by social breakdown. The non-medical worker, if he is wise, will never attempt to make a medical diagnosis, even of the most tentative kind, but he will utilize promptly every opportunity to bring together the possible patient and the expert medical diagnostician. Early diagnosis is a very important element, for instance, in the cure of syphilis, cancer, stomach ulcer, and lead-poisoning, while the prevention of infant blindness is a matter of hours not days. This is no plea for a general interest in health campaigns, which is almost universal and often most in evidence in those very family agencies that are neglectful of their opportunities to cure and prevent in the individual case. The important thing to emphasize here is the daily exercise of our interest by leaving no stone unturned, by making the concrete application in the detailed work of whatever kind for which we stand responsible to the community.

Comment on one of the case records of a large family agency reads as follows: "Visitor has certainly shown patience and sympathy, and has tried to align all available sources for relief. Is it not possible, however, that time and money might have been saved if a careful examination of the man had been made at once, instead of trying for two months to help him get work which he was physically unable to do?"

"I remember with shame," writes a supervisor of case work, "a case that I had myself years ago where a man who was thought to be very lazy really had intestinal tuberculosis. In these days a good many case workers would be quick to see the possible significance of symptoms such as his and would arrange for a medical examination promptly, but there are hundreds of others all over the country who would not. We cannot emphasize too strongly, it seems to me, the importance of securing medical examinations in all doubtful cases, as one of the most important principles of social treatment."

A charity organization society secured surgical care for a woman whose health had been injured, according to the society's record, by running a foot machine in a factory. As soon as she recovered she returned to the old job, where she could make good wages, and her daughter was permitted to start at the same kind of work.

Any list of the particular things relating to health that are to be kept most in mind by the non-medical worker will change yearly with the rapid advances in medical knowledge and with the equally rapid gains in the public control of disease. Since the preparation of this book was begun, there has been a marked change in the matter of workmen's compensation (to take an illustration that is both industrial and medical), but the responsibilities and awkwardnesses from which these new compensation laws have released the social case worker will enable him to make his work for individuals tell all the better in the allied field of occupational disease.[1] Social case work will continue to show, in its future development, this frequent throwing off on the one side and annexing on the other. To those who may be tempted to complain that too much is expected of the social case worker, this is the answer. His task contracts in a cheering way only as he deliberately extends it in directions that are carefully chosen and then steadily advanced.

Owing to the rapid changes just referred to, not even the most tentative list of health matters to be kept in mind by the social diagnostician can be given here, but medical men are beginning to write for social workers, and their statements should be studied carefully at first hand. There are excellent manuals relating to tuberculosis, and recently we have had a Layman's Handbook of Medicine prepared "with special reference to social workers" by Dr. Richard C. Cabot,[2] in which, among many other things of use to us, he is at pains to name those diseases in which, owing to the

[1] For illustration of the type of case work still needed in the compensation field, however, see Chapter XII, Employers and Other Work Sources, p. 248.

[2] Cabot, Richard C.: A Layman's Handbook of Medicine. With special reference to social workers. Boston, Houghton Mifflin and Co., 1916.

importance of past history in their diagnosis, the social worker can be of especial service.

IV. METHOD

It remains to gather up, from notes made in the course of case reading, such criticisms and suggestions with regard to the relations of case workers to Medical Sources as will possibly help to strengthen social diagnosis on the health side.

1. Ask for Prognosis. It is not enough to learn the name of our client's disease; even more important are the medical predictions as to duration and probable outcome—the physician's prognosis. We should also be at great pains to learn what social treatment will hasten recovery and what will help him to avoid a recurrence of the trouble. In this way the medical prognosis may become the cornerstone of the social diagnosis.

2. Economize Resources. This lesson is needed at every stage of treatment and in the use of every source of information, but it is especially needed at this point by workers in the larger cities, for in these Medical Sources multiply very rapidly, and are sometimes consulted wastefully and heedlessly by the social agencies. The very willingness of doctors, hospitals, and dispensaries to serve is a temptation to the social worker. They should be consulted freely, of course, but should be chosen with care, and for better reasons than the social worker's own convenience. A knowledge of the special facilities and the limitations of medical agencies in the worker's own city is essential; and once consulted, these should be utilized to the full; should be given the benefit, that is, of whatever is known already, and should be given a free hand to make as complete a diagnosis as possible. The medical diagnosis given with encouraging promptness is not always the fullest or the best, and social workers should have a special respect for the physician who hesitates to pronounce judgment hastily.

Nowhere, perhaps, can the scientific axiom, "observations are not to be numbered but weighed," be more fittingly applied than to the following of medical dicta. The testimony of one physician who knows is worth the testimony of fifty who do not know. We should discourage the needless multiplication of Medical Sources, therefore, by consulting, at whatever cost of time and trouble to ourselves, the very best available, and then should abide loyally by their findings.

In the small community, even the mediocre specialist may not be available for mental and nervous examinations, and it may devolve upon the social workers there—little fitted as they may feel themselves for the task—to interest one of the younger doctors to make special studies in this field. Many similar gaps remain to be filled; there are communities in the South where no physician has any special knowledge of the treatment of pellagra, and others, both North and South, where, even now, no expert diagnosis of a case of tuberculosis can be had.

But in the city of many physicians and medical agencies, how shall we discover who are the best available? Often doctors have been consulted before the social agency appears upon the scene, and it is necessary to turn to medical judgments already formed and to act upon these. Consequently it will sometimes be necessary to make inquiry about the standing of the doctor in a given case among his own fraternity. The etiquette of the social worker's relations to a reputable but relatively incompetent private physician who is in charge of a difficult case requiring the best diagnostic skill has yet to be worked out, but the patient's interests demand a not too easy withdrawal from a situation which calls for both tact and persistence. It is disheartening to read in social records—even in those showing the deepest concern for the welfare of the client whose treatment is recorded—entries of hasty and contradictory opinions given by doctor after doctor, hospital after hospital, with blind faith in all on the part of the recorder, and with no consciousness of failure, apparently.

Dr. Cabot comments upon a social record submitted to him as follows: "The lack of medical co-operation, that is, lack (in the first place) of ability and (in the second place) of frankness on the part of the doctors concerned in the Boyle-Carey family, has been pointed out by various of our social workers at the Social Service Department, and doubtless by many others. But the point that I want to make about it is this: It may very well have been impossible to secure adequate medical co-operation, and the workers on the case may therefore have done everything that could have been done to avert the evils that came from the lack of such co-operation. *But* it is not at all evident that the workers were themselves aware that they were being checkmated and put on false scents so frequently owing to the shortcomings of the doctors. When a person is quite unavoidably balked by such means, it seems to me that the records should show some indication of his rueful awareness thereof, just as, when a surgeon tells a patient that he should be operated on and the patient refuses, the surgeon is careful to make it clear in his record that the subsequent disasters are not his fault but are due to lack of proper co-operation."

3. Seek First-hand Information. This also applies elsewhere, but when the statements are as technical as medical diagnoses and prognoses are likely to be we must guard this point especially. In the gathering of medical evidence we must avoid both oral and second-hand reporting, whilst using every possible device that will save the time of the physician and his busy hospital and dispensary assistants. The written diagnosis is no substitute for a personal interview with the doctor, in which his suggestions as to social treatment and his fuller statement as to prognosis are procured; it saves many misunderstandings, however, and should not be omitted. The secretary of a state commission for the blind now asks for a written statement of diagnosis, and, when this is refused, indicates on the record that the diagnosis came by word of mouth only.

It will not always be possible to follow this rule, but it is quite possible to foreswear the gathering of medical information by hearsay. To ask a patient what the doctor said about his condition and write down the answer is to quadruple the chances of error, for the doctor may not have told him the whole truth, fearing that it would unduly alarm him; the patient may not have understood what was said; he may not remember accurately; or he may have reasons of his own for not telling all that he remembers. Some one or more of these objections applies to all evidence at second hand, and its use when the source is accessible is a sign of faulty technique.

A worker in a child-placing agency heard a rumor that Mrs. B, with whom twins had been placed to board, was tuberculous. Accordingly, fearing for the health of the agency's charges, she telephoned the charity organization society's district secretary, who had known Mrs. B. The secretary stated that Mrs. B had been treated at a certain hospital three years before for tuberculosis and that one of her children had had tubercular glands. Knew nothing more recent of physical conditions, but felt there was absolutely no danger at this time. Agreed with child-placing agent that it might not be a good place for a long residence. The twins were removed from the home immediately, though, save for Mrs. B's health, it was a suitable one.

A case reader comments upon the record of this treatment as follows: "I find fault with this action, first because the hospital record was not consulted, and second, for the unsound deduction that the home might be safe temporarily but not permanently. If the woman was in an infectious stage of the disease, there was danger to the children during every minute of their stay with her; and if she was not, they could stay with her indefinitely provided she was examined from time to time."

4. A Medical Diagnosis Should Have a Date. The illustration just given serves to emphasize the further point that physical and mental conditions change, and that a diagnosis of six months ago must be brought up to date before we can safely make it the basis of social action.

5. Beware the Medical Opinions of the Non-medical. It is only natural, perhaps, that non-medical social workers who see much of sickness should not only become alert to its signs and symptoms—this much they should always be—but that they should also begin to pride themselves upon this alertness, and air their views of matters strictly medical. "There is nothing," writes a hospital social worker, in commenting upon a group of case records in which this tendency appears, "that will more quickly antagonize a physician than for the social worker to make even a suggestion of a medical diagnosis. The more medical training one has, the more cautious one grows about this." We should be at great pains to give the doctor any social facts that seem to be significant, but we should spare him, in so doing, our medical guesses. Otherwise, we are likely to find in him, at the very moment that we most need an open mind, a closed one.

A medical-social worker says of her instructions to new assistants, "I always caution them, in asking a physician to examine a patient, not to make a diagnosis. For example, instead of taking a child to the doctor and saying, 'I think Johnnie has adenoids,' say, 'Johnnie sleeps with his mouth open. Is there any obstruction in his nose?'"

A nurse records that a certain woman is "extremely thin and delicate looking;" a non-medical social worker describes the same woman as "thin and consumptive looking." This last term should not be used until after a physical examination.

A district worker in a charity organization society sent a girl to a nerve clinic with this memorandum: "Mary has a delusion that she is pregnant." She was found to be three and a half months pregnant and a shocking condition of neighborhood immorality was unearthed by the discovery.

6. Doctor to Doctor Is More Frank. The Hippocratic oath[1] is now interpreted more broadly than formerly, and doctors are often

[1] It may interest social workers to know the exact terms of the Oath of Hippocrates. They are as follows: "I swear by Apollo the physician, and Aesculapius and Health [Hygeia] and All-heal [Panacea], and all the gods and goddesses, that,

willing to give information, in confidence, to social workers whose use of it clearly will be not only social but for the best interests of the patient. As court procedure becomes more and more socialized, physicians will probably be more willing than now to place their information at the service of judges, especially in cases involving the welfare of children or the protection of the community. As social work is more skilfully done, they will treat social practitioners with a still larger measure of confidence than at present. Meanwhile, social workers must recognize that, in difficult cases, doctors who do not know them well or understand their methods of work and are therefore unwilling to give them information are more likely to deal frankly with doctors who do understand and who are enough interested to act as intermediaries.

The social service department of a dispensary sought the report of a diagnosis made three years before by a large public hospital, explaining that it might throw light on the problem of present treatment. They received promptly a diagnosis of "pelvic disturbance." But the dispensary doctor who was treating the case, by communicating directly with the hospital later, secured a diagnosis of "venereal infection."

The secretary of an agency for the care of girls reports that she always prefers to get a medical opinion, especially in perplexing cases, through a wellknown physician who is an active member of her directorate. One letter sent by the head of an

according to my ability and judgment, I will keep this oath and this stipulation—to reckon him who taught me this Art equally dear to me as my parents, to share my substance with him, and relieve his necessities if required; to look upon his offspring in the same footing as my own brothers, and to teach them this Art if they shall wish to learn it, without fee or stipulation; and that by precept, lecture, and every other mode of instruction, I will impart a knowledge of the Art to my own sons, and those of my teachers, and to disciples bound by a stipulation and oath according to the law of medicine, but to none others. I will follow that system of regimen which, according to my ability and judgment, I consider for the benefit of my patients, and abstain from whatever is deleterious and mischievous. I will give no deadly medicine to anyone if asked, nor suggest any such counsel; and in like manner I will not give to a woman a pessary to produce abortion. With purity and with holiness I will pass my life and practice my Art. I will not cut persons laboring under the stone, but will leave this to be done by men who are practitioners of this work. Into whatever houses I enter, I will go into them for the benefit of the sick, and will abstain from every voluntary act of mischief and corruption, and further, from the seduction of females or males, of freedmen and slaves. Whatever, in connection with my professional practice or not in connection with it, I see or hear, in the life of men, which ought not to be spoken of abroad, I will not divulge, as reckoning that all such should be kept secret. While I continue to keep this Oath unviolated, may it be granted to me to enjoy life and the practice of the Art, respected by all men, in all times! But should I trespass and violate this Oath, may the reverse be my lot!"—Genuine Works of Hippocrates, trans. from the Greek by Francis Adams, Vol. II, p. 278–80. New York, Wm. Wood and Co., 1886.

institution for the feeble-minded in answer to the inquiry of this physician is as follows: "It appears that —— is about two years behind in school work, perhaps a little more, but her defect seems quantitative rather than qualitative, and I do not believe that she is defective enough to warrant her commitment at this time. I told the young lady who brought her that I thought the problem would have to be worked out further before anything could be done. Her responses to the laboratory tests were not convincing, but she has the natural feminine subtlety and reticence, and I do not believe that a single examination would begin to map out the entire field. Should her dishonest habits continue [the girl had been stealing money] she might be committed to the reform school, and there they would have the opportunity and are properly equipped to make a thorough study of the problem."

7. Careful Reporting Wears Away Prejudice. An unco-operative attitude on the part of physicians, where the social worker needs their help in securing social action (whether in individual cases or in other ways), can sometimes be accounted for by the inability of the non-medical social worker to make his daily contacts with Medical Sources as helpful as they should be. Written summaries of the social side of any case reported for diagnosis or treatment are aids to this, provided they are accurate, clear, and without irrelevant detail.

Dr. Adolf Meyer, in commenting upon the same record that was submitted to Dr. Cabot,[1] points out the shortcomings of certain medical reports in the case and adds: "They probably also never had a written summary of the type of the one sent Mrs. Scott [superintendent of the girls' reformatory]. . . . Now a consulting alienist such as was to be appealed to would really have been unjustified in making a far-reaching estimate without such documents or copies of documents."

A critic of this criticism submits that, while it is well to present a written social summary, the doctor does not always read it. A better way, according to this second critic, would be to make a report orally to the doctor, to interest him in the material that the social worker has to give, and then hand him the written summary before leaving. At the time, it might mean little to him, but two months later, when he knew his patient better, some part of it might mean a great deal.

When a Medical Source has been helpful in a given case, it would be well worth while to report briefly to that source later in just what manner the help had furthered social treatment, thus strengthening the relations of the two kinds of work at their point of intersection.

8. Miscellaneous Suggestions. The following suggestions as to the detailed use of Medical Sources need no illustration:

[1] See p. 214.

To establish the identity of a record or of a patient in a large hospital the name or number of the ward, and, in large dispensaries, the number of the patient's dispensary card, will be found useful.

The lodge doctor can frequently give some medical report and other information about the men of the family. This is especially true in foreign families, where it often happens that no other physician has been consulted.

Medical records sometimes contain non-medical information of value. New York hospitals, for instance, record the names and addresses of the two nearest relatives or friends of the patient. A tuberculosis sanatorium, by recording the name of the person responsible for the payment of board, helped a non-medical agency to discover several years later a co-operative relative. One hospital record brought to light the approximate amount and the whereabouts of money in bank.

The physician who has treated some family regularly for years is able to throw light on other home matters than the health of its members. At times of sickness and death relatives appear who have not been heard of before, and the family doctor is in a good position to estimate the depth of their interest, as well as the closeness of the bond within the immediate family group.

SUMMARY OF THIS CHAPTER

1. So marked is the emphasis now put upon data about health and disease in nearly all forms of social case work, that any failures of Medical Sources as witnesses stand out in bold relief. These failures fall under the three heads of (1) non-social attitude; (2) conflicting diagnoses and prognoses; (3) faulty medical records.

2. Parallel failures should be noted in the witness of social work sources to the medical profession. Conflicting diagnoses and prognoses are even more common in social work than in medicine.

3. The two types of data—social and medical—are complementary. It follows that social workers might hold a strategic position, were they better equipped to recognize and report upon the early signs of impending physical or mental breakdown. Earlier reporting of these signs would add materially to the number of cures. It is impossible to overstate the importance of cultivating a habit of awareness at this point, of being alertly watchful for the more obscure signs of breakdown.

4. In all relations with doctors, hospitals, etc., we should

(1) Ask for prognosis as well as diagnosis, for the probable duration and outcome of the disease, and for ways of helping to hasten recovery and avoid recurrence

(2) Economize medical resources, by selecting the best sources and using them to the full

(3) Seek first-hand information, and not depend upon hearsay statements of "what the doctor said"

(4) Note the date of a medical diagnosis before making it the basis of social action

(5) Beware the medical opinions of the non-medical

(6) Seek the mediation of a physician in securing important medical information not otherwise procurable

(7) Report with special care the social side of medical cases.

CHAPTER XI

SCHOOLS AS SOURCES

HERE are sources of information that seem to have been imperfectly used as yet by social workers. It is true that many of the agencies studied consult school officials (they were consulted 687 times in the 2,800 cases already referred to), but an examination of the individual items seems to show that both family agencies and those for the care of dependent children do not confer with educators often enough.[1] The children's agencies have many charges that are under school age, but, even after allowing for this, consultations with School Sources are too infrequent, if the statistics at hand are at all representative of the usual practice.

A formal school report giving a child's grade, and his marks for scholarship, attendance, and deportment, leaves many of the most important questions about him unanswered, as the following comments, written by one who was making a survey of the case work of a certain charity organization society, indicate:

> A driver, supposed to be intemperate, a wife, and four children, thirteen to three. Known to the society since December 24, 1908. An unsatisfactory record culminating in a "sob" story in the newspapers. I notice that what to me is the most important source of information—more important than landlords and former residences—was not consulted at all, namely, the school in which two or three of the children must have been entered. The physical condition of the children, any evidences of the moral background of their home which came out at the school, indications of their mental condition, whether they were laggards or not, whether they came to school looking well cared for—all of this would be extremely valuable in further treatment. In other words, is there a leverage upon this family through their love of the children revealed in proper care, or will more coercive remedies be necessary? For the children's sake, this family cannot be dropped.

[1] This impression has been strengthened recently by the findings of the Springfeld (Ill.) Survey. The failure of the Associated Charities of Springfield to consult School Sources about the families in which it was interested had kept it ignorant of one of the most serious evils permitted by the city administration; namely, irregular school attendance. See Francis H. McLean on The Charities of Springfield, pp. 89-93.

An Italian couple with three children, eleven, eight, and six. The man has open sores, but earns $4.00 a week; the wife is supposed at first to be tuberculous but afterwards this is found to be incorrect. It is determined that there is no hope of this family itself, and an attempt is made to have the S. P. C. C. take the children away by court proceedings. They are now with their parents on parole to March 8. Here again I notice that one of the most important sources, the public school, was not consulted regarding the condition of the children, though what would have been gathered there would have been of the utmost importance either in strengthening the appeal to have the children taken away, or in indicating, as so often happens in Italian cases, that there are unrevealed sources of income and of strength (through family connections) which could be utilized. This might have required specially arranged observations on the part of the school teachers.

Societies for the protection of children from cruelty seem to consult teachers habitually—some of them to the exclusion of other equally valuable sources, and nothing that is said in this chapter as to the great value of school evidence must be interpreted as an argument for the exclusion of other points of view. The "neglect case" is one that especially attracts the teacher's attention. The child comes to school ill clad, unclean, suffering often from pediculosis, and sometimes sick. The medical inspector's reports have not been heeded at home, the parents have been sent for and interviewed with no effect. Naturally, in such cases, teachers have direct evidence to give to agents for protection from cruelty and to probation officers. They are able to see direct benefit, moreover, from their co-operation with both, for the very terms of probation require, in the case of school children who have been delinquents, a satisfactory report to the court by the probation officer of school attendance, conduct, and scholarship.

These are the marked social failures, however—failures in which the family neglects the most elementary duties to the child, or in which, through lacks within the home or outside, the child and society are brought into apparent conflict and there is obvious need of readjustment. At many earlier stages, before such neglect develops, school evidence could come in with even greater effect than it can later to prevent these sharp collisions. The early symptoms of social breakdown are quite as important as the early symptoms of bodily disease, and the teacher is in an admirable position to observe these social symptoms—in so admirable a position, indeed, that many social activities may be centered in the schools temporarily, some of them to be very soon removed again. For in the long run teachers themselves will see the importance of concentration upon their own task: they will realize that they can give better social evidence and make a better contribution to social welfare when their time is freed from a variety of social work items —such as home visiting, vocational guidance, health matters, etc.—for teaching under conditions that make a very high grade of individualized instruction possible. A public school system in a large city lists seventeen points upon which its teachers are marked for renewal of license, but unfortunately the ability to individualize their pupils is not one of the seventeen. Our case reading shows that many teachers are already eager to win the co-operation of those who know the home background intimately, because the home background will help them to do this very thing, to adapt their teaching to the needs and capabilities of each child.

I. THE SOCIAL EVIDENCE OF TEACHERS

What are some of the things that teachers who individualize their pupils can tell the social worker? What light that cannot be had elsewhere are they able to throw on social situations? And what can the social worker do with this information that will bring direct benefits into the school room? These questions are considered under the subheads of grade, scholarship, attendance, behavior, physical condition, mental condition, home care, and results of social treatment.

1. Grade. Taking the simplest thing first, grade is a matter of record, and the mere fact is one about which the individual teacher need not be troubled.[1] Some agencies seek records of grade and the other school marks as a matter of routine. This is good as

[1] Cumulative, individual record cards giving the school history of each child have been introduced into most of the progressive city school systems. The form used is one agreed upon by the United States Bureau of Education and the National Education Association in 1911. These records pass from teacher to teacher and from school to school as the pupil is promoted or transferred. They give for each child information under the following headings: Last name, first name and initial, place of birth, date of birth, vaccination, name of parent or guardian, occupation of parent or guardian, residence, school, date of admission, date of discharge, age, grade, room, regularity of attendance, health, conduct, scholarship. These records may be found in the individual class room, in the principal's office, or in the superintendent's office; hence careful inquiry should be made before assuming that they are not kept.

far as it goes, but the routine entry of a child's grade upon a social record has little significance except in relation to other facts, such as the age of the child when first entered at school, the family removals from city to city, and from one city neighborhood to another, school absences due to sickness and to other causes if any, the child's knowledge of the English language, etc. The general school standards of the community must also be known, such as the usual age for each grade and the extent to which school overcrowding, seat overcrowding, and part-time classes enter into and modify the particular condition under review. If these facts are all at hand, they can be co-ordinated and inferences of a certain value can be drawn from them without a personal interview with each teacher.

It must not be forgotten that a child gets much more out of school if he is in a grade with children of his own age. The waste of social efficiency that comes through failure to win promotions at the normal rate makes this question of school grade an important one in itself; as a symptom it is even more important, related as it is to all the items that here follow. It will be seen that most of these need the personal interpretation of the teacher or principal.

2. Scholarship. A general scholarship mark is not so significant as are marks showing relative standing in different studies, and these again are not so significant as the teacher's own observations of the child's mental reactions. Often these observations come out when the social worker asks questions based upon his own inexpert inferences from school marks.

A charity organization society was helped by three school principals in its treatment of a widow with three children, who was in receipt of a private allowance from the society. First a grammar school principal induced the society to undertake the training of the girl of eleven for the profession of teaching. She had unusual ability. Then the older boy in the family was found to be a number two student at the high school. He was taken to the principal of a mechanical high school for advice, and, after a long interview between the boy and the principal, it was decided that the boy would probably do better in commercial studies. He was taken also to the principal of the commercial high school, who confirmed this judgment. After a year's trial, it seems to have been a wise one, as the boy has done much better than in the academic course.

In more progressive communities, scholarship, grade, and attendance tests are combined with physical tests to replace age requirements in determining the time at which children shall be permitted to have their working papers. But there are other and better reasons for keeping informed about these school matters. Social workers can be too eager to get children ready for the minimum work requirement; they cannot be too eager to get them ready for life.

3. Attendance. Non-enrollment is not the chief evil, even in communities that have no compulsory attendance laws; irregular attendance is a still greater evil, and one which most cities are dealing with through special departments and special officers. In the 2,800 cases reviewed, attendance officers had been consulted 77 times as compared with 485 consultations with teachers and school principals. Educators feel that the attendance officer's task is in need of reorganization. As now interpreted his is undoubtedly a narrow specialty, and his social evidence is crippled by this fact.[1] He can testify to the condition of the home as he saw it at the time of his visits, and, if the visits are well timed, this yields something, but not very much. No such revealing observations by attendance officers have been discovered in the course of our case reading as the following from a school principal:

Visit made to school in the interest of an Italian widow's family; five children, three in one school as follows: Maria fifteen, John eleven, Angelo eight. Maria's report for September, "Deportment excellent, scholarship fair, attendance two half days excused." Principal says she is in high seventh grade and will pass into eighth in February. He looked up her grades for last year and said she must have done very well, as the teacher she had was a very strict marker. Regards her as a wonderful girl, very straightforward and competent.

John, now at the truant school, was a chronic truant, a cigarette fiend, and generally incorrigible. The former principal, whom this one succeeded nine months ago, used to let the boy stay away from school without hindrance, as he was so great a problem when there. The present principal found that John was roaming the streets and made every effort to keep him in school; would send for Maria and she and her mother would scour the streets until they found the boy. Was a boy of nomadic tendencies that must be reckoned with, so gave him permission to leave the school whenever he came to the office and asked for it. Later gave him the task of watching and entertaining the kindergarten children between 11.15 when they were dismissed and 12 o'clock when older brothers and sisters called for them. He was remarkably successful in this, but it did not solve the cigarette smoking or the truancy entirely.

[1] From one city, however, comes the testimony of a competent social case worker that the only effective case work that she could find there was being done by the attendance officers.

The principal found that an eighth grade boy in another school was leading John and a companion in all their misdoings. They used to go to the home of one of the boys and "cut high capers." . . . Boy was kind and lovable at times but had a bad temper and was vindictive when crossed. A physical examination had brought out the fact that he had rheumatism and heart trouble and the teachers were afraid to discipline him. This, with a number of other factors, contributed to the thorough spoiling of the boy. At one time a charitable lady had taken a great interest in him—gave him money to buy candy as an antidote for the cigarettes, perhaps, but dropped him later more spoiled than ever. Finally principal had sent him up for truancy in order that he might have to do without cigarettes for a while. He was in the third grade at the time. [Report on one other boy in the family follows.]

In families that are in receipt of regular allowances from an agency, public or private, it is possible for the agency to regulate school attendance by arranging with the children's teachers to furnish a written school report each week, and then making relief conditional upon a good attendance record.

4. Behavior. This should be taken to cover a good many personal characteristics not usually covered by the more formal word "deportment" or "conduct." If a girl seems to have the idea that the world is against her and shows it by repelling friendly advances from her classmates, that is a more important fact than that her deportment is "poor." We must learn to seek for the description of the child's acts, motives, desires, tendencies, instead of for the reactions of the teacher to her more or less unpleasant experiences. Sometimes it is necessary, as tactfully as possible, to push beyond the initial school statement.

A probation officer reports a boy of eleven who the teacher thought was feeble-minded but the doctors said was not. His teacher was urged to try a class in raffia work and so give the boy a chance with his hands. General statements as to this work and as to his mental work were analyzed, by close questioning, into the following: In the first hour he did fairly well; second hour, work less satisfactory; third hour, nothing. By probing still further, it was found that the boy came without any breakfast. This was not due to poverty but to carelessness and to the boy's lack of appetite. Both parents were seen about it, and, by special permission, the boy was sent home at recess for extra feeding.

Her stepmother had decided to put a girl of thirteen away, but the parish priest urged the judge not to commit the girl and appealed to the child's school principal to justify his judgment by doing her best to make a good girl of one who screamed wildly on the streets until the neighbors complained, stayed out to play with rough boys after ten at night, refused to do any work at home, etc. The girl was referred every day for two weeks to the principal's office for bad behavior in the class room, and was then referred to a home and school visitor, who had quiet talks with her in which the before-mentioned acts were discussed in detail. The visitor decided that she needed the advice of a neurologist. Consultation with one brought a diagnosis of the early stages of St. Vitus's dance. Treatment, a course of dieting, salt baths, long hours of rest, temporary withdrawal from school, country outing for two months, two more months with an aunt in the suburbs. Result, return to school in good mental and physical condition.

5. Physical Condition. A teacher who has had a few such experiences as the foregoing is tempted to suspect "the early stages of St. Vitus's dance" in all her more troublesome pupils. Social workers make equally hasty generalizations. Among the earliest of the physical disabilities to win a commanding position as an explanation of trouble in the school room were positional defects; but adenoids, eye strain, and now (among the mental difficulties) feeble-mindedness either have been or are very popular. Needless to say, the discovery of all these conditions is of the gravest importance in the right place—in the place, that is, where they really exist. The teacher must not play physician, but, like the social worker, he can help to get his pupils to the right specialist at the earliest possible moment, suspending judgment meanwhile, and keeping watch for the evidence that disproves his explanation. Medical inspection in the schools is neither thorough enough nor frequent enough at present to relieve the teachers entirely of this duty. Certain individual variations in children that are due to physical or nervous disturbance are evident, moreover, only to one who has them under observation continuously.

From a hospital social service department comes this memorandum: Diagnosis of a girl was epilepsy, and our department was asked to follow this up by inquiries at the home and the school. Teacher said, "Child has far fewer attacks when she is not noticed." This gave a clue. A period of observation in a hospital was arranged for, and the suggestion that the child had hysteria was confirmed.

6. Mental Condition. The illustration just given might very well have been placed under this heading instead of under "physical condition," but it has been allowed to stand where it is because observations of physical habits and temperamental dispositions, of aptitudes for one or another study, of variations in response to stimuli at different times of day, days of the month, seasons of the year—all these things have a direct relation to both physical and mental states.

A case worker, in commenting upon the record of a difficult girl who was later committed to an institution for the feeble-minded, calls attention to the fact that the girl received low marks in arithmetic, grammar, domestic work, and sewing, all requiring reasoning and action based upon reasoning, while in memory studies—geography, history, spelling—in deportment, which may be largely imitation, and in the mere mechanical keeping of things in place in her room, she had much higher marks. Until the psychologists can speak with more assurance, however, it would seem unwise to put great confidence in comparative marks in different subjects. The teacher's own observations concerning the child's abilities are more trustworthy.

Commenting on another history of a girl also committed later, another case worker writes, "The visits to the teachers brought nothing but generalities. Not an illustration is given, merely obscure terms, such as 'on the whole consider her bad,' 'of average ability,' etc."

Writing about the questionnaire on a Child Possibly Feeble-minded in Part III, a distinguished psychiatrist says, "In reality, the questionnaire of a Feeble-minded Child is a list of all the questions that may be asked about *any* child"; and if the questionnaire about which this comment was made had been intended as a blank to be filled out, instead of as a series of suggestions to be examined carefully by the social worker, the criticism would have been a damaging one.

At the time that the study of case records for this book was proceeding, agitation for the segregation and humane care of the feeble-minded child was just beginning to make new headway under the impetus given to it by recent eugenic studies, so that a good many illustrations are at hand of school initiative in trying to secure transfers to institutions for the feeble-minded. The records studied show that some of these children were feeble-minded and that some were not.

A probation officer was asked by a teacher to interest herself in a boy who was "certainly feeble-minded, for nothing could be done with him in the school room." Under probationary treatment, however, and with the heartiest co-operation of the teacher, the boy began to bring better and better reports. For instance, on a certain day the boy appeared at the probation office with a report of which he was particularly proud, to find only a substitute in charge. His disappointment was so obvious that his teacher was at great pains to communicate with the probation officer promptly, and to make the boy feel that both teacher and officer regarded that report as a matter of real moment.

In a case submitted for study by a child-saving agency the agency, after a period of observation in a hospital, had placed a girl of seven at board in one of the smaller towns of the state. The diagnosis was "a mild form of chorea. With proper management in a home outside will improve rapidly." Four months later, the child was reported as taking great interest in exciting the other children in school. Next month, the superintendent of schools, with the endorsement of the school physician, writes to the agency that child is mentally defective. Again, three months later, he writes more urgently, and a physician of the state institution for the feeble-minded is consulted. The girl is taken there under observation. First report, "Brighter in many ways than most of the children at the school. She seems to have no moral sense." Report after seven weeks, "I am convinced that the little girl is deficient mentally."

The choice between leaving a child who can be described as having "no moral sense" in contact with normal school children for months, and branding her as feeble-minded when there is reasonable doubt, is not an easy one to make. In cases such as the one just cited, of a child bright in some ways but abnormal, the highest available authority should be consulted promptly. The school superintendent urged that the little girl had "the attitude and the motions of many of the school for feeble-minded children," but was not more specific in his statements. He was correct in his inference, however, and school evidence will have to play an important part in the discovery and segregation of defectives.

7. Home Care. It has already been suggested that teachers are excellent witnesses as to the signs of home neglect.[1] They are equally able to give testimony as to good home nurture. This is partly due to the fact that they have a basis of comparison in the procession of classes coming under their care. It is also true that, as regards home matters, teachers belong in the group of "supplementary clues" mentioned on page 174; they are not included usually in the list of neighbors and personal references put forward in the first interview by a new client as prepared to vouch for him. Seeing things from a less acute angle, teachers are able to throw a clearer if less intense light upon the family characteristics than comes from more personal sources.

In nearly all of 100 widows-with-children records examined by the writer, the school had been visited, though only once, by investigators who were studying the administration of a public pension to mothers. Twenty of these records have been taken at random and examined with reference to this question of the new light, if any, that can be thrown on home problems by a single visit to the school. There were 52 children of school age in the 20 families. The department administering

[1] For a questionnaire regarding a Neglected Child, see Part III, p. 405.

the pensions had consulted the school previous to the special inquiry in one of the 20 cases; and in 9 of the 20 no new light on the home as a whole was had by the special investigator's school visit. In the remaining 11 the following results were obtained: In one the teacher agreed to see that there was no longer an excuse for the absence of an older sister by taking the youngest child into the school. In five the need of these enumerated readjustments was made evident: (1) change of mother's work, (2) mother must show more interest in children's condition, (3) children's breakfast must be prepared, (4) older children must be sent to school much more regularly, (5) special care needed in diet of children. In five families the home care was discovered to be especially good, and in one of these five the mother had been to the school on her own initiative to discover how the children were progressing. It will be seen that all of these items have a direct bearing upon any plans for family relief or other care. They are fairly representative of the contribution that the school can make in case work. Three-fourths of the schools visited were public and the rest parochial.

A boy whose conduct in class was excellent but whose attendance was irregular made his teacher suspicious that home conditions were not all right by often falling asleep in school. A home and school visitor was asked to look into the matter, and discovered that the boy's stepfather was sending him out early to sell papers, and punishing him severely when he failed to return with a certain amount daily. Many interviews were held with the stepfather himself, who found the visitor willing to listen to his own difficulties and to help him to more regular work, but quite determined to protect the boy. The newspaper selling was stopped, the boy sent to the country for a month, and his scholarship after his return markedly improved. The investigation as to the home's share in the boy's condition did not center around this one fact of neglect—it could not if he was to remain with his own people—and, by pushing beyond into the industrial and other factors, the home itself was very much improved.

8. Results of Social Treatment. The elements with which social work has to deal are so many and so intermingled that any tests of the results of the work itself are applied with difficulty. It is possible for our clients to fulfill one or another condition urged upon them from without, or to appear to fulfill it, without any essential change of goal. Here once again, in this matter of measuring results and testing the efficiency of case work, the co-operation of the teacher who knows his children well would be invaluable, especially to the family agencies. On such a date, at the beginning of social treatment, the children of the family exhibited, from the school point of view, such and such characteristics. After so many months of family treatment, the children, under conditions of observation that are practically identical, show what changes, if any? Not all of these changes, favorable or unfavorable, could be credited to or charged against the family agency, but the connection between its work and this group of results could be studied carefully and a reasonably accurate balance could be struck.

In so far as general inquiries and requests for special observations put any new burden whatsoever upon the teachers, we must be at great pains to see that the thorough putting through of our own task really helps theirs. In some cities there have been board of education rules requiring that all access to teachers must be by letter. In one, for a little while, the rule was promulgated, even, that no public school teacher should give any information to a social agency. The results were so disastrous in their effects upon school work that the rule was soon set aside. No teacher should be called from his class-room work to answer a question that someone else can answer just as well; when the record contains what is wanted, the record should be made to serve. No routine questions asked for the sake of filling out a face card and leading nowhere should be allowed to interrupt his busy day. But the co-operative result in which the social agency helps the school quite as much as the school the agency is the thing to aim for. Anything that influences the character of a child must concern its teachers. They are concerned with, though not directly responsible for, improvement in home conditions; they are interested in the segregation of the mentally defective; in the cure and prevention of physical and mental disease; in the reduction of irregular school attendance, improper and under-feeding, and dead-end occupations; in the abolition of premature employment; and in the prevention of that waste of unusual ability which comes from lack of longer training. It would be foolish to make teachers responsible for these reforms, but they are vitally interested in them. From the illustrations already given it is evident that social workers are interested too—are deeply interested in all of them, and have already borne no small part in the improvements achieved in these very directions. To utilize to the full this common interest is a fundamental part of the technique of consultation with School Sources.

School Sources of information are among the very best, but every source has the defects of its qualities. Teachers see home conditions from one point of view only, and, unless they have had occasion to think of human relations in disadvantaged families from other angles also, they are liable to fall into the error of thinking that any home adjustment which meets school needs, even temporarily, must be the right one.

A large institution for orphans or half-orphans finds that the testimony of teachers, though absolutely necessary, is often biased by the idea that certain statements will get the child into the institution and that certain others will keep him out. If the teacher is "sorry for his mother," or eager to get a troublesome pupil out of her classes (to give two reasons often encountered), her personal bias even leads sometimes to suppressions or misstatements of fact. A number of records submitted for study illustrate this. The misstatements are more often made on the application blank, however. When seen face to face, with an opportunity to have explained to her the real uses of the institution and the possible alternative plans, in case the application is rejected, she is usually quite frank, both in her description of the pupil's characteristics and in her explanations of her former statements.

II. METHOD

A probation officer finds that she secures definite vantage ground for a first interview with the parents of a boy or girl of school age who has been arrested, by going first to the school. She gets what she can about age, disposition, physical, mental, and moral calibre, from the child's own teacher, and also such information as the teacher has, though this is often very incomplete, about relatives and home conditions.

Needless to say, such inquiries—any inquiries in fact—must not be made in the hearing of the other children, or in such a way as to attract their attention. Sometimes school officials do not seem to realize the dangers of public questioning and public discussion of home and personal affairs—a principal will send for a child and question him, if not before his own class, then before another. This must be discouraged, of course.

It is difficult to make any suggestions about the choice between seeing principals and seeing individual teachers that could be applied to all school systems. In some cities, social workers always go to the principal first, who calls the teacher if necessary. The principal may know other children in the family, and the teacher only the one child; the principal has the record, but the individual teacher, on the other hand, has had better opportunity of observing evidences of home training, and of noting the health and personal characteristics of his pupil.

Whenever information of value has been procured from a teacher that has later been put to use with definite results, or whenever new developments or new plans might possibly be of interest to him, the opportunity should not be lost of showing how his work is related to that of the social worker. A letter written, a message sent, or a visit paid may increase co-operation later. Many failures in co-operation are directly due to the failure to knit more closely the temporary contacts and natural introductions that come through case work.

It sometimes happens that a social agency is able to justify and explain a teacher's position, where it has been misunderstood, as in the following instance:

A boy of twelve who became insane seemed to have been particularly excited over his school teacher's cruelty. The family and the family doctor (a neighborhood practitioner) were inclined to feel bitterly toward the school. The medical-social service department interested in the case made an investigation and became convinced that the boy's school treatment had been good. The department's record adds, "Letter written to family doctor explaining to him that investigation made by social service does not reveal any abuse in the school. Social service is anxious for him to understand this, as he might be influential in the neighborhood in correcting any misapprehension."

Whatever has been said here about the utilization of the educator's experience and point of view applies equally, of course, to home and school visitors, to teachers in settlements, to boys' and girls' club workers, directors of playgrounds and recreation centers, librarians of children's rooms in public or special libraries, and to Sunday school teachers. Fellow pupils must be consulted in a few child-protective tasks, and the characteristics of companions and of the gang leader (where there is one) must be taken into account in many of them.

Last of all, it should be noted that a certain lack of sympathy and understanding as between home and school has been due, in part, to the very scale upon which our educational processes have been carried on. Definite steps, also on a large scale, are being taken to overcome this, but every social worker who enters a home often and also knows the school to which its children are sent should be striving to make the home more helpful to the school.

SUMMARY OF THIS CHAPTER

1. The teacher who is the best educator, who is able to individualize his pupils and adapt his teaching to their needs and capabilities, is the best social witness.

2. The failings of teachers as social witnesses are traceable to those school conditions which make any individualization of their pupils impossible, and to their tendency to think that whatever social adjustment meets school needs, even temporarily, must be the right one.

3. The social evidence of teachers may be classified under evidence about (1) grade, (2) scholarship, (3) attendance, (4) behavior, (5) physical condition, (6) mental condition, (7) home care, (8) results of social treatment.

4. Grade means little except in relation to other facts, such as age of child when first entered at school, the family removals from city to city, school absences due to sickness, child's knowledge of the English language, etc.

5. A general scholarship mark is not so significant as are marks showing relative standing in different studies, and these again are not so significant as the teacher's own observations of the child's mental reactions.

6. Behavior covers something more than can be shown by a conduct mark. We must learn to seek for the description of the child's "acts, motives, desires, tendencies."

7. Certain individual variations in children that are due to physical or nervous disturbance are evident only to one who has them under observation continuously. Teachers are in a better position to give this evidence than anyone else, unless some members of the child's family happen to be good observers.

8. School evidence must play an important part in the discovery and segregation of defectives.

9. Teachers who have never seen the homes of their pupils are able nevertheless to give excellent witness as to the signs of good home nurture and those of home neglect.

10. As a measure of the results of social treatment in the home, a teacher's testimony taken at the beginning of treatment and at intervals later would have definite value.

11. As with medical sources, careful social reporting to School Sources by case work agencies and brief supplementary reporting on new developments later, strengthens co-operative relations.

CHAPTER XII

EMPLOYERS AND OTHER WORK SOURCES

EVERY period of the world's history is a period of transition, of course, yet the institutions with which the social worker has to deal seem to be changing at a far more rapid rate in our own day than in any other. Developments that have been continuous but hidden are now at last bearing visible fruit. In the hospital, the school, and the workshop reorganizations are in process that should soon make the doctor, the teacher, and the Employer more effective agents of social advance and better witnesses in the gathering of social evidence than they have ever been. The Employer differs from the teacher and the doctor, however, in that he is farther removed in daily habit from socialized action, and is often controlled by quite another set of motives. Even when, as sometimes happens, his motives are completely social, this fact is not easily recognized, because he is hampered by imperfect forms of industrial organization. By the earlier kinds of social work, Employers were used habitually as a favorite "reference" to vouch for clients in a general way as worthy or unworthy, industrious or lazy, sober or drunken. Like most things that we have always done, our regular practice of consulting with these industrial sources has become perfunctory. The case illustrations at hand show even less constructive planning on the industrial side than on the health and educational sides. There are probably other reasons for this than that the social agencies have been doing an old thing in an old way. Changes from small industrial plants to large ones, with the corresponding multiplication of middlemen, and the almost complete failure to individualize the laborer in most of our wholesale processes, have made it increasingly difficult to get the information that may be had about his work, and the information that may be had is less revealing.

There are signs from many quarters that the handling of labor as though it were scrap iron is soon to end, and that the workshop of the future will be supervised by trained observers, who will be far more keenly alive to mental and temperamental differences than the small Employer ever was. Our immediate business, however, is not to indulge in prophecy, but to consider, first, the scope and use of a work record; second, certain failures of Employer testimony regarded as social evidence; third, differences in the social worker's relations to former, to present, and to prospective employers; fourth, methods of approach in different types of cases; and last, miscellaneous work sources—those other than Employers.

I. USES AND SCOPE OF A WORK RECORD

1. Uses. The least constructive use of any source of information is merely to verify another source. An extreme instance would be that of the visitor who returned to a family agency with an air of satisfaction and the sole statement, "Well, I find the man *did* work for the firm that he said he worked for." Verification is necessary, but usually it should be merely the by-product of more fruitful inquiries.

The ancient Teutonic trials (which were not trials in the modern legal use of the word) were often by ordeal. If the accused performed the ordeal, he won; if he failed, he lost.[1] Comparable to this rude justice is the work test of modern charity, which soon ceases to be a test, even, and becomes a doling out of woodyard or other work tickets as a substitute for discovering the right thing to do. There is, however, a place for the test which is carefully planned to reveal capacity when it is not discoverable by other means—for investigation by experiment, as it may be called. An interested Employer, who understands the end in view, may be helpful here in creating conditions that make the test a fair one.

Beyond the formal verification of a statement or the testing of a man's willingness to do any work whatever, the reasons for studying a client's work record are many and various.

In the first place, if unemployed, that fact alone does not classify him. He may be a man who has held a permanent situation for a long time and lost it through some change in the nature or organization of the industry; he may be accustomed to discontinuous work lasting longer or shorter periods but with necessary breaks between

[1] Encyclopædia Britannica, Eleventh Edition. Article on Evidence.

the jobs; he may be a casual laborer who is chronically underemployed, who works only a few days in each week; or he may be unemployable.[1]

In the second place, industrial conditions, though we speak of them in the mass as good or bad, are, within limits, as various as the conditions of the composite group of the unemployed, and are quite as much in need of analysis if we are to replace or to advance an unemployed workman. Studies made within the last decade show how little work conditions have been standardized[2] and how various are wages and industrial environment in the same processes of the same industry. "The bearing of this on individual case treatment," writes Miss Mary Van Kleeck, in a paper addressed to charity organization workers,[3] "is obvious. Because the average wage of women in factories in our community is $6.00 a week is no reason for being content with supplementing from charitable sources a working woman's earnings of $6.00 in a cigar factory, when a

[1] For a discussion of these classes of the unemployed from the English point of view, see second volume of Minority Report of the English Poor Law Commission: The Public Organization of the Labor Market, Chapter IV, pp. 163–230.

[2] Thus, from the 1912 report of the Massachusetts Commission on Minimum Wage Boards it appears that in the candy industry one factory paid no woman or girl less than $5.00, while 69.6 per cent of its women and girl employes received $8.00 or more; in two other factories, on the other hand, 30 per cent and 47 per cent respectively of the women employes received less than $4.00 while only 7 per cent and 3 per cent were paid as much as $8.00. Not all of these factories were situated in the same community, but the contrast was nearly as great in the case of six department stores in Boston where the percentage of female employes receiving under $4.00 varied from 1 to 24 per cent, while from 13 to 58 per cent received $8.00 or more; and in the case of 13 laundries in Boston and Cambridge, in which from 0 to 29 per cent of women and girls received under $4.00 and from 0 to 45 per cent, $8.00 or over. (See pages 62, 118–119, and 160.) A similar state of affairs in the millinery trade was revealed by the New York State Factory Investigating Commission (Fourth Report, 1915, Vol. II, pp. 437–439); and the United States Bureau of Labor's Report on Conditions of Employment in the Iron and Steel Industry in the United States (1913) gives the results of a study of wages paid in the Pittsburgh district which reveals notable contrasts as between the different concerns. (Vol. III, pp. 261–267.)

Furthermore, factories in the same industry differ greatly in the extent to which the size of their working force varies from month to month. Thus in 12 Massachusetts candy factories the minimum force employed in any month varied from 22.7 per cent to 76 per cent of the maximum force. (Minimum Wage Report, p. 67.) A similar variation in 18 large retail stores in New York is revealed by the New York Factory Investigating Commission's Fourth Report (p. 607), where it appears that the minimum force employed forms anywhere from 47 to 85 per cent of the maximum force. Similar conditions prevail in the men's clothing trade, as may be seen by consulting the United States Bureau of Labor's Report on Condition of Woman and Child Wage-earners in the United States, 1911, Vol. II, pp. 174–179.

[3] One of the short, unpublished papers referred to in the Preface.

frank talk with her employer or her transfer to another factory would increase her wages." Fatalism is too common on the industrial side of social case work.

"This is a case," says a critic of a certain family record, "where the husband is working as driver for a trucking company and is only paid when there is work on hand, but has to report every day. No attempt is made to straighten out this matter by making a further investigation into the man's industrial record, to learn whether the case committee should not advise him to look for other work and possibly assist in this direction. His is just the sort of irregular work in which his tendency to drink may get the better of him, and he appears to be of good stuff, well worth rehabilitating now instead of waiting until things get worse."

The same critic says of another case, "This man has been allowed to get down to a $12 a week income, and is in an occupation which does not hold promise of advancement. I believe there should be a consultation with the former employers to learn how skilled he is, and whether at a later date he should be encouraged to make efforts to get back into his former occupation."

And of still another case he writes, "Here is a man who has been in this country for twelve years, and is said to be earning only $3.00 or $4.00 a week. That is something which requires righting. Somewhere and somehow the real life of the family and condition of the man can be revealed."

In the third place, advancement as well as reinstatement must be the aim, and for this the facts are needed. The prospective employer is more easily interested by one who has the facts of work history. Even where the Employer is indifferent to them, there is loss of influence with him and nothing but loss to the workman when we recommend the latter for a kind of work that he is incapable of keeping.

In the fourth place, the former employer is not merely a means of completing our work-history record, he is not just a source but is often a resource, and, in most interviews with him, the possibility of reinstatement must be kept in view. With the present employer, where sickness of the workman is not the trouble, but where he is failing to spend his wages on his family, the chance of persuading his Employer to "trustee" the wages or to bring influence to bear in some other way is worth considering. Thus the two purposes of social diagnosis—first to arrive at as exact a definition as possible of the difficulty, and second to assure that this definition is so procured that it can be followed by effective and co-operative action—help one another and are to be developed simultaneously.

2. Scope. Having regard to the gathering of data only, the following is a fuller outline than will be necessary in the study of any one work record. Like all the outlines in this book it is intended to be suggestive and is not a schedule to be filled out. Nor is all the information indicated to be procured from any one source —a comparison of the statements of client and of Employer will lead to correction of the inaccuracies of each.

Names and addresses of former employers.

Nature of occupation or occupations with each former employer (first the industry, then the exact process engaged in, for it is necessary to have both).

Between what dates employed.

If large concerns, worker's number, department, and foreman.

Wages earned at each place.

Worker's record at each for speed, accuracy, regularity, sobriety; relations with fellow workmen; peculiarities of habit and temper revealed.

For present occupation, the foregoing, and—

- Week's work or piece work.
- Full, seasonal, occasional, or part-time work (if seasonal, how many weeks lost in a year).
- Hours of work daily and weekly, and amount of overtime.
- Nature of the material worked in and healthfulness of the process.
- Sanitation and safety of surroundings.
- Opportunities for advancement.
- Full analysis of wages (how much when working full time, amount of fines, of overtime pay, of gratuities, commissions, or bonuses; earnings at present allowing for part time if any, etc.).
- Is there a mutual benefit society or an insurance system in connection with the establishment?
- If the employe is sick, what assistance has been given by Employers? by fellow workers?

If out of work, how long and cause of leaving last employment.

Time out of work during last twelve months.

Age at which first went to work, nature of work, nature of preparation.

For the relation of the facts suggested in this outline to the other social facts of a family history, see questionnaire on Any Family in Part III and the questionnaires that follow it on a Deserted Family, Inebriety, and a Homeless Man. Where any of these three conditions complicate the task, there are important variations in the ground to be covered.

Under a Deserted Family, for example, these questions among others: What opportunities for development did man's earliest occupations give him? Has his wife worked since marriage and if so the effect on her health, on his wage-earning, on the home, on the children? Have his children's earnings had any effect in lessening the father's sense of responsibility?

Under Inebriety the following: Has the patient met with business reverses? Does the nature of his employment expose him to temptation? Does he work long hours in extremes of temperature? Does he work under trying conditions of dust or ill ventilation? Has his wife been forced to become a wage-earner?

Under a Homeless Man: Was he ever a newsboy or messenger? First occupation, its nature and wages. Did he ever learn a trade? Longest time at any one job. What does he consider his true occupation? How long ago was his last work? If his work has usually been seasonal, how has he been accustomed to live between jobs?

II. CERTAIN FAILURES OF EMPLOYER TESTIMONY

The comparison of sources on page 166, Table 2, shows that (omitting other social agencies as a source, since these bear a different relation to diagnosis) Employers stand, in frequency of use, as follows:

	First City	Second City	Third City
Former employers	5th	7th	6th
Present employers	10th	10th	9th

This shows greater uniformity of practice than in the use of any other one source, with the possible exceptions of dispensaries and relatives. Present are not consulted so frequently as former employers. Is this due solely to the fact that, in cases of unemployment, there are no present employers, and that former employers are, case by case, more numerous? In the 2,800 cases examined, former employers were communicated with 470 times as against 232 consultations with present employers. Interviews with case workers and a study of their records reveal another reason for the difference. Former employers can be seen with far less danger of injuring a client's industrial relations and status. They are accustomed to be used as work references, and no prejudice is created by the inquiry if it is made with any discretion. The information that they are able to supply often makes communication with a present employer unnecessary, though this is not invariably the case, as will appear later.

What can be said, in general, of the social evidence value of Employer testimony? Employers' statements have greatest value in matters strictly industrial, and are too often quoted in social records as conclusive with regard to matters about which their knowledge is merely hearsay.

As to home conditions, the character of the wife, etc., the "shop" usually know what the breadwinner of the family has told them and no more. This does not mean that work references can give no evidence of value on these matters, but that the usual tests should be applied—the identity of the original informant must be known, and any signs of bias must be noted.

An Employer sometimes states the maximum earnings at full time, or names the rate at which a workman is paid, without giving (unless specifically asked) the number of hours actually worked. "The most accurate way," says Miss Sears, "is to know what his [the employe's] last pay envelope contained."[1] The only way to be absolutely sure of this, of course, is to see the envelope.

Letters of former employers about a workman addressed "to whom it may concern" are valueless; they express too often the good natured relief of one who is well rid of a burden, while a present employer is sometimes tempted to conceal the truth about a particularly useful employe. These two forms of bias are illustrated in the following instances:

A man's Employer wrote, "This is to certify that ——— has worked for me off and on for the last four years. His work has been very satisfactory, and he is a thoroughly good, all-round man, and I think you will find him very valuable." The man's foreman, when seen later, said that he was a plausible fellow who impressed everybody favorably at first, but who spent his money as fast as he got it on drink and on women. Had once said that he was married but later denied it. His Employer wrote the letter because he was "down and out," and no one wanted to give him another knock. This client had tuberculosis and needed care, but the form that the care took had to be modified by the existence of a wife and children (he had claimed to be single), and by the presence of inebriety and syphilis—conditions all brought to light in the course of inquiry.

An Italian widow with children, who claimed that their only support came from a sister of hers who worked for a tailoress for $2.00 or $3.00 a week, had her story confirmed by the sister's Employer. Later the payrolls of the shop showed that these two women and the daughter of one of them (whose whereabouts had been reported unknown) had been earning steadily from $10 to $18 a week, and that their average earnings had been between $12 and $13. Various charities and individuals had supported the family meanwhile, at the request of the charity organization society. The tailoress explained that she knew that help which was not needed was being given; but the women were so valuable to her that she could not afford to offend them.

[1] The Charity Visitor, p. 31.

III. THE CO-OPERATION OF EMPLOYERS

1. Former Employers. The former employer may be an unsatisfactory writer of letters of recommendation, but when seen in his own surroundings, where payrolls, foremen, and shop mates can be consulted, or where it is possible to refer the inquirer to one or the other of these, his evidence assumes a very different character, especially when he is not too busy to hear, in a few words, the circumstances and plans that give his own statement a definite value. By showing the relation of his testimony to constructive work that is in progress, it is often possible to interest him in the future of his old workman and in the family's future too. Sometimes the former employer becomes the prospective employer. Where there is a good chance of this, he should be seen quite late in the course of the outside inquiries, to spare him a second visit, if possible, and to make his co-operation fit in with the other plans developed by consultation.[1] The degree of interest felt and exhibited by the inquirer, and the amount of knowledge of the real situation that he shows will have a direct relation to the kind of co-operation secured.

An office for the care of the homeless and transient poor reported one of its applicants as the "raggedest creature that ever came in here." The man had only one leg, his artificial leg was broken, he last worked for a contractor as teamster, and had a record of drink. The former employer was induced to take him back and to pay $5.00 a week out of the man's wages toward $50 advanced by the agency to buy another leg. This was in May. In August the man had one lapse, was arrested for drunkenness and neglected to pay his fine. When re-arrested the Employer paid his fine and took the fellow's habits actively in hand. Three months later he was doing well, and his Employer was looking for another man to work with him—one of steady habits who would not lead him into temptation.

The former employer who has not been mentioned in a first interview, but whose name comes to light in the course of outside inquiries, is what has been called a "supplementary clue."[2] He is often a valuable witness.

It has been said that Employers and fellow workmen know little about home conditions, but the matters about which they do know are intimately related to the home, and their items of evidence have all the more value because they are circumstantial and indirect. If we know how to piece them together and weigh them as against

[1] See p. 170 on the order in which outside sources should be visited. [2] See p. 174.

other testimony, our work in the home will be better rounded. Just as the teacher who studies her pupils gives revealing evidence about home conditions and habits, though she may never have entered the home, so the Employer's facts and first-hand observations have a relation to these same things, though his inferences and opinions may be of little value.

In attempting to gauge the possibilities in the father of two boys (aged eleven and three) who was said to be neglecting them, a charity organization society received the following estimate from a naval station: Man was in the marine corps for fifteen years, was promoted to sergeantcy and in charge of a prison guard. Began to drink some, and they felt he would be better in the Philippines. While there, saved the life of his commanding officer and received commendation and a medal. On his return to this country, was again given the post of sergeant of the guard. At this time, was drinking more and more and was less reliable—mixed up in a number of scrapes. At the end of enlistment was honorably discharged. Then went into the labor department, where he held an important clerkship. Discharged for being drunk in working hours. Conduct was poor but work was excellent. Fine fellow, above the average in intelligence, and could have been advanced considerably in the service but for his drinking habits.

The same society was able to get a portion of the family background needed in planning for an Italian widow with three children from an Employer's report on the work record of her deceased husband, who was a stone mason: Not like the ordinary Italian; began with low wages but worked up to $2.75 a day. Got into debt and used to ask for extra work, so that he sometimes earned $19 or $20 a week. If the Employer wanted anyone to help him set up a gravestone always asked C, and he was ready and willing. Non-union man, no benefit society so far as known, worked at this one place until a few days before his death. Debts were contracted first, it was thought, owing to illness of little boy and of wife, who was sick a good deal. Then his brother got into trouble by buying on the installment plan, and C had to help him out.

A boy of fourteen complained to an S. P. C. C. of the treatment that he received from his father. His case was taken into court, but, under questioning by the judge, his statements were contradictory. The boy's former employer was then seen, who said the boy had lost money while working for him, and had been discharged for carrying tales about the office which were without foundation—he was very untruthful, in fact. No doubt about his neglect at home, however, as his clothes and shoes would hardly hold together, and they were obliged to fit him out themselves. The young woman stenographer, seen separately, agreed that the boy was untruthful, but added that his parents bought him no clothing whatever during the whole winter of his employment. This warning as to the boy's romancing and the confirmation of his neglected condition would both have been useful in preparing the case for its first presentation in court.

The same S. P. C. C. was dealing with a non-support case, involving four children under the age of six. The proprietor of a garage reported that he had given work to the children's father at the request of a former employer who knew and felt sorry for the family. No signs of liquor during the eight weeks that the man worked for him, but he often failed to come to work. Shiftless and lazy. Was warned that if he did not do the work properly he would be discharged. But for his carelessness might have had the work indefinitely. (This last statement had a direct bearing upon proof of non-support.)

2. Present Employers. Workers in family and in child-saving agencies agree that inquiries of the present employer are difficult and to be avoided if possible, unless the head of the establishment or its foreman is known to be one who can be interested. Complete avoidance of the risk, however, would work great hardship to innocent people.

Upon a complaint from a wife with two children that her husband drank and did not support his family, a letter of inquiry was written to the office by which the man was employed, stating the wife's grievances. This brought a request for further particulars, but soon after a second letter came stating that the man had been discharged because they could not keep anyone in their employ who drank. The discharge may have been hastened by the inquiry, and the possibility of some such action ought to make agencies very careful about sending letters to unknown Employers, though a simple request for the man's work record might have been harmless enough.

Probation officers find that they have to be very careful about seeing the Employers of their boys and girls. With some firms the mere discovery that a child has been brought into court leads to immediate discharge. There are others, however, who take more interest in a boy on probation than in one who needs no oversight. Obviously, an important part of a probation officer's equipment is a knowledge of the attitude of the factories and shops of his district toward their young people.

In non-support cases requiring court action the evidence of present employers is even more important than that of former employers, for the prosecuting agency must be able to give the man's exact earnings, the duration of his employment, the number of times that he has been absent from work, and the supposed causes of absence, as well as the occasions and amounts of wage attachments for debt. Often the man exaggerates the number and amount of these attachments.

An S. P. C. C. received a complaint that a father was leaving four children, ranging in age from four to eleven years, alone at home not only in the daytime but all night. The father's present employer was not seen before the trial, and the judge decided that the neglect was not wilful, because, when a witness testified to the fact of night absences, the father claimed that he had been away only one night, when he had changed shifts with another man. After the trial, the contradicted witness obtained a letter from the man's Employer giving thirty-six dates on which he was recorded as having done night work during the last six months.

The following are instances of co-operation with present employers whom it was possible to interest and from whom useful information was had:

A public department for the care of dependent children had as its wards two children aged eleven and nine whose mother had eloped with a man not their father, the whereabouts of the father being unknown to the guardian of the poor who committed the children. A journey the length of the state by the department's visitor brought no trace of the father, save a statement that he used to be well known in a certain town. The police station of this town reported that the man had been favorably known for years, and had formerly worked there for a barber. This barber knew the present employer's address, which happened to be in the city in which the children's department had its headquarters. Personally seen, this Employer gave the man a good name; said that he worked faithfully and well, had little initiative, and drank very occasionally. The Employer was interested in the story of the children, offered to increase the man's wages at the first opportunity and to encourage him to make a home for his children. This last the father has not done, but he has paid for their care regularly for three years.

A charity organization society was able to interest a group of present employers in a family in which the chief breadwinner had developed tuberculosis. The Employer of the man had known nothing of his illness. He undertook to move the whole family to the country and to aid in other ways. The firm employing the oldest boy gave a good report of his work and prospects. The girl's Employers increased her wages upon hearing of her father's illness, but gave reasons for thinking that she would do better at other work in the long run. The case reader who studied this record says, "Its investigation also seems to show what I miss in many others—the possibilities in the particular work, and the suggestion (where this is the case) that the employe might do another kind of work better."

Since it is a delicate matter to establish relations with present employers, necessary though their help may be in the treatment of certain cases, a good general rule is to seek their help late in our inquiry, when it must be sought at all.

3. Prospective Employers. Sometimes a prospective employer is so well known to a social agency and so interested in its work that his establishment becomes an experiment station for the testing of unknown capabilities, the training of handicapped or difficult people, and the interviewing of unemployed men whose work record can be secured better by a business man than by a social worker. Sometimes a prospective employer may know our client well already, and may have a real interest in his welfare.

But usually a prospective employer should not be seen. His interest is slight, and the one fact that he alone can bear witness to is the offer of work. Sometimes it is necessary to have this fact. If, for instance, an agency dealing with homeless or non-resident men is asked to pay the board of a number of them until they can get their first wages, the statement that work awaits them must be verified in some way, and it cannot always be verified without inquiry of the prospective employer. In such cases, the client's interests must be safeguarded; the promise of work must be confirmed without telling anything of the worker's affairs.

IV. METHOD

In addition to the analysis of a work record and the discussion of the social worker's relations to Employers, past and present, certain details of method should be mentioned, some of which apply generally and some only in accident cases, or to the work of the foreign day laborer.

1. The Approach. Addresses of Employers can be made fuller and more accurate by reference to the city directory. In choosing among a number of former employers, those for whom a client has worked the longest in recent years and the one for whom he worked the longest of all are the most important to see, though contradictory evidence may make it necessary to see all the others. Sometimes an Employer knows our client in other ways, as fellow member of some church or social organization, as an old friend of his family, etc. These relations that are outside of business should be noted.

There is need of communication with the Employer direct, instead of through the former or present worker or his family.

An Italian widow told a family agency that her daughter of seventeen was earning from $5.00 to $6.00 a week in a stocking mill, and the girl herself confirmed this. At the mill she was found to have averaged $8.50 a week for the last eight weeks.

A boy of eighteen, who was believed by his mother, a widow with a consumptive daughter, to be earning $4.00 a week, and so was paying only $3.00 into the home, was found, upon inquiry, to be earning $8.00. An interview with the boy confirmed the social worker's opinion that the mother did not know.

Often a wife does not know her husband's earnings, and her statements, made in good faith, are not accurate.

From what has already been said it is evident that personal visits to industrial establishments are far more fruitful than telephone messages or letters. An appointment, though, to see the best member of the establishment at the best hour for him should usually be secured over the telephone. Unfortunately, letters are the only means of communication in some large establishments and in some large communities. Rules forbidding personal interviews may possibly be set aside, however, by seeking the co-operation of proprietors through channels that are particularly influential with them. Perfunctory responses should not be accepted as the only ones procurable without making a determined effort to win social interest higher up. On the other hand, good service can be had through letters and telephone messages when all inquiries about work records in a large concern are handled by one person, and the agency or worker inquiring happens to have already established a good understanding with this interested source. In industrial establishments employing a social worker the fact should be known, of course, and the approach be made through him.

Get the Employer's point of view before deciding how much can safely be told of a client's affairs, though more of what he knows will be revealed, usually, after he has been told a good deal. Often a reference to the foreman is the best result that can be had from the business office of a firm. "In our dealing with a certain railroad," writes Miss Florence Hutsinpillar,[1] "we invariably get a negligible result by telephoning to the office, but never yet have we failed to get information of value when we pick our way through the yards to the shops where we can find the foreman."

Equally emphatic testimony is at hand as to the value of forewomen. One social worker believes that the forewoman of a factory has a rare opportunity to do constructive social work for girls, and cites instances of the influence of certain forewomen who are still the exception.

2. Accident Cases. In cases of accident coming under the new compensation laws, procedure must be regulated by the provisions

[1] In one of the short, unpublished papers referred to in the Preface.

of the state law. Social case work in what used to be a most unsatisfactory group of cases has been greatly facilitated by these new laws. They have not done away with the need of individual social work altogether because there are countless adjustments to be made, and social case workers who have the detailed facts and are seeking no personal advantage can be of great service, moreover, to the arbitration boards responsible for fixing standards. A group of case records brought to the attention of the writer illustrates the way in which one family case worker was able, by energetic inquiry, to challenge with success an unfair ruling of the accident insurance companies as to the average wage of longshoremen. The decision of an arbitration board in the first of these cases established a new and higher standard of compensation.

For cases not coming under a compensation law and for which no lawyer has been engaged, Miss Hutsinpillar warns the social worker to distrust his own legal knowledge. It is necessary to hear the Employer's side of the accident, but, in doing so, to compromise the employe's interests in no way, and to commit him in this first interview to no settlement. "However pressing the necessity of the family, let the need be met in some other way until the evidence is fully in hand. When the employer assures us that there is no case but says that, because we come in the name of charity, he will give the employe's widow $100, it is here that the long sight, the view into the future, is much needed." Miss Hutsinpillar recommends compromise later, however, in those cases in which, after good legal advice, it is evident that no legal claim can be established under existing laws.

3. Foreign Workmen. Occupations in the old country furnish clues to industrial aptitudes and possibilities over here. If a man has been a skilled basket maker in Italy, it is a pity to let him continue to sort rags in New York or Chicago. Often the foreign workman is known by another name arbitrarily given to him by his foreman or mates at the shop, and it is necessary to discover what this name is before he can be identified at his work place. In large concerns he has a number, and may have his number tag or metal check with him at the time of the first interview. If he speaks no English, it may be necessary to name over the leading Employers of his neighborhood in order that he may recognize his own place of employment. He may have a preference for seasonal work instead of a steady job; he may object to working in midwinter, for instance. If so, how has he made out before at dull times in his kind of work, and how are his fellow workers managing to get on?

Sailors (foreign and native) are given discharge papers from the boats on which they have served, stating, among other things, seaman's name, age, place of birth, date of entry and discharge, place of discharge, character, ability, capacity in which he served, and seamanship. The usual entries regarding character, ability, conduct, and seamanship are "G" for good and "V G" for very good; the Cunard Line uses only "G." "D R" (decline to report) is used when a record is unsatisfactory. Discharge certificates containing anything less than "V G" (or "G" from the Cunard Line) have a way of getting lost. Inability to produce a certificate may be due to another cause, however, for in the American service, especially the coastwise service, the law requiring the issuance of these certificates is very slackly enforced; in the English service it is strictly enforced.

The work record of a day laborer is more difficult, because he may work for contractors whose operations are now in one place and now in another. Every day laborer knows where he was last paid and by whom, however, and it is possible, as Miss Sears points out,[1] to get his Employer's name in this way. The Italian bank may be mentioned, in passing, as a place that is often the employment agency for Italians, and often closely related to the padrone.

In the family of an Italian day laborer which applied to a charity organization society, the woman was sickly, there were four children under twelve, the man came and went as he pleased, and seldom supported his family. Upon one of his periodic returns he claimed to have earned only $60 in six months over and above board and travelling expenses to and from a small place 628 miles away in which he had done pick and shovel work on the railroad. The local office of the railroad that employed him provided the society with the name and address of the construction department chief in the city nearest to the small place where he claimed to have worked. A night letter dispatch to the charity organization society in that city secured the interest of this construction department. The dispatch had asked length of time working, pay, cost of board, reason for leaving, whether he worked full time, and whether cold weather had interfered with his work. All of these points were covered in the answer, which showed that the man had been earning enough, over and

[1] The Charity Visitor, p. 30.

above his expenses, to have sent money home regularly, and that he left of his own accord.

V. MISCELLANEOUS WORK SOURCES

The miscellaneous work sources consulted in the three cities studied were trade unions, fellow workmen, welfare managers, store detectives, employment offices, and, in one case, the superintendent of a school for telephone operators. Store detectives appear in the records of adult probation departments only. Employment offices, as now organized, are of little value in any search for detailed knowledge of a worker's possibilities.

Unions and fellow workmen are the most important members of this miscellaneous group, though neither seems to have been used very frequently. One reason, perhaps, for the infrequency of consultations with unions is the difficulty of discovering where and when the union secretary may be seen.

In one of the cases studied, a bricklayer's union helped a child-saving agency to discover a deserting father; in another a Russian cigar maker who was incurably ill was given complete support through union sick benefits and through special subscriptions from union members; in another case, also that of a cigar maker, the man was not a union member, but was suffering from a disfiguring and progressive skin disease, and the cigar makers' union raised $60 which it turned over to a hospital social service department to be spent for him, also offering to be responsible for his funeral expenses. In this same hospital social service department was found the record of a man who had been expelled from a trade union because he had accused its officers of dishonesty. Later it came out that, at the time, he had had the morphine habit. After the hospital had practically cured him of it, his union agreed to reinstate him if the hospital doctor would state in writing that the man's inability to tell the truth had been due to the habit. This the doctor was able to do.

Fellow workmen are especially generous in cases of sickness, either the sickness of their shop mate or of one of his family. A visit to the shop of a sick breadwinner often brings out the fact that "the boys in the shop" have taken up a subscription for the man. The one who has this subscription list, as Miss Hutsinpillar notes, is a valuable source of suggestion and co-operation. He knows the sick man and has a warm personal interest in his affairs; the social worker, on the other hand, knows more than he about the medical and social resources of the community and how to use them.

In preparing the questionnaire on desertion in Part III the

writer received from Mr. C. C. Carstens, of the Massachusetts Society for the Prevention of Cruelty to Children, the important suggestion that deserters rarely cut themselves off from all communication with their former surroundings, and that this communication is often through "cronies" in their former shop or former neighborhood. Appeal to these friends is more successfully made for the children than for the wife. If she has lost her hold, the man is still eager for news of his children, and even when this interest does not bring him back, it leads him to write to mates who can send news of them.

At the beginning of this chapter it was said that the material gathered for it seemed to show less constructive relations on the part of social workers to Employers than to physicians or teachers. As case workers realize more fully the need of making their case work better by linking it with a knowledge of mass problems, and as they see that one bridge between the two is supplied, in the field of industry, by an intimate knowledge of conditions in the establishments that they themselves visit, their work will broaden. It will become more intensive and more inclusive—more intensive as they seek the precise items that show the relation of their client to the particular bad condition discovered, and more inclusive as they ask advice and co-operation from those who are studying conditions of this type. This co-operation would mean the substitution of a developing program for a static one. The use of Employers to get and record a few routine facts about wages and habits, or to secure for our clients an occasional contribution or an occasional job, is surely a static program in a field which presents infinite possibilities of usefulness in return for greater discrimination and deeper insight.[1]

[1] A critic of these pages writes, "If this point of view were in the mind of the case worker in every interview with an employer, it would mean the accumulation of exceedingly valuable information for the social agency with which the worker was associated. The information procured would be not merely a contribution to the study of mass problems, but would constitute material for constructive work in individual cases. This suggests the possibility of indexing interviews with employers in a file, referring back to the original case record entries. I hesitate to make this suggestion, since it would appear to increase the amount of clerical work, but it would surely be of value to the case worker to be able to refer quickly to former interviews held by other case workers with an employer unknown to him and to whom he may now be turning with a specific problem."

SUMMARY OF THIS CHAPTER

1. The reasons for studying a client's work record in detail are (1) the great variation possible in degrees of employment, unemployment, and employability; (2) the lack of standardization of wages and work conditions in the same processes of the same industry; (3) the possibilities of advancement for a client; (4) the possibilities of reinstatement.

2. A case worker who studies the work record of a client with the aid of the outline given in this chapter (p. 239) should interpret the facts thus secured in the light of the other facts of his client's history—facts of health, training, family background, etc. A work record has little significance in case work without this context.

3. Employers are often quoted in social records as authorities upon matters concerning which their knowledge is hearsay, such as home conditions, character of an employe's wife, etc. Other drawbacks of Employers as witnesses are that their statement of wages earned may be the maximum of possible earnings unless the hours actually worked are asked for; that their written letters of recommendation "to whom it may concern" may be valueless; and that they may sometimes be tempted to conceal the truth about a particularly useful workman.

4. Former employers can be consulted with far greater freedom than present employers, and the information that they are able to supply often (though not invariably) makes communication with the latter unnecessary. The most important former employer witnesses are those for whom a client has worked the longest in recent years.

5. In certain cases the evidence of present employers is essential. In non-support cases, for example, it is necessary to know exact earnings, duration of employment, number of times absent from work, supposed causes of absence, and number and amounts of wage attachments for debt.

6. As a rule, though there are exceptions, prospective employers should not be interviewed.

7. Personal visits to industrial establishments and interviews with foremen especially are far more fruitful than communications by letter, though some firms refuse to give information in any other way than by letter.

8. In accident cases not coming under the compensation law care is necessary to avoid compromising the employe's interests.

9. The work record of a day laborer working for contractors, especially when the laborer is foreign, presents certain difficulties, but every worker knows where he was last paid and by whom.

10. Aside from Employers, the most important work sources are trade unions and fellow workmen.

11. An intimate knowledge of work conditions in the industrial establishments visited by the case worker will make him a better diagnostician and also a better co-operator with those who seek to improve conditions of industry.

CHAPTER XIII

DOCUMENTARY SOURCES

A STUDENT of social work would find it an illuminating exercise to make a list of the numerous places in which some one or more of the facts of his own life are on record, and then examine the entries, in so far as this is possible. He would find that the most personal of these, such as the date of his birth, his standing in school, his inheritance, purchase, or transfer of certain forms of property, his marriage, his fatherhood, the deaths of those dear to him, are matters of public record; and that in many professional and business records besides—those of physicians, dentists, insurance companies, banks, and retail dealers, to name only a few—some of the most intimate facts about him are neatly indexed and filed away. In addition to the witness of these unprinted documents, he would find himself recorded, perhaps, in city and telephone directories, in professional directories and periodicals, in church year books, in the advertising and news columns of the daily papers, and in the membership lists of professional, graduate, political, benefit, and social organizations. However uneventful his life, however retiring his disposition, he would discover that he was already very much on record; he is destined to be still more so, indeed, as community life becomes more highly organized.

In the course of his inquiry, he would also find that the documents in which his name appears fall into two large classes—into documents of original entry and those that are copies or in some other way derivative from the originals. The documents of original entry would not always be accurate, perhaps, but the copies could not possibly be so unless their originals recorded the truth about him. In fact, everything that he had learned, in the course of his work, about the superiority of first-hand information would be found to be applicable in his scrutiny of these documents. He might have been in the habit of regarding himself as the best possible source of information about everything that concerned him individually. In that case, he would soon find that he was mistaken; that the record made at the time corrects not only inaccuracies but aberrations of memory. If the experiment is tried with any degree of thoroughness, he will be less afflicted thereafter by what one case worker calls "clue blindness," and will have learned to consult documents oftener in his daily work, despite a prejudice against them which is common among social workers.

This prejudice against the written word is due, probably, to the too great confidence often reposed in it by the case worker's clients, with many of whom anything that is written and signed is regarded as satisfactory proof. The "testimonials" that are proffered by clients, and the blank forms that are so cheerfully filled out by their "references," are often worthless because they have been prepared, however honestly, for the occasion and with conscious or unconscious bias. Then too, even where the document tells truthfully all that it purports to tell, and even where it is not proffered by the one most concerned but reaches the social worker in some other way, it often conveys only a small part of what is needed and of what its writer could reveal if seen face to face.

There would seem to be a distinction, then, between the documents that record in a colorless way events, dates, and places, and those that sum up more or less subjective experiences and impressions. The social worker is fortunate in that, dealing for the most part with contemporary data, he can seek the source behind the document in the many cases in which the document does not suffice, and the document itself in those many other cases in which the memory of an individual cannot be depended upon. Generally speaking, the individual's testimony is least satisfactory in regard to those matters of time, place, amount, and procedure in which accuracy is vital; and the document is least satisfactory in those matters of personal experience and human relation in which the motives and capacity of the witness, the atmosphere and spirit of his statement, are all important.

For objective matters of fact, the more impersonal our sources the better. It is foolish to listen to the conjectures and opinions of a dozen witnesses, none of them wholly disinterested, about a matter that was recorded under circumstances that precluded all thought of the point now at issue, when this colorless, disinterested, and, perhaps, accurate record is accessible. Disinterestedness and accuracy are not synonymous, of course; records are to be handled critically, as all our evidence must be; but it marks a tendency to consult the wrong sources for objective matters that the social agencies in two of the three cities studied were found to be consulting original documents in the rarest instances. Out of 1,600 case records examined in these two cities, there was found not a single instance of the consultation of a marriage record; birth records were examined 14 times (11 of these records were foreign); baptismal records, 6 times; property records, 5 times; court records, 29 times; immigration records, 6 times; passports, 3 times; and miscellaneous records, 11 times. In the other city (see analysis of sources in Appendix II, Table B) the value of records had been discovered. Out of 1,200 cases examined, the consultations of records were as follows: Marriage, 143; divorce and legal separation, 16; birth, 139; baptism, 36; property, 36; death, 28; contagious disease, 19; insurance, 15; guardianship, 7; insanity commitments, 30; court records not otherwise counted, 21; immigration records, 4; miscellaneous records, 7. An examination of a number of other cases in this same city in the course of the case reading for this book shows a firmness of texture in treatment that can be traced directly to this habit of consulting Documentary Sources. The habit should be formed wherever such records are available, and, wherever they are not, social workers should be as much interested as the bar and the medical associations in securing better public records.

It may be noted, in passing, that here also is an opportunity to relieve the overburdened case worker. The work of consulting records either in person or by correspondence can be delegated without the loss of efficiency that often results when other important parts of social diagnosis and treatment are delegated. In an agency employing a number of workers, some one of these can master the details of consulting records near by and at a distance, and can do all of this work that needs to be done.

I. PRESENT USE OF DOCUMENTS

As brought to light in our case reading, the present social work uses of documents are fairly obvious ones. They fall, roughly, under a search for facts about birth, death, marriage, divorce, whereabouts, property, immigration, and conduct. The documentary evidence of social agency records will be considered separately in Chapter XVI, Social Agencies as Sources.

1. Birth and Death Records. Reasons for discovering the exact age of a child—not merely the year and the month but the day of the month—have already been given.[1] The documents in the family's own possession that are used to establish births are family Bibles, certificates of baptism, and passports. The original records are usually those of churches made at the time of baptism, or of doctors and midwives, who are required by law, in many places, to report all births to the public department of health or, in smaller places, to the town clerk or the health officer.[2] The church register of baptisms is, in some countries, the sole source. When any question arises as to a child's age, it is always well to try to procure a transcript of the birth record.[3]

Some states have established state archives, in which the birth records of the entire state are assembled. These are not the original documents, but direct transcripts from them, subject only to the kinds of error due to copying.

An S. P. C. C. records several cases of moral danger to girls in which, before any steps could be taken or any extended inquiry made, it was necessary to consult the public records and discover whether these girls were over seventeen (as they claimed to be), or seventeen or under. Because of certain legal restrictions, a plan of treatment could be much more effectively carried out in the latter case than in the former.

A public department for the care of children notes that, in one case, where the father and mother were named John and Mary and their last name was a common one, it would have been impossible to identify the birth records of their children

[1] See p. 154.

[2] A social worker who examines applications for work certificates in a large city instructs her assistants to address inquiries about birth certificates in any American city to the registrar of births. Even where there is no official so named the letter is delivered and answered.

[3] Birth certificates in New York City cover the following items:

Name of child	Father's name	Mother's birthplace
Sex	Father's birthplace	Mother's age
Color	Father's age	Number of previous children
Date of birth	Father's occupation	How many now living in all
Place of birth; that is, street and number	Mother's name and maiden name	
	Mother's residence	

without the maiden name of the mother. Marriage records seldom can be identified without this item.

The four kinds of documentary evidence named in New York's child labor law are (1) certificates of birth,[1] (2) certificates of graduation accompanied by evidence from school that the child is fourteen years old, (3) passports or baptismal certificates, (4) "other documentary evidence" satisfactory to the board of health. Until the board is satisfied that no certificate of birth can be obtained, no other evidence is accepted.

The "other documentary evidence" that has proved acceptable to the board includes (1) the manifest sheet at the immigration station, (2) father's naturalization papers, (3) insurance policies, (4) Bible records, (5) Bar Mizvah certificates, (6) circumcision records, (7) confirmation records, (8) court records, (9) hospital records, (10) children's institution records, and (11) other social agency records.

The board finds that the record at Ellis Island is more likely to understate than overstate a child's age, because parents often seek to avoid paying fare for their children. Bible records are good if the Bible is not too new and the entries are in ink. One family Bible presented as evidence of a birth supposed to have been recorded in 1895 was found to have been published in 1904. The Bar Mizvah certificate testifies to the performance of a Jewish ceremony which usually takes place when a boy is thirteen, but may take place, if his father has died, at twelve. Circumcision records (the ceremony is usually on the eighth day after birth) are good evidence, but difficult to obtain when, as often happens, they are in the custody of elderly men unwilling to make an affidavit. Confirmation and first communion records are regarded as good evidence; so are hospital records when the treatment was given more than two years before the application for an employment certificate. Day nursery records are better than those of other social agencies, because they were made when the child was very young.

Among the kinds of documentary evidence of age that the board of health has found unsatisfactory are statements of private physicians, personal affidavits, and school records. Some parents

[1] See How to Obtain Foreign Birth Certificates, a leaflet printed by the New York Child Labor Committee.

overstate their children's ages to get them into school before they are of school age. In general, the board regards records made less than two years before the application for work certificates as likely to be untrustworthy. Where facts were recorded a number of years before the work certificate question was a pressing one, this particular incentive to misrepresentation probably was not present.

Death records present few difficulties, and are usually accepted as proof that the death actually occurred on the date recorded. Entries of death as filed at the board of health and in hospital records often give clues to other needed evidence besides proof of death.[1]

2. Marriage and Divorce Records. Marriage records vary in form and in place of custody with the marriage laws of different states. In some, a religious ceremony is the only legal one; in others, civil marriage and even common-law marriage, or public acknowledgment of the relation, constitute a legal bond. Civil records of marriage licenses and church records are the chief sources; both are better than marriage certificates. The existence of a record is not conclusive proof of the legality of a marriage. It may have been solemnized when one or the other was married already, or when one was of an age which requires the consent of parent or guardian. If the marriage took place in another state from the one in which both parties to it resided, a search for the reason sometimes reveals serious irregularities.

A young couple with two small children were under the care of a charity organization society for some months before the disappearance of the man, who had committed a felony. After his disappearance the woman acknowledged that they were

[1] New York City death certificates call for the following items:

Place of death; that is, borough and street number
Character of premises
Full name
Color or race
Single, married, or widowed
Date of birth
Age
Occupation
Birthplace
If foreign born, how long in the United States and how long in New York City
Name of father
Birthplace of father; that is, state and country
Maiden name of mother
Birthplace of mother
Former or usual residence (This is given in cases where deaths occur in hospitals or institutions and when the deaths are those of non-residents or recent residents)
Cause of death
Physician's name and address
Where was the disease contracted if not at the place of death
Place and date of burial
Undertaker's name and address

not married. A much earlier search for evidence of marriage would have saved the woman, who was apparently far better than the man, from months of abuse and humiliation.

A legal aid society bestirred itself, in one of the cases reviewed, to procure and actually obtained a separate support order for a woman from her alleged husband, who drank and neglected her. It came out later that the woman's record was even worse than the man's and that there had been no marriage.

One woman, whose affection for the man whom she called her husband seemed slight, refused to swear out a warrant for non-support. The hospital social worker interested in her affairs discovered that the pair were not married.

In one case, where a marriage record was not at first discovered, the man had been married, as the public department interested in his children found out later, under an assumed name. He had deserted from the Navy, and so wished to conceal his identity.

Proof of legal marriage is very necessary in family desertion and in separation and non-support cases. It is also a protection to children whose legitimacy is in question.

A child-saving agency had moral but not legal proof that a child was exposed to moral danger in the custody of its mother. A search for her marriage record led to her acknowledgment later that she was not married and to the commitment of the child.

In the same agency a search of both birth and marriage records established the paternity of a child and reunited its parents. The father, who had been at sea at the time of its birth and for some months before, had been told, probably with malicious intent, that it was born five months after his marriage. The public records proved that the child had been born eleven months after the marriage.

In looking up marriage records it must be borne in mind that there are various reasons for minor differences of date. The date of the public record may be that of the issuing of the license, whereas the license may have been held a good while and the date of the marriage (the date given by the client) would thus be a later one. Sometimes a marriage has taken place, but there has been tardiness in making the return to the bureau of licenses, or no return whatever has been made.

Divorce records may sometimes have to be consulted to establish the rights of children or the legality of a later union.

A case committee was asked to suggest the best thing to do for a couple living together as man and wife. There were two children—one by a former union of the woman's to a man who had left her years before, and to whom she claimed to have been married. Some of her advisers, feeling that there was real affection in the present home, offered the aid of a lawyer to obtain the annulment of the woman's marriage on the ground of her husband's long continued absence, and thus make it possible for her to marry. But the wife took no steps to this end, and later it came to light that there had been a third and earlier relation to a man who must have been married to her because he had obtained a divorce. These facts raised two questions in the minds of the committee, who decided that no suggestions as to treatment could be made until they had been answered. First, had the woman been married to the father of the older of the two children? The record had not been looked up. Second, what were the circumstances of the still earlier marriage and divorce? The record had not been examined.

3. Records Indicating Whereabouts. Frequently it is difficult to discover the present or previous whereabouts of a relative of a client, or some other interested person. Directories are the first resource in such cases, and their use is discussed in some detail on p. 265, but a number of unpublished lists and records have also been found to be useful. Besides formal records of birth, death, marriage, property, etc., which often reveal the whereabouts of someone other than the principals, illustrations are at hand of reference to voting lists, enlistment records, police precinct books, receipts of foreign drafts, and cemetery records.

The social service department of a dispensary failed to find a patient at the address given when he did not return for much needed treatment. The *voting list* of the district was consulted, and this showed his transfer to another voting district. In this second district he had not yet registered, but it was suggested at the registration office that the *ward boss* be seen. Through him the man's address was discovered.

A family case worker reports that, when the city directory fails to make an approximate address more definite, she usually consults the voting list before attempting a house to house inquiry.

Voting lists are also consulted by an S. P. C. C. to discover the whereabouts of fathers who have left their families but are believed to be in the city. This same society often consults the Army and Navy *enlistment office records* in seeking a deserter who is young enough and strong enough to have been enlisted. He often gives an assumed name at the recruiting station, but can sometimes be traced by his description and by the date of enlistment. He claims to be single, of course. In one such case, where the man had enlisted in the Navy, the society got a prompt and satisfactory reply to the following letter: "We learn from the enlistment office in this city that you enlisted August 10 after taking an oath that you were a single man and, therefore, can be arrested for perjury. You left your wife and two children under two years old without support. We learn that you will receive your first pay October 10. Now if you will write your wife saying you will send her a large portion of this money, so far as we are concerned there will be no further action taken."

A postal card from Fort Slocum written by a runaway boy to his father said nothing of enlistment but furnished a clue which was followed up by a letter to the commandant of the fort. This brought the reply that the boy had enlisted and given his age as twenty-one years and two months. His real age was seventeen.

Information about the character of a particular neighborhood or house or store can sometimes be had at the police station in that district, where the *police precinct book* may reveal police relations with the place in question. This form of inquiry has been found especially useful just before helping to move a family into new quarters.

Some large police departments have a *lost and found bureau* which consults ambulance and hospital records on request in cases of sudden disappearance.

A young Armenian was returned to Constantinople by an agency for the care of homeless men. There was some doubt as to whether he would go to his destination, but a *foreign draft* for his use in getting established there was found to have been paid and duly receipted for, which established his whereabouts.

After a factory fire in which many foreign girls lost their lives, the records of *banks* in the foreign quarter revealed the addresses of the families of some of those who had been sending money home through the banks. The records of foreign drafts at the post office were also consulted.

A social worker who has been making some eugenic studies finds *cemetery records* of value. This is research work, which has a technique different from that of case work, but the suggestion may well be used by case workers in difficult situations. Writing of a certain cemetery that keeps good records, the investigator says, "Given one name and the approximate date of death, the records show names and dates of burial of all persons buried in a certain grave or family plot. Then still other records show, for each interment, age, place of birth, occupation, cause of death, residence at time of death, name of attending undertaker. This makes vague information more definite and introduces to relatives not named."

A few illustrations of the incidental use of more formal public records as a means of revealing whereabouts follow. The first bears indirectly upon a matter that often puzzles the social worker, especially in the use of public resources, namely, upon legal residence. It often happens that a long and difficult social treatment process is suddenly checked and made of no avail by the discovery that the proposed inmate or beneficiary has no legal residence in the state in which he is living. The use of private resources is not so rigidly restricted, and the settlement laws that limit the action of public agencies in some of our states will undoubtedly become less rigid in time. Meanwhile, it is necessary to have legal residence in mind and to know how to establish it.

A state department for the care of children discovered in the course of verifying the ages of the 11 children of a certain family by means of the state registry of births, that several of them were born in a town in which their parents were not known to have lived, but in which they had had a legal residence.

In a manuscript on Investigation at a Distance, Miss Alice Higgins (Mrs. Wm. H. Lothrop) tells how the examination of a *marriage record* revealed the maiden name of an absent wife and her birthplace in a small town in another state. A letter to a clergyman there led to his advertising for her in the local newspaper. This advertisement was seen by the wife's cousin, who promptly notified her, and caused her to visit the offices of the associated charities. She was able to give information and intelligent advice in a perplexing situation.

Consultation of the *court records* in a town where a family had lived only a few weeks revealed to a charity organization society the earlier movements of the family's deserting head.

A record of death in a hospital's files brought to light the whereabouts of the only responsible relative of a deceased Italian, whose family were in distress and applying to a charity organization society. The accuracy of the return on the death record had been attested by a cousin of the man, and this cousin was able to give other needed information.

A family case worker reports that a *baptismal record* often reveals a valuable source of co-operation by giving the name and address of a child's godfather or godmother.

A child labor committee reports that *school census records*, where they are frequently amended, are useful in searching for addresses.

4. Property Records. Facts about property are far more completely on record than facts about people; the less highly organized the community the greater the disparity in value between these two kinds of record. The use of property data—of records, that is, of real estate, inheritance, insurance, bank deposits, pensions, and cemetery lots—is so well understood that it need not be dwelt upon at any length, though social workers are still too likely to take hearsay evidence and rumor with regard to property instead of having the records searched.[1] Their examination can be effected more quickly and accurately with the aid of someone in a law office who is accustomed to this work.

Mr. L. H. Levin, secretary of the Hebrew Benevolent Society in Baltimore, gives an instance of this tendency as follows:[2]

Not long ago an investigator reported that an applicant was supposed by the neighbors to own the house in which he was living, and this belief was strengthened by the fact that he had sold a house a few years previously and had moved into this one ostensibly as landlord. The applicant and his married son, who with him

[1] See footnote, p. 123.

[2] In one of the short, unpublished papers referred to in the Preface.

occupied the house, gave conflicting statements as to its ownership, and as the result of numerous conferences and parleys, the investigator reported the applicant as the probable owner, basing his judgment on the opinion of the neighborhood, reinforced by the conflicting statements of the occupants of the house. After the report was in, the matter of the ownership of the house was referred to the Legal Aid Bureau, which reported that it had belonged to the applicant, but had been sold a short time previously for a small sum above its encumbrance. If the investigator had known that the ownership of the house was a matter of record, and that the information could be ascertained in a few minutes, not only would he have saved time and trouble, but he would have been able to bring in an accurate report.

It is especially difficult to get any clue to the possession of property by members of certain foreign groups. Their standard of living is low, they are apparently destitute, and are more than willing to add to their resources by seeking help from funds that seem to them inexhaustible and to be intended for the aid of such as themselves. These people are not necessarily adventurers, but they are aliens and their sense of individual responsibility toward our country's social institutions has not yet been developed. A charity organization society in a large city furnishes the following illustrations of the concealment of property in the Italian quarter; the habit of mind referred to is, of course, not confined to Italians.

An organ-grinder with four children, oldest aged nine, complained to the society of the laziness of his wife, who refused to accompany him on his street journeys. She was found to be seven months pregnant and in wretched physical condition. Hospital care was secured at once, but the child was born prematurely and its mother died. The widower continued to apply—for relief in winter, for aid when his organ went to the factory for new records, and for the correction of his children, who were being cared for by his aged mother. The Italian-speaking agent of the society, happening to pass the family's door one day soon after relief had been given, remarked to the grandmother that she would never be able to raise vegetables in the small flower pots over which she was working. Whereupon the old lady replied that their contents would soon be transplanted to the lot that they owned. Public records showed that the man had already paid $146 on a lot upon which he still owed $89.

A woman recently widowed claimed to have received only $10 after the Italian benefit society had paid her husband's funeral expenses. Records of the court showed, however, that the mother had been appointed guardian of her eleven-year-old son's estate and had given bond in the sum of $1,000. This led to the discovery that the benefit society had paid her $200 and that there was a $1,000 insurance policy besides. The widow had been granted a mother's pension of $20 a month from public sources, but this was revoked after these matters of record came to light.

A fruit peddler was always claiming that he was too sick to work and received, accordingly, sick diet orders, clothing for the children from their schools, free day nursery care for the younger ones, etc. It was learned later that sick benefits had been paid by his Italian society at the same time. Finally a dispensary doctor (not Italian) examined him, said that he needed work, and that his trouble was nervous indigestion which would be helped by outdoor employment. Started in a fruit stand, he seemed to prosper and to have a good stock, but continued to appeal for relief. After repeated but unproved rumors that the man had $600 in bank, it was suggested to him that he sign a paper turning over his property before further relief was given to his family. This he refused to do.

Bank accounts are private records, of course, and as such cannot be consulted at will. In some states, however, public relief officials are given by law the right to obtain information from banks about the deposits of any recipient of public relief.

The pension bureau at Washington is willing to give information regarding recipients of government pensions, but not only the name and address of the soldier or sailor inquired about must be given, but the full name of the organization in which he served, with the dates of enlistment and discharge.

Property, pension, and bank account records are consulted, of course, not only to discover what clients have in the way of resources, but to find out what they are entitled to have. In a certain case where the damages awarded a workman against his employer had not been collected, the record of a transfer of property by the employer to his wife had to be looked up to learn whether the transfer had been made at about the time of the institution of the suit. This was done in order to lay the basis for a suit to set the transfer aside.

5. Immigration Records. Records at the port of entry give not only the immigrant's age and last residence, but the name and address of his nearest relative in the country from which he came and the name and complete address of any friend or relative whom he may have been going to join in this country; also a statement regarding the money in his possession on landing, and many other data less likely to prove of value to the social worker. In order to tap successfully this source of information it is important to be able to give the immigrant's full name, his nationality, the name of the steamer and line that brought him to the United States, the port of embarkation, and the exact date of arrival; though information from the records is known to have been obtained when it had been possible to furnish an approximate date only.

Neither the immigration record nor the passports and other papers in the possession of the immigrant himself are first-hand documentary evidence as to age or birthplace. The passport contains all data needed for the identification of the immigration record.

6. Records of Conduct. If the question has to be settled of placing a delinquent boy or girl on probation in his own home or elsewhere, the court records of father, mother, or older brothers and sisters have a direct bearing upon the decision. If our client has broken the law and been arrested, his previous arrests if any must be taken into account. All work for prisoners and probationers, adult and juvenile, is very much hampered, at present, by the condition of court records, especially those of the minor courts. Police records of arrests are equally unsatisfactory; the names given on the docket are often *aliases*, and other arrests may be recorded in any one or more of a dozen different places. There is need of a central registration of arrests and trials, with identifying data that will be accurate and unmistakable. Lacking this, public officials and social workers must know how to use such facilities as are now at their disposal, must know where to go or write for a copy of a court entry, must know the shortcomings and possibilities of the records of indictment, the docket entries, etc.

II. USE OF DIRECTORIES AND NEWSPAPER FILES

Before turning to the few suggestions under the head of method that are sufficiently applicable to the use of documents in different parts of the country to be given here, the consulting of printed lists of names and addresses and of the files of newspapers should receive some attention.

City directories are the most useful printed lists—not only the current directory of one's own city, but the directories of earlier years and of other cities. These may be consulted for a small charge at the local directory publication office, which keeps on its shelves the directories of all the larger cities at least. Some large manufacturing concerns have collections of directories and the current directories of other cities can often be consulted at the local board of trade.[1] Business directories are less satisfactory than telephone directories, which contain all the business concerns of any size and are revised oftener. There are also special telephone directories in which subscribers are classified by the nature of their business.

In some states year books are published that contain lists of the public officials of the state and counties, lists of city and town officers, salaries, terms of office, the membership of the legislature, its committees, the court calendars, the banks and newspapers of the state, county maps, etc. A few cities publish a civil list of all city officials and clerks, with their addresses and salaries.

There are a number of trade directories such as the one issued by the American Iron and Steel Association, Hendrick's Commercial Register of the United States for buyers and sellers, etc.

Professional directories of the clergymen of a given denomination, of the lawyers of a given city, of the physicians, of the public school teachers, etc., are valuable. Many religious denominations publish a year book for the whole country which may not only be used in getting more accurately the name of a clergyman in a distant place, but may discover there a very serviceable correspondent. A few cities publish special directories of their social agencies, public and private, and of the medical, educational, remedial, and custodial resources of the community.

The following instances illustrate both the value and the method of using directories:

A charity organization society telegraphed to a sister society a thousand miles away in the East that it had been applied to for a loan by two women who formerly lived in this eastern town at addresses unknown. Search of a city directory five years back gave an entry of removal to another state, but an earlier directory gave a city address. Inquiry in the neighborhood revealed their former church attendance, and the minister of the church was able to give a sympathetic picture of the background and characteristics of these clients.

The head master of an English school wrote to an American charity organization society to discover the whereabouts of a brother, who had left England eighteen years before and had not been heard from for fifteen years. At that time he was living in a small town in the same state as the society, but had his mail sent to a railroad office by which he was employed in the society's own city. The town

[1] The New York Public Library has a large collection of the directories of American cities, going back in some instances as far as the '60's. It also has many Canadian and English directories.

directory of nine years back in the smaller place gave the man's address at a hospital where he had served as porter, but the hospital had lost all trace of him. A clergyman in the town was appealed to, who learned that the man went to a large city in another state after he left the hospital, and had married there, maiden name of wife unknown. The charity organization society in that city was written to and asked to search marriage records and back numbers of its city directory. The marriage records revealed nothing, but the city directory did give an English family of the same name, who became interested in the search and found the missing brother after two months' delay.

On p. 196 the story is told of a homeless man, Albert Gough, who was found to have escaped from an insane asylum and whose whereabouts was revealed to his relatives sixteen years after he had last been heard from. The process of finding these relatives is what now concerns us. Gough's address sixteen years ago in another state and city was sent to the charity organization society there, with the name of a suburb in which he had also lived, and the name of the husband of his sister Martha, one Joseph Flynn, who had formerly worked for a firm of Jones on Water Street. Another sister, Alice, was the wife of Peter O'Brian. These relatives were all found in five days, and the method used was as follows:

All the names mentioned in the letter of inquiry were first carefully looked up in the confidential exchange.[1] None of the names was found there, and the inquiry was turned over to one of the society's least experienced workers with the sole suggestion that a city directory was often a case worker's best friend. After a careful search of every city directory between the years 1890 and 1910, a list was made of the Joseph Flynns, Peter and Alice O'Brians, and Albert Goughs contained in each, with their occupations and home addresses. The total entries thus listed were 56. Notwithstanding Gough's statement that he had not lived in the city for sixteen years, it seemed worth while to search the directory for his name as well Nothing was found, however, more recent than 1893, when an Albert Gough had been employed as carpenter and had boarded on Camden Street, in the neighborhood of Norton, the suburb where Gough claimed to have been. This gave some hope from the very start that his story was true.

Then came the important task of drawing the right inferences from this mass of material. The investigator put her wits to work and decided that only Flynns and O'Brians who were living in the city sixteen years ago would surely warrant a following-up, and that of these only those recorded as still living there could easily be traced. Only one Joseph Flynn clue fulfilled both these conditions. The following day, therefore, with lively expectations of at once discovering Gough's brother-in-law, the worker made a call at this one address, to find that the family had moved. She made another call at their new address, discovered with difficulty, to find that they were all out for the day. To save time, therefore, and to allow for the possibility that this Joseph Flynn might not be the one that she was seeking, she decided to work also from the other end and try to discover whether this Flynn, an upholsterer, was identical with a Flynn, a belt maker, who from 1890 to 1904 had boarded in another part of the city.

[1] See p. 303 sq.

The neighborhood proved Jewish, and children volunteered the information that "no Christians live down here." Proprietors of nearby grocery and clothing shops were also ignorant of Flynns, but at last a young woman in a bake shop was found who remembered the family very well; the father, an upholsterer, had died nine years ago, and his son, a belt maker, had moved to Duane Street. The young woman did not know whether the younger Flynn's wife was named Martha or not, but her age corresponded with the probable age of Albert Gough's sister. Duane Street corresponded with an address found in the directory for 1905, and assured the investigator that this was the same family that she had been seeking the day before. As they would not be home until the following day, she devoted a part of the afternoon to looking up a Mrs. Alice O'Brian and making sure that she was not Gough's sister. Early the next morning a visit to the first family of Flynns left her very downhearted, as, despite the fact that her name was Martha, Mrs. Flynn proved not to be the sister. Thus the clue offered by the case worker's best friend, the directory, proved elusive. There remained, however, the Jones firm on Water Street, for the letter of inquiry had mentioned this additional clue, fortunately, and it was found from an old directory that a hardware firm, Jones Brothers, had been situated there eight years ago. From an elderly clerk in a nearby book shop it was learned that one of Jones Brothers' former clerks had a little office on the top floor of the building formerly occupied by the firm. Here he was found in a little attic room. He had known the Joseph Flynn employed by Jones Brothers, thought that he was now living at Glenside, and knew that he was working for the Multiple Insurance Company. A telephone message to the insurance company brought the Flynn address at Glenside. Less than twenty-four hours later Albert Gough's sister had had her first news of him in sixteen years, during the greater part of which time he had been an inmate of a hospital for the insane in a state in which he had no friends or relatives.

"We have had occasion several times to use the year books of the various religious denominations," writes Miss M. L. Birtwell.[1] "A few years ago we were trying to help a widow with an aged mother and an obstreperous young son dependent upon her. The woman was peculiar; we did not feel that we understood her and she would give little definite information about herself. The old mother was feeble, almost in her second childhood, and much inclined to beg, so not helpful in enabling us to get at the real needs of the family. The woman had a sister, but she declared she did not know her exact name and address. She was married, she said, to a Universalist minister named Taylor, whose Christian name was a Bible name, and she lived 'somewhere in Vermont.' We telephoned a request to the Harvard Divinity Library to consult the Universalist year book. They found an Amos Taylor listed as pastor in the village of K. Mr. Taylor's wife proved to be the sister of the woman we were interested in, and by following up this clue we learned the story of the woman's life, which enabled us to deal with her with a far more sympathetic understanding than had been possible previously."

The case reading for this book brought to light no illustrations

[1] In one of the short, unpublished papers referred to in the Preface.

of the use of newspaper files and news indices to establish the date of one event by associating it with another, or to discover the notice of an accident, an arrest, an award, a death, a disappearance, or any of the thousand and one happenings that are recorded in the daily press. Such clues are now made more accessible to the case worker by N. W. Ayer and Son's annual list of all newspapers printed in the United States, by the publication of indices to some of the leading papers, and by Bowker's Index to Dates of Current Events. The latter aims to cover news in the United States which is of permanent interest and has more than a local appeal. The date given is that of the event, not of the report of the event. The index goes back to 1912 only as a separate publication. Indices to the following years and newspapers, which include their personal news, are also available: 1863–1904, New York *Times;* 1875–1906, New York *Tribune;* 1891–1902, Brooklyn *Daily Eagle;* 1903–1904, 1908–1909, Street's Pandex of the News; 1913 to date, New York *Times*.[1]

III. METHOD

"In the early days," says Thayer,[2] "they did not stick, it would seem, at showing the jury any document that bore on the case, without even thinking of how the writer knew what he said." This is the first question to ask of ourselves—How did the writer know the truth of what he says? The second is quite as important; namely, What interest, if any, had he at the time that he wrote in representing things as they were not? And the third, Was he trained to be accurate or did his lack of training render inaccuracy probable? These questions for the document in the writing, but its custody since also has a bearing upon our discussion. We may say that there is no record because we do not know how to spell the key words that would identify it, or because it has been misplaced, wrongly indexed, or not indexed at all by its custodians, or because, since it came into their custody, it has been changed or stolen. Public records have been well kept for a long time in some places, in some they have been well kept for a little while only, and in many they are still abominably kept. If

[1] The list is of indices on the shelves of the New York Public Library, omitting those that index no personal news.

[2] Preliminary Treatise on Evidence, p. 520.

a document is printed, a new element of error creeps in. It is obvious that the mere failure to discover a record after diligent search is negative proof at best and not final. The record, when found, is usually evidence, sometimes proof, but seldom a conclusive demonstration.

"There are three principles which apply to the use of records, whether public or private," says Miss Zilpha D. Smith.[1] "First, to get a general knowledge of what records are available, and, in order to determine their value, of the methods by which they were gathered. Second, to use the earliest record of a certain fact as the most trustworthy. Third, to consult the record when it will serve our purpose instead of seeking an interview, because use of a record does not stir other people to prejudice or action."

Public records in other parts of the country may be consulted through public officials. There is a charge in most states for transcripts, especially certified transcripts, and care must be taken, in writing to mayors, town clerks, clerks of court, chiefs of police, and others, to give all possible identifying information with accuracy and to offer to repay the necessary expenses of the search.[2]

A search for a record should not be limited to one spelling of names or to one date. The dictionaries used to remind us that, in order to find a word, we must know how to spell it. This is not strictly true, of course, if we are able to think of a number of spellings each of which might possibly be the right one. For foreign proper names, more especially, no small degree of ingenuity is necessary in the searching of records, because the owners of the names do not always know how to spell them, and the custodians and indexers of documents certainly do not. Then too, when an Italian barber named Cellini suddenly changes his name, under influences social or political, to Kelly, the effect upon an index is disastrous. The list of variable spellings given in Appendix III was prepared by the registration clerks of the New York Charity Organization Society from the much more extended groupings in daily use in their Social Service Exchange. Each community should work out its own list, with reference to its local needs.

[1] In one of the short, unpublished papers referred to in the Preface.

[2] The New York City Bureau of Records, which is under the Department of Health, now assures greater accuracy by issuing photographic copies of its records.

With the list given in Appendix III in his pocketbook, the agent of a child-saving agency would have been saved a second visit to the public record office in the following case:

A girl seeking separate support from her husband asked the children's society to take her case into court. As there was some doubt about her marriage, the records were searched, but without avail. A few days later a letter was received from her signed Margaret Koch. She had spelled her husband's name as Cook at the time of her visit, or so the agent had understood it. Going back again to the record office, the agent found the record of marriage under the new spelling.

A worker in an agency that has had much experience with forced marriages instructs her assistants, in their search for elusive public records, to look forward of the date given when they are looking up marriages, and back of the date given when they are examining records of births. This would not be a safe rule if the birth or marriage record of a girl who claimed to be over eighteen when she was not so old were in question; in fact, it is not a rule at all, but it contains the suggestion that we should look both before and after the date given, looking first in the direction in which the variation is most likely to have occurred.

A word of caution about translators. When a document is in a foreign language and no trustworthy translator is at hand, it may be well to seek the aid of the consular office of the country whence the document came.

In the foregoing statements about public records and where to find them, it has been impossible to give more than a generalized view, because there is no uniform record system in our 48 states. A social case worker should know what public records are available in his own city and state, should know in general their lacks in fullness, accuracy, and accessibility, and should be prepared to do his part in procuring a better system of records.

SUMMARY OF THIS CHAPTER

1. Documents both printed and unprinted may be divided into original and derivative. The derivative record, when a copy, cannot be accurate if the original is not.

2. Documentary Sources are most satisfactory in those objective matters of time, place, amount, procedure, etc., in which accuracy is vital. They are least satisfactory in those matters of personal experience and human relation in which the motives and capacity of the witness, the atmosphere and spirit of his statement, are all important.

3. Social case workers consult documents most frequently for facts about birth, death, marriage, divorce, whereabouts, property, immigration, and conduct.

4. Many documents are utilized in establishing dates of birth, such as certificates of birth, baptismal certificates, immigration records, naturalization papers, insurance policies, Bible and other religious records, court records, hospital records, children's institution records, and the records of other social agencies. Not all of these are of equal value. The record made at or near the time of birth is the most trustworthy.

5. The chief sources for proof and for date of death are the records of the board of health and of hospitals.

6. The sources for proof and for date of marriage are the records of marriage licenses and marriages (civil) and of marriage ceremonies (church). There are often minor differences of date, such as differences between the date of issuing the license, the date of the ceremony, and the date of reporting the ceremony.

7. Records of birth, death, marriage, property, etc., often reveal the whereabouts not only of members of the immediate family but of their friends and connections. Other sources for whereabouts are directories, voting lists, enlistment records, police precinct books, receipts of foreign drafts, and cemetery records.

The most useful and accessible source of all is the directories, both special and general, for current and earlier years. Boards of trade, certain large manufacturers, the publishers of directories, and a few large libraries have files of the directories of other cities. Every case worker should learn to consult directories promptly and skilfully.

8. Property data appear in records of real estate, inheritance, insurance, bank deposits, pensions, and cemetery lots.

9. Records of arrest and of trial often give important data as regards conduct.

10. The date of an event may sometimes be established by its association with another event, the date of which is matter of record. Newspaper files and an index to dates will be found useful in this connection. Back files of newspapers and their indices also bring to light notices of such personal incidents as an accident, an arrest, an award, a death, a disappearance, etc.

11. In the search for and use of documents we must consider in each case the disinterestedness of their authors and the carefulness of their custodians. How did the writer know the truth of what he wrote, and what interest had he in writing it thus and not otherwise? Then failure to find a record may be due to our or to the writer's misspelling of the key word, to wrong indexing, or to theft.

12. A search for a record should not be limited to one spelling or to one date. Lists of variable spellings, especially of foreign names (see brief example in Appendix III) will be found serviceable.

CHAPTER XIV

NEIGHBORHOOD SOURCES

WE come now to a group of sources that, measured by their value to the diagnostician, are on a lower plane than any that have yet been discussed. Neighborhood evidence is often the synonym for gossip and inaccuracy. There are situations in which the testimony of a present neighbor may be indispensable, but in social work these are the exception, and no fact could better illustrate the crudity of much of our social treatment than the discovery that, at the time that our statistics of outside sources were gathered, present neighbors were found to be more frequently consulted in one of the three cities studied than any other one source.[1] Neighborhood Sources in order of frequency of use in the three cities ranked as follows:

	First City	Second City	Third City
Present neighbors	9th	3rd	1st
Present landlords [2]	18th	4th	5th
Present local tradesmen	29th	24th	20th
Former neighbors	13th	12th	15th
Former landlords	16th	5th	16th
Former local tradesmen	33rd	36th	27th

Reference to Appendix II, Table B, shows in the first city (where no evidence was found of a general tendency to lean too heavily upon Neighborhood Sources) a good deal of diversity of use as between one agency and another having the same general purpose. One placing-out agency consulted present neighbors not once in its 50 cases, and another consulted them 27 times. On the whole, however, their use in this city seems to be largely confined to the protection of children from neglect, to the public care of children, and to adult probation. They are usually avoided by the family rehabilitation agencies and still used, apparently, by other relief administrators.

[1] Excluding social agencies as a source.

[2] Including owners, agents, and janitors.

In the sections that follow, the use of Neighborhood Sources is considered under the subheads of present neighbors, former neighbors, landlords, and other Neighborhood Sources.

I. PRESENT NEIGHBORS

The worst example of interviewing present neighbors that has come to the attention of the writer is that of a public outdoor relief agent who habitually visited neighborhood tradesmen, janitors, etc., before seeing the family, and tried, by leading questions, to draw out anything unfavorable about them that could be either suggested or uncovered. These are the methods not of the diagnostician but of the inquisitor. Such abominable practices are not confined to public outdoor relief departments, of course. Unfortunately the reaction against them, wherever they are found, easily takes the form of protest against every kind of inquiry.

The objections to present neighbors as sources of information may be stated in a word. They are likely to be biased by a desire to do a favor or to pay off a grudge. Their questioning works undue hardship, moreover, to the subject of the inquiry, exposing him to gossip and humiliation without securing any insights that could not be arrived at better in some other way. "My mere appearance at a family's door," said a probation officer, "advertises to the whole neighborhood that there is trouble in the family, and I have as little to do with the neighbors as possible." "We have to use them for court evidence," writes the head of a society for the protection of children, "but we use them as little as possible, and always try to secure other evidence in addition, realizing that their evidence is of the most prejudiced kind, either strong for the family or else harboring a grudge."

The circumstances under which we are justified in seeing present neighbors have been so well described by Miss Amelia Sears in a short paper[1] that it is given here practically in full:

The visiting of present neighbors has been compared to that last resort of the surgeon—the exploratory incision, permissible only when every other means of diagnosis is exhausted and the condition of the patient admits of no delay. Perilous situations permit of untoward measures; danger inherent in the family situation so serious as to necessitate immediate and decisive action justifies recourse to any expedient. Physical and moral danger within the family indicates one of two condi-

[1] One of the unpublished papers referred to in the Preface.

tions—mental instability or moral turpitude. Illustrative of the former we have the spectacle of an epileptic insane father of three small children. He suffers from frequent seizures and is shielded by the mother who, by her defense, blocks all efforts to have him judged insane. He is finally placed under confinement by the testimony of present neighbors.

In spite of the harshness incident to the visiting of present neighbors, it is conceivable that the process may prove beneficial to families needing legal protection. A refined German widow and her son, a mechanic of thirty, were both possessed of fixed delusions of persecution, delusions which precluded their giving information about friends or relatives. The mother, when interviewed by a physician, who had called at the visitor's request, was sufficiently cunning to conceal her mental state and send him away convinced there was no condition which justified his interference. The next step, a deliberate and systematic canvass of the neighborhood, revealed many startling facts about the couple but nothing sufficiently conclusive until a neighbor stated that a physician had been seen to enter the home some weeks before. The clue was followed up, and upon the evidence of this second physician, who was an alienist, both mother and son were placed in a state hospital for the insane.

Many as are the manifestations of mental instability which threaten family integrity, they do not present the intricacies of investigation which are offered by the various types of immorality, including licentiousness, theft, fraud, begging, begging letter writing, abuse of children other than physical, brutality, and extreme intemperance. These latter conditions not only justify but they demand recourse to any and every means that may give needed protection to children.

The investigation of such family situations, besmirched as they often are, presents exceptional difficulties; not only must the truth be discovered regarding people who are interested in evading discovery and many of whose associates are of questionable character, but also the truth must be discovered so conclusively that it is possible to provide witnesses possessing first-hand knowledge of the degraded conditions and willing to testify to the same. Often only through a united effort of the charity organization society and the court agencies is there a chance of discovering the facts and of securing evidence sufficient to safeguard the children whose welfare is involved.

For instance, the investigation of the cause of disintegration of the D family began in the court and was carried thence to the charity organization society. The original action was brought by the father, who requested that the judge of the juvenile court place his children in institutions, claiming that his wife drank heavily and failed to give them proper care. On the first hearing, Mrs. D was exonerated, the children sent home, and the father ordered to contribute weekly to their support. Mrs. D instituted the second hearing, claiming that Mr. D was disobeying the court order, whereupon Mr. D was incarcerated in the county jail for contempt of court. Interviews with the wife in the home and the husband in the jail were contradictory in the extreme, and relatives and references of both were so partisan as to make it well-nigh impossible to learn conclusively if the wife drank to excess, which seemed to be the crux of the situation. An unsophisticated drugstore clerk interviewed during a canvass of the neighborhood cleared up this whole matter by naïvely stating he was in the habit of selling liquor to the D children for their mother's use; a statement of quantities, dates, and hours at which it was sold brought, when produced in court, the first conclusive evidence to the attention of the much troubled judge.

Similarly, court officials and the charity organization society united to secure data sufficient to satisfy the judges of two courts in which various members of the C family were simultaneously arraigned. Pending the collection of evidence, Mrs. C was released from the municipal court on suspended sentence, having been charged with open and notorious adultery, and the children were paroled from the juvenile court, pending the disposition of their mother's case. The school and the landlord and various relatives were willing to give general statements; it remained, however, for the neighbors in the rear tenement on the same lot to produce the evidence of an eye witness necessary to convict the mother.

The rule of visiting present neighbors only in cases necessitating court evidence holds in relation to families in which possibly there is little viciousness, but where the abuse of the children is the result of ignorance and of low standards.

The old grandmother and the drunken uncle to whom Grace and Johnny M were paroled from the juvenile court never meant to harm the children, but still the home was unfit and a menace to the children, both of whom were subnormal. The efforts of the probation officer to secure sufficient evidence to remove the children from this home were curiously frustrated by the fact that during the last months Johnny had improved continuously and unaccountably in health, appearance, and even weight, in view of which fact it was difficult to persuade the judge that the home was entirely unfit. The explanation came when the visitor seeking evidence of carousals in the home unexpectedly found the "good neighbor" in the baker's wife, who proudly accounted for Johnny's improvement by the fact that she had fed him regularly for weeks and, of late, mightily interested in his improvement, had also been weighing him regularly.

The justification of the use of any method of investigation as harsh as this visiting of present neighbors exists only in its beneficent results to the family. If we grant that, as stated in the beginning, the use of this method is limited to such family situations as contain inherent dangers, and keep in mind the solution of the family difficulties compatible with the best and lasting interest of all concerned, it is conceivable that this conquering, this gaining the ascendancy through force—mental not brute, it is true, but still through force—may prove the only means of aiding the family.

This was written when Miss Sears was the district secretary of a charity organization society and it gives the point of view of a family rehabilitation agency. Its findings are confirmed by our case record reading in other social agencies.

The records of an S. P. C. C. show many instances of the usefulness of present neighbors in securing proof of insanity, of immorality, of the need of other guardians for children, or of their physical abuse. These records also show that neighbors are capable, out of pure spite, of lodging unjustifiable complaints against parents.

A hospital social service department finds neighbors invaluable in insanity cases. One such case was that of a woman about whose daily ways, as evidence of her insanity, it was difficult to get any information. A neighbor in the same house helped the department to procure a clear picture. Another patient came to the hospital in such an excitable state that she was probably too dangerous to leave at large. One of the hospital social workers took her home, but found no one there. A neighbor in the same tenement house gave the necessary addresses of the patient's children.

A woman who was keeping a disorderly tenement petitioned the court for a revocation of the decree that made a social worker the guardian of her thirteen-year-old daughter. The mother's petition was denied after a long hearing. She afterwards told a probation officer that the case was going her way at the trial until a neighbor testified whose apartment was immediately over hers. When seen before the trial, the woman's landlord and the police had denied that anything was wrong, though the tenant had been in jail before on the charge of keeping a disorderly house. In court, however, the police confirmed the neighbor's story.

There is great difficulty in persuading neighbors to tell in court what they know about the neglect and physical abuse of children, and often no other witnesses can be secured to testify to the specific acts of cruelty justifying removal.

A school principal complained to the S. P. C. C. that a stepmother was suspected of abusing her husband's children. One neighbor said, when seen, that the stepmother had been drinking and carousing for more than two years back. A second, a city employe, said that he could tell a horrible tale if he would, but that it was none of his business. A third had seen the small girl hard at work before 5 a. m. The city employe was summoned at the trial but did not appear, and the court returned the children to the home to see whether they would not be treated better. But how was this to be ascertained? The wife of the witness who failed to appear was seen and reported further fighting, indecent talk, and the girl's being dragged into the house by the hair of her head by the stepmother, but this informant would not go into court because she was afraid of the woman in question. Another neighbor confirmed this story, but also refused to testify. There was no difficulty in getting a number of statements that tallied in all important particulars, but there was not a court witness among them.

The same society received an anonymous complaint that the children were neglected in a certain family. Their mother said that the complaint must have come from colored neighbors with whom she had quarreled. The policeman on the beat, the visiting housekeeper of the charity organization society, and the children's teacher all believed that the charge was unfounded. The family was persuaded to move to a better neighborhood, and the charity organization society continued its visits.

Critical comments on the records of a large family agency contain the following: "Much of the information gathered from present housekeepers and janitresses is contradictory and of negative value. Often it is one-sided, and often totally misleading. The reason for using this source and statements from previous residences which are near the present one is that they are easiest to get." Consultation with such sources to the exclusion of better ones, or their frequent use at all in cases not requiring court action, marks a low degree of social skill.

II. FORMER NEIGHBORS

Under the head of former neighbors may be included the tenants at each former residence, the neighbors living nearest to these who were there at the same time as our client, the local tradesmen, and the landlords or real estate agents who rented to our client, also the housekeepers, janitresses, etc., connected with the properties. Landlords and tradesmen will be considered separately.

When removal has been only a short distance away, or when the community is a small one, some of the objections made to interviewing present neighbors apply also to seeing former ones. In neighborhoods well removed from the present residence inquiries quietly made do no harm and sometimes reveal facts of value, especially in those obscure cases in which the evidence is very contradictory or in which clues are not plentiful. The former neighbor's experience is removed from the enthusiasms and irritations of daily intercourse and has acquired a certain degree of perspective. It is still open to the objection, however, that it is liable to be the experience of one who is not a good observer. Especially important, in recording such statements, therefore, is the habit of writing beneath them an evaluation of the witness's personality. Such brief impressions must be clearly set apart as impressions only, though it is often possible to add to them the testimony of others, such as, "has a good name in the neighborhood for trustworthiness," "said by the local tradesmen to be quarrelsome," "standing in the community unusually good; regarded as a leader by his fellow-countrymen," etc.

When our list of clues includes five or six previous residences, a good principle of choice is to select those in which the client has lived the longest during the last five years. It may be necessary, should we obtain contradictory statements from these, to visit all the others.

If a family has arrived from another city and has immediately become dependent, previous residences in other places may be our only clues outside the family group at first, and out of these scant materials a plan of treatment must be devised. Where there have been many changes of both residence and neighborhood within the same city, the character of the different neighborhoods is some indication of an upward or downward trend in standard of living—often too the very time at which the stream of the family life was bent from its natural course is thus suggested.

Sometimes unfavorable rumors in present neighborhoods are disproved by a former neighborhood record. Sometimes, on the other hand, the withholding of all clues to trustworthy information is one sign among others of an anti-social purpose, and it is necessary, for the protection of innocent people whose welfare is directly involved, or even for the protection of the community in some cases, to push forward with whatever slender thread may be discoverable. Here, too, the first clue is likely to be a previous residence. Thus, we are able to utilize former neighborhoods in a number of ways that are not only different from but less hazardous than present neighborhood uses.

The matron of a children's charity reported of a certain cobbler whose family were in distress that a relative of hers, who lived in the neighborhood, heard that the man was employing three assistants and doing unusually well. At the cobbler's former residence and shop this rumor was discredited.

In a city in which the charitable work for families had recently been reorganized and an attempt made to substitute the idea of rehabilitation for the old, promiscuous dosing, a citizen asked the reorganized agency to visit a woman who had been a persistent beggar for many years, adding, in the letter containing the request, this suggestive sentence: "Our agencies have looked after her many times, but I feel that some action should be taken to change the general condition of her life, *so that neither an organization nor individuals should be called upon to make so many decisions per year in her behalf.*" Expert after fifteen years of experience with the aimless questioning of many different givers, the woman would give very little information about herself, except a long recital of misfortunes and the statement that her only child was feeble-minded. She did happen to mention one previous residence, however, and near it was found a housewife who had lived in the same place for years and knew that her former neighbor had several children, one of whom was a policeman. When the policeman was seen at his home, he told of three married brothers and sisters, and of seven uncles and aunts, some of them well-to-do. So far as could be discovered, none of these had ever been conferred with before by the agencies that had been making the "many decisions per year," nor had any evidence been brought to light before that the woman's begging was a monomania, as proved to be the case.

These supplementary clues to other sources (in the case just cited clues furnished by the former neighbor to the married children and by them to the other relatives) are among the best results of former neighborhood visits.

There is a great deal of evidence at hand, as a result of case reading, of the extreme untrustworthiness of the ordinary run of former neighborhood opinion. The following are fair examples:

"At 302 E Street landlord not at home; neighbors said family were a hard lot; man and woman drinking all the time; evicted on account of non-payment of rent. Had lived in house five years. Man had been discharged from the railroad because he ran over a child and killed it. Said he was all right except for drink, but woman was a wicked, bad creature." The evidence of the former landlord, seen later, of the former employers of the man and of the woman, and of the family doctor proved that these statements were altogether untrue.

The janitress at the former address "has lived there about five years. Knew all about the family. Says she is a beautiful lady, and that the husband gambles. 'She drank a little but nothing to hurt,' and more in the same strain." Further inquiry brought out the truth—the janitress and the subject of the investigation used to drink together, and both were untrustworthy.

"It is necessary to remember," writes Francis H. McLean, "that while others whom we consult may mislead . . . here we enter the domain of mere gossip. . . . Is it not fair to say that one ordinarily cannot expect to receive a just picture of the whole family from the angle of the old neighborhood connections, but that they may bring certain concrete elements into relief?"[1]

So much for neighborhood statements, but we must not forget that neighborhoods, both past and present, speak for themselves, that the physical condition of the house lived in[2] and its environment—the character of the shops, the streets, the local amusements, the play facilities—are all eloquent to one who brings to them an observant eye and a good basis of comparison.

III. LANDLORDS

Here as with employers and neighbors we must discriminate between present and former. The present landlord is to be avoided,

[1] In one of the short, unpublished papers referred to in the Preface.

[2] See p. 151.

usually, by any agency whose connection with a tenant, if known, would be liable to create prejudice against him. The landlord has been known, also, to take advantage of any new philanthropic interest to secure better returns from his property, and, as the relation between landlord and tenant is a business one, it had better remain undisturbed. When this statement was made to a group of social case workers, two of them protested. One of these worked in a small southern city where, in his experience, landlords were actually more lenient with their tenants when they knew that the associated charities was trying to help them. The other worker was a district secretary in the Polish section of a large city, where many of the Polish landlords reported their tenants to the district office for assistance as soon as they failed to pay their rent promptly. The first knew best a group of landlords who wished to share the social agency's burden; the second had in mind a group who wished the society to help them rather than their tenants. The divergence of view illustrates the importance of knowing local conditions and of accepting no social formula without testing it anew with reference to these conditions. A kernel of truth remained unchallenged, however; it was that the social worker must protect his client from all unnecessary annoyance, and must get the needed facts from sources that will assure this protection.

Like foremen in large industrial establishments, the agent of the property is often the right person to see, instead of the landlord. He collects the rent and so is in and out among the people. Sometimes the landlord is also a tenant and sublets. In that case he is a neighbor and is to be dealt with as such. In addition to the neighborhood causes of bias, he is likely to be influenced by an additional one in that the tenant who has paid his rent is a model citizen, and the one who has not is under grave suspicion. The landlord who is not a neighbor can show this same bias. An unfounded complaint made to a society to protect children from cruelty that a certain man's family and children were neglected came from the man's landlord at a time when the rent was unpaid.

On the other hand, there is evidence at hand that landlords, former ones more especially, can often give the one needed clue —the name and address, or information about relatives, work connections, etc.—that leads to helpful co-operation and a possible solution. In addition to this, their account books are evidence of the amount of the rent, of the way in which it was paid, and when.

In writing of janitresses or caretakers, Miss S. F. Burrows points out[1] that we cannot draw conclusions from information secured at former addresses without taking into account the type of housekeeper interviewed, the differences between the family that formerly lived there and herself in nationality and religion, and the loss to her if the tenant moved away in arrears for rent. Despite these drawbacks, Miss Burrows feels that such caretakers can give us some insight into "the attitude of the members of the household toward each other as well as toward their neighbors; the class of relatives or friends frequenting the rooms; their habits of cleanliness, temperance, and morality." She would agree with Mr. McLean, of course, in urging the most rigid analysis of all evidence from old neighborhoods.

IV. OTHER NEIGHBORHOOD SOURCES

The local tradesmen are the most important Neighborhood Sources not yet mentioned. The grocer, the druggist, and the saloon keeper are the best known of these. The grocer is preeminently a neighbor, but his account books reveal purchasing habits and food habits. The druggist's value is illustrated by Miss Sears, who is quoted on page 275. We should know the laws regulating the sale of opiates, and realize that the druggist who observes such laws strictly, especially while they are still new, is a very unpopular man in some neighborhoods.

In most foreign neighborhoods there is some one man who stands out as the representative member, the spokesman of the foreign group. His position is not an official one, though he is often interested in local politics. He is a mine of information about the family life of his compatriots, but he must know and sympathize with the inquirer's interest before he will be frank. This fellow-countryman need not always be a present or a former neighbor. In the smaller foreign groups, he is likely to know any of his own people who are living in the same city.

One very important Neighborhood Source—the social settlement—is not included in this chapter because the valuable evi-

[1] In one of the short, unpublished papers referred to in the Preface.

dence that it can give about the neighborhood background and other important matters is considered under Social Agencies as Sources.

SUMMARY OF THIS CHAPTER

1. A tendency to lean heavily upon evidence from Neighborhood Sources marks a low degree of diagnostic skill.

2. Present neighbors are often biased witnesses, because they wish to do a favor or to pay off a grudge. In questioning them there is also risk of humiliating a client.

3. Certain difficulties cannot be solved without the evidence of present neighbors, however. These situations usually center around the need of legal protection or of physical protection for someone whose welfare is seriously endangered.

4. It is possible to utilize former neighbors in a number of ways that are less hazardous than are consultations with present neighbors, especially in cases in which other evidence is contradictory or in which clues are not plentiful. In the latter case a former neighborhood will often supply a supplementary clue.

5. The evidence of neighbors aside, neighborhoods speak for themselves, and their physical, moral, and social characteristics—those of the house lived in, of the shops, the streets, the local amusements, the play facilities—should all be noted.

6. Present landlords should be avoided usually by representatives of any agency whose connection with a tenant, if known, would be liable to create a prejudice against him.

7. The local tradesmen—the grocer, the druggist, the saloon keeper—are Neighborhood Sources.

8. In foreign neighborhoods there is often some one man whose co-operation is valuable because he stands out as the group leader, as the natural spokesman and representative of his compatriots.

CHAPTER XV

MISCELLANEOUS SOURCES

THIS review of outside sources of information and their uses is nearing its conclusion. One of the most important sources of all is the social agencies themselves, but treatment of this source has been reserved for the next chapter for reasons there explained. The other sources to which no attention has yet been given fall into three groups: (1) public departments not directly engaged in social work, (2) business sources other than employers and neighborhood tradesmen, (3) fraternal orders. None of these requires very extended notice.

It was hoped that even a limited inquiry into the outside sources now being used by social agencies would discover some useful ones which were still quite generally neglected. As a matter of fact, a number of these have been unearthed. Every new source evaluated and held in reserve for the right occasion enriches social case work and gives it greater flexibility. There is crudity everywhere in the processes of an art so new, but the only discouraging case work practice is that which settles back into a certain routine, a certain round of things invariably done, without any fresh thought or spirit of adventure. By comparison with the efforts of those who are less experienced, such routine work may seem, on first examination, fairly good, but there is a blight upon it; closer scrutiny shows that no experiments are being tried, no established method is being revised or discarded. Work not half so good may contain far more promise, therefore, if it bears marks of dissatisfaction with the tool and its manipulation.

One of these marks is the habit of seeking unusual sources of knowledge and co-operation. Without imagination we do not find even the obvious source that has been overlooked. Like Mr. Deland's advertiser of carpets,[1] who realized that families were

[1] Deland, Lorin F.: Imagination in Business, p. 43. New York, Harper and Brothers, 1909.

more likely to buy floor coverings when they moved to another house and then, after repeated experiments in wrong directions, discovered that the one man who always knew when people were going to move was the moving van proprietor, we must be able to think of familiar things in a fresh and unfamiliar way. The unusual sources mentioned in this chapter under business sources are mentioned not so much for their value in themselves as for the process by which they were brought to light. The same enterprise that, in the agencies studied, discovered and used these will discover and use others.

I. PUBLIC OFFICIALS

Educational and health authorities have been discussed in earlier chapters,[1] and public charitable and correctional agencies and institutions are more appropriately considered under social agencies than under miscellaneous public agencies.

1. Police. From one point of view the police seem an important neighborhood source, so identified are they with the neighborhood life. Nor are they infrequently consulted. In two of the three cities studied, they rank seventeenth and eighteenth respectively and in one even third in frequency of use.

The idea has often been advanced that the police forces of our cities should be made up of men with the point of view and the training of social workers. Boies in 1893 was probably the first one to take this view,[2] but even a quarter of a century later the actual situation hardly justifies the classification of police departments under social agencies, though advances in that direction have been made, notably in New York City, under the administration of Police Commissioner Woods. A probation officer some of whose case histories were studied for this book declares that the policeman is a too much neglected factor in social endeavor, that he knows the families on his beat thoroughly, and is very sensitive to the critical attitude taken toward him by some social workers; after his personal friendship is won, there is nothing that he will not do. True enough, but the attitude thus described

[1] See Chapters XI, Schools as Sources, and X, Medical Sources.

[2] Boies, Henry M.: Prisoners and Paupers, p. 241. New York, G. P. Putnam's Sons, 1893.

is not the professional but the neighborhood state of mind. It is only in the capacity of social witness, of course, that the policeman is here considered, and even so the country as a whole, not any one of its cities, is in mind. Often the policeman holds so many relations, political and other, to the people who live on his beat that he is not willing to tell what he knows when the telling would have great social value and would be in no wise subversive of discipline; nor is he always willing to discover the things which it is his special task to discover.

A worker in a child-protective agency suggests that, in cases where such personal and political complications are likely to interfere with the patrolman's usefulness, it is often better to seek information through the sergeant of police. He is in line for promotion, is anxious for court work for that reason, and, though still closely in touch with his district, is no longer so dependent upon the good will of its people. The individual policeman has been known to withhold testimony against a family whose children were neglected, for the reason that he was indebted to them for a useful tip or for some other favor. Moreover, the statements of those members of the force that are known by the judge to be untrustworthy are likely to be discounted in court.

After these drawbacks are given due weight, it is still not only necessary to consult patrolmen in a good many instances, but perfectly possible, often, to establish an understanding with them which will win very valuable co-operation.

Usually three men patrol each beat, one in the daytime and two who alternate at night. There is no record system. What each one knows is known to him only, so that, where it is important to cover the whole ground, each one of the three must be seen. It is necessary to know the hours at which patrolmen and different special officers can be found at the police station. The night officers are particularly useful in child neglect cases, as the disorderly conduct that will be accepted as proof of neglect often takes place at night.

In the search for runaway boys and mentally disturbed adults who have disappeared, it is necessary to communicate with the police both in town and elsewhere. The chief of police in smaller places is consulted a great deal by social workers at a distance, who seek from him information as to the standing of former and present residents, as to records of arrest, etc. If it is possible to judge by case record reading, the police departments in these communities are giving a better grade of social service than in the large cities. They deal with many problems that are divided among the varied agencies of the large place, and this fact alone develops in them a degree of social experience.

2. Other Officials. The list of Miscellaneous Sources actually used in the 2,800 cases reviewed shows occasional consultations, though these are by no means frequent, with the following state and city departments or officials: *State,* employment bureau, department of labor, controller, board of insanity, penal commissioner. *City,* district attorney, city solicitor, assessor, treasurer, sheriff, street inspector, store inspector, superintendent of newsboys, town clerk, chairman of the board of supervisors.

Courts are not included here because, often, they have probation officers and other social workers associated with them and are consulted as social agencies. More often still their official records are the real source, and these are considered under Documentary Sources. When it is necessary to consult an official of the court it will usually be found that the clerk remembers the case in question better than the judge. In like manner, the *town clerk* in small communities, or the official whose duties correspond to those of the town clerk, is the one who knows most about his fellow citizens. The *town librarian* is another possible source of community information, though he does not appear in the statistics gathered.

Social workers must remember that most of these city officials are desk men and take a desk point of view. The impressions that they get, aside from the documentary evidence that passes through their hands, are the impressions not of those who work in the open but of those who hear only the client's stories usually, and who accept or reject these without the analysis or the readjustment of view that follows naturally upon frequent home and neighborhood visiting. Whereas the policeman is too much exposed to neighborhood influences these others are not enough so. It is often the social worker's task to explain to them the modifying circumstances of an individual case as the facts come to light. Only in personal interviews, where the desk man has the opportunity to explain his own point of view at length, can he be induced to modify it. Again, the official who is already interested in a personal problem is antagonized by letters and telephone messages, unless he has had enough experience with social work processes to understand their details without careful preliminary explanations, which are given much better face to face.

The federal officials most often consulted are those in the bureau of immigration, postmasters,[1] United States consuls,[2] and officials of the War and Navy Departments.

Foreign consuls appeared frequently in the case records read for this volume. Here are a few of the matters about which they were consulted:[3]

A German consul in an American city was appealed to about a young German officer who claimed that he had been obliged to leave the army because the death of a relative had reduced his income. He asked to be sent to New York, where he was sure that he could get work with the Hamburg-American Line. The consul was able to throw some light on the young man's finances and on his chances of getting work in New York.

An Austrian consul knew the region from which a miner, blinded through his own carelessness, had originally come. There was no provision for the blind there and the man had no family. The consul's first-hand knowledge of this Austrian province determined a hospital social service department against deportation and in favor of training for work in this country.

A Greek consul in one of our states undertook to get information in another about the mother of a Greek girl who had run away from home because, as she claimed, her mother had abused her. The consul, after inquiry by letter, gave the woman a very good name, but a social worker, sent to the mother's own community later, discovered that the girl's charges were more than justified.

A Greek consul helped a widow whose children were still in Greece, first by paying her board while she received special treatment to recover the use of her arm; second by asking his own sister in Athens to secure certain information about the children.

II. CERTAIN BUSINESS SOURCES

Employers and neighborhood tradesmen[4] by no means exhaust the list of business sources that may be used in social diagnosis.

[1] See p. 336. [2] See p. 326.

[3] These were all consultations before August, 1914. The European war may have modified the method of approach and the service procured in some instances.

[4] See Chapters XII, Employers and Other Work Sources, and XIV, Neighborhood Sources.

A firm with whom our client has had business dealings in the past, or someone who is an authority on the fluctuations of a certain market, or on a certain industrial process may be an invaluable witness.

Sometimes it happens that the business dealings may have been of the most casual kind—the moving of furniture, its storage, its purchase on the installment plan, the collection of an insurance premium, the delivery of an express package—but the details of the transaction may reveal some bit of evidence that is all the more valuable because it is circumstantial and not originally related to the matter at issue.

A charity organization society was helping the drinking wife of a workman employed in another city. The wife was on probation, and the husband was sending money to the society for the support of his family. Two *insurance agents* who called to collect weekly premiums at the woman's home were able to give clues that aided later in the protection of the children. The relation of such agents with the homes that they visit is, of course, only a business one; these men were not willing to have the information obtained from them used as evidence in court. It was treated as strictly confidential.

A girl who came to a dispensary was so dangerously ill that she was transferred to the city hospital. The medical diagnosis was obscure, and the only social information was her address. This was a lodging house to which she had recently come; the landlady knew nothing but the name of the *expressman* who had brought the girl's trunk. From him was procured an earlier address and from that previous residence a pertinent history.

A summons for the father of six neglected children could not be served because the family had moved, present residence unknown. The former landlady was able to give the license number of the *moving van* that took their goods, however, and through the police this number was traced to a local firm. They kept no record when a family paid for the moving in advance, as this family had, but they obtained the address from the driver of the team.

A charity organization society over 1,100 miles away wrote to an S. P. C. C. in the interest of a child whose mother had deserted her home in the society's city, had taken her little boy with her, and was living with a man not her husband. A neighbor known to the S. P. C. C. was asked by them to take the number of the moving van, if this couple moved away. As a matter of fact, however, they were found in another city through the records of a *sewing machine company* from which they had made an installment purchase. The father of the boy was sent to this third city and there secured the legal custody of his child.

An Italian family, upon its first application to a relief agency, often claims to have no relatives whatever. Where there has been a death in the family, the *undertaker* often knows the name of the male relative that managed the funeral.

One visit to an undertaker in a large city brought an unexpected piece of information. A middle-aged man with a young wife and one small child had applied to a charity organization society for relief and help in getting work. As the background of his story was very scant, a memorandum was made of the name of the undertaker, in a neighborhood five miles away, who had "buried" his first wife. This information had been volunteered, not sought. The undertaker knew all about the first wife; she was a neighbor of his, still living and in excellent health. There had been no divorce, her husband had simply disappeared one day, but she had no desire to see again the man whom she had formerly had to support.

A somewhat unusual use of a business source of information is the following: A hospital social service department was interested in an alcoholic case, a woman whose only near relative was a daughter. The mother was unable to give this daughter's address, as was also a cousin who was visited. The latter knew, however, that she was engaged to marry a professional baseball player whose name he was able to give. The *sporting editor* of a daily paper supplied an address at which the player was found.

III. FRATERNAL ORDERS

Benefit societies of the insurance type often have to be consulted. They belong halfway between references of a business and those of a social nature. The fraternal feature is more marked in the foreign benefit orders, for in these the ties of a common past are more binding. A point worth remembering is that the one who proposed our client for membership in the order is usually a person well acquainted with him and with his family.

Of the fraternal societies, not of the insurance type, the oldest and the one that appeared most often in the case records studied was the Masons. This society's relations to social workers may well stand for those of the whole group of sources to which it belongs. Membership in the Masonic fraternity, even if a generation or more back, is a fact worth knowing, as the society interests itself in the descendants of members who died in good standing. In some of the cases studied, members not in good standing were helped generously, if not by their own home lodge, then by one in the city of temporary residence. This generosity is so generally known that it has been imposed upon in the past, and the society has found it necessary to establish a "black list" of those who are making fraudulent claims of membership and are begging from city to city. The best approach for information with regard to a client who is a Mason is by letter to the master of the particular lodge of which he is or has been a member. If this is not known, a letter to the grand secretary for the state will usually bring the name of the master of the particular lodge and its address. Inquiry of the client's lodge should include a definite statement as to the reasons for asking information, give the possibilities of his case so far as known, and ask for advice. Non-resident Masons in need of assistance are usually cared for by a local Masonic relief association; the order is not a relief body, however, but a fraternal one.

A hospital social service department was interested in a man whose arm had been disabled by a fall. A Masonic lodge in another city sent assistance, but explained (through the local Masonic relief association) that the recipient had often been dependent before the accident. As his arm got better, he showed little inclination to find work for himself, and the relative and the Masonic lodge that had been helping both agreed to give their aid through an agency for homeless men which tried to stimulate his powers of self-help.

SUMMARY OF THIS CHAPTER

1. The unusual source newly discovered and evaluated and then held in reserve for the right occasion is one test of diagnostic skill. It is a better test than the attainment of a certain minimum (even of a fairly high minimum) of ground invariably covered in every case.

2. The policeman's strong points as a source of information are his intimate knowledge of neighborhood standards and his first-hand witness of the goings and comings within the neighborhood. His weak points are his political and other relations to the people, which tend to make him as unsatisfactory as any strictly neighborhood source.

3. If the policeman is too much exposed to neighborhood influences, many public officials, who are desk men, are not enough so. As a means of arriving at a common understanding, personal interviews with them, in which their exclusively desk point of view can be supplemented, are far better than letters.

4. Among the business sources cited in this chapter are some implying relatively slight contacts, such as insurance collecting, the moving of furniture or trunks, the sale of a sewing machine, etc. These are mentioned, not because they are frequently of value, but because they illustrate the process by which an item of circumstantial evidence may be so used as to uncover important data.

5. Benefit societies of the insurance type have more marked fraternal features in the foreign groups. The one who proposed a given person for membership in such an order is frequently well acquainted with him and with his family.

CHAPTER XVI

SOCIAL AGENCIES AS SOURCES

WITH some of us the team sense, which is the psychological basis of co-operation in social work, never extends beyond a rather mechanical and listless "belonging"; with others it develops and attunes every faculty. The team, according to Joseph Lee, "is created by assuming that it exists and acting boldly out from that assumption. It grows as its members have power to imagine it and faith to maintain, and act upon, the reality of that which they have imagined."[1] All co-operation is primarily an act of faith. It implies vision, trust, and a common goal.

Though this theme is an inspiring one, which invites digression, its consideration here must be confined to its relation to social diagnosis.

The writer was at one time chairman of an informal committee of charity organization workers which attempted to give advice by correspondence to colleagues in widely scattered communities. One such fellow worker, who had just become executive secretary of a society long established but with a none too prosperous past, wrote for suggestions about co-operation and added, "The investigations made by this society are very good indeed, but there is no co-operation whatever among the social agencies of the community." As gently as possible, an attempt was made to discover the diagnostic habits of this organization, which had so completely failed to establish relations with its social environment. Inquiries were fruitless. The reply came back that their investigations were "all right," and that what was wanted was light on an entirely different subject.

Case work co-operation of some sort is possible, perhaps, with-

[1] Lee, Joseph: Play in Education, p. 339. New York, The Macmillan Co., 1915.

out intelligent diagnosis, and a very poor sort of diagnosis is possible without the co-operation of case workers in other social agencies, but, wherever the processes of co-operation and of investigation have progressed far enough to have genuine social betterment for their aim, they might almost be described as one piece of goods. In its relations with client, client's family, and outside sources, diagnosis with a social aim is a fine exercise in working together. Gross is quoted at the beginning of this book as saying, "The trained man understands how little the mind of an individual can grasp, and how many must co-operate in order to explain the very simplest things." Working together in order to understand and achieve is always a more fruitful process than co-operating in order to co-operate.

There seem to have been in this country four stages of development from competition to co-operation in social work. Needless to add, all four of these stages exist today—just as the phrenologists still exist (and prosper apparently) in the very communities that have given to the world some of the important discoveries of experimental psychology.

(1) The first or competitive stage was chaos. Some of the charitable conditions of that earlier time actually created a demand for child inmates among certain groups of institutions, and stout objection to any reform that "cut down their figures" extended to many charities besides those for children. The absence of common understandings, of any unwritten code governing the behavior of social practitioners to one another, was another ugly characteristic of this competitive period in social case work.

(2) The earliest approaches to social co-operation were like the earliest approaches to social diagnosis—they were made *in vacuo*. The competitive period was succeeded by a series of extremely awkward attempts—most of them unrelated—to replace competition by co-operation. As a result of this awkwardness, the latter word came to have some unpleasant associations. Miss Birtwell has noted[1] that at this stage our facts were gathered together, then our plans were made, and later the investigating agency appealed for co-operation "wherever there was promise of support for those particular plans. We took to heart," she adds, "the mild

[1] In one of the short, unpublished papers referred to in the Preface.

reproach of a Catholic priest, who once said to one of our young workers: 'You make your investigation and form your plans, and then assign me a part in them; but I want to come in at the very beginning, where my people are concerned.'" The method thus complained of was characteristic of the period of co-operation *in vacuo.*

(3) Further attempts to conquer chaos were by a routine division of cases on the basis of territory, of nature of need, etc. Here belong also the beginnings of any systematic interchange of information through registration bureaus, confidential exchanges, or social service exchanges, as they have been called at various times and in various places.[1] These emphasized the avoidance of duplication, at first, but now regard elimination of waste as a by-product of more constructive gains. Some of the agreements and reforms of this period have led to excellent results, and co-operative development would have been impossible without them, but traces of their inauguration as found in the case records of organizations that made the mistake of leaning too heavily upon the new devices suggest that all such arrangements have their dangers. Through unimaginative or selfish use, they may develop the characteristics of those agreements in the business world which ignore the interests of the consumer—with us the client. The social diagnostician must, of course, consider his relations with his client as of even greater importance than his relations with the social agencies of his community. To accept every statement of a social agency at its face value, to regard every professional opinion as equal in specific gravity to every other, may be a convenience when the confidential exchange first becomes available; this acquiescence may save trouble to the consultant and to the agency consulted, but the assumption can do the social case worker's clients grave injustice nevertheless.

Just after "joint traffic agreements" among social agencies have become popular in a community, one may expect to find in its case records the conclusions of co-operating agencies accepted without any of the data upon which they are based, may expect to see recorded many duplicate descriptions of the present situation of clients, and may observe the gossip and guesses of workers with

[1] Described p. 303 sq.

differing standards promoted to the dignity of "an investigation." All of this is part of the price of progress, probably, but no time should be lost in progressing beyond it. It is distressing to find unfavorable data overemphasized. Perhaps records of arrest and imprisonment were not open to the social agencies previously; when they became accessible through the exchange it was easy at first to put too much emphasis upon the mere fact of a previous arrest, without seeking the details that would have explained its possibly accidental nature. Or perhaps a previous application for relief had come to light automatically under a new plan of interchange between agencies, though the client had denied having made any previous application for help. Is he a fraud? Not necessarily. Many harmless men and women might be given a bad name in this fashion, or, to take the opposite possibility, a client's record might bristle with respectable social authorities and endorsers, yet contain few facts and fewer insights. What is needed—and this need, be it remembered, cannot be well met without complete interchange of information among agencies—is a sense of the main drift of a client's life, a summing up at some one stage, preferably an early one in each case, of the assets and liabilities in character and environment with which social agencies have to deal if they would win their way to a helpful result. Variations in points of view, provided that each is based upon a real experience, help us to think. We are most helped, in fact, by the experience of the agency least like our own, but the right of each to compare its experience with other experiences and to reason about it should not be abrogated. When it is, we encounter the chief danger of the period of joint traffic agreements.

(4) These frankly stated drawbacks are no argument, however, for a return to chaos. They urge us, rather, to push on toward the logical next step in co-operation—toward the kind of honestly evaluated sharing, toward the increased social responsibility, which not only avoids mischievous interference with the client's best interests, but can be of inestimable value in furthering them.

Devices have their place in such a development; understandings of a formal sort have their place. At one stage it may be necessary to have a more or less arbitrary division of work. For example, it may be wise to have an agreement between the charity organization society and the visiting nurse association that the nurses will turn "family problems" over to the family agency, and that the family agency will turn over all "health matters" to the nursing agency. It is illogical to assume that there is any clear line of demarcation between these two things, but some such division may be a working necessity.

A truer co-operation will soon cut a gateway in the fence thus put up, however, and will be sure to find in addition a section of ground which must be occupied in common, if the best work is to be done. When this more highly developed stage in working together is reached, the understandings growing out of it will defy statement in a bald formula.[1]

Co-operation based on responsibility for the result of our social acts, co-operation advanced by sound and thorough professional training, fostered by good will, by social zeal, and by unhampered freedom of discovery, leads us away from "understandings" and into a daily deepening understanding. This latter is a matter of the spirit. Freedom to learn, to grow, and to serve is fostered by co-operation of the spirit. This is the fourth and highest period of social co-operation, for which the other periods are only preparatory.

I. TWO DISTINCT FUNCTIONS OF SOCIAL AGENCY TESTIMONY

Returning to the statistics of outside sources once more and for the last time, we find that, even when the medical, social, and school sources considered in other chapters are excluded from our total of social agencies, there remains a larger number of consultations with this latter group than with any other. Relatives (next in order of frequency) were consulted 1,187 times, whereas public and private

[1] My apple trees will never get across
And eat the cones under his pines, I tell him.
He only says, "Good fences make good neighbors."
Spring is the mischief in me, and I wonder
If I could put a notion in his head:
"*Why* do they make good neighbors? Isn't it
Where there are cows? But here there are no cows.
Before I built a wall I'd ask to know
What I was walling in or walling out,
And to whom I was like to give offense.
Something there is that doesn't love a wall,
That wants it down."—Robert Frost in North of Boston. London, David Nutt, 1914.

social agencies—the deductions just named having been made—were consulted 2,243 times, or, if we include church sources, 2,748 times. If the plan of presentation adopted for outside sources had been followed strictly, social agencies would have been presented first of all. But, as sources, these agencies seem to belong upon another plane. In order to emphasize this difference, they have been reserved for separate treatment at this much later stage.

Somewhat different tests must be applied to the evidence given by social agencies to social agencies from those applied to the statements of any other outside sources: first, because the relation that these organizations have held to a client is in many respects similar to the relation now held by the inquirer; and second, because of the variety both of the tasks that social organizations perform and of the attitudes that they at present take toward the processes leading to diagnosis. The variety of their tasks is shown by Table 5, on the next page, and the nature of their relation to their clients brings us to the most important distinction to be made in evaluating social agency testimony.

This distinction is based upon the fact that social agencies can be called upon to fulfill two different functions as witnesses:

1. To Supply Data from Their Own Experience. They may have had a social experience of their own with a client, and we may need to know that experience. Even when the service undertaken for him was quite different from that which we ourselves are about to attempt, it may have fulfilled all the difficult conditions of an "investigation by experiment";[1] in that case, it may help us to know the client's reactions and may give us a key to certain of his personal characteristics. Social agencies are often at their very best as witnesses, when they are reporting, without bias, a first-hand experience of this kind—an experience acquired in the course of treatment. Of course, the better they understand their client's background, the more intelligent will be their interpretation of this experience.

Institutions for adults and for children frequently supply just this experience type of data. They have the advantage, when they are not too large, of being able to control the conditions under which their observations are made far better than these can be

[1] See reference to this term on p. 86.

TABLE 5.—SOCIAL AGENCIES (EXCLUSIVE OF HEALTH AND SCHOOL AGENCIES) USED AS SOURCES BY 56 AGENCIES IN 2,800 CASES

Type of social agency	Consultations	
Private agencies		
Family agencies		
Charity organization societies	645	
Foreign relief societies	92	
Other relief societies	219	
Total		956
Homes for adults		48
Children's agencies		
Homes for children	143	
Societies for the prevention of cruelty to children	122	
Children's aid societies	118	
Day nurseries	47	
Total		430
Settlements		119
Unclassified		204
Total for private social agencies		1,757
Public agencies		
Charities departments (including public outdoor relief)		275
Adult probation departments		81
Juvenile probation departments		72
Municipal lodging houses		6
Almshouses		31
Unclassified		21
Total for public social agencies		486
Total for public and private social agencies		2,243

To which, for the purposes of this study, may be added the following church sources:

Type of source	Consultations
Clergymen	345
Fellow church members	101
Church visitors	35
Sunday school teachers	24
Total	505

controlled by the society or department engaged in field work only. They have the corresponding disadvantage, however, of a more rigid and artificial standard of measure. In the freer give and take of the field, an artificial standard is more easily corrected.

Plenty of evidence is at hand that, when case workers can see the asylum official who knows their client, they get valuable data as to the client's personal habits. The temporary homes utilized by children's agencies during a period of observation (investigation by experiment) are also useful aids in diagnosis.

Children's institutions that are excellent witnesses as to their own experiences with inmates may still have only the vaguest of extra-mural data about them. They may admit them, discharge them, send them home temporarily at vacation time, and place them permanently with relatives or with strangers on knowledge that would be regarded as inadequate by any humane person who was seeking a home for a stray cat or dog. It follows, of course, that institutions of the type that Miss Florence L. Lattimore describes in her study of Pittsburgh are not competent witnesses as to family conditions either past or present. Nor is their investigation of placing-out homes any better. In 1907, the date of Miss Lattimore's study, one of the largest homes in Pittsburgh allowed children to be taken out "by any woman of respectable appearance who applied at the institution, filled out a blank, and waited for the child to be dressed." [1]

Even in our estimate of an institution's intra-mural testimony the point of view of the institution witness must be taken into account. In fact, the personal point of view must be probed for and allowed for everywhere. One amusing instance of this appears in a medical-social record:

A temporary home for working women was asked to report upon the conduct of a certain girl. The home replied that she was troublesome, unruly, and hard to control. When asked for detailed examples of her behavior, they wrote as follows: "We told Mary that she could not crochet in this house on Sunday. We had to speak a second time about this and send her to her room. Later, we found her disobeying upstairs. We do not allow gaiety of any sort in this house on Sunday, not even light music. You know we must keep up a certain standard."

A very different point of view—one that is also based largely on experience, but upon experience of a more flexible kind—is that supplied by the social settlement. The settlement thinks instinctively in terms of neighborhood reactions. This is a type of evidence so little known to numbers of case workers that they do not consciously seek it, as they should, or recognize its absence.[2]

A head worker in a settlement, who had formerly been for a year in a charity organization society, writes, in reply to a question about changes in her point of

[1] "Pittsburgh as a Foster Mother," in the Pittsburgh District, Civic Frontage, p. 348.

[2] For a good illustration of the type of neighborhood evidence that a settlement worker of experience is able to give, see the descriptions of foreign neighborhoods in Boston in Robert A. Woods' Americans in Process. Boston, Houghton Mifflin, and Co., 1902.

view: "The settlement worker is continually gauging cause and effect in neighborhood reactions, and by continuous experimenting in lines of action tending toward a fuller citizenship comes to develop a sort of intuitive sense of the practicability of plans. Because of this on the part of the settlement worker and the training in analysis and deduction on the part of the charity organization society worker, the two should work together closely—far more closely than they do.

"From the settlement I have gained that subtle, interpretative method of dealing with facts which I believe can only come by steeping one's self in the standards, manners, and customs of races, and by entering into the community life of a neighborhood. By so doing one becomes sensitive to the varying tendencies of a district, and hence one comes to interpret the lives of individuals with all the gradations of shading which make fact true. Had I entered as fully into the lives of the working people when in charity organization work as I have the past two years, I know I could have done much better in my charity organization contacts."

To still another group of sources, to the churches, social case workers may turn for personal experience more freely than for objective data. The degree and variety of contact with parishioners are very diverse, however, in the different religious denominations and in the churches for different nationalities. A pastor or priest of the foreign community in an American city is often the one to whom members of the community most naturally turn for advice in temporal matters also—for the interpreting of letters and for a variety of other services, each of which gives him added insight into the daily lives of his people. Parishes are sometimes so large and their clergy so overburdened that this ceases to be true, but in smaller communities it often holds true of both the foreign and the native American clergy.

In court work, both clergymen and settlement workers hesitate to give the testimony that they have to give, even when this would substantially aid in assuring a much desired result. The ground of their hesitation is the possibility of estrangement in future relations with the families involved. Social workers who are eager to bring about a certain beneficent result—the protection of children from neglect, the punishment of a deserter, etc.—must learn to respect this point of view, and to protect the parish and neighborhood representative from involvement, whenever this is possible.

Like the judge, the clergyman leans to a too great faith in conversion on the spot. In fact, the latter often takes a deliberately optimistic view which impairs his value as a witness in court and out.

In churches which employ a pastor's assistant, deaconess, or church visitor, this worker often knows more of the things that the case worker seeks information about than the minister does.

2. To Supply the Results of Their Inquiries. There is a second function of social agencies as witnesses; namely, to supply those objective data of a fundamental sort about clients which seldom change. Gathered originally by a particular organization for its own purposes, these facts may, if collected carefully in the first place, serve equally well, and with substantial economy of time and effort, the purposes of a second organization. A more important saving, even, is the wear and tear to the sensibilities of a client who might otherwise be harassed by needless questioning.[1]

It will help us to evaluate the evidence of social agencies more justly if we can keep quite distinct in our own minds these two functions of theirs as witnesses. In their testimony from personal experience they are witnesses of their own knowledge; in testimony based upon data that they have gathered they are often witnesses to matters of hearsay. Even in this second capacity, they have the advantage sometimes, though not always, of a certain skill in the weighing and testing of evidence. If their items of outside evidence have been recorded and duly credited to their sources *at the time that they were gathered* with sufficient fullness and accuracy to make them clear, and if the written record is always consulted before reporting to another agency, the danger of error is materially reduced. Danger of error in the original observation remains, however, and no one agency is ever an equally good judge of all kinds of data. Agencies that habitually neglect certain observations may be very keen about certain others. Such differences can be discovered by practical experience only. The particular type of social work engaged in, with its natural limitations, is one guide; the history not only of the individual agency but of the form of effort of which it is a part is another; the past relations of the given agency to the one seeking information is still another; but the most important factor of all is the native ability and professional equipment of the individual case worker who made the original observation or who represents the agency as witness, and this is a changing factor.

[1] See also the discussion of duplicate investigations on p. 311.

A case worker who removes from one city to another must revise all his standards of measure of social agency testimony. A charity organization society or associated charities, for example, is usually an agency that thinks of and knows a family as a whole. Relatively speaking, it has an unusually clear idea of the family histories and background of its clients, is well grounded in the habit of conferring with relatives, health agencies, former employers, schools, and the social agencies interested. It is not so strong in ability to gauge neighborhood influences; it too often neglects to individualize each growing child in the family; it sometimes emphasizes health and self-support at the expense of less measurable but very important social gains. But in certain cities the societies bearing the name of charity organization society or of associated charities are only rudderless, small-dole agencies, operating without plan or purpose. Obviously, it is necessary to look beyond the name and the avowed objects of a society in accepting its testimony.

A case worker may have been well trained, but may be employed by an agency under conditions that make it impossible for him to do trained work. These conditions limit his competence as a witness, of course. Some public departments, for instance, investigate chiefly with reference to the question of ability or inability to reimburse the state, or with reference to legal settlement. Others have rules that so many references—three or four—are to be consulted. Limitations of this order must be known and allowed for.

A radical change of management in an agency often makes it necessary to note whether a particular investigation, together with the inferences and plan of treatment drawn from it, was made before the change or after. One of the case readers for this volume spent two months in a society to protect children from cruelty in which there had been a change of management. After reading a large number of its records, she wrote:

"Even those cases in which only one or two or three interviews are thought to be necessary show an absolutely new way of approach since the change. I think I mentioned before that, under the old régime, unless the evidence of the investigator's eyes, backed up, perhaps, by a policeman or a neighbor, showed obvious neglect, the entry 'Nothing for us to do' was by no means uncommon. I have not found one case, under the new régime, where this sentiment is expressed in letter or in spirit. There is always something for the S. P. C. C. to do, though this is not always taking the case into court."

This last illustration might also point the moral that agencies skilled in the gathering and recording of objective data are usually the ones most likely to continue treatment long enough to gather also a rich store of personal experiences. This is not always true, however. Resourceless treatment, together with inability to recognize the significance of reactions to treatment, may follow a fairly good social diagnosis. It should be repeated, therefore, that the two types of evidence—as to actual, first-hand experiences with clients, and as to objective data gathered outside about them

—must be distinguished, and that from each social agency must be had the type of witness that it is best able to give. Social agencies are not what Francis H. McLean calls a "single-headed" source.[1] They are so far from being this that they presented, in the material studied for this book, examples of the very best and of the very worst social reporting.

With the increasing activity of social organizations and with their marked tendency toward specialization, has come a new need of some systematic exchange of information. This has become a prime necessity, if only to fix responsibility for social treatment, though it has many other advantages. As we have seen in the chapter on The First Interview, the first step, upon receipt of an application from a new client, is to discover what other social agencies, if any, are acquainted with him. This discovery is facilitated by the regular exchange of information among agencies, or, better still, by an exchange of the identifying data which will lead us to sources of information. Very easily and conveniently these identifying memoranda lead to an exchange of information when it is needed and not otherwise.

II. THE CONFIDENTIAL EXCHANGE

Some years ago the writer had occasion to consult an oculist in a strange city. He proved very skilful, so that when she removed her home from Philadelphia to New York and needed to choose another regular oculist, she asked the advice of this one. Upon her first visit to the New York practitioner thus selected, she tried to give the history of former eye treatments, first in her old home, then in the city only visited, and so on, making a sincere effort to do this as accurately as she could. But the new doctor received these communications with an air of skepticism. It appeared that he had been supplied with more trustworthy data already; the specialist who had recommended him had sent him a detailed statement of the Philadelphia prescriptions, and of his own findings and prescriptions. These were more truthful than the oral witness of the patient for two reasons: they were taken from memoranda made at the time, and, more important, they were taken from memoranda made by expert refractionists.

[1] See p. 175.

Such communication direct from practitioner to practitioner greatly reduces the percentage of error in every profession, and upon the need of some such direct interchange of experiences in social work is based a system now widely adopted, especially in our larger cities, and already referred to in these pages more than once. It was known first as the "registration bureau" and later as the "confidential exchange," or the "social service exchange." Its use brings other minor advantages, such as a checking of the tendency (not confined to the clients of social agencies) to run around from adviser to adviser. Doctors, lawyers, architects, and many other professional men, probably, know the type of nervous indecision, of speculative fever, of which such running around is only a symptom.

The Confidential Exchange was devised by the charity organization societies and is still financially supported or administered or both by these societies in most places. Better diagnosis, better treatment, better understandings among agencies, are its outstanding achievements, but incidentally it has reduced duplication of effort, has increased the sense of responsibility of the social agency definitely in charge of the individual case, and has been, moreover, a real economy. Its advantages are not confined to the processes of social diagnosis, for, long after treatment has begun, an inquiry at the Exchange from another agency about one of our clients may enable us to prevent unnecessary interference or may assure much needed co-operation; but the present account of the Exchange is limited to its uses in diagnosis.

Wherever there has been no Exchange and then one is established, its possible usefulness is soon vividly illustrated by such instances as the following, taken from Miss Margaret F. Byington's pamphlet study of Exchanges:[1]

> In another city a Confidential Exchange is just being started, and the infant mortality nurses and the tuberculosis nurses have not yet learned to use it. One family was badly infected with tuberculosis, the father dying, and the mother in an advanced stage of the disease. There were seven children, the youngest a nursing baby. The tuberculosis nurse kept urging the mother to stop nursing the child, but she refused to do so. Finally the tuberculosis nurse found that the infant mortality nurse had been visiting the family and, not knowing that the mother had

[1] The Confidential Exchange, p. 8.

tuberculosis, was insisting that she nurse the child. When the two nurses got together on the case, it was too late, for the baby died of tubercular meningitis.

Here was failure to consult owing to ignorance of the other agency's relation, but our case reading shows many instances of such failure where the other agency's relation was known. This sense of self-sufficiency, this tendency to operate in a vacuum, is worn down by the successfully administered Exchange. Not all who have the advantage of a local Exchange use it, as the case just cited also shows, but a few such happenings as this one (and oversights quite as serious are brought to light as soon as an Exchange is started) convey their own lesson.

The following brief description of Confidential Exchange machinery is Miss Byington's:[1]

"The mechanism of the Exchange is an alphabetical index with a card for each family or unattached person known to any of the inquiring agencies. This card gives the 'identifying information' —the names, ages, and occupations of the members of the family group, names and addresses of relatives, and the names of agencies interested, with the date on which each inquired. No facts about family history or treatment are included. When a co-operating society becomes interested in a new family, or in any one of its members, it inquires at once whether the Confidential Exchange knows the family or person. This inquiry is made either by telephone or by mail on printed slips furnished by the Exchange. The Exchange looks up the family in the index, and then reports to the inquiring agency the names of any societies that have been previously interested and the dates on which they inquired. If the information given by the inquirer is not sufficient to make identification possible, the agency is so notified, with the request that it inform the Exchange when further facts are secured.[2] The Chil-

[1] The Confidential Exchange, p. 5 sq.

[2] The following on the subject of identifying information is part of a longer passage in Wigmore's Principles of Judicial Proof, pp. 64–65. "The process of constructing an inference of identification . . . consists usually in adding together a number of circumstances, each of which by itself might be a feature of many objects, but all of which together can conceivably coexist in a single object only. Each additional circumstance reduces the chances of there being more than one object so associated. . . . It may be illustrated by the ordinary case of identification by name. Suppose there existed a parent named John Smith, whose heirs are sought; and there is also a claimant whose parent's name was John Smith. The name John Smith is associated with so many persons that the chances of two

dren's Aid Society, for example, inquires about Mrs. Mary Jones, and is informed that the North End Mission 'inquired' in January, 1910, the S. P. C. C. in December, 1910, and the Social Service Department of the Massachusetts General Hospital in March, 1911. The Children's Aid Society then calls up, or, better still, personally interviews, all these agencies, and secures directly from them what data they have about Mrs. Jones and the story of their relations with her. Experience has indicated that it is wiser to have *no information* in regard to the family pass through the office of the Exchange; that it should give only the names of interested societies."

It will be noted that agencies no longer "register" but "inquire," thus placing the emphasis on the more important part of the process. No one not directly and *disinterestedly* concerned, no one who cannot prove that social betterment is his aim, should be entitled to even the colorless data that the Exchange can supply. Its facts should be carefully guarded from those who might put them to other uses, such as installment collectors or other creditors. Instead of invading privacy, the Exchange assures it. Where there is no such aid to co-operation, or where agencies whose lines may cross refuse to make systematic inquiry of an Exchange already established, it becomes necessary, in order to be sure that effort is not being duplicated and that useful insights are not lost, to inquire directly of each agency that might have known a given client. Each such repetition of a client's name to an agency that does not know him is rendered unnecessary by the existence of an Exchange in which all the social agencies are participants.

supposed persons of that name being different are too numerous to allow us to consider the common mark as having appreciable probative value. But these chances may be diminished by adding other common circumstances going to form the common mark. Add, for instance, another name circumstance,—as that the name of each supposed person was John Barebones Bonaparte Smith; here the chances of there being two persons of that name, in any district, however large, are instantly reduced to a minimum. Or, add a circumstance of locality,—for example, that each of the supposed persons lived in a particular village, or in a particular block of a certain street, or in a particular house; here, again, the chances are reduced in varying degrees in each instance. Or, add a circumstance of family,—for example, that each of the persons had seven sons and five daughters, or that each had a wife named Mary Elizabeth and three daughters named Flora, Delia, and Stella; here the chances are again reduced in varying degrees, in proportion to the probable number of persons who would possess this composite mark. In every instance, the process depends upon the same principle—the extent to which the common mark is capable of being associated, in human experience, with more than one object."

In a small city where the Confidential Exchange is still a new thing, a worker in a family agency reports that she must also call up the overseer of the poor about each new application to her office, because he does not use the Exchange. She has found it necessary to communicate besides with a missionary who is often working in an unrelated way with the same families. The confidential character of the work of the family agency, the overseer, and the missionary would have been conserved if all three had used the Exchange, for then no client's name need have been mentioned to an agency not already acquainted with him.

The reason most often given by a social agency for refusing to use the Exchange is that its relations with its clients are too confidential.[1] As just shown, this objection is based upon a misapprehension. Nor does an agreement to make systematic inquiry imply obligation to inquire in every single instance. There may be exceptional cases in which no inquiry need be made or should be made, though these exceptions will not be many after the true nature and value of the Exchange have been made apparent by its frequent use.

It will of course be understood that the Exchange is not confined to an indexing of the recipients of material relief. It is a key to the knowledge and activities of those who have rendered or are rendering social service in any form, and its usefulness is being rapidly extended far beyond the boundaries of relief societies and other charitable agencies.

Both of these objections—that their work is confidential and that it is not relief—have heretofore held back many of the social settlements from making inquiry. In so far as their work is with a whole neighborhood, inquiry of the Exchange is not practicable, of course, but case work of any kind—social betterment work, that is, with individuals—is helped by the Exchange, whether it radiates from a settlement, a church, or a private family as its center. "To the casual onlooker," says Miss Byington, "the Confidential Exchange, with its files of cards, must seem to embody the maximum of red tape with the minimum of 'charity.' We must kindle his imagination, that he may see as we do that behind the machinery is a constructive force; that the Exchange is not a device for preventing overlapping of relief, that it is not a benevolent detective agency, but that it does conserve and render

[1] See The Confidential Exchange, p. 13.

more efficient our service to an important section of the community."[1]

III. THE USE OF EXCHANGE DATA

The old adage about bringing a horse to water has been illustrated in the course of our case reading by the very perfunctory use made of the Exchange by some of the agencies studied. It is necessary to inquire of the Exchange *before* acting instead of after, if the clues suggested by its reports are to be of any real service. And there is no particular merit in consulting the Exchange, even with great promptness, if the clues which it furnishes are not intelligently followed up.

It is true that, in a city in which the Exchange is well established and widely used, the clues furnished are sometimes bewilderingly many; some of them may yield little of value; and always the time element makes necessary an intelligent choice of the order in which social agency clues shall be consulted.

In the case of Boston, where so many agencies inquire of the Exchange that this is particularly true, the writer has had the opportunity to examine a group of reports on the practice of a large number of agencies using the Exchange.[2] Some send letters at once to all clues furnished by the Confidential Exchange, some select for a first consultation the agency most like their own, some consult first the one that is most conveniently situated for a prompt personal interview, some go first to those in whose methods they have the most confidence, many consult at once the agency that inquired last of the Exchange, and many others consult first the Associated Charities, when its name appears in the list of clues, consulting next the agency most like their own. These reports cannot be taken as proof of the wisdom or unwisdom of any definite principles of choice—they were gathered too informally—but they are suggestive. The agencies that always consulted the Boston Associated Charities first usually gave as their reason that

[1] Miss Byington makes it clear that something more than good clerks and a sound office system is needed in a successful Exchange. It must be administered by social workers who are fully alive to its progressive case work possibilities. It must be assured continuity of policy, and that policy social in the highest sense.—The Confidential Exchange, p. 22.

[2] Contained in notes of two informal conferences held in April, 1915, by students of the Boston School for Social Workers, for which the writer is indebted to Miss Zilpha D. Smith.

this particular agency studied the general family history very carefully, and always covered the clues furnished by the Exchange, thus rendering first-hand consultations with each and every one of these clues unnecessary. The agencies that invariably consulted first the Exchange inquirer of latest date usually gave as their reason that this source was most likely to know about the present situation.

Here we have somewhat divergent tendencies, which recall the principle of choice suggested in Chapter VIII, Outside Sources in General, that sources rich in history only be sought before those likely to prove rich in co-operation. It is to be expected that some agencies will be most occupied with the present situation, and that others, seeking a broader basis for what may prove a longer treatment and one looking to more permanent results, are eager to get a good family background for their diagnosis and prognosis. A placing-out agency is unquestionably more likely to get the special information that it needs from another placing-out agency, and, more important still, it is more likely to find that some one capable of taking full charge has already accepted the responsibility or wishes to do so. There is much to be said for propinquity also. For instance, an agency in a charities building on the next floor but one can be seen at once, and the direct communication, with its fair chance of seeing the particular worker in the agency who knows the client best and its further chance of hearing him detail, with case record in hand, the agency's information and experience, has very definite advantages.[1] In theory, the agency that last inquired has either left the case in charge of another willing to assume full responsibility or else has inquired of all the previous inquirers, and is in a position to pass on their data; but with each remove such information tends to become diluted, so that the most that can be hoped for from the best of social agency witnesses is a hint as to what kind of information we are likely to find from the other agencies reported by the Exchange. If we consult only those whose methods of investigation we approve, a process of in-breeding and of separation begins at once, which may have serious effects upon our own work and upon community co-operation later.

[1] For a discussion of the telephone as a medium of communication in the processes leading to diagnosis see the next chapter.

In summing up these conferences, Miss Zilpha D. Smith gives, as the first purpose of calling up previous inquirers, "To find out if any other organization holds itself responsible for the social treatment of the family or person, or responsible for making a plan. If so, to report how their affairs came to our notice and why. Also, to help, if need be, the family or person to co-operate with the other organization." When no such responsibility has been assumed and treatment therefore becomes necessary, the second purpose is to profit by the experiences of the agencies reported as having inquired, and to utilize any items of history that they may have gathered.

After treatment of a case has ceased, the notifications that continue to come in from the Exchange that the former client has been inquired about by successive agencies are often thrust aside or destroyed. Even if no attention is paid to these notices at the time, and sometimes they require attention, they should be saved for future reference, for treatment may have to be resumed at a later date.

It is well to remind ourselves, in leaving this subject of the use of Exchange data, that no system of indices can take the place of a quick and resourceful summoning of concrete case experiences into consciousness. Some social agencies would have been satisfied to return a prompt negative to the following inquiry:

A woman calling herself Sarah Collier Potter, who claimed that she was recently widowed and penniless, applied to a child-protective agency. She had with her a two-year-old boy named George and was soon to become a mother. As the in-town addresses she gave were false, the agency wrote to the overseer of the poor in a nearby town on the chance that Mrs. Potter might be known to him, at the same time adding some descriptive details. The overseer replied that he knew of no Sarah Collier Potter, but that some items in the story suggested that she might be Bridget Karrigan, who had sometimes given the name of Collier, and who was an unmarried woman now pregnant and mother of a boy of two named George. Then followed a clear account of Bridget's occupations, application to court for support of her child, etc. These cases were found to be identical. An index alone could hardly have established the fact.

IV. SOME FURTHER DETAILS OF CO-OPERATION

Almost every aspect of the ethics and technique of consultation is involved in the right use of the confidential exchange. There are, however, certain details of co-operative relations that require separate treatment, such as the knotty problem of duplicate investigations, the advisability of investigation that probably will be followed immediately by transfer to another agency, and certain daily helps in the practical working out of co-operation as it relates to diagnosis.

1. Duplicate Investigations. In the earliest stages of this inquiry into social diagnosis, a meeting of representatives from 31 local social agencies was held in one of our large cities. Again and again, in the course of the frankly informal discussion of co-operative relations with which the evening was filled, the topic of duplicate investigations was returned to. Some present felt that overlapping of investigation was quite as great an evil as the overlapping of relief—an evil not traceable to any failure to use the local confidential exchange, for all present inquired of it systematically, but due, rather, to unwillingness to accept the investigations and recommendations of others as a satisfactory basis for action without supplementary inquiry.

Inquiries that cover the same ground needlessly and repeatedly are undoubtedly not only a hardship to our clients but an injury to them, for under the experience they can become as abnormally self-conscious and self-pitying as are certain of the more well-to-do who flit from doctor to doctor.

At the same time, no general arrangement to pool our social diagnoses will furnish a way out of the dilemma, so long as standards of investigation are so capriciously variable. One reason why agencies cannot agree at present to accept the investigations of others wholesale is that they cannot trust them to be good, though they should be perfectly willing to take the facts of another agency in so far as they can be assured that they really are facts. The slow development of a sound technique in common is the only sure way of overcoming the worst results of over-inquiry. Duplication will seem inexcusable in a community in which such a technique has been mastered by all case workers. If, however, by duplicate investigation is meant *any* inquiry by more than one agency, there is little doubt that, for the best interests of our clients, such duplication must continue. The idea of one broadly comprehensive inquiry, covering all the social aspects of a family's life, made once only and then placed forever after at the service of all social workers interested in any of the family's members as a substitute for further investigation, is a doctrinaire conception originating probably with the charity organization societies but now for the most part outgrown by them. As a basis for social inquiry the family point of view is valuable beyond question, and certain data so gathered will not need to be regathered, but there will have to be reinquiry as circumstances change, as new questions arise, and as a new form of social service, requiring its separate skill and separate data, is needed. The new agency called in should utilize the older experience, of course, but it will not only have to bring this experience up to date, but must seek besides the particular insight into the situation and the personality which is necessary for the new task in hand. The oculist already referred to (p. 303) did not rest back upon the very satisfactory data furnished, but made his re-examination with those data in mind.

Practical illustrations of most of these difficulties were presented at the meeting at which the elimination of inquiry by more than one agency was urged. A medical-social worker—to take an extreme instance—stated that, in certain cases, the most important single item of her inquiry was to discover what a patient had had for breakfast that morning—a matter which obviously could not be referred back to someone who was supposed to have a more comprehensive knowledge of the patient. The after-care agent of a girls' reformatory, whose cordial relations with the local society to protect children were based upon many case work views held in common, pointed out that written reports from the society inevitably emphasized those aspects of a girl's history for which the community held that particular society responsible, whereas a visit to the agent of the society who had known the girl usually brought out useful information that, for the original investigator's purposes, had not seemed even worth recording. In addition to these items, however, new questions had usually come up that made reinvestigation necessary—a new decision had to be made, and its very nature suggested lines of inquiry not already covered, such as further detailed characteristics of a certain relative now willing to take the girl, the more recent physical and mental history of the girl herself, etc.

Neither confidential exchanges nor uniform record cards, nor the businesslike agreements sometimes suggested by efficiency experts who know little or nothing about social case work, will succeed in eliminating supplementary investigation, but, with such efficient aids as a thorough standard of diagnosis, re-enforced by thorough use of the confidential exchange, the duplicate investigation which really duplicates and to which, therefore, there can be reasonable objection, will gradually disappear.

2. The Transfer to Another Agency for Treatment. When the first steps in our relations with a new client indicate that he is probably in more need of the services of another agency than of our own, how far should we go with our inquiry preliminary to diagnosis before referring him, and what should our further relations be to him and to the agency after the transfer has been effected? Evidence on the first of these two questions is very conflicting. Some of it seems to indicate that the first agency should go far enough at least to be quite sure that the transfer is a justifiable one. Emphasis on this side could be defended, in part, by the fact that under pressure of work most case workers tend to accept quite readily any indication that a particular demand upon their time and sympathy can, with decency, be set aside or passed on to others. The unfortunate results of this tendency are aggravated, sometimes, by another transfer, made for much the same reason by the second agency, to a third. A further argument against the ill considered reference is that it is one of the greatest bars to co-operation. Obviously, we cannot co-operate with an agency the purposes and limitations of which we have never concerned ourselves to discover; but however well we may know these purposes and limitations, unless we know also something more than can be learned at an application desk of the clients whom we refer to the agency, we shall continually be asking it to do things not at all within its scope.

On the other hand, the social organization which tries to do thorough work likes cases referred to it promptly. One of the most cheering developments in connection with tasks formerly undertaken only at the eleventh hour is that they are now developing a preventive side; but preventive measures seldom succeed without the early reference. This is notably true of various forms of what was formerly court work or nothing. The case records of one society for the protection of children show a good deal of work in co-operation with other agencies and with parents themselves, in which, by timely treatment, court intervention was rendered unnecessary. Dr. William Healy, working exclusively at first with the Chicago Juvenile Court, was later often appealed to by parents, clergymen, and teachers for an expert opinion on a difficult child that had no court record.[1] We cannot always be sure, of course, that our first reference will be the right one, and any tendency to delay too long in seeking co-operation may make effective treatment more difficult.

Another possible argument against investigation before transfer is that a client who must be transferred goes more readily and gives a second agency his confidence more freely if he has not been visited, interviewed, questioned by the first agency just before the transfer was made. The more complete the understanding between the two agencies, the less will be the difficulty from this last obstacle.

As with so many other questions raised in this book, there can be no one conclusive answer. The matter of investigation before transfer cannot be settled by a formula. We can be on guard, however, against the very natural tendency to relieve ourselves of trouble by hasty transfers, and we can be sure that no endeavor put into strengthening the relations of our client to the agency to which he is being transferred will be wasted.

Says a critic of a group of case records: The entry "disposed of through the juvenile court," or "removed to ——" (another city or town or some place in the country), is a form of social bookkeeping entry that may indicate no real conclusion of the social difficulty. All environmental changes need analysis, if we are to be thorough.

There can be no two opinions, of course, about the folly of taking up the case of a transferred client anew, later on, without consulting with the organization to which we transferred him.

A single woman in need of light work, for example, was referred to a family agency by a medical-social department. The family agency provided convalescent care and later found work for her. About a year and a half later she applied to the hospital again for medical care and was visited by its social service department. Following this second application, an auxiliary of the department provided sewing

[1] The Individual Delinquent, p. 14.

for six months and rendered other service without making any inquiry of, or attempting to confer with, the family agency previously called in.

3. Additional Suggestions. Communication with other social organizations should be direct and not through clients or any other intermediaries. Statements and messages are often repeated inaccurately in all innocence, and sometimes they are colored by the interest of the messenger.

A conference of representatives of several agencies—of all interested in some one case which happens to present special difficulties—may save valuable time, promote good understanding, and bring the solution appreciably nearer. A certain agency has refused, perhaps, to accept the point of view of another. It is not impressed with the reasons given and believes the diagnosis or the prognosis or both to be mistaken. At the conference of all interested, however, it is impressed, or else the organization from which it has differed is impressed, by the point of view of a third, or by the new light thrown upon the matter by a doctor or teacher who is present. The outcome is not necessarily the one intended by the agency calling the conference; a better policy may be adopted than that originally favored by either of the two disputants.

Since co-operation is based upon trust, one final suggestion under this head may well emphasize the importance of teaching co-operating agencies that we are as good as our word always. If we have said that we will do a thing, it should be known to be as good as done.

SUMMARY OF THIS CHAPTER

1. The process of arriving at a social diagnosis is a co-operative one. Properly conducted, moreover, it often leads to the intelligent co-operation of relatives, employers, social agencies, etc., in the treatment which is to follow diagnosis.

2. As regards social agencies, the four stages of development from competition to co-operation in their social work are (1) the competitive period, (2) the period of co-operation *in vacuo*, (3) the period of "joint traffic agreements," (4) the period of co-operation in spirit.

3. As outside sources, social agencies belong upon a different plane from all others, and to their evidence somewhat different tests must be applied. They fulfill two distinct functions as witnesses: first, they can supply their own social experience with a given client; second, they can often supply certain objective data about him. Some agencies excel in the one kind of testimony, some in the other, and a small group in both.

4. In evaluating its testimony, the point of view of the individual agency must be considered and allowed for. Other things being equal, that type of social experience which is least like our own is most valuable—the agency developed on the neighborhood unit helps most the one that regards the family as its unit of measure, etc. If there has been a complete change of management in an agency, it is important to know, in each instance, whether its case report refers to work done before or after the change.

5. A systematic and confidential exchange of identifying information among social agencies assures better diagnosis and treatment, promotes better understanding between agencies, reduces duplication of effort, and increases the sense of individual responsibility for work undertaken.

6. Prompt consultation of the exchange is essential, however, and a prompt following up of the clues which it supplies.

7. The order in which the social agency clues so followed up should be consulted depends upon a number of factors; but, in general, the first thing to seek is assurance that the entrance of our own agency into a given case would not duplicate effort or interfere with the treatment of some other agency; second, when this first point has been settled, history useful in our own diagnosis; third, co-operation in treatment.

8. Additional investigation is not necessarily a duplication of effort, but over-inquiry will best be done away with by a high and widely accepted standard of diagnosis.

9. Communication between social practitioners should be direct and not through their clients or other intermediaries.

CHAPTER XVII

LETTERS, TELEPHONE MESSAGES, ETC.

OUR review of outside sources is ended, but before leaving this part of our subject for an analysis of the last stage of all in the processes leading to diagnosis, there are certain things to be said about the various means of communication with outside sources and the relative uses to which these means may be put. Of the statements procured by different means, which ones (other things being equal) are most satisfactory—those that are (a) written replies to the questions on a form or schedule, (b) written replies to letters, (c) telephone replies to questions asked by telephone, (d) telegraphic replies to inquiries made through the same medium or (e) replies by word of mouth secured in the course of a personal interview? Many other combinations of these means are possible, of course, but taking these five main forms of communication without their variations, from which one, on the whole, does the social case worker win the best results? The personal interview has become his main reliance. There are exceptions to this, but to an increasing degree it is true in most forms of case work.

Oral testimony fails us when accuracy is vital, as in matters of time, place, amount, etc., but so does written testimony, unless we seek the original documents.[1] The distinguishing characteristic of social evidence is not, however, its handling of objective matters, but its ability to evaluate human relations. It is justified as a separate type of evidence by its possible usefulness in gauging the interest, capacity, and whole atmosphere and spirit of the individual witness, including his capacity to become more interested than he now is. In subjective matters such as these there is no satisfactory substitute for the personal interview.

A policeman wrote from a small town to an associated charities secretary about a family in which the husband was very abusive. After giving certain information,

[1] See Chapter XIII, Documentary Sources.

he added, "If I could see you, I could say many things which I think it would be just as well not to write, for the reason that the explanation would take a lot of time and paper and then perhaps would not be very satisfactory—you know how it is."

A woman probation officer was asked to inquire into the story of a young girl arrested for immoral conduct who gave the name of Emily Burton. The girl said that she came from the town of G——, about sixty miles away, and that her people were French Canadians and Catholics. Her name seemed unmistakably Anglo-Saxon, but she persisted that she had no other, so the probation officer decided to go herself to G——, and follow personally the very slender clues that were in her hand. First, she saw the police captain there, and interested him to assign an officer to accompany her on her search, but the girl's parents could not be found at the address given or anywhere in that street or neighborhood. School records revealed nothing, nor could the parish priest identify the family from the description. The mill in which the girl claimed to have worked was the next to the last clue, but it yielded nothing. Returning to the captain of police, the probation officer told him of a brother George who worked for a farmer (or so the girl claimed), but the only George known at police headquarters who worked for a farmer was named Lodie, and the probation officer did not even attempt to see him.

On the day of the trial, and just before it began, the girl begged hard for mercy, but the probation officer was forced to point out in all kindness that she did not even know who she was. Whereupon the girl said that her name was Lodie and that she really did live in G——. The identification of this one name more than justified what had seemed a futile journey, for it gave promise that there was further truth in the girl's story. A second visit to G—— brought to light five respectable brothers and sisters, with four of whom the officer was able to consult. This led to plans of co-operation with the girl's mother, to the return home of the wanderer, who had been denied a welcome earlier and to plans for her continuous supervision under suspended sentence.

Where such serious issues are involved as in the case just cited, it is no unusual thing, now, for case workers to travel from one end of a state to another or into other states to make an inquiry in person. At one time this would have been regarded as a very wasteful procedure, but much footless endeavor—expensive in time and money, and expensive in its results—has been saved by such journeys.

I. BLANK FORMS

Many charitable institutions still select their inmates on the basis of statements filled out on application blanks, to which are appended certain letters of endorsement. The formality of these blanks is believed to secure greater accuracy in the replies. Where inaccurate replies are a statutory offense, punishable by fine or imprisonment, there may be justification for this view, but such powers seldom reside in social agencies, either public or private, and where they do they are not always used. The logically arranged and categorically framed questions of an application blank suggest the answer that will lead to the decision desired by the applicant. This is the chief objection; another is that no formal set of questions, however full, can cover all possible contingencies; a blank may be carefully and accurately filled out by a witness and yet omit important items. As regards the letters of endorsement which usually accompany such applications,[1] written by merchants, teachers, clergymen, doctors, and other presumably responsible persons, these are too often found to be not worth the paper upon which they are written, as some of the cases cited in this volume show.[2]

II. LETTERS OF INQUIRY

The author's examination of case records indicates greater advances during the last decade in the art of conducting personal interviews than in the art of letter writing. This is natural, perhaps, for the attempt to make social diagnosis a more flexible and understanding thing has been pushed forward under many disadvantages, of which time pressure, public impatience, and inadequate preparation are only a few. Under these handicaps the substitution of visits for letters has diverted attention from the possibilities of letters in those cases, still numerous, in which they should be used. As a result, many of the carbon copies of letters found in case records have the air of having been written or dictated in a most perfunctory and absent-minded way.

A case worker's letters, in so far as they relate to diagnosis, fall into the two large groups of those that ask information about clients and those that give information. Those that ask information may be divided into letters that ask it of the witnesses direct and letters that ask it of intermediaries who are requested to see the witnesses or to communicate with them in some other way. Again, letters that ask information direct may be divided into those that ask it of persons near enough at hand to make a personal interview with them later quite easy or at least possible, and those in which

[1] Some institutions and agencies provide a form of recommendation requiring nothing but the signature of the endorser.

[2] See, for example, pp. 232 and 241.

the opportunity for such direct communication later is remote or non-existent. Obviously, each one of these divisions and subdivisions demands from the letter writer a somewhat different method of presentation, though attention will be given here almost exclusively to letters of out-of-town inquiry and their replies.

In respect of letters of inquiry (to take this half of the subject first) the question that precedes every other is (1) What other means of communication, at command, would serve the purpose better? This settled in favor of the letter, as the best available means, the next question is (2) Have the preliminary inquiries that would make the writing of this letter the logical next step all been made? And (3) Has the definite relation of the part of the inquiry to be covered by the letter to the whole of diagnosis and treatment been thought out by the inquirer as clearly as it can be at this early stage? Only when this has been done can be found the answer to the next question, which is (4) Has the best possible correspondent been chosen for the particular information or the particular service desired? (5) If so, what method of presentation will most interest him, and so win the information or the service? (6) How, for instance, can the trouble to which he will be put by the inquiry be justly measured, and every effort be made to anticipate his difficulties and give him the details that will help him to overcome them? (7) If the correspondent is not personally known, as often happens, what circumstances of his occupation, experience, education, and of his relation to this particular problem should be borne in mind and turned to account in the attempt to make the significance and possibilities of the inquiry clear to him? Each of these questions deserves amplification.

1. Should the Letter Be Written at All? The advantages of a personal interview have been made clear. When letters are the sole means of communication with persons who do not understand the case worker's point of view or whose attitude and characteristics are unknown to him, his work is seriously handicapped from the beginning. Some letters are merely preliminary to an interview; others follow it, to secure in black and white data of a technical or of a purely objective nature,[1] in which accuracy is

[1] Many hospitals refuse to give a diagnosis unless written application is made for it.

of the first importance. These present no difficulties, but less direct means—letters, long distance telephone messages, telegraphic dispatches—must often be the only approach. In more than 11 per cent of all the outside sources consulted in the 2,800 cases included in our special study, the agencies and persons communicated with were out of town. Letters to out-of-town sources tax the case worker's ingenuity far more than does his other correspondence, and except when otherwise specified this discussion is limited to them.

2. Should the Letter Be Written Now? A favorite time for writing letters of inquiry is just after the first interview has been held. When no one living in or near the city in which the client makes his application has had any but the most casual contacts with him, letters to those at a distance who have known him well, or to others who will visit these witnesses, are a necessary procedure and such letters must be written at once. A safe general rule to follow, nevertheless, is this: Write no important letter to a place at a distance which is not based upon and shaped by all the obtainable evidence near at hand. Much of the growing dissatisfaction among agencies which receive many out-of-town requests for inquiry service—notably among the charity organization societies upon which this demand has fallen the heaviest—may be traced to the fact that many requests are made upon very inadequate data when it is known that more data near at hand are readily obtainable. On the other hand, it must be conceded that there is real danger in delaying out-of-town inquiry until after plans have been made and the case treatment has actively been started.

A flagrant instance of the inquiry that should have been made, and yet was made too soon, will be found on page 174, where the public charities of a German city were asked to seek out relatives, to interest them in a case of distress, to get their advice as to the best method of treatment, and to obtain from them material assistance. All of this was asked without providing them with any data save the impressions of a first visit supplemented by the impressions of the agency that referred the family for care. The family had lived in the same American city for eleven years, yet no history was procured before setting in motion a process which, if unsuccessful in its outcome the first time, could not easily be repeated.

The inquirer might well have reasoned as follows: The public department of charities in a large German city has many inquiries from America, probably. It has its own work besides. This matter will receive only perfunctory attention unless I can show that I know whereof I write. The relatives of this woman have not seen her for many years, probably, and about her life in America they know what she has told them. I must seek information covering this long period elsewhere, and out of the clues now in my hand, must construct her past in this country as best I can. Since I shall be fortunate if I get one reply from my German correspondent, I must make that one count for as much as possible in shaping treatment aright by letting the inquiry overseas grow out of the history nearer at hand. But the line of reasoning actually followed would appear to have been this: It will take several weeks to hear from Germany, so a letter must be written at once—the visits here can be delayed. Besides, there are no relatives over here, or so the mother of the family says, and relatives are always the best references.

3. What Relation Does This Particular Inquiry Bear to the Whole Process? The need of asking this further question is illustrated by the letter of inquiry just referred to. It is also illustrated by many letters to relatives, copies of which have been found in the case records studied. Instead of showing that the inquirer is thinking of his client's life as a whole, of the great gaps in his understanding of that life, and of the kind of insight that the relative would best be fitted to give, they show an almost automatic drift into requests that the brother pay a month's rent, that the grandfather furnish milk for the baby, that a home be supplied for a family of six, etc. These are services all of which may be appropriately undertaken by relatives under certain conditions, but what is the purpose in paying the rent and furnishing the transportation? Permanent betterment presumably, or at least some better foothold, some more effective adjustment for the client or for his whole family. The following inquiry shows this relating of the simple question—the question of willingness to receive a relative—to some of the more important issues involved. The reply is given on p. 324.

We are anxious to have a call made upon Mrs. Jane Seymour, who lives in Bedford [a small town in the same state as that of the agency addressed]. Will you be kind enough to forward this letter to your correspondent there? [The enclosure read as follows:]

We have become very much interested in Arthur Brown, a private in the United States Artillery stationed at Fort ——— in this harbor. He comes from Bedford, where his mother, stepfather, and brother have a farm. He has been in the army nearly three years and has five more months to serve. Last summer he married a girl in this city whom he is unable to support, as his pay is only $18 a month. Consequently he has been running into debt ever since his marriage and owes about $40. At the present time he has drawn a month's pay in advance. He tells us that his mother, Mrs. Seymour, is very willing to take his wife and baby into her home. We are afraid that Mrs. Brown is a difficult girl to get on with and for that reason are particularly anxious to know whether Mrs. Seymour is a tactful and intelligent woman.

Can you send someone to see Mrs. Seymour and can you find out anything about the family? If you are able to see Mrs. Seymour will you tell her that we are going to help Mr. Brown to pay his wife's rent until we hear from her? If this address is not accurate enough will you please let me know?

This letter was not addressed to Mrs. Seymour herself for reasons that are evident; the inquiry was sent through two intermediaries —through a family agency in Mrs. Seymour's state, which found a correspondent in her town of Bedford. It would have been easy enough to write to Mrs. Seymour direct and ask, Will you take your daughter-in-law and grandchild into your home? But it was not possible to ask, Are you responsible enough and tactful enough to care for a girl who needs especially good care? Which brings us to our next question.

4. Has the Best Correspondent Been Chosen for the End in View? The real end in view must be clearly grasped before this query can be asked or answered. It must be confessed that the very uneven development of social case work in different cities and in different parts of the country often reduces the inquirer to Hobson's choice in the matter of correspondents. It is not always possible, for instance, to avoid direct communication by mail with the Mrs. Seymours, and certain things that they cannot tell us must remain unasked and unanswered. In choosing the method of inquiry through an intermediary, moreover, there is always the risk that a private matter may be made public, that the pride of sensitive people may be wounded, owing to lack of tact and discretion in the intermediary selected. Nevertheless, direct replies from illiterate witnesses are often so unsatisfactory, and the observations and estimates of an intermediary are so much needed that this risk has frequently to be taken.

The correspondent found in Mrs. Seymour's town replied as follows:

I have just received the report of the chairman of our investigating committee of the case of Mrs. Jane Seymour, as requested in your communication of the 18th. She reports Mrs. Seymour to be a quiet, modest woman of average intelligence and fair education, who she judges could get along with her son's wife if she is at all reasonable. Mrs. Seymour is a woman of few words, a good housekeeper, in comfortable circumstances, with plenty of room in her house for Mrs. Brown, and she is quite willing to have her come so she can help her son in this way to get on his feet after his enlistment expires. She said she did not have money to send for Mrs. Brown, but could and would take care of her until her son was able to take care of her himself. I think the ——— society need not hesitate to send Mrs. Brown to Mrs. Seymour's. There will be plenty to eat, a good home, with wholesome surroundings, and from all I can learn a thoughtful woman to live with and take care of her.

This is not the report of a trained social worker—it is not so concrete as such a report should be—but it contains a general common-sense estimate by a kindly householder, and this estimate makes the answer more satisfactory on the whole than direct correspondence could have been. It cannot be denied, however, that the choice between direct and indirect communication is a difficult one to make, and one requiring tact and consideration. The letter of inquiry (p. 323) speaks of Mrs. Brown as "a difficult girl to get on with." This is a vague description, but it may have been purposely so in view of the fact that the correspondent to be selected was unknown to the writer.

One letter about the relatives of a skilled workman known to be drinking heavily and to be despondent and destitute was sent to an overseer of the poor in a small town. He promptly handed it to the man's brother and told him to answer it. The kind of reply thus obtained could have been had as well or better by direct correspondence. The intermediary had failed to grasp the purpose for which he had been called in.

Local correspondents can be secured in a number of ways. Through the use of the professional directories and the year books described in the chapter on Documentary Sources a state or county official, lawyer, teacher, physician, or clergyman may be found who may prove a valuable intermediary in an important inquiry. When we are seeking the kind of information likely to be known to a local merchant or manufacturer, wholesale houses in our own city may have correspondents in smaller places to whom they can give us letters of introduction, and some such approach might be found to the other out-of-town sources mentioned in this paragraph.

Miss M. L. Birtwell writes[1] as follows of clergymen as correspondents:

In localities in which we have no regular correspondent we may use some local clergyman, preferably of the same denomination as the family in regard to whom we are inquiring. Often we use the Episcopal clergyman, as the organization of that denomination on the parish system gives their clergymen a sense of responsibility in regard to any need within parish boundaries. If the inquiry is to be made in a locality of which we are entirely ignorant, we have sometimes written to the postmaster, enclosing a letter which he is requested to give to the nearest or most influential local clergyman.

Our local Home for Destitute Children once asked us to investigate the application of a widow for the admission of her two children to the home. Her husband, she said, had been drowned some months before in Nova Scotia; she could find no work there by which she could support herself, so had come to a sister in Cambridge in the hope that the latter would care for her children while she went out to work. The sister had children of her own, however, and her husband would not consent to the additional burden. The woman said she had a place at a restaurant at $5.00 a week, which she would lose unless she could get her children cared for at once. We found the woman with her sister in a neat, comfortable home with every appearance of respectability, but she seemed unable to give references from her home town. The owner of the mill where the husband worked had gone out of business, they had lived too far out in the country to go to church, so knew no clergyman well enough to give his name as reference, etc. We advised the Home against hasty action and refused to make any recommendation till a thorough investigation could be made. A letter was at once written to the local Episcopal clergyman, asking him to look up the family history, the record of the man's death, and resources in the way of work for the woman. A prompt reply was received saying that the man was alive and well; that there had been a family jar, and the woman in a fit of temper had gone to the States to visit her sister; that the man had told her to go if she wanted to, but had said that she would have to get back as best she could. We wrote the clergyman to stimulate a forgiving spirit in the man and urge him to send at least part of the fare of the family, and promised to do what we could to help the woman earn her share. We got her a place at service with one child, the employer knowing it was a temporary arrangement, leaving the other child with her sister. She saved her wages of $2.00 per week, and in a few weeks, with her husband's help, the traveling expenses were met and the family reunion took place.

An exasperating practice of some social workers which is usually

[1] In one of the short, unpublished papers referred to in the Preface.

without excuse is to write directly to a relative or other witness, asking for advice and service, and at the same time to write to another correspondent, asking that the person thus addressed be seen, without mentioning to either that a letter has been sent to the other. Presumably the idea behind this procedure is that, if either source fails, time will have been saved by duplicate inquiry. There may be cases in which both letters should be written, but in these circumstances both correspondents are entitled to an explanation.

Sometimes a client will suggest that he himself do the writing to relatives or others at a distance who know him, showing the replies when received to the case worker. Usually this is not a good plan. A letter of reply is of little value as evidence without the contents of the letter to which it is an answer, and moreover the client's failure (innocent failure often) to ask the right questions may cause unnecessary delays.

The choice of foreign correspondents has always presented difficulties, and these difficulties have been increased since August, 1914, though time will bring better adjustments, of course. The following general suggestions about foreign letters are made by the American Association of Societies for Organizing Charity:

> Letters written in the language of the country to which they are going may be addressed to the mayor of the town or to the parish priest; the consul in your city who represents this country may be willing to forward a letter for you or write himself to some local official; inquiries may be sent to the American Consul in the city nearest the town where the visit is to be made. While the department of state has stated that this is a logical service for the consuls to render, the societies have not always received prompt or satisfactory replies from them. In France and Italy the mayor of the town has proved to be the best source of information.

5. What Will Interest the Correspondent Selected? An intelligent choice of out-of-town sources of information follows as far as possible the line of their natural interests. A kindly woman, herself a householder, can enter more fully than many another into the deeper meanings of the request made of Mrs. Seymour (p. 322) that she receive an unknown daughter-in-law into her home. A clergyman is fulfilling one of the true functions of his pastorate when he seeks to stimulate a forgiving spirit between husband and wife (p. 325). This was not the first request made in this instance, but family estrangement is suggested by the story of a woman of apparent respectability who will give not a single clue to sources of information in her home town. The looking up of records was only preliminary to the real task developed by the facts of the case. This longer view not only helps in the choice of correspondents, but it enables us, in writing to them, to leave a window open, to suggest a prospect beyond the immediate details about which we are concerned. It is this prospect, this relating of small details to helpful and constructive results in the near future, that will most surely interest them in our request, and fire them with a desire to have a share in this particular social undertaking. Not many words will be necessary, but something of our real interest, something more than mere processes, must be suggested.

The avoidance of technical terms, a choice of words at once direct and human, an ability to think imaginatively of our task and to convey its large spirit of service to our correspondent—these are methods that emphasize the need of varied approach, for no one form of approach will interest all correspondents equally. It is worse than folly to write to the prosperous father of a wayward son—to a father who might have been not only the most valuable single source of information but the best of co-operators—and seek to interest him by saying, "We are very anxious to obtain the previous record of this young man." One such inquiry, to which reference has been made earlier, brought no reply, and the following, also found in a case record, did not deserve one: "I am anxious to have your advice about your brother, John Smith, now in this city." This was the entire letter, but extreme prolixity is quite as bad. A letter that is practically a case record summary and a chronological one at that may be serviceable as part of another social agency's case record, but it will never interest a correspondent.

Every little while someone proposes that, in order to systematize out-of-town inquiries, they should all be centralized, should be handled for each community by some one agency. The maximum of interest will never be developed in this way, however, and it is likely that order can be introduced into our inquiries by some other plan not so liable to destroy their serviceableness.

6. What Presentation Will Save the Correspondent Unnecessary Trouble? Every witness from whom we seek co-operation should be assumed to be socially minded and willing to do his fair share until there is conclusive proof to the contrary. He is entitled, therefore, to protection from annoying publicity. Inquiries should not be sent on post cards, and in small places, or in neighborhoods in which our letters may be handled by gossiping fellow tenants, they should have only a return address printed on the outside instead of the full name of the social agency.

Whatever data will aid in the full identification of our client and of the places or people locally involved in his story, whatever details will make clearer the items to be verified or discovered, will surely save time in the long run for the inquiring agency. But even more important is the consideration that a clear setting forth of these things in the original inquiry will save unnecessary annoyance to the correspondent, will further excite his interest, and will make him a more competent reporter, whether of his own first-hand information or of the data obtained by visits made at our request.

In writing to relatives, for instance, it is not enough to dwell upon the specific things that we wish to know, or even to suggest the future helpful uses to which their information will be put. Relatives are often consumed with anxiety to know just what has been happening lately, and what are the present circumstances of one from whom they have not heard in a long while. Our statements should be specific rather than general, moreover, though they should not be technical. This applies also to letters in which we ask a correspondent to see relatives.

A family agency found a man ill in the almshouse hospital with tuberculosis, who confessed to a prison term for forgery. Though he told thus much, he gave the agency an assumed name and added a false address for his immediate family in a distant city. A kindred agency there was asked to visit. They could not find the man's family at the address given, but did find the firm of employers whose check he said that he had forged. All knowledge of him or of the circumstances was denied, however, by the clerk in charge at this establishment, until mention was made of the fact that the man was now very ill. The clerk, who, it appears, was an old chum, immediately became alarmed, told the sick man's real name, and took the case worker making the inquiry to the family's right address. The visits made in this case would have been of no avail without the mention of the client's present condition contained in the letter of inquiry.

An associated charities was asked to see the relatives of a one-legged man who, with his family, was destitute in a distant city. It replied that these relatives refused to be interviewed or to give any information. The inquiring agency wrote again, giving more details and asking more specific questions, but with no better result. When the agency protested to a referee later about what seemed to be poor inquiry work on the part of its correspondent, the referee replied in part as follows:

Without knowing anything more than the letter reveals, it seems to me possible that the unwillingness of the Jacks family in Wickford to give any information, and the unwillingness of the Wickford society to push an already exasperated relative further at the present time may be due to the fact that, doubtless through hurry or some oversight, you failed to ask any of the questions in your first letter that you did ask in your second. The visitor of the Wickford Associated Charities had a commission from you to find out whether the Wickford relatives would contribute toward the purchase of a new leg. This was a perfectly concrete demand upon them which seems to have brought an indignant response. In my own experience it is a mistake to begin an approach to relatives with a demand for service on their part. The initial demand should be for advice and any experience of theirs that will increase your own insight. It is very clear that you realize some of this, or you would not have written the questions contained in your second letter, but unfortunately they came rather late and after the damage had been done. . . . In your first letter you do not even supply Jacks' first name, and, upon reading the two letters side by side, I think you will agree with me that your second would have been a much better guide to anyone visiting the Wickford relatives for the first time than your first letter was.

One letter of inquiry reads as follows: "Will you kindly forward the following information to your correspondent in Cranford? James Harvey, American, aged thirty-three, came to us this morning to obtain work. His mother, Mrs. Kate Harvey, lives at 20 Saunders Street, Cranford, with her married daughter. There are several other brothers and sisters of Mr. Harvey, and we would like to find out if they are able to give him some assistance.

"Will you also look up the following business references for Mr. Harvey? He has worked for the Cranford Tunnel Company and for the Electric Works as wireman. During the past winter he says that he was ill in the Cranford Hospital with hemorrhages of the stomach. Any information which you may obtain for us will be greatly appreciated."

About which the case worker responsible for the inquiry in Cranford writes: "There is no explanation here as to how Harvey came to the society, what his plan for himself is, how he is being cared for—in fact nothing that has any human interest. When the mother was interviewed, she began to ask questions which we were unable to answer. The mother felt and expressed herself as unable to suggest anything unless she had further information, and the interview was a failure from every angle."

Another letter of inquiry to a kindred agency out of town describes the present situation of a family quite fully and then asks that visits be paid to a tax collector, a minister, a trust company, a farmer, and to a Mrs. Carter on B Street. The street is several miles long, and neither street number, first name of woman, nor relation to the family written about was indicated. In fact, the particular information sought of each informant and his supposed relation to the case were not named in a single instance.

The following is a better example than any given so far of the type of inquiry which saves delay and trouble, and secures socially valuable results. It was written by a state board of charity to a child-protective agency in the same state.

I do not know whether you are the proper person to whom to address the following inquiry, but if you are not, I trust you will forward my letter to the appropriate society.

We are interested in a girl named Jessie Smith, who is at the State Institution at Fairview. She was sent there by the House of the Good Shepherd of Preston for confinement. She had been arrested in Knightsbridge and put on probation for a year, the year to be spent at the House of the Good Shepherd. She entered Fairview on September 2, 1910, and her child was born about the middle of November. Her year on probation will not be completed until the latter part of this month, January, but the Sisters had no way of taking care of a woman with a baby, and so would receive Jessie again only on condition that her child was taken from her first. Neither of Jessie's two sisters nor her aunt will receive the mother and infant, or even the baby without its mother.

The doctors at Fairview have had this girl under observation for some time. She has a violent and ugly temper, provoked by trifles. They consider that it is quite possible that she is insane, but they would like us to get more of her family history to help them in their diagnosis. I am writing to ask whether you will not assist us by getting some skilful visitor to make certain inquiries for us.

Jessie tells us that she was born in Franklin, West Virginia, August 5, 1887; that she lived in that city with her father for fourteen years. Her mother died when she was a little child. At fourteen her father placed her in the Industrial School of that state at Perry, and she remained there for seven years—until she was twenty-one. This school is a reform school. When twenty-one she was placed out in Jefferson, near Perry, by the Industrial School. From there she was shortly taken by a Rev. Mr. Baer of Clayton in this state. Mr. Baer had, as I understand, brought up her sister Jane (Mrs. Albert Dawson, Exeter Street, in your town) and so was anxious to take Jessie, Jane in the meantime having married. Jessie stayed with Mr. Baer a year and then went to be with Mrs. Dawson. From there she came down to Beaufort to stay with her aunt, and later returned to the eastern part of the state. She worked as a waitress for a Mrs. Jenkins who runs a dining room for your girls' seminary, and was also a waitress for a time at the Eastern Hospital.

Can you put on foot an inquiry of Mrs. Jenkins; of the Eastern Hospital; of the police in Knightsbridge; and of the sister, Mrs. Dawson? We should be glad to know how good a worker she is, why she left her places, and how she conducted herself. And of the sister we should like to know whether there is anything in her inheritance which would explain her possible insanity. She told me that her father lives in California because of asthma, but she also said that he had had a cough for many years. If there is any other taint in the family, such as alcoholism or epilepsy, this or tuberculosis, according to the present opinion of doctors, might be a contributing cause of mental disorder. Some uncle or aunt may show the taint, even if her immediate forebears do not.

I fear that I am asking a great deal of you, but the information may be of the greatest value to us. This girl is certainly not normal, and I know I don't need to say to you how almost hopeless it is to try to get such a girl—plus a baby—established respectably. For the sake of the child, and of future children that ought not to be born, we want to do everything we can towards having this mother committed. We shall ourselves, of course, get the information from Clayton and Beaufort.

7. What Facts relating to the Correspondent's Occupation, Education, etc., Should Modify the Approach by Letter? Where a correspondent is personally known to us, we have a definite advantage in our choice of method of approach, but often our only guides are a few stray facts as to his occupation, his educational advantages, and his alleged relation to the client about whom we write. We fall back upon these slender clues because we lack an intermediary whose point of view is known, whose discretion can be trusted, and whose face-to-face intercourse with the witness can overcome our own handicaps.

Letters to business men should be as brief as is possible without sacrificing definiteness and clearness. Letters to former employers of a client should give his name in full accurately, and state definite dates and the exact kind of information sought, while at the same time explaining the reason for the inquiry in such a way as to create no unreasonable prejudice. Where the client's service has been of a personal kind, involving direct daily contacts with the correspondent, the letter can safely be more personal.

Inquiries of physicians have been considered in the chapter on Medical Sources. It may be repeated here, however, that no letter asking for a medical diagnosis should attempt to give one, that the relation of medical diagnosis to the social treatment of which the letter of inquiry is a part should be made clear, and that family history and the specific circumstances, acts, etc., that might have a bearing upon medical diagnosis should be stated. To say that we think our client is mentally deranged is futile; to state the observations that have created this impression is a possible help.

A worker in a public agency for the blind whose work is statewide takes for granted, in writing to priests about their parishioners, that they have a deep interest in the things she is trying to accomplish. In her experience, the interest already exists or is very easily aroused, and her letters usually convey a recognition of this fact. The following is a characteristic beginning:

"You probably will be glad to know that, learning of a child in your parish who has inflammation of the eyes, I went to see her and found the family willing to let the child come to the city and attend the Eye Hospital." And this is a characteristic letter ending: "Remember me should you hear of one who is blind or in danger of becoming so. I should like not only to do what I can to help them, but, in doing for your parishioners, to be able to serve you."

This same worker, in addressing the parents of a client, always puts the names of both on the outside of the envelope as well as on the enclosure, doing this in order to make both parents feel an equal responsibility for answering her inquiries and for carrying out her suggestions.

A case worker in a children's agency once said, after looking over a group of letters addressed by workers in another agency to a wayward girl, that they were so dignifiedly and elegantly expressed as to make her hesitate to show her own. She was accustomed, when writing to uneducated people personally known to her, to address them in simple and familiar language, some of it almost childish. It may be questioned whether letters of inquiry to simple folk are always intelligible to them. Short words and sentences, and an ability to see both the form and the content of the letter through the eyes of the receiver would bring better results. Even the form of the letter—its typewriter script on official letter paper—may put a barrier between its writer and the least businesslike of his correspondents; a letter written by hand on unofficial paper sometimes makes a better beginning.

Sometimes, on the other hand, a formal rather than a familiar tone is justified by the nature of the contents. This is true in the following to a father from a child-protective agency:

"A complaint has come to this office that you are not properly providing for the support of your wife and minor child, that most of your time you are idle, that your wife is obliged to go out to work leaving your child in the care of your mother. I called at your home yesterday to talk this matter over with you, found the house empty and the door unlocked. The outside appearance was very disorderly and dirty. I would like to hear your side of the story and would be glad to have you call at this office Saturday morning at 10 o'clock." The recipient did not come, but went to work the next day and, a month later, was found to be still working steadily and doing better in every way.

In all of the foregoing, emphasis has been put upon letters to those who are not themselves engaged in social work. When we are writing to social agencies, our statements must be full enough to enable them to co-operate intelligently. If we are writing about a family, the names and ages of all its members, the wife's maiden name, and the husband's full name (even though deceased) should be given. In asking to have an employer visited, do not omit to mention the approximate dates of employment, the kind of work done, and, if a large firm, the department in which the worker was employed, his work number, and the name of his foreman. When marriages, births, or deaths are to be verified, always give the dates. Dates should be given also for the period of residence when institutional connections are to be looked up or former addresses are to be visited. When addresses are given us it is an easy matter, before asking an out-of-town agency to visit, to discover whether the addresses are at all possible by consulting the nearest file of out-of-town city directories, or the nearest set of street guides for other cities.

"When I have a name given me without the street address," writes a family case worker, "and I want to ask another society to investigate for me, I have been able to give the exact address by consulting the directory of that city, so I do not often ask for investigations at addresses that do not exist. Recently I had a client who said that his brother-in-law had a restaurant in Los Angeles, and he gave the street address. Instead of writing to a Los Angeles social agency and waiting two weeks for their reply, I went into our board of trade rooms and consulted the directory. I could not find either the brother-in-law's name or that of the street. When my client found that I could not accept all of his first story, he told me the true one." [1]

The time of social case workers in other cities is quite as valuable as our own. More care in calling upon them for service, a clearer realization of the uses to be made of that service, and a better statement of our own case would greatly enhance the value of information received from these sources.

III. LETTERS OF REPLY TO INQUIRIES

The quality of a letter of inquiry has much to do with the fullness and satisfactoriness of the reply. For this reason more space

[1] For use of directories see also Chapter XIII, Documentary Sources.

has been given to this first half of letter writing. The second half, which we must consider only in so far as it relates to the replies of social case workers—to the letters, that is, in which they send information already at hand and those others in which they send information secured especially for the inquirer—need not detain us long. The worst failings of such letters of report are traceable to failings in the investigations themselves, but some few are due to faults of the social diagnostician as correspondent.

In the first place, his letters, like those of other modern correspondents, often contain internal evidence that they have been written in reply to inquiries that have not been read, or, if read, have not been fully apprehended.[1] It follows, in the second place then, that his reply fails to cover all the points raised. When it is impossible to cover them he could at least indicate the items not supplied and the reasons for the omission. This precaution would save the annoyance of further inquiries, further replies, apologies, etc., with all their avoidable delays. In the third place, he gives too often only the inferences drawn from information gathered, whereas the information itself, with its source or sources and some evaluation of the witnesses quoted, is needed. The inferences are useful too, but they should be recognized and stated as such, thus giving the inquirer a chance to use his own judgment. Statements such as, "I am informed," "I understand," without saying by or from whom, leave the mind confused and unsatisfied. What is said elsewhere[2] about the use of general terms in case records applies to letters also.

Letters of report to correspondents in the same city are easily followed by directer communication, which supplements or corrects their deficiencies. There is something so tangible about a letter, however, that an error may survive the correction and make trouble a good deal later.

[1] "My dear old grandfather. . . taught me never to attempt to answer a letter without placing it before me and reviewing it scrupulously, paragraph by paragraph. Hundreds of times have I devoutly blessed his memory for that lesson in the common-sense of correspondence."—Anonymous Contributor in the *Atlantic Monthly*, June, 1913, pp. 856–7.

[2] See p. 349.

IV. SOME TECHNICAL DETAILS

The foregoing sentence might seem to contain an argument for destroying letters as soon as their immediate purpose had been served. In one family agency a business men's committee recommended that all correspondence about any given case be destroyed as soon as the case was "closed"—this being the agency's technical term for the discontinuance of treatment. Medical men would have seen by analogy the folly of this, but business men could not, and the attempt to carry out the decision caused endless trouble. It is important in case work to keep all letters received and copies of all letters sent that have any bearing upon case diagnosis and treatment. The originals of letters written by a client who, at the time of writing or later, suffers from some form of mental disease are sometimes important items in the diagnosis of the disease. This is also true in the diagnosis of mental defect, but there are equally important inferences to be drawn from the letters of the normal, such as their fitness for certain work, their degree of education, etc. It is often found wise to preserve copies of letters not addressed to the case worker but shown by the client as having an important bearing upon his affairs. One child-protective agency is accustomed to have such letters copied at its office while the client waits.

Letters of inquiry or report should not be forwarded by the client's own hand. One letter so sent to a hospital contains the following sentence: "No doubt you will notice at once upon talking with her that she is not mentally normal." Apart from the danger of suggesting a diagnosis, it was a mistake, of course, to send this by a client. The report should have gone by mail, and only a short, unsealed note of introduction, referring to the letter, should have gone by hand.

Letters addressed "to whom it may concern" should not be written at all. The worthlessness of such letters has already been referred to (p. 177). Circular letters of inquiry are often used with good results in cases involving the discovery of the whereabouts of runaway boys or of adults who are mentally disturbed. These forms should indicate that duplicates are being sent to a number of places. They should contain a careful description of the person sought and suggestions as to the kind of story that he is likely to tell.

Another very useful device in establishing whereabouts and even identity is the registered letter. The special delivery letter is not so good, because the post office authorities are not so careful to demand, for its receipt, the signature of the addressee or of someone holding his power of attorney. The registered letter receipt is used as evidence in court. Here its signature can be disputed, of course, in which case the handwriting expert may have to be called in.

One medical-social department tried to find the mother of a hospital patient, a child who was on the dangerous list. A letter addressed to her had just been returned "not found." The post office authorities were consulted, with the practical guarantee from them that a registered letter would reach her in two days' time. It did, in a suburb several miles away from the original address.

A regulation of the post office department forbids letter carriers to give information about addresses, but it is possible to get such information higher up when satisfactory reasons can be given for seeking it. In large cities application can be made to the division superintendents, followed, when this fails, by appeal to the postmaster himself. Any supposed irregular use of the mails should be reported promptly to the post office inspectors, who are always ready to investigate such complaints.

As has been said already, a letter is better evidence when accompanied by the inquiry to which it is a reply. A letter is somewhat better evidence when accompanied by the addressed and postmarked envelope in which it was received. In the case of letters returned, the envelope marked "address not found" should be saved. It is evidence that the attempt to find has been made.

V. COMMUNICATION BY TELEGRAPH

In a good many minor matters, where necessary details can be stated briefly and where promptness rather than fullness of reply is the important thing, communication by telegraph is more satisfactory than by letter alone. A telegraphic dispatch should always be followed by a letter the same day, and in cases in which this procedure is not well understood and therefore taken for granted by the recipient, the dispatch should state that a letter is on the way. The follow-up letter should contain a copy of the dispatch, which may have been mutilated in transmission. Sometimes, when a letter alone would suffice if given prompt attention, the psychological effect of the dispatch is to assure prompter answer of the letter. The "night letter" form of dispatch, which carries 50 words without extra charge, is often better than a letter alone, when a correspondent is more than twenty-four hours' journey away.

A large group of social agencies (about 800 at the present writing) use a telegraphic code in matters pertaining to the transportation of their clients within the United States. The preliminary inquiries by telegraph that often precede the furnishing of transportation are thus made at lower cost, and there is also a general understanding among these agencies, which are all signers of a "transportation agreement," that such inquiries shall take precedence of others and be answered with especial promptness.[1]

VI. COMMUNICATION BY TELEPHONE

The question of whether, in a given case, the long distance telephone would not be a better means of communication than the telegraph is one that must be answered with a knowledge of all the circumstances of each inquiry in mind. The possibility of a choice should not be lost sight of, however. The mere existence of a telegraphic code, for instance, may lead the signers of the transportation agreement to use it when some other means of communication would be better. For data already in the possession of the one communicated with, the telephone response is prompter and fuller, though it is not always accurately received. For information that must be gathered, reply by telegraph, with all its shortcomings, is better, therefore, and especially so for names, numbers, etc. All such data should be repeated by letter, however, when originally communicated either by telephone or by telegraph. The promptness of the long distance telephone in putting us in communication with those who already know is illustrated by the following instances, the first supplied by Miss Alice Higgins (Mrs. Wm. H. Lothrop), and the second by Miss M. L. Birtwell:

> A business man asked us to send a young fellow to his father in a city 200 miles distant, and thought us a bit fussy when we talked over a long distance telephone to learn if such return would help the man. We learned the father was a chronic drunkard and a most undesirable guardian, but that an uncle in an adjoining city to our own would be a wise and interested adviser. Consultation with the uncle

[1] See pamphlet, Passing On as a Method of Charitable Relief. Russell Sage Foundation, New York, 1911. (Now out of print.)

resulted in a good position and a home for the nephew; and the business man then appreciated that knowledge before action meant wiser action.

A man of fifty-three wandered into our office one morning at about 11 o'clock and asked for work. He did not seem strong or intelligent and we felt that he was hardly a promising subject for the labor market. We could get little out of him, but on rather close questioning he mentioned Palmer as a recent place of residence. Knowing that the State Hospital for Epileptics was located there, we telephoned to the State Board of Insanity to inquire whether such a man had been a recent inmate. The reply came that according to report from that hospital a man of that name had left the institution two days before. A telephone message to Palmer, eighty-four miles away, brought word from the superintendent that the man had left against the advice of the authorities; that he was entirely unfitted to earn his living out in the community, but that he could do some work about the institution; and that they would like us to use our utmost efforts to persuade him to return. He refused for a time and shed tears at the prospect; but after much kindly persuasion on the part of one of our workers, who shared her lunch with him, he consented. He was put on the train in care of the conductor, the superintendent was telephoned to that he was coming, and at half-past five in the afternoon he was in safe hands again. He wrote us a day or two later that the doctor met him, that he had a good bath and a good supper, and was back at his old job at the stable.

As a means of communication within the city, especially with other social agencies, the telephone is very popular among case workers and will probably continue to be so. Its dangers and shortcomings are only beginning to be noted, and they deserve enumeration for this reason. No one will use the telephone too little, because it is so convenient, but the facts brought to light in the course of our case reading should lead everyone to use it, in diagnosis, with more caution.

It is comparatively easy to get in communication with even a very busy person over the telephone, which still has the right of way in household and office alike. But this very fact means that the one telephoned to may have been interrupted, with the result that he is somewhat irritated and has little conscience about putting off the interrupter with an inadequate and hastily expressed statement. Are the ordinary run of people as frank in their telephone intercourse as they are in intercourse face to face? The question is not without interest. When an attempt is made to answer it, this factor of interruption will have to be taken into account. Another consideration will have to be the fact that the one telephoned to cannot always be sure of the identity of the person at the other end of the wire. How can he know that this questioner is just what he claims to be? The one telephoning, on the other hand, cannot know who is in the same room with his informant, and the informant cannot always be sure, unless he has a private wire, who else, besides the people in the room with him and the questioner, may be listening to the conversation.

Two other elements increase the chances, not of suppression or untruthfulness, but of error. Over the telephone, as we now know it, proper names are very frequently and other words somewhat less frequently misunderstood. In case work this is a serious drawback. In addition to this, case records seem to show that the eye helps the ear in noting what is said, and that telephone conversations are less accurately reported on our records than are personal interviews. The following comments and case items illustrate these drawbacks:

A critic of case records writes of one as follows: I should say that the telephone communication with the minister on September 16 had been ill advised. With a minister who does not understand our methods one of two systems of approach is generally advisable; first, and preferably, the personal conference; second, a letter, possibly followed by a telephone call. Direct approach by telephone is pretty risky unless we know our people.

The husband of a tuberculous wife asked a medical-social department to communicate with him by telephone, when necessary, at the factory where he worked. But in this way the fact that his wife had tuberculosis became known there, and the fear among his fellow employes that he might infect them made it so uncomfortable for him that he was forced to leave.

A former newspaper reporter became the client of a certain social agency. Soon after, the agency received a telephone message purporting to be from the night editor of a daily paper asking that the reporter's application receive immediate and careful attention, and that whatever inquiry was made be conducted without inconvenience to him. Seen later the same day, the night editor denied all knowledge of this message. Far from commending the reporter in any way, he considered him an adventurer and "hold-up man."

A family agency was asked by a society in another city to see the relatives of one of its clients and his physician. The agency telephoned to the physician to find that the client's brother was in his office at the time. While the treatment of the case was not hampered by this fact, it made an additional difficulty for the brother, who was extremely sensitive about the client's misfortunes.

A child-protective agency operating in a rural area reports that, in the small country towns included in its district, half the town may be on one telephone line, and that it is considered an innocent and legitimate diversion to lift the receiver and hear all about one's neighbors. This is especially true if a particular neighbor is known to have had a visit from the agency's case worker.

The registrar of one of the confidential exchanges reports that a hospital telephones each morning all the names about which it wishes to make inquiry, and that a written report is sent to the hospital later in the day about each one, indicating whether it is known or unknown. Usually a note comes from the hospital still later to say that certain of the names previously telephoned were misunderstood, and that the correct spelling is so and so. Thereupon the exchange often finds that these names about which "no information" had been reported are really in the exchange.

The use of the telephone to obtain medical data led to the following results in one Polish family: (1) Dispensary reported by telephone after examination of the three children that Dominic had been given a positive diagnosis of tuberculosis. (2) Three days later a visit to the dispensary brought out the fact that this diagnosis belonged not to Dominic but to Almena, his sister. (3) A year and four months later, dispensary telephoned that the mother of the family had an advanced case of tuberculosis. (4) Three weeks later, the doctor, when seen at the dispensary, said that she had an early case.

A family was referred by a medical-social department to an associated charities with certain data, including the statement of the man of the family that he was earning $14 a week. The society visited the employer and reported over the telephone to the medical agency after this visit (or was understood to have reported) that the man was earning $17 a week and had been doing so for the last six years. As a matter of fact the record of the associated charities quotes the employer as saying that the man had been earning $14 a week for six years but that his weekly wage had just been increased to $17. The record of the medical-social department did the man unintentional but serious injustice, as it suggested the inference that he was not trustworthy.[1]

Some case workers are so unwilling that their work should be represented on the records of other organizations by someone's recollection either of a telephone conversation or of one face to face that they always offer, when information is requested, to send a written summary of what they know instead. If inquirers are in special haste, they make a brief statement at the time and send the written summary for purposes of verification and for its fuller and more carefully considered details. Such workers, in asking information from others—in following up the clues supplied by the confidential exchange, for instance—are careful to ask for written summaries from those agencies which prove, when telephoned to, to have some definite information to give. When supplemented

[1] A critic points out that this same error in reporting or recording might have happened in or after a personal interview, though there are more errors when the telephone is used.

by the written summary, the telephone becomes a far safer means of communication.

SUMMARY OF THIS CHAPTER

1. The best means of communication for most case work purposes is the personal interview; the worst is the blank form.

2. The letter of inquiry is too often a matter of routine. The value of such a letter may be tested by the following questions:

(1) Should the letter be written at all or would some other means of communication serve the purpose better?
(2) Should the letter be written now? Have the preliminary inquiries that would make its writing the logical next step all been made?
(3) What relation does this particular inquiry bear to the whole process?
(4) Has the best correspondent been chosen for the end in view?
(5) What will interest the correspondent selected?
(6) What presentation will save him unnecessary trouble?
(7) What facts relating to this correspondent's occupation, education, etc., should modify the approach by letter?

3. The case worker's letter of reply to an inquiry should bear internal evidence that the inquirer's letter has been read and its contents fully apprehended. When it is impossible to cover all the points of an inquiry, a reply should name the items not covered and give reasons for the omission.

4. A letter of reply to an inquiry should not confuse the inferences of the writer with the information on which they are based. The letter should give both, but it should be possible for its recipient to distinguish them.

5. A telegraphic dispatch should always be followed by a letter the same day; this follow-up letter should contain a copy of the dispatch.

6. The telephone as a means of communication in case work is too convenient to be abandoned, but its drawbacks are not always understood and guarded against. There are good reasons why people are not so frank in their telephone intercourse as they are face to face, nor do they understand what is said as well. The eye aids the ear in getting names and numbers accurately; over the telephone these are frequently misunderstood.

CHAPTER XVIII

COMPARISON AND INTERPRETATION

WE come now to the fourth and last of what for convenience we have defined as the stages leading to diagnosis. Workers will continue, in many cases, to find their way to a correct and sufficiently amplified diagnosis without consciously arranging the preliminary steps in groups, but in cases presenting difficulties they will find this separation and the further analysis attempted in this chapter an aid to thinking. The processes already described have been (1) the first full interview with a client, (2) the early contacts with his immediate family, (3) the search for further insight and for sources of needed co-operation outside his immediate family.

To emphasize the essential unity of these three processes, to bring out a few of their salient features and to establish more clearly the relation of these to the final process of Comparison and Interpretation now to be described, it is necessary at this point to review briefly a part of the ground that has already been covered. Since each item of this restatement has been more fully developed in earlier chapters, no more than a regrouping of the main ideas is necessary.

I. CERTAIN ASPECTS OF EARLIER PROCESSES RESTATED

We have seen (1) that certain methods and points of view are common to all interviews, (2) that different types of interview call for changes of emphasis, (3) that discrimination in the choice of outside sources of insight is an economy of time as well as an indication of skill, (4) that the risks involved in different types of evidence and the nature of these types must be kept in mind in gathering the facts and in weighing them, and (5) that the characteristics of human beings as witnesses should be our constant study.

1. Methods Common to All Interviews. Our methods and point of view are in many ways the same whether we are meeting a client for the first time, visiting members of his immediate family, or seeking insight from outside sources. In all these cases we should

(a) Strive to procure from each the evidence that each is best able to give. Some facts come best from our client, some from our observation of his home surroundings and neighborhood, some from the testimony of employers and comrades, and some from documentary sources.

(b) Utilize any natural avenue of approach to a client presented at the beginning of the interview, and as the interview develops avoid the temptation to shape it in accordance with preconceived ideas of its probable content. The same caution applies to any questions that we may have to ask—the way in which we put our question should not suggest the answer.

(c) Give the person interviewed ample time, therefore, in which to explain his own point of view, and give him also a sympathetic hearing.

(d) Keep the goals of fuller knowledge of the client's problem and of the future co-operation of relatives, employers, etc., in its solution always in view. Our ability to show genuine interest will play an important part in procuring both information and backing.

2. Changes of Emphasis in Interviewing. Generally speaking, we are justified in narrowing our inquiry, somewhat, as we approach the sources farthest away from our client's personal life, and in broadening it in our talks with him and his family. As between the client and his family group on the one hand and certain outside sources on the other, this difference becomes a marked one. In talking with our client, the whole man, for any diagnosis that deserves to be called social, must concern us. We must be alert to every possible clue to his personality, or, in other words, we must note the current of events in his life as well as his social relationships. What has been the main drift of that current? Who are the people and what are the social institutions that have most influenced him?

To win these insights as promptly as possible without endangering our future relations with him we must avoid, in our interviews, all dictation, hurry, and overquestioning; we must give our client a patient and fair hearing, merely guiding the trend of talk enough to encourage a full development of his story.

This same painstaking method may be necessary with all the members of the client's family group. Knowledge of the main drift of the family life may be the key to a diagnosis of the client's situation. In studying that drift it will be found useful to note the difference between the power of cohesion in a united and in an unstable family.

Passing to outside sources, we find some, more especially those whose relations to our client have been personal and unbroken, from whom we shall need guidance and help during the period of treatment. A number of others, however, we shall see only, as a rule, before our diagnosis is made, and thereafter not at all. With these latter we can afford to save time by narrowing the inquiry to the special information which this or that source is likely to supply, though always with the possibility in mind that, at any moment, the person interviewed may show himself able to throw unexpected light on other aspects of the problem. We do not see even the least important outside source merely for verification of items already learned elsewhere; verification should be a by-product of more fruitful intercourse. Success in the interviewing of outside sources depends partly upon taking time to explain briefly to teacher, physician, church visitor, etc., the relation of the items of information sought from him to the constructive work which is in process.

It is evident that the multiplication of interviews in which inquiry is thus narrowed may be carried too far. If undertaken heedlessly, without a clear conception of the weaknesses and strengths of the evidence already gathered, they may add little to our sum of knowledge. On the other hand, there is always a degree of risk in omitting any source. One of the ways of economizing means is to strive to get from sources that are being consulted sidelights upon the probable value of those that have not yet been seen.

3. Discrimination in the Choice of Outside Sources. Economy of means is a lesson still too little heeded by case workers. They should beware, it is true, of using in every case the same two or three kinds of source and no more; but, in choosing varied sources for varied cases, they should learn to seek the source of each kind which is likely to yield the facts they want—the most skilful physician, for example, the employer for whom a client worked longest, the one for whom he worked longest during the last five years, the previous residence at which his family lived the longest during the same period, the social agency that has had the least casual contacts with his family, etc. It may even be that some social agency has already assumed responsibility for treatment. This fact would come out after consultation of the index at the confidential exchange or social service exchange, and would render unnecessary further work with the client in question.

Every such discrimination gives a more assured and economical use of sources. Thus

(a) Some sources are known, even before they have been seen, to be rich in history—they are familiar with our client's early life from observation instead of hearsay. These witnesses may or may not be so associated with the client's present as to be likely to be rich also in co-operation. In choosing the order in which sources should be seen, it has been found useful to see first those who are likely to be rich in history only, in order that our first conference with a possible co-operator may be conducted later, when we can meet him on more equal terms as to a knowledge of relevant facts in the client's history and therefore with greater likelihood of achieving a social result.

(b) Another useful discrimination is that between clues to outside sources obtained from a client or his immediate family, and such clues when obtained elsewhere. The latter are called supplementary clues, and, since usually they have been revealed more disinterestedly, are less liable to be prejudiced.

(c) A further discrimination divides social agencies as witnesses into those agencies that have had a personal experience with our client which has a bearing upon diagnosis, and those agencies that, with or without such an experience, have gathered certain objective and fundamental data with regard to the client—data which are not likely to change. Previous experience of the work of certain social agencies may serve here to guide us to those that usually gather carefully the facts of family and personal background.

(d) Still another discrimination is between the uses to which documentary and personal sources can be put. The impersonal document is more satisfactory for objective matters of fact, such as events, dates, places, amounts; and individual testimony more satisfactory for subjective matters, such as personal traits, in which the motives and capacity of the witness, the atmosphere and spirit of his statement, are all important.

4. Types of Evidence. There are discriminations to be made not only in the types of source but in the types of evidence which sources supply. Real evidence, it will be remembered, is the very fact at issue presented to our senses. Testimonial evidence is the assertions of human beings, to which must always be applied tests of the competence and bias of the witnesses. Circumstantial evidence is any indirect evidence whatsoever which tends to establish the point at issue. The tests applied to it have to vary, because the subject matter is infinitely varied. Any fact in the material universe or in the mind of man may become the basis from which some other fact is inferred.

There is an important distinction in testimonial evidence between the assertions of those who say that they saw or heard the supposed facts themselves and the assertions of those who have the facts only from what others have told them. This latter is hearsay evidence, and in all our interviewing we should discover the extent to which the assertions of the interviewed are founded on observations or on mere rumor.

5. Characteristics of Witnesses. The first, unrehearsed statement of a witness is often the most trustworthy. This first statement can be made less reliable, however, by a careless use of "leading questions," which are a danger not only in the first interview but everywhere. "Every one of us," says Gross, "has made the frightful observation that by the end of an examination the witness has simply taken the point of view of the examiner, and the worst thing about this is that the witness still thinks that he is thinking in his own way."[1]

A witness may be quite sincere also in thinking that he knows more about an event or a person than he really does. His good faith, therefore, is not the only thing to establish. His competence includes both his opportunity to know the facts and the way in which he has used his opportunity. This latter is conditioned by his powers of attention, memory, and suggestibility. What ideas had he in stock, moreover, which would have made him a

[1] Criminal Psychology, p. 163.

good or a bad observer? What reason had he for observing carefully?

Apart from his competence as a witness, what risk is there of bias in his testimony? Bias may be racial, national, religious, political, environmental, or some element of self-interest may enter in. Important forms of environmental bias are those of a man's occupation and of the particular habit group to which he belongs.

Obviously it is not enough to add statement to statement, as a phonograph would. The processes of inference, of comparison of material, begin with the first interview and continue through all the steps leading to diagnosis.

II. THE COMPARISON OF MATERIAL

"I am astonished," says Dubois, "to see how many young physicians possessing all the working machinery of diagnosis do not know how to make a diagnosis. It is because the art of diagnosis does not consist merely in gathering together a great many facts, but in co-ordinating those that one has been able to collect, in order to reach a clear conception of the situation."[1] And we are told that the historian first collects his material, then collates it, and only after it has been collated attempts his final interpretation. He weighs his evidence, of course, as we do, item by item when it is gathered, but a reweighing of the total is necessary when all the items are in. "After a student has learned to open his eyes and sees," writes Dr. Richard Cabot of clinical teaching, "he must learn to shut them and think."[2] So must we. Nevertheless, this stage of assembling our material, of relating its parts and trying to bring it up into consciousness as a whole, will not be easy to illustrate, since it is the most neglected part of case work technique.

Speaking broadly, the social case worker of an earlier day did little visiting of anyone except his client and so observed only within those narrow limits. He was mentally sluggish, moreover, and guilty of much thoughtless prescribing. The case worker of today is more active physically—sometimes doing too much running around, one is tempted to believe—but his advance in useful-

[1] The Psychic Treatment of Nervous Disorders, p. 277.

[2] Case Teaching in Medicine, Introduction, p. vii.

ness over earlier workers would be greater if he would oftener "shut his eyes and think," if he would reduce the visible signs of his activity and assemble his forces in order the better to deliberate upon his next move before he makes it. Case records often show a well made investigation and a plan formulated and carried out, but with no discoverable connection between them. Instead, at the right moment, of shutting his eyes and thinking, the worker seems to have shut his eyes and jumped. On the other hand, however carefully the inquiries are recorded and the diagnosis which grew out of them indicated, however carefully a plan of action is decided upon, etc., the processes by which the diagnosis is arrived at—what parts of the evidence have been accepted or rejected and why, what inferences have been drawn from these accepted items and how they have been tested—can none of them be revealed in a record.

Some case workers feel that their conscious assembling of material comes when they present a summary to the case committees of volunteers who assist them in making the diagnosis and the plan of treatment. This is especially true if any of the members of the committee have a social experience that has made them both critical and just in their valuing of testimony. One worker writes, "Repeatedly, flaws in my investigation have not occurred to me in reading over the record, but they have become only too evident at the moment of presenting the case to my committee. The standard in my mind of what the committee ought to know in order to make a fair decision has then suddenly revealed weaknesses to me before they were brought out in the discussion."

The same bracing influence comes from submitting findings at this stage to a case supervisor who is responsible for the work of a group of social case workers. Indeed, the process of comparison, in so far as it can be studied at all at present, is found at its best in the daily work of a few experienced supervisors. Unfortunately they are usually persons who are much overburdened. Although committees, at their worst, can be useless as critics, when well chosen they have an advantage over any one referee in that they bring not only less jaded minds but more varied experiences to bear upon each problem. Either supervisors or committees have the advantage over the worker who makes his analysis unaided, that they do not know the client or his story, and that consequently they are not already so impressed with any one part of the story as to be unable to grasp the client's history as a whole.[1]

1. Suggestions for Self-supervision. In the absence of a competent supervisor or of a committee, the case worker will often have to take the place of both by consciously setting aside some time in which he will strive to look at his own work as if he were a critical outsider.[2]

(a) He can try to review each item of a case with all the others in mind. When each particular piece of evidence came to him, he judged it by what he then knew. How does he judge it now in the light of all the evidence?

Gross suggests another way of testing our material which is psychologically more difficult; namely, to consider a part of it with other material deliberately excluded.[3]

This is what a probation officer had to do, probably, when a father lodged complaint against his boy for stubbornness and for thieving from his older brothers. The home seemed so satisfactory that she was inclined to seek the cause of the trouble in outside influences that would have led the lad to take first small sums and then much larger ones. When, however, the time came for planning, the explana-

[1] A case reader of wide experience suggests here that, in fields of work where no committee is possible and no supervisor is at hand, someone with a keen mind be introduced to case record reading and that current problems be "tried out on him." Even where there is a committee it is important that someone on the committee besides the case worker read the record before the case comes up for discussion.

[2] Any detailed discussion of the worker's case records must be reserved for a separate book on that subject, though self-supervision might well include not only the case work but its recording. Charles Kingsley warned a young writer that he should never refer to anything as a "tree" if he could call it a "spruce" or a "pine." If that lesson had been impressed upon the present generation of case recorders, the task of writing this book would have been an easier one.

Among the general terms against which collectors of family histories for eugenic study are warned by the Cold Spring Harbor Eugenics Record Office (see Eugenics Record Office Bulletin No. 7, p. 91) are *abscess,* without cause or location; *accident, decline,* without naming the disease; *cancer,* without specifying organ first affected; *congestion,* without naming organ affected; *convulsions,* without details and period of life; *fever; heart trouble* and *heart failure; insanity,* without details; *kidney trouble; lung trouble; marasmus; stomach trouble.*

The social case worker's Index Expurgatorius would have to cover a much wider range of subjects; but some of the commonest substitutions are *relative* for the word expressing the exact degree of relationship; *Italian* or *Austrian* or *German* for the term descriptive of a native of the particular province or other political subdivision; *day laborer* or *salesman* or *clerk* for the particular occupation; and *bad, dull, unsanitary, shiftless, incompetent, unsatisfactory, good, bright, industrious, proud, refined,* and a host of such adjectives for the specific act or condition.

[3] Criminal Psychology, p. 12.

tion had not been found, and, having a mind that demanded specific data instead of falling back upon an unsupported theory, she began her search anew and excluding from her mind for the time being the favorable family appearances, found two court records of the arrest of the father, one for buying junk from minors and the other for peddling without a license. These may seem small offenses, but they were serious enough in the father of a boy who was also developing a tendency to lawlessness.

(b) Sometimes, as Gross suggests also, the grounding of a fact has been so difficult, has taken so much time, that we slur over the task of establishing its logical connection with the whole, or do that part of our work "swiftly—and wrongly."[1] Or sometimes the slurring is due to the desire to make a definite report with promptness, as in the following case:

A charity organization society was asked in August by the state's attorney to interest itself in a non-support case, in which the man of the family had been arrested for not making weekly payments to his wife on the separate support order of the court. A week later the society submitted a report of its inquiry upholding the wife. In October, however, when the man made application to have his children removed from the home, an exhaustive study of the case revealed bad conditions there. A critic of this case record writes: "Before your first report to the state's attorney was sent, contradictions in the evidence had developed that should have made it clear to you that further investigation was needed. The sources of information were at hand and the winter's rush was not upon you."

(c) As was the case in the foregoing example, a review of our material will often reveal unsuspected contradictions in the evidence. Where these contradictions cannot be reconciled we may safely infer that further evidence is needed; where, though all the evidence points one way, no explanation of the difficulty or guide to its solution has been revealed, we must again look for additional facts.

(d) The rhetorics tell us that the first and last paragraphs of an essay are the two that make the deepest impression upon the reader. It may be well to ask always, therefore, whether the story as told by the first person seen, or the first theory adopted by the worker has received undue consideration in shaping the final conclusion; or whether the last statement made has been allowed this advantage. Anyone who has had occasion to note the eagerness of each of two complainants to tell his grievance first will appreciate that

[1] Criminal Psychology, p. 143.

we have an intuition that first impressions are lasting. Where there have been matters in dispute, however, the strategic position—second only in value to the first—is the last. In short, we must guard against the impression made by first and by last statements in an investigation.

In all this analysis of data the suggestions made in Part I in the discussion of inferences will be found useful.[1] What is there said about the testing of inferences applies to their retesting by the case worker, and is so fundamental that it has seemed best not to restate in abbreviated form the conclusions of that chapter at the beginning of this. There are, however, many of the details in the later process of comparison—in the process of examining critically, that is, the gathered testimony—which are best summarized on the assumption that someone besides the case worker himself is to review a mass of evidence.

2. Suggestions for Comparisons Made by a Supervisor. What should a supervisor look for in a case record in which the work has reached the stage of evidence gathered but not yet compared or interpreted? For convenience of reference the treatment of this topic has been reduced to questionnaire form and added to the series of questionnaires in Part III,[2] but every other questionnaire in this volume should be understood to have a relation to supervisory work and to the comparisons made in self-supervision. The questionnaire for supervisors summarizes material scattered throughout this volume and rearranges it under the heads of (a) the case worker's relations with client, (b) with client's family, (c) with outside sources, (d) the conduct of the inquiry as a whole, and (e) wider aspects of the inquiry.

Good supervision must include this consideration of wider aspects. We have seen that the habit of keeping in mind the bearing of each individual fact on general social conditions gives added significance to the statements in a record. This habit may also open broader avenues of usefulness. Every case worker has noticed how a certain juxtaposition of facts often reappears in record after record, and must have suspected that this recurring juxtaposition indicates a hidden relation of cause and effect. Or else he must have noted that some twist in the affairs of clients showed again

[1] See p. 81 sq.

[2] See p. 449 sq.

and again a marked similarity of outline such as to suggest a common cause, though no rational explanation came to hand. It is here that the "notation of recurrence," as it is called, becomes a duty of supervisor and case worker. Not only should these repetitions be noted but they should be compared carefully. Some situations that seemed similar will be found upon examination to be different in essence, but the remainder, if they are likely to throw light on social conditions or on the characteristics of any disadvantaged group, should be submitted to those specialists in social reform who can make a critical and constructive use of them. The getting at knowledge that will make the case work of another generation more effective may be only a by-product of our own case work, but it is an important by-product.[1] The wider significance of case work data is illustrated incidentally in the analysis of the Ames case, which follows:

3. The Ames Case. On page 84 will be found the face card of a family record of the Ameses, begun in 1909, together with a discussion of some of the inferences drawn from it by a case worker who had not read the record itself. This process of drawing inferences from a face card and then testing them by the record or by further inquiry will be found useful in review procedure.

Let us now see, without attempting to reproduce the Ames record,[2] how a few of the suggestions in this section may be applied to the story of that family:

[1] Dr. Adolf Meyer, addressing a group of after-care committees for the insane, just after having read some of their records, says, "I had to put a big black cross in my mind over the town of Waterloo. There is a town which evidently contains centers of infection, which the community cannot afford to tolerate, and which can be attacked if one has sufficient material against them. . . . The authorities and the good and bad people may not pay much attention to remonstrations until sufficient material accumulates and is plunged at the right time, and then you may be able to do something. These are difficult tasks, I know, but there is no way of doing anything by keeping quiet or by making abstract complaints."—After-care and Prophylaxis, p. 16. Reprint of an article in the State Hospitals Bulletin, March, 1909, authorized by the State Commission in Lunacy, Albany, N. Y. Utica, N. Y., State Hospitals Press, 1909.

[2] Study of the original case record would be more satisfactory, for case workers will always disagree as to what is important and what is not in the making of a summary. On the other hand, a social case record which is fully adequate for study is such an identifiable thing that the writer has never been willing to publish one. The few that have been privately printed for class study only have been excellent teaching material, though even in the use of these few the danger of violating the confidences of clients has not been completely avoided, and the problem of reconciling their use with the highest case work ethics has been a puzzling one.

Thomas Ames is a tuberculous hatter of thirty-eight with a wife of twenty-eight and two children, girls aged six and nearly two. Mrs. Ames' mother lives with them. The family had been reported as in distress to a charitable woman, Miss Delancey, when she happened to be visiting some of their neighbors. After one visit to the Ameses, she sought, on May 10, the advice and aid of the nearest district office of the charity organization society. One of the society's case workers held the first interview in the home that same day, noting on the record that she was obliged to interview Ames, his wife, and his mother-in-law together.

Mr. Ames gave at this time his story of work at Caldwell's hat factory ever since his marriage, and stated that the tuberculosis dispensary had advised him to apply for admission to the state sanatorium, but that he could not leave his family. He was seeking work as an insurance solicitor, hoping in this way to become stronger. The mother-in-law was not working for reasons unstated. The church had helped but was too poor to continue, or so the family believed. Mrs. Ames had never been strong since the younger child's birth. She showed some hesitation about having any of her own or her husband's people seen. Mr. Ames, however, said that he understood the case worker's desire to consult them and furnished the addresses of his four brothers and sisters and of his wife's two sisters.

The outside visits were then made in the following order: Tuberculosis dispensary, Mrs. Ames' two sisters, her doctor, the school principal of the older child, one of Mr. Ames' brothers, and his two sisters, then the tuberculosis dispensary twice again, followed by an interview with Mrs. Ames alone. Only after all these visits had been made were the manager of the hat factory and the pastor of the church seen.

What did these outside visits reveal? An unusually simple family history, which for that reason is used here for illustration. The dispensary doctor was not found until the third visit to the dispensary, which, aside from sending a quart of milk daily, had had no contact with the home. The medical record showed that Ames' condition was grave, that he was running a high temperature and was unable to work.

Mrs. Ames' two sisters spoke in high terms of Ames' industry and kindness to his family. The older child was reported by the school principal to be quiet, well trained, and diligent, but "by no means bright." Mrs. Ames' doctor had known the family a long while, spoke well of them, but was vague about the wife's health, describing her as "always frail," and did not state how long it had been since he had last treated her.

Joseph Ames and his wife had not realized before the seriousness of the situation. On learning it, they offered Mrs. Ames and her children a home if her husband would go to the sanatorium. (The case worker said on the spot that she thought the plan an excellent one, though the interview developed that both Joseph and his wife were sure Mrs. Ames should go to work and that she was "too high-toned.") Their sister, Clara, seen on May 15, was found to know the Ameses better than the other relatives of the husband. She dropped a hint that Ames was willing to go away, but that his wife was holding him back and urging him to find other work.

The case worker had had no intimation of this, but it proved the key to all the treatment that followed. A private interview was had with Mrs. Ames. She could not believe at first that her husband's condition was as grave as represented, and moreover was worried as to what was to become of her home and her children. It was possible to convince her that Ames was a very sick man, and to reassure her as to her household. The explanation of Ames' attitude having been passed on to the dispensary, the doctor there was able to persuade his patient to apply for admission to the sanatorium.

It had taken ten days to accomplish this. Thereafter followed quickly visits to the two important sources of co-operation in the case—the employer and the church. Although Caldwell's had aided, the firm did not know that Ames had tuberculosis or was incapacitated for any work. They agreed, in the light of this development, to pay $5.00 a week until Ames could be admitted to the sanatorium. (The period of help was extended later to the date of Ames' return.) The pastor of the church agreed to supply whatever food was needed.

During an interval of some months before Ames could be admitted, Miss Delancey served as a regular visitor to the family, with the immediate object of suggesting the necessary precautions for the invalid. With a sleeping tent in the back yard, Ames actually made some slight gains at home before his five months away.

This social diagnosis and treatment, which was successful in the promptness with which it got at the heart of the difficulty—a personal as well as an economic one—and rallied the outside sources to meet it, had some weaknesses which a competent supervisor would quickly discover. Ames came back well enough to take and keep more healthful work under his old employers. But just after he went to the sanatorium in September, Mrs. Ames developed an incipient case of tuberculosis. Fortunately the infection was discovered in time; but the fact is there had been such concentration upon the problem of the sick man that preventive examinations of wife and children—a precaution more often neglected in 1909 than now, it is true—had not been made. And why was a woman described as frail left with no more definite diagnosis for four months? The opinions of the relatives on both sides of the house as to her health, her ability to work, etc., were set down in the record, but no competent professional judgment was procured.

Then, before the inquiry had been completed, the offer from the Joseph Ameses of a home with them for Mrs. Ames and the children had been accepted by the case worker as a definite solution without weighing the arguments for and against. Probably it was so received because it was the first concrete offer made. Its abandonment later may have been because other resources became available, and may have had no reference to the real objections to this solution on the score of health, incompatibility, the difficulty of re-establishing the home once it had been broken up, etc.

What does the school principal mean by her statement that Alice Ames is "a diligent student, although by no means a bright child"?

Even in so relatively simple a case as this one, a comparison of all the items of evidence, both by the case worker and by someone who did not know the Ameses, would have saved motion in useless directions and have started it in helpful ones. A supervisor skilled in the notation of recurrence, moreover, would have learned from the study of other cases that not only in the hat factory where Ames worked but in certain branches of the whole industry did an unduly large proportion of tuberculosis cases have their origin. This feature of the case noted, all available data should have been placed at the service of students of occupational disease in its legislative and other aspects. Not satisfied with search in this one direction, the supervisor should have sought for possible causal factors of Ames' disease in his family history and his home sanitation.

At the same time it must be admitted that both case worker and supervisor might have made all these comparisons painstakingly, might have secured the necessary medical diagnoses of mother and children, and the mental examination of the older child, might have organized a committee to investigate the relation between hat making and tuberculosis, and might still have failed utterly in the social diagnosis and treatment of the Ameses. "They go through all their paces," said a social worker of certain trained assistants, "they attend to all the latest things listed in our modern social programs, and then miss, far too often, the most significant point in the whole case." This is another way of saying what Dubois has said—they possess all the working machinery of diagnosis but do not know how to make a diagnosis.[1] Painstaking comparison of all the items of evidence aids and leads up to interpretation, it often reveals the interpretation, but it cannot provide the imaginative insight which can make interpretation more than half of treatment.

III. THE INTERPRETATION OF MATERIAL

Ability to form a judgment is more important than ability to suspend judgment. We are between the horns of a dilemma here, for the diagnosis too promptly made, even when not erroneous, may be only the one-word diagnosis which roughly describes the general type of difficulty, and leaves undefined every individualizing particular. The delayed diagnosis, on the other hand, may miss the critical moment for effectiveness in treatment. With all the

[1] See p. 347.

defects apparent in the social handling of the Ames case, it shows ability to grasp promptly the significant factor in a human relation—in this instance, the wife's unwillingness to have her husband leave home, and the reason for it. It is this insight into human relations that distinguishes social diagnosis from all other kinds.

The dispensary had known Ames for a number of weeks and had diagnosed only the disease, his church and his employer had known him for years and had observed only the distress, when a social case worker, called in more or less by chance, found the true situation, simple as it was, still undefined and unanalyzed. Some fumbling followed. The social diagnosis might have been swamped by the premature remedy proposed by the Joseph Ameses. The check, however, was momentary, and five days after the original application the key to the situation had been found. The highest success, of course, would have been to find and hold to this main theme without losing grasp upon the other and related matters that were already in evidence. Miss Delancey was at hand and eager for direction. Assuming the possibility of her success in aiding the family to rearrange home conditions for the invalid father, this could have been counted upon to make her all the more influential in looking after the physical and mental health of the two little girls and the health of their mother. That these were not included in the program from the very beginning was a waste of time and opportunity.

Sometimes where there has been frequent change of social agency or of worker in a case, every type of diagnostic habit will be found in a single record—the one-word diagnosis, the situation-of-the-moment diagnosis, the painstaking but fumbling kind, the clear-on-the-main-difficulty type, as well as the type which is both clear and full.

Take, for example, the family of Braucher, the man with a South American wife and two small children, whose story is told in part in the chapter on Relatives.[1] The family, it will be remembered, had been treated in four different districts of one charity organization society. First, the situation was summarized as "man unable to work because of flat-foot; distress of family due to this cause." Later, when Braucher had neglected the medical treatment offered,

[1] See p. 188.

and when routine efforts to verify his story had failed, it was summed up in the phrase, "family shows industry as beggars, but in no other way." A local charity in another city had offered, as a definition of the characteristics of the man's relatives, who lived there, the statement that they were people with "a discouraging record." But the secretary in the fourth district, dissatisfied with this report, had sought out Braucher's people and brought back to him a message from them. The message appealed to an unsuspected side of the man's nature—a fact which this fourth social diagnostician, unprejudiced by earlier verdicts, was prompt to recognize. The renewal of Braucher's relations with long estranged kindred became the worker's starting point in the attempt to develop his social and industrial ambitions, these ambitions becoming in turn the keynote in a long and successful treatment. With all this, Mrs. Braucher's separate needs were not overlooked. Social diagnosis should not limit itself to the naming of one cause or one disability.

It would be possible to maintain, of course, that the worker who succeeded where three had failed had a stronger faith in human nature or a more winning personality. Unquestionably these were factors in the success. As has been said elsewhere, faith in the possibilities of our clients and of social treatment is fundamental. But the turning point was the discovery of the relatives by one who knew how to weigh evidence and to follow slight clues. Success was due to technique and insight in combination.

1. Diagnosis Redefined. Social diagnosis, then, may be described as the attempt to make as exact a definition as possible of the situation and personality of a human being in some social need—of his situation and personality, that is, in relation to the other human beings upon whom he in any way depends or who depend upon him, and in relation also to the social institutions of his community.

Medical diagnosis leans more and more to the inclusion of a certain amount of social context; diagnoses of mental states will in time do the same. Each, however, will continue to be based upon a body of experience which is not primarily social, which has a different starting point and develops a different skill and emphasis. The fields overlap but are by no means coterminous. As social diagnosis becomes more expert it will be, incidentally, a serviceable adjunct of medicine and of psychology, and there is no need to add that both of these will continue to furnish invaluable data to the social diagnostician.

Since this book is not addressed to the specialist in any one branch of social case work, it cannot narrow its field to suggestions which would not apply to all branches. With this limitation, it will not be possible to dogmatize about the content of a diagnosis, about the making of diagnostic summaries, or even about the time element in this part of case work; it will only be possible, in bringing the discussion of this final stage to a close, to add under these various heads a few general suggestions.

2. Diagnostic Content. A poor social diagnosis errs by being too general, by being too detailed and therefore confused, or by overlooking some of the important factors in a case though clear on the main disability; whereas good social diagnosis includes all the principal factors standing in the way of social reconstruction, with emphasis placed upon the features which indicate the treatment to be followed. This emphasis the worker should allow no predisposition toward some favorite causal factor to disturb.

A diagnosis may be mistaken. It is humiliating to find that a case of mental disease or of tuberculosis can still be diagnosed by a social agency as a case of unemployment due to laziness or inefficiency. On the other hand, it is exasperating to find that a tuberculosis nurse can still tell a patient, upon her first visit, that his is the worst case of overwork she has ever encountered, when the facts are notorious that he has never supported himself and his family, and that he has undermined his health by years of dissipation. This absorption of the worker in the superficial aspects of a case is responsible for many mistaken diagnoses.

A diagnosis may be a mere classification. It may be no better than pigeon-holing. The one-word diagnosis, even when it names the general type of difficulty with correctness, is not social. In the days of disorganized social dosing, a woman with children and no male head in her household might be recorded by different agencies as a widow, a deserted wife, or an unmarried mother without any of them having verified her civil condition. Although the affixing of the correct label is an advance, no such label standing by itself has a practical bearing upon prognosis and treatment.

Widowhood, desertion, illegitimacy—these are only isolated social facts having no diagnostic significance until their context in the particular instance is given. How varied that context may be is partially indicated by the questionnaires bearing upon these three disabilities in Part III.

A diagnosis may be too detailed. As the purpose of diagnosis is to throw into high light the factors most influential in bringing a client to his present pass, it follows that the including of details is apt to spoil the perspective and so give either a distorted or a confused picture of the situation. In other words, the defining of a client's need calls upon the worker to distinguish in the evidence collected what is relatively important for successful treatment from what is relatively unimportant. A worker may have gathered the evidence in a case with care; he may have had his perceptions awakened in many directions by the ablest books on the causes of poverty; yet he may have failed to recognize the factors working most mischief in the case under consideration. In short, his work may be painstaking but without penetration. The remedy lies in experience under skilful supervision, where this is possible, as well as in a deepened sense of fellowship with one's clients.

A diagnosis may be partial, although clear on the main difficulty. This was true in the Ames case; it is true today of much of the work of case workers with method and experience above the average. The saving strength in their work is that they are testing diagnosis continually by that knowledge of the consequences of a given treatment as applied to a given diagnosis which comes only from long familiarity with social practice. The weakness in their work is that they are apt to note and to treat merely some one conspicuous need in a number of cases too large to allow of more thorough work. True as it is that the results of treatment must be the usual test of a diagnosis, practical experience in observing these results will not save a worker who is under the pressure of too many cases from getting but a partial view of their complexities and possibilities.

A diagnosis can be full without loss of clearness. It is wasteful to gather ample evidence and then, in our eagerness for quick results in dealing with some urgent need, lose sight of the facts significant for a more searching treatment. A fuller diagnosis would bring these into the picture of the case without obscuring any immediate issue.

Thus far, emphasis has been placed upon the defining of the difficulty in the client's situation. We must, however, remember that, while making a comprehensive diagnosis which is to be followed by treatment, we must keep the clues to possible remedies in view. The diagnosis itself should bring together those elements in the situation which may become obstacles or aids in the treatment. We have no word for this summing up of assets and liabilities. Its inclusion in diagnosis is justified only on the ground that the diagnostician, who must have had social treatment in view from the very beginning, has been measuring at every stage of his work the treatment value of each circumstance, each human relation, and each personal characteristic. Here then is the place to sum them up.

The diagnostic summary, or the diagnosis put in black and white, should give the content of a diagnosis in orderly form, although that form may have to be somewhat varied for different types of social case work. Most types will have to include, in addition to a general description of the difficulty, a statement of those peculiarities of circumstance and personality which differentiate the case under review from all others. Then should come an enumeration of the causal factors, so far as known, in the order of their importance. It is a help to clearness of thinking to set them down though they must be understood, at this early stage of treatment, to be only tentative.[1] And last should come the just mentioned appraisal of the assets for reconstruction discovered in the course of inquiry—those within our client, within his immediate family, and outside. The inquiry has had this for one of its chief objects. Not only the assets but the special obstacles to be overcome and guarded against in treatment should be included. All of this must be dated and must stand, like a bill of lading, "errors and omissions excepted." There would be few more dangerous things

[1] This listing of factors recognized as causal in the individual case should not be confused with the attempt to establish statistically *the causes* of poverty, crime, or any other of society's outstanding failures. To any such generalizing other tests must be applied. The two undertakings may be related or may become so some day, but they cannot be assumed to be identical.

than a social diagnosis that was not subject to review in the light of further facts.

How do these suggestions apply to the Ames case? The following summary attempts to embody the criticisms and review of that case already given in this chapter:

DIAGNOSTIC SUMMARY

May 19, 1909

Ames, Thomas (38) and Jane (28), two girls, 6 and 2, and Mrs. Ames' mother

DIFFICULTIES DEFINED: Illness of breadwinner from tuberculosis, no savings. Ames unwilling to take needed sanatorium treatment, wife seconds him. Mrs. Ames described as "frail" (competent report needed).[1] Older child "not bright" in school (mental examination needed?).

CAUSAL FACTORS: *Of the tuberculosis*, not definitely known. (Family history? Housing? Conditions of man's work?) *Of the refusal of sanatorium care*, Mrs. Ames' failure to realize man's condition, and her fears that home may be broken up. *Of Alice's school record*, not known.

ASSETS AND LIABILITIES: *Assets*—(1) Man's temperate habits and affection for family. (2) Excellent home standards of family. (3) Dispensary's willingness to co-operate in persuading Ames to go away. (4) Miss Delancey's interest. (5) Mrs. Freeman, the wife's sister, and Joseph Ames are able to help with relief; other relief resources are Caldwell's and the church. *Liabilities*—(1) Man not a skilled worker, highest weekly earnings $12. (2) Needing immediate attention—Mrs. Ames' opposition to sanatorium care as above.

3. The Time Element. The omissions in the Ames record that are indicated in the foregoing diagnostic summary could have been accounted for, probably, by pressure of other work. Those who know most about the well-nigh intolerable conditions under which case work is done—conditions, that is, of too many clients and of continual hurry—will make large allowance for shortcomings. Even in normal seasons the demand for good social case work is so fitful that it cannot assure the conditions essential to good work. In periods of industrial depression, of war, of epidemic, or of other abnormal pressure, standards that have been established laboriously are not only battered down by the stress of the time but remain down long after the occasion has passed. This is owing in part to the tendency to carry over into ordinary times habits of work created by emergent periods.

In spite of these discouragements the case worker who depresses

[1] Entries in parenthesis indicate omissions in the inquiry.

himself and others by an attitude of skepticism toward progress forgets that he is not alone in facing difficulties. Most of the world's advances in skill have been made under pressure. They have been made by the exceptional man or woman who has developed judgment in eliminating matters of lesser importance from the work before him through sheer strength of desire to work out his ideas. The exceptional teacher, physician, social worker has repeatedly established and advanced standards in this way. And one need not be unusually gifted to try two experiments in connection with his own work which will have a steadying influence upon standards.

The first experiment has just been suggested; namely, that as soon as a period of special pressure is passed the worker should set himself to overcome those lax methods and mental habits which emergency conditions have forced upon him.

The second experiment is suggested by Dr. Adolf Meyer, professor of psychiatry at Johns Hopkins. Dr. Meyer teaches students specializing in mental diseases that there is a subjective reaction toward better work in all their cases if they are careful to get a complete picture in a minority of them. In social work, also, experiment shows that the habit of covering the ground with especial thoroughness in a few cases affects a worker's standards with all. He may not be able to give any more time to the majority of his clients after this tonic exercise than before, but his judgments about them will be more penetrating. This result is so beneficent and far-reaching that every case worker should contrive to secure at some time during his crowded days a few undisturbed hours, a little center of quiet into which he may bring selected tasks to be worked out studiously, and, if possible, to a successful issue.

Such concentrated attention produces another reaction which extends beyond the worker himself and his own achievement. Good work creates a demand for more work of the same grade, thus exerting an influence which tends, as it spreads, to change for the better the conditions under which social work is done. Boards of directors become awakened to the fact that thorough work means results, and are then ready to do their part toward supplying enough workers to maintain standards.

An after-care worker for a girls' reformatory found that the reformatory authorities were satisfied with meager reports of the girls' previous histories. In special instances at first—instances in which the authorities could see at a glance the significance of a fuller history—she began to supply written data. The result was that gradually the management came to demand and to make provision for obtaining more detail for all inmates. By assuring a better understanding of each girl's individual problems not only the after-care work but the treatment of inmates of the institution was reshaped.

4. Full Diagnosis Not Always Possible. Last of all, full diagnosis—any correct diagnosis in fact—is not always possible, even when there is ample time. We are dealing with human factors and we too are human. We cannot hope that the processes here described will always bring the truth to light or reveal the possibilities of treatment. Try as we may, certain cases will remain obscure. When this happens we must trust in part to further acquaintance with our client and in part to temporary treatment of some kind which will itself become a form of investigation.

Be it repeated, no diagnosis is final. Since later developments in a case may clarify the social practitioner's insight into its causal factors, there is a sense in which investigation continues as long as does treatment.

SUMMARY OF THIS CHAPTER

1. First we collect our material, next we compare each part with all the other parts, and then we interpret it. This last is diagnosis.

2. Social diagnosis may be described as the attempt to make as exact a definition as possible of the situation and personality of a human being in some social need—of his situation and personality, that is, in relation to the other human beings upon whom he in any way depends or who depend upon him, and in relation also to the social institutions of his community.

3. There has been too little relation, heretofore, between material gathered and its interpretation. This is due to neglect of the process of critical comparison.

4. Comparison of data should include review of each item with all the others in mind, and sometimes review of each with all other items deliberately excluded. It must guard against overemphasizing the fact established with difficulty, against hidden contradictions, and against overemphasizing first and last statements and hypotheses. It must retest carefully the inferences that have underlain the conduct of the inquiry so far. The questionnaire for Supervision and Review in Part III gives detailed suggestions for the comparison of data.

5. It is possible to make all these comparisons painstakingly and arrive nowhere. The "working machinery" of diagnosis does not assure results where imaginative insight is lacking.

6. A good social diagnosis is at once full and clear, with emphasis placed upon the features which indicate the social treatment to be followed.

7. The one-word diagnosis which is a mere classification is of little value, but a detailed diagnosis can also be valueless if it misses the very factors that are working most mischief in the case under consideration.

8. Not only must a social diagnosis define clearly the difficulty or difficulties; it must also bring together those elements in the situation which may become obstacles or aids in the treatment.

9. The form of diagnostic summary may have to be varied for different types of social case work, probably, but generally it will include (1) a definition of the difficulties, (2) a listing of the causal factors, so far as known, that enter into these difficulties, (3) an enumeration of the assets available and the liabilities to be reckoned with in treatment.

10. There are two experiments that may help to control, in part, the troublesome time element in diagnosis: (1) To watch for and check the tendency to carry over emergency period habits into times that are not emergent. (2) To cover the ground in a minority of cases with especial thoroughness.

11. Full diagnosis—any correct diagnosis in fact—is not always possible, and no diagnosis is final.

CHAPTER XIX

THE UNDERLYING PHILOSOPHY

ALTHOUGH mention has been made more than once in earlier chapters of the interdependence of individual and mass betterment, it will not be amiss, in bringing this long discussion of the diagnostic process to a close, to re-enforce briefly the position already taken that social reform and social case work must of necessity progress together. We have seen, for example, that the diagnostic side of case work received a great impetus when the plans of reformers began to be realized, and that social work immediately had at its command more varied resources than it could apply without further knowledge of the differences between men.[1] To understand these differences and adapt its working programs to them, account has had to be taken of men's social relationships.

Less emphasis is placed in these pages upon the other side, upon the number of social reforms that have been direct outgrowths of case work, and the number that owe to this work either effective amendment or successful administration. There are few administrative tasks in the social field, in fact, which do not have to utilize some form of social diagnosis and treatment. A new piece of social legislation may give case work a new direction, it almost always modifies such work, and sometimes renders it unnecessary in a given field. This last eventuality, however, is predicted many times for once that it is realized.

When, for example, the restriction of child labor was made possible, several new kinds of case work became necessary, one of them involving greater skill in sifting the various evidences of age, one involving the development of other family plans to take the place of children's earnings, etc. The methods of many agencies engaged in case work were modified by these child labor measures. In some states, on the other hand, data supplied by the agencies pointed the way for improvement in the new laws. Discussing this subject of the relation of case work to social reform at a recent

[1] See p. 32.

session of the National Conference of Charities and Correction,[1] the writer ventured the opinion that workmen's compensation laws belonged to the type of social legislation which rendered further case work for one group unnecessary. But in the debate which followed several people were on their feet at one time to bring forward instances in which case workers had not only had to make adaptations of the existing compensation laws to individual cases, but, in so doing, had discovered points at which these laws should be amended.

In any consideration of the readjustments necessary from time to time between social diagnosis and treatment on the one hand and social research and prevention on the other, analogies drawn from recent developments in medical science and practice are inevitable. As between laboratory discovery and bedside practice, for instance, Dr. Lewellys F. Barker summed up the situation a few years ago,[2] making among other points the following: Many of the teachers and investigators in the purely laboratory branches of medicine are men of limited clinical experience or none at all, while the clinical branches themselves are becoming more highly specialized. As everyone knows, there has been almost explosive progress in the laboratory branches, but laymen are not so familiar with the important fact emphasized by Dr. Barker that new medical discoveries may, and often do, lie unapplied for long until clinical medicine has been developed to a point where it can adapt and apply them. "The Wassermann reaction may be primarily worked out in a non-clinical laboratory, but the determination of its real significance for the diagnosis and treatment of disease demands, subsequently, long years of clinical research." Scientific clinical work will suffer loss, in Dr. Barker's opinion, "if the men who are presumably cultivating the clinical sciences of diagnosis and therapy overlook their own legitimate problems." These problems are "tasks set by the patients themselves . . . these living patients are, primarily, the objects of study of the clinical scientist." Meanwhile the air is thick with "*applicable* facts, of the most diverse origin," and "only the younger clinicians

[1] See Proceedings of the National Conference of Charities and Correction for 1915 (Baltimore), p. 43 sq.

[2] Presidential address before the Association of American Physicians. *Science*, May 16, 1913.

have had opportunity for securing a training permitting of an understanding of even a part of them."

It would be easy to push this analogy too far, to urge too insistently that applicable knowledge is not being applied in the social field because we have failed to stimulate original and progressive work among social practitioners to the extent that we should. The important fact for us is that, while readjustments are clearly necessary, diagnosis and therapy do assuredly assume, with each advance in social reform, each gain of scientific medicine, not less but more importance in both fields. If, as we have seen, the one-word diagnosis of our case work cannot be social, neither can the single reform put forward to cure all the ills of society. There is, in fact, more resemblance than either would admit between the mental habits of the case worker who contentedly treats one individual after another, one family after another, without giving a thought to the civic and industrial conditions that hedge them about, and the mental habits of the reformer who is sure that the adoption of his particular reform will render all social case work unnecessary. Both ignore the complexity, the great diversity, of the materials with which they are attempting to deal.

This diversity of man's life is made clearer on its mental side and in its relation to our subject by certain concepts of modern psychology. Two of these, in fact, may be said to constitute the underlying philosophy of social case work; they explain the necessity for its continuing survival in some form. The first relates to the fact of individual differences, the second to the theory of "the wider self."

I. INDIVIDUAL DIFFERENCES

Not that the resemblances among men are socially unimportant; resemblances have made mass betterment possible, while individuality has made adaptation a necessity.[1] In the early stages of a democracy, doing the same thing for everybody seems to be the best that administrative skill is equal to, but later we learn to do

[1] "Even if man's nature included only five traits, *a*, *b*, *c*, *d*, and *e*, and even if each of these existed in only five degrees, 1, 2, 3, 4, and 5, there could be over three thousand (3,125, to be exact) varieties of men. . . . Hygiene, medicine, education, and all social forces have to reckon with original differences in men." E. L. Thorndike, Individuality, pp. 19 and 43.

different things for and with different people with social betterment clearly in view. Our public schools of a generation ago prided themselves upon treating all alike—whereas reports of recent school investigations show that it is the differentiated treatment of the school child which now possesses the minds of educational reformers.[1]

It seems unnecessary to illustrate further the truth of this first concept, but that of the second one, relating to the wider self, is not so obvious.

II. THE WIDER SELF

Individual differences must be reckoned with in every field of endeavor, but the theory of the wider self, though it has of course other implications, seems to lie at the base of social case work. We have seen how slowly such work has abandoned its few general classifications and tried instead to consider the whole man. Even more slowly is it realizing that the mind of man (and in a very real sense the mind *is* the man) can be described as the sum of his social relationships.

Mrs. Helen Bosanquet expresses this for the layman more clearly—perhaps because she is a social worker—than others who have written about it. She says:

> The soul literally is, or is built up of, all its experience; and such part of this experience, or soul life, as is active at any given time or for any given purpose constitutes the self at that time and for that purpose. We know how the self enlarges and expands as we enter upon new duties, acquire new interests, contract new ties of friendship; we know how it is mutilated when some sphere of activity is cut off, or some near friend snatched away by death. It is literally, and not metaphorically, a part of *ourselves* which we have lost.[2]

[1] For example, take the following by Leonard P. Ayres in the Proceedings of the Fifty-second Annual Meeting of the National Education Association, 1914, p. 278: "In every school system there is greater difference in class room ability between different members of the same grade than there is between the abilities of the average children in the lowest and the average children in the highest grades. . . . This means that . . . we must differentiate our courses because our courses are made for our children, and our children are differentiated by nature."

Or the following by Paul H. Hanus in School Efficiency, A Constructive Study Applied to New York City, p. 15: "Over and above the foregoing suggestions for the improvement of the course of study in certain details is . . . the adjustment of the entire course of study to individual and local needs throughout the city. The differences in respect to individual and local needs in New York City with its heterogeneous population are very great, and they are not now satisfactorily taken into the account." Yonkers, N. Y., World Book Co., 1913.

[2] Bosanquet, Mrs. Helen: The Standard of Life and Other Studies, p. 131, London, Macmillan and Co., 1898.

That we may know a man by the company he keeps is a maxim of which Polonius might have been the author. But it has a deeper meaning than the conventional one. A man really is the company he keeps plus the company that his ancestors kept. He is "co-extensive with the scope of his conscious interests and affections." These interests change inevitably. In fact, change is one of the conditions of their continuing healthfulness, though change may mean either contraction and loss or the widening of interests, the strengthening of social ties.[1]

Although the preliminary inquiries of social agencies are still conducted from other motives, many of the more thoughtful case workers of today are learning to study the relations of individual men in the light of this concept of the wider self—of the expanding self, as they like to believe. In so doing, they are allying themselves with the things that "move, touch, teach"; for where disorders within or without threaten a man's happiness, his social relations must continue to be the chief means of his recovery. Many years before these ideas were formulated by science they

[1] This conception of the wider self is described in varying terms by different psychologists. The two following passages may be taken as representative:

James Mark Baldwin: The thought of self arises directly out of certain given social relationships; indeed, it is the form which these actual relationships take on in the organization of a new personal experience. The ego of which he thinks at any time is not the isolated-and-in-his-body-alone-situated abstraction which our theories of personality usually lead us to think. It is rather a sense of a network of relationships among you, me, and the others, in which certain necessities of pungent feeling, active life, and concrete thought require that I throw the emphasis on one pole sometimes, calling it me; and on the other pole sometimes, calling it you or him. Social and Ethical Interpretations in Mental Development, p. 508 sq.

Edward L. Thorndike: About fifteen years ago the point of view of students of human nature showed the first clear signs of what has been a rather abrupt change —toward thinking of a man's mind as the sum total of connections between the situations which life offers and the responses which the man makes. Up till then the mind had been thought of primarily as a set of magical faculties or powers—attention, memory, inference, reasoning, choice, and the like—or as a collection of certain contents—sensations, images, thoughts, volitions, and the like. Today the progressives in psychology think of a man's mind as the organized system of connections or bonds or associations wherby he responds or reacts by this or that thought or feeling or act to each of the millions of situations or circumstances or events that befall him. Their customary name for the mind is the *connection-system;* their ideal of psychology is a science which can predict what any given situation or stimulus will connect with or evoke in the way of thought, feeling, word, or deed; their offering to education is an offering of knowledge of the laws whereby connections in thought and behavior are made and broken, are preserved and weakened, and are of help and hindrance one to another. The Foundations of Educational Achievement, *The Educational Review,* December, 1914, pp. 487–8, Vol. 48, No. 5.

were applied to housing reform, to neighborhood improvement, and to case work by Miss Octavia Hill, whose relation to the beginnings of social diagnosis has been described in the first chapter. Hers was a conception so sound and so inspired that science came later not to correct but to fulfill it.

It will still be necessary to do different things for and with different people, and to study their differences, if the results of our doing are to be more good than bad. It will still be necessary to study the social relations of people, not only in order to understand their differences but in order to find a remedy for the ills that will continue to beset them. These ills will change their form, some will be blotted out, and the whole level of life, as we have a right to hope, will be lifted. Although the level upon which the case worker operates will also be raised, case work will still be needed; its adaptation of general principles to specific instances will not be automatic nor will good administration become so. It may also be predicted that the forms of organization now responsible for case work will change, that its scope and skill will advance far beyond the present-day practice described in this study. The methods and processes here dwelt upon will subordinate themselves to a larger whole. It is only through devotion to that whole—not through any narrow insistence upon technique alone—that we can submit ourselves in the right spirit to the task of analyzing individual situations. But we must come under the law before we can rise above it.

PART III

VARIATIONS IN THE PROCESSES

CHAPTER XX

SOCIAL DISABILITIES AND THE QUESTIONNAIRE PLAN OF PRESENTATION

WHEN the case worker has gone only a short distance in his preliminary inquiries, or sometimes at a later period, he discovers a certain disability or a combination of disabilities. What are the implications of his discovery? How should it modify his method? By what means can a large number of possible modifications be indicated and made accessible for reference when needed? This, next to the discussion of evidence, has been the most difficult problem with which the present study has had to deal. Our discussion of the methods and points of view common to all social diagnosis is ended, but there remains to be treated this baffling topic of the variations in method demanded by different tasks and by the presence of different disabilities.

I. OBJECTS OF THE QUESTIONNAIRES

1. Their Dangers. In determining to present in questionnaire form most of the material gathered for this final division of the subject, the writer is aware that the device is clumsy and that it has its dangers. The purposes and limitations of these questionnaires are bound to be misunderstood by some who attempt to use them, no matter how clearly it is set forth that none are sets of questions to be asked of clients and that none are schedules the answers to which are to be filled in by anyone. They are merely long lists of queries which, when gone over by the social case worker *with a particular case in mind,* may bring to his attention, out of the many presented, a possible four or five that may contain suggestive leads.

Leading questions are dangerous things, as already indicated; the questioner, ignorant of the true answer, suggests one nevertheless to the person who is being questioned. Here the case worker is asking *himself* questions. He is merely doing more formally, in fact, what he is forced to do all the time, for social diagnosis moves forward by calling up before the mind one possible explanation after another, one alternative after another, before putting each to the test. It is in the suggestion of alternative situations and explanations that these questionnaires will, it is hoped, prove of some help. Their very extent and elaboration should make it evident that no one of them could apply in its entirety to any one client or any one family. But it may be added that they have no significance and will seem only a confused mass of detail unless they are examined with a particular case in mind. In a case in which the first interview has been held and certain data have been gathered elsewhere, the choice of questionnaires to be examined should not be difficult. The preliminary questionnaire regarding Any Family takes precedence (if there is a family) of the questionnaires covering the particular disability or disabilities.

2. Their Use Illustrated. Thus, the Angelinos are a family, and that fact may justify taking the time to read over the first questionnaire in order to be sure that no important point which seems to bear upon their present difficulties has been omitted. Many of the questions are disposed of at once as not applying, as applying but unimportant, or as already followed up, but a few of those which remain may raise a doubt of the course that the inquiry has taken so far and suggest another way. The Angelinos are not just a family, however, they are a family recently arrived in this country. What does that fact suggest with regard to their background and foreground? The Immigrant Family Questionnaire is necessarily general, but it may yield a few ideas. The oldest girl is blind and has had no care. Unless the case worker knows just where to turn for guidance in dealing with this disability on its social side, Miss Lucy Wright's carefully framed questions, as given in Chapter XXV, may have something to teach him. A good deal later Angelino leaves home without giving any clue to his destination, or so his wife says. Possibly the Deserted Family Questionnaire may throw some light on the first steps to be taken. Neither in this case nor in any other, however, are these questionnaires to be heavily leaned upon. Anyone who has had the patience to follow the earlier discussions of this book will realize that it does not put forward the treatment of separate disabilities as the whole of social case work by any means. The Angelinos are not just an immigrant family or a deserted family, and the case worker who knows *them* as well as their disabilities is the one who will have most success in the diagnosis and treatment of their social situation.

II. WHAT IS TRUE OF EVERYBODY?

Requests often came to us, in gathering our material, for a good, comprehensive outline of the ground that should be covered in any social diagnosis whatsoever. No single question of the outline thus asked for was to be unimportant, and all were to apply quite universally to human situations. This was, in effect, a demand for a short cut, and there are no short cuts in diagnosis. Between a clear conception of the things that are true of everybody and an equally clear conception of the things that are true of that complex of human relations and experiences represented by an individual client, anything might be important, and there are few things that might not become in certain circumstances unimportant.

Studies yet to be made will undoubtedly give case work a more solid basis of formulated and applicable experience, but such studies, if they are to be of value, cannot begin with uniform schedules, filled out by different agencies and workers—each with a different notion of what social evidence means or with none at all. When answers obtained in this way are added together to make a total, the result is meaningless. A more fruitful method of case work study, and one adaptations of which will probably be tried in the near future with different groups of cases, is that already illustrated by Dr. Healy's Individual Delinquent and by Dr. Cabot's Differential Diagnosis. The former gives the results of diagnosis and treatment in 1000 cases of juvenile delinquency selected on the basis of "repetition of offense plus sufficiency of data"; the latter classifies 383 case histories of disease by what its author calls their "presenting symptom"—by the one, that is, of which the patient was most acutely aware when he asked medical aid, such as a backache, a chill, a headache, etc. "Cases do not often come to us systematically arranged," says Dr. Cabot, "like the account of typhoid in a text-book of practice of medicine. They are generally presented to us *from an angle*, and with one symptom, generally a misleading one, in the foreground. From this point of view we must reason our way back into the deeper processes and more obscure causes which guide our therapeutic endeavor." With Dr. Cabot "we" means the medical practitioners, but it is illuminating to us as well as to them to see diseases of the most diverse origins and degrees of curability thrust in shoulder to shoulder, jostling one another, because their victims all happened to complain chiefly of a headache, for instance. As a lesson in social diagnosis, the book carries two meanings—its obvious meaning, which is that the symptoms of physical disease encountered daily in the course of social work need the most expert medical diagnosis, and its deeper meaning, that social diagnosis must also be expert, must also reason its way back "into the deeper processes," and push beyond surface symptoms to their causes.

The social worker needs for his daily task two kinds of equipment. To be a good case worker, he must have a generous conception, and one filled with concrete details, of the varied possibilities of social service, and this conception must be a growing one. It must grow with his growing experience and also with each year's freight of social discovery. And quite as vividly, quite as progressively, he must have a conception of the possibilities of human nature—of the suggestibility, improvability, and supreme value of folks. The former conception can be acquired; it comes in part from sympathetic study of the constructive programs of service already well represented in the literature of social work, in part from the use of such technical material as has been compiled here, and in part from practical work under progressive leadership. But the latter conception is, in a sense, part of himself. What he thinks of human nature is bounded by what he knows of human nature, and what he knows, in this field, is bounded by what he is.

What are the things that are true of everybody? Or, to narrow the question somewhat, What is true of everybody living under the conditions which a modern civilization imposes? No two people will answer this question in the same way, but the mere exercise of trying to answer it will clear the mind, or will at least make it impossible to continue to record as facts statements that cannot possibly be true of anybody.

The writer used to give this question as an exercise to workers in training with interesting results. What a case worker "thinketh in his heart" about the life of the individual and about society's responsibility for it is going to be a matter of commanding influence in his daily work. The question is one which each worker must answer for himself and in his own way, but the following rather matter-of-fact answer is given here as being more or less in key with the point of view of the present volume:

We all have a birthday and a place of birth, and have or have had two parents, four grandparents, etc., with all that this implies by way of racial and national characteristics, of family inheritance and tradition, and probably of family environment. Our place of birth (assuming here and elsewhere the conditions of a modern civilization) was a house of some kind, and we have continued to live in this or in a series of other houses ever since. The characteristics of these houses, their neighborhood and atmosphere, have helped to make us what we are.

We all have bodies that need intelligent care if we are to keep them in good repair. Their condition has influenced our minds and our characters, though it is equally true that these, in turn, may have influenced profoundly our bodily health.

We have all had an education, whether through instruction in the schools and in the churches, or through means less formal.

We have all had some means of subsistence, whether through gainful occupations of our own, through dependence upon the gainful occupations of others, or through assistance public or private.

We all modify, and are in turn modified by, our material and our social environment. The body of social traditions, institutions, equipments of every sort that man has built up has left a deep mark upon him. This implies, among other things, an emotional responsiveness to the society of our fellows—responsiveness whether shown in marriage and the founding of a second home (in which case, of course, all of the foregoing things are true also of the one married), or in other associations of personal loyalty with our fellows, individually and in groups. These attractions imply repulsions. We are remoulded by the discords of the one, the concords of the other.

We are all going somewhere and have not yet arrived. Our character is "not cut in marble," but is the sum of our past experiences—a sum which is to be changed, inevitably, by our future experiences.

III. WHAT IS POSSIBLY TRUE OF ANY FAMILY?

As already said, most of the questionnaires that follow are applicable to a particular disability, and are confined to the diagnostic aspects of that disability. But the line between diagnosis and treatment cannot be drawn strictly, so a few questions bearing more especially upon treatment are included; and the first and the last questionnaire do not treat of disabilities at all. The first relates instead to the basic facts likely to be true of most families; the last is framed for one who reviews the entries of a case record before advising as to the next steps leading to diagnosis or as to the diagnosis itself.

The family rather than the individual has been made the subject of this preliminary questionnaire, because the work to be undertaken is social, and the individual in whose interest the lists of questions will be consulted must be considered primarily—whatever his disabilities may be—in his social relationships. The questions of this preliminary list are not as a rule repeated in later lists, though sometimes, where they have seemed especially applicable, they have had to be repeated for emphasis. It is assumed, however, that where a special questionnaire has to be consulted this first one will also be included. The eleven lists which follow it are not poured into any one mould. Their classification is not uniform nor is their treatment. It will be seen that they are the product of different hands and that the subjects are too diverse, moreover, to have made uniform treatment advisable.

QUESTIONNAIRE REGARDING ANY FAMILY

This is not a schedule to be filled out nor a set of queries to be answered by a social agency's client or clients. For an explanation of the purpose of these questionnaires see p. 373 sq.

A star (*) indicates that the answer to the question may be found in, or confirmed by, public records.

I General Social Data

1. Family's name? Wife's given and maiden name? Husband's given name? Full names of children? Names of all other members of the household, and their relation to the family?
2. What was the birthplace of husband, of wife, and of each child? Nationality of each of the four grandparents?
3. What was the date of birth of husband, of wife, and of each child?*
4. What were the conditions, economic and moral, in the husband's childhood home? The wife's? What was the effect of these conditions on his or her health, character, and industrial status?
5. How long have they been in the city, the state, and the country? Reason for each migration? Do they both speak English?

6. What was the date and place of their marriage?*
7. What previous marriages had either contracted, if any?*
8. Has there been any divorce or legal separation and on what grounds?* Have any of the children been placed under guardianship?* Adopted?*
9. What relatives outside of the household have husband and wife (including married and unmarried children, and children by previous marriages)? What are the circumstances of these relatives, their interest in the family, degree of influence with the family? Names, addresses, degrees of relationship?
10. What is the point of view of such other natural sources of insight as friends, former neighbors, former tradesmen and landlords, priests or pastors, fellow workmen and lodge members, etc.?
11. Has the trend of the family life been upward or downward? What characteristics of husband or wife, or what circumstances of health, employment, etc., have determined this trend? What were the family circumstances and characteristics when the family was at its best? How do these compare with its present standard?
12. What is the attitude of the members of the family toward one another? Do they hang together through thick and thin or is there little cohesion?
13. Have the parents good control over the children? Have they their confidences? Are the children taught consideration of the rights of others?
14. What are the children's aptitudes, chief interests, and achievements?

II Physical and Mental Conditions

15. Did the parents or other relatives of husband or wife have marked mental, moral, or physical defects? Unusual gifts or abilities? What facts, if any, about the husband or wife or their parents would indicate physical or mental dangers to be guarded against or special capabilities to be developed in the children?
16. How many children have they had? Did wife have any miscarriages? How many children have died? When and from what causes?
17. What attention is given to personal hygiene and health in the family? Are there regular meal hours? Do the food expenditures give a sufficient and well balanced diet? Is the importance of regular sleep, bathing, care of the teeth, and regular action of the bowels appreciated?
18. If there is a baby, how is it fed, where does it sleep, how much is it in the open air during the day? If the wife is pregnant, is she receiving good care?
19. What is the present physical condition of each member of the family, including also bodily and mental defects?
20. What treatment has been and what is now being given the various members by physicians and medical agencies, and with what results?

III Industrial History

21. What is the business or employment, both previous and present, of each worker in the family? What are the names and addresses of employers, previous and present? Between what dates was worker employed by each? What were his

earnings, maximum and usual, when regularly employed? What was his work record at these places for speed, accuracy, regularity, sobriety? What were his reasons for leaving? To what trade union, if any, does he belong? Is he in good standing?

22. At what age did each member of the family go to work, what was his training, and what was his first occupation? Have his occupations since been, on the whole, a good fit? If not, is he capable of developing greater skill at something else?

23. What was the occupation of the wife before marriage, if any, and wages then?

24. Is present occupation of each worker regular, seasonal, or occasional? Is there any chance of advancement? If out of work, how long and why?

25. Are the conditions under which each member of the family works good? If not, in what way bad?

IV Financial Situation (exclusive of charitable relief)

26. *Income.* What are the present wages and earnings? What proportion, in each case, goes into the family budget? Is this proportion too large or too small? Present income from other sources, including lodgers, boarders, pensions, benefits, contributions from relatives, etc.? Is the present income adequate? Could the present income be increased in any wise way?

27. *Outgo.* What are the monthly expenditures for food, rent, clothing, fuel, insurance, carfare, recreation, sundries? What is the amount of debts, to whom, for what? Are any articles in pawn, where, amount due? Are any articles being purchased on the installment plan? Weekly payments? Amount still to be paid? With what insurance company are members of family insured? What is the total of weekly premiums? Are they paid up to date? Could the present expenditures be decreased in any wise way? Should they be increased, and how?

28. Is there any court record of inheritance, of property, of insurance, of damages recovered?* Has the family, or did it ever have, savings? When, where, and how much? Do any members belong to benefit organizations? Amount of dues, possible benefits?

V Education

29. What was the education of parents? At what ages did they and the older children leave school? Did the children have any vocational training? How does the education of each member of the family compare with the standards of the community in which each was reared?

30. What is the school and grade of each child of school age? His teacher's name? School evidence as to scholarship, attendance, behavior, physical and mental condition, and home care?

VI Religious Affiliations

31. What is the religion of each parent? Name of church? What signs are there of its influence?

32. Do children receive religious instruction in Sunday schools, or otherwise? Where and from whom? Where were they baptized?

VII Recreation

33. What social affiliations have the various members of the family? Do any of them belong to clubs or societies—church, settlement, fraternal, political, or other? What forms of recreation do the family enjoy together? What separately? How does each member employ his leisure time?

VIII Environment

34. Does family occupy a whole house? If so, has it a yard? A garden? If not, on what floor do they live? At front or rear? How many rooms? Name and address of landlord or agent?

35. Are the rooms adequately lighted and ventilated? What are the toilet and water facilities? The general sanitary condition of the house?

36. Are the rooms comfortably furnished? Are they clean, or sordid and dirty?

37. What is the character of the neighborhood? Has it undesirable physical or moral features? How many other families in the house? Their general character?

38. How long has family lived at present address? At what previous addresses has family lived? When and how long? Character of each neighborhood and house?

IX Relations, If Any, with Social Agencies

39. Have any social agencies or institutions had relations with the family? If so, of what kind and with what results? If first contacts have been with the wife, is the husband known also, or vice versa? To what extent has the family received charitable aid, if at all?

X Basis for Treatment

40. What are the family's plans and ambitions for the future? What moral and temperamental characteristics and what aptitudes of each member can be reckoned with as assets or must be recognized as liabilities in the shaping of that future?

CHAPTER XXI

THE IMMIGRANT FAMILY

THE RECENT immigrant has been mentioned a number of times in these chapters in connection with such topics as the "funded thought" of peasant witnesses, the attitude of the alien toward our social agencies, the search for data in foreign birth records, in immigration records, etc. These comments will not be repeated; they can be readily referred to with the aid of the index. Passages in earlier pages bearing upon topics discussed in the chapters which follow are made available in the same way.

In dealing with foreign clients, the case worker finds himself in danger of falling into one of two errors: he may think of them as members of a colony or of a nationality having such and such fixed characteristics, or he may ignore national and racial characteristics and try to apply to them the same standards of measure that he would apply to his fellow-countrymen. He is liable to surprises if he adopts the latter course. Before long, he will have learned that he cannot ignore national characteristics altogether. But only extended experience will teach him to be as discriminating in ascribing such characteristics to others as he would wish his own adviser to be were he a stranger in a strange land and in difficulties. Generalizations about Americans, applied to himself in such a case, might strike him as beside the mark.

Let us suppose instead that he is suddenly transferred from service in one of our city districts or in a town that happens to have few foreign residents, to a crowded immigrant quarter where he is made responsible for shaping the child-protective activities or the family case work of the neighborhood. In addition to the obvious duty of studying the quarter as he finds it, he will be confronted with the further one of trying to acquaint himself with the old world background of his neighbors—not merely the characteristics of their native country as a whole, but those of the different provinces and localities from which they came.

I. STUDY OF THE GROUP

Only general suggestions are possible here as to how such a study might be undertaken. Following the questionnaire plan already adopted, a list of queries has been prepared relating to the group background and another list relating to a family of recent immigrants. The latter is given further on (p. 387); the former follows here. Its questions should be understood to apply to native country, province, and town. From this, a student of the subject may be able, after omitting those questions that obviously do not fit either the particular group in mind or his own individual needs, to make a modified outline which will serve as a starting point for his reading and thinking.

I Characteristics of the Inhabitants

1. Are they thrifty and industrious? Are they as a whole law abiding? What is their attitude toward the courts? Does the character of the laws or the manner of their enforcement explain any criminal tendencies in the community? Are there any community customs which are popularly recognized as substitutes for law? Where is the line drawn between fellow citizens and strangers?

2. Are the people stolid or excitable? Warlike or submissive? Jealous? Hot-tempered? Given to intemperance? Superstitious? Suspicious? Are there any superstitions which in any way affect their life in this country? Are family relations affectionate? How deep a hold has religion?

3. If there are peculiar and striking characteristics which are puzzling to Americans, is there anything in the history or traditions of the people to explain them?

II Occupations and Recreations

4. What are the chief occupations of the place? Agriculture? Manufacturing? Fishing? What stage of development have industries reached? Are there many skilled workmen? A large professional class? Is there only one means of livelihood in the community? Is there any marked discrepancy between wages and the cost of living?

5. Do the women engage in wage-earning occupations? If so, what is their industrial status? Do they ordinarily work in the field? Do they carry on home manufacturing? What is their attitude toward domestic service?

6. What are the national songs and dances, the special holidays and fête days? What are the favorite recreations and sports of the community? Do they develop the team spirit? Are games of chance prominent?

III Education and Culture

7. What opportunities for education are accessible to the peasant? What is the percentage of illiteracy in the country? Among the peasants? Is education secular or religious? Public or private? Is it given in the native language?

Is it compulsory? To what age? How many weeks comprise the school year? Are there trade schools? Is there any legally established apprenticeship system or other system of trade training? What training are the women given, at home or at school, in sewing, knitting, weaving, lace-making, embroidery, etc.?

8. How do the attainments of the educated class compare with those of other countries? Have there been notable literary achievements? What are the national arts? To what extent do they form part of the life of all classes?

IV Religion

9. Is there a dominant church, politically? Is it a large factor in the social and community life of the people? Does it figure chiefly in ceremonials or does it influence the thought and life of the people?

V Family Life and Woman's Position

10. What is the relation of parents and children? Does the father have any patriarchal authority over his family? Is the tie of kinship particularly strong or weak? Does it extend beyond the immediate family? To relationships by marriage? Is intermarriage of relatives common?

11. What is woman's position in the home? What is the customary age at marriage? What amount of freedom do women have before marriage? After marriage? How is the marriage arranged? What are the dowry customs?

12. What is the general attitude toward irregular relationships formed by young girls? By married women? Is betrothal equivalent merely to engagement, as in the United States, or is it regarded as a sort of trial marriage?

VI Community Customs

13. What are the usual living conditions among the peasants as regards housing, sanitation, cleanliness, etc.? What are the peculiar customs of dress, cooking, etc.?

14. Is there a strong community feeling? If a family is in need, how is it usually relieved? By relatives, friends, public assistance, private organizations? What is the popular attitude toward medical agencies, toward institutional care, toward outdoor relief and begging?

VII Laws and Government

15. Is the land held in large estates or small holdings?

16. Is the country (or was it until very recently) under a liberal government? An oppressive government? Is taxation heavy? To what extent is the community self-governing? Is national patriotism strong in the community? Local patriotism? What are the government's requirements regarding military service?

17. How progressive and competent is the government in its handling of sanitary and health matters?

18. What is the nature of the laws regulating labor—wages, hours, equipment of factories, etc.? Are there laws prohibiting child labor, and how well are they enforced?

19. What are the most important legal regulations relating to the family? What legal rights do women have? Are both civil and religious marriage ceremonies required? Is divorce or separation permitted? What is the legal status of the illegitimate child? What are the laws of inheritance of wife and children? Of trusts for minor children?

20. What governmental provision is there for old age, unemployment, sickness, accident? For dependents, for delinquents, for defectives?

VIII Emigration

21. Has the emigration from this community been a recent development? What causes have led to it—racial, religious, economic (necessity or experimentation), political? Has the desire to escape military service contributed? Is exile used as a substitute for imprisonment?

22. Has emigration been unduly large? Has it drained the community of the able-bodied? What effect has emigration had on standards of living and wages in the community? Do members of the community receive much money from America? Has the emigration been mainly directed toward one destination? If so, what?

Answers to these questions will not be found in any one place. Some will be in books, some can be learned from people, and a few of the most important of those remaining unanswered will come gradually in the course of one's daily work. No one way of proceeding can be urged, but if the writer found herself suddenly responsible for social work among a foreign group, she would be eager to get well in mind the history of their nation in the last hundred years. During that period there have been momentous political changes the world over, and it would be necessary to understand those that had most closely touched the particular group with which she was dealing. Sometimes the clearest understanding may be had from the "life and times" of a great national figure. No one who has read Thayer's Life of Cavour,[1] for example, can ever forget the strikingly dissimilar characteristics of the natives of the different Italian provinces, or forget the background of oppression and anarchy that is only half a century away from the Neapolitan or the Sicilian of our own day. Another view of a given foreign group may be had from whatever native poetry and legend best illustrate folk ways. Some of their modern fiction too would be illuminating, though much of it would be of no

[1] Thayer, William Roscoe: Life and Times of Cavour. Boston, Houghton Mifflin and Company, 1911.

use whatever. Books of travel help, unless written by men of one idea, determined to prove their point.

The history of the coming to this country of the immigrant group which is being studied, and the sum of its achievements and failures here, are often matters of record. If, of the people under consideration, such an admirable study has been made as Miss Emily Greene Balch gives us in Our Slavic Fellow Citizens, this part of the inquiry will be made easy. The social settlements in America have done a great service to their country by interpreting immigrant life in its cities to a preoccupied public. From the appearance of Hull House Maps and Papers[1] in 1895 to the present time, they have labored unceasingly and with rare discernment in this particular field. The various stages of Americanization are made clear, for example, in a book mentioned earlier—in Robert A. Woods' Americans in Process.

Advice upon the right books to read may well be sought of some of the settlement leaders, especially where there is a settlement in the foreign quarter which a worker is studying, or where there is one in another quarter of the city of like character. Advice may be sought of this leader not only upon books but upon the people who can help—upon representative men and women of the colony, and educated fellow-countrymen in the city. Some of the latter hold themselves aloof, however, taking an unsympathetic attitude toward the struggles of their less sophisticated compatriots. The case worker who reads the language can get many insights from the newspapers and periodicals which are printed in it in this country.

II. STUDY OF THE INDIVIDUAL

As already said, our questions will not be fully answered by any or all of these means. It should also be repeated that individuals and families cannot be treated merely as recent immigrants exhibiting certain racial and national characteristics. They are human beings first of all. Even the detailed questions which follow, outlining not only their early history and their migration to this country but the period of attempted adjustment here, do not necessarily bear upon the most important part of the client's story in every case.

[1] Hull House Maps and Papers. New York, T. Y. Crowell and Company, 1895.

IMMIGRANT FAMILY QUESTIONNAIRE[1]

This is not a schedule to be filled out nor a set of queries to be answered by a social agency's client or clients. For an explanation of the purpose of these questionnaires see p. 373 sq.

A star (*) indicates that the answer to the question may be found in, or confirmed by, public records.

The questionnaire regarding Any Family (p. 378) precedes this one. Its more general questions are repeated here only in rare instances, when it has seemed necessary to give them special emphasis.

I Parents and Early Home in Old Country

1. In what country, province, and town were the husband and wife born and brought up? Was birthplace (or early home, if different) in highland or lowland country? Inland or a seaport? Isolated from foreign influences? In country, town, or city?
2. Was the family home comfortable? How many rooms were there? Of what, in general, did the family's food consist? Was it meager in quantity or variety? Was it limited by custom or by economic conditions? Was the income of the family sufficient for family needs?
3. Did the father work in the field, factory, shop, or at a profession? Did he work on share or by the day? Did he hold any government position? Did the mother work as well? At what?
4. Did the family belong to a dominant or a subject race? What was the standing of the family in the community? Was the standard of living in any respect above or below the general level? If so, how and why? Did the father own property? What was its nature and value? Has this property deteriorated in value? Has it been sold?
5. Was the family a united one? Had the father patriarchal authority over the children? What was the attitude of the family toward the mother? Were religious influences strong in the home? Is any history of religious persecution involved? What was the family's attitude toward the government under which it lived?
6. Was there any family history of insanity, feeble-mindedness, tuberculosis, deaf mutism, eye disease, goitre, or syphilis?
7. Had either parent, or any members of their families, a criminal record?* A record of unusual immorality?
8. How many brothers and sisters have the husband and wife had? How many are now in this country, how many abroad? What is name, address, age, occupation, social and economic status of each? Influence with these clients of each?
9. If parents or brothers or sisters have died, what was age and cause of death in each case?*

[1] This questionnaire is for a family in which the parents came to this country as adults, after marriage. If they came as children or young people, some of the questions and their grouping would have to be modified; the questionnaire might in that case be regarded as applying in part to the parents belonging to the preceding generation.

II Individual History prior to Marriage

10. What type of school—public or private, church or secular—did the two heads of the present family attend? Did they learn to read and write their own language or any other? At what age did each leave school?

11. What was the age of each at beginning work? Was it for the father, or was he or she apprenticed, or put to work for a regular wage? What was the nature of the work? Was it too hard for his or her years? Did the man ever serve in the army or navy?* How long?* Was service compulsory?

12. When did each first break away from home ties, and why?

13. Had either been married before the present marriage? If so, what were the circumstances, time, and place?* Did the former wife or husband die? If so, when and where?* Under what circumstances? Did he or she leave any property* or insurance? If still living, has a divorce been secured? If so, when, where, and for what cause?*

14. Was the earlier marriage a happy one? What period elapsed before remarriage? Was remarriage for economic reasons? Were there any illegal relationships before the present marriage?

III Marriage and Family Life

15. Are husband and wife from the same community and class? Are they related? In what degree? Are they of different races, religions, or nationalities? Of widely different ages?

16. What was the period of acquaintance before marriage? Was the marriage negotiated by the respective families? If so, what were the guiding principles of the choice?

17. When and where did marriage take place?* Was there both civil and church ceremony? Have they a certificate? Who were the witnesses?*

18. When (exact date) and where was each child born?* Christened? Who were its sponsors?

19. What is the relation of parents and children? Does the father have any patriarchal authority over his family? What is the mother's position in the home? Is the tie of kinship particularly strong or is it weak? Does the tie extend beyond the immediate family?

20. Has the marriage been a happy one? If not, did the trouble begin before emigration? When and how? Was there any evidence of unfaithfulness?

21. Did the home, after marriage, compare favorably with those that the husband and wife had known before? Did the husband support the family to the best of his ability?

IV Circumstances Pertaining to Emigration

22. Had there been any change in the family's circumstances which made emigration desirable? Did they come to earn the necessities or the comforts of life, or was it to accumulate savings to take home? Was it to escape justice? To avoid military service? Was it because of racial or religious persecution? Because of domestic difficulties or infelicities?

23. Did the husband have regular work at the time of emigration? What was he doing at that time?

24. Had relatives or friends preceded them? Did the impetus come from a steamship agent, or from printed matter sent out by steamship companies? Was work promised by an employment agency or a steamship company?

25. How were the necessary funds secured? From savings, from selling or mortgaging property, by borrowing from relatives or friends, from a steamship agent, from a banker? For how long a period were they planning and saving for the journey? What was the destination on embarking? Why had the emigrant chosen that particular town or city?

26. If money was borrowed, how much, and what were the terms of payment? What household belongings, if any, did they bring with them?

27. Did the husband leave his family behind? If so, what provision did he make for their support? Did he send money? Did relatives care for them? Did they have income from property? Did the wife work? How long before the family joined him? How was the money secured?

28. From what port did he (and his family) embark?* Name of steamship?* Did he follow route ordinarily taken from his town? If not, why?

29. What was the port of entry, date of landing (and other items on passport)?* Had husband (or family) received instructions regarding answers at port? What, why, from whom? Was he (or were they) detained?* Why, how long, how released?* Were there any reasons why any member of the family could not be admitted?* What was done?* Who befriended and who took advantage of the family? To whom were they assigned?* Did they go first to a relative or friend? What address?

V Industrial Adjustment in This Country

30. How much money did the husband have on landing? Was it his own? Did it last until he was able to earn his way? If not, how did he manage?

31. What work did he expect to do in this country, and why? If he had been promised a job before coming, what was it, and by whom promised? Did he get it? How long before he went to work? How did he get his first job? What was the nature of work? Was he fitted for it by previous training or experience? What were his wages?

32. How did this occupation compare with work formerly done by him in the old country as regards skill or strength, healthfulness, remuneration, hours, and chances for future development? Was he handicapped by not speaking English? Was he at an advantage or disadvantage over Americans in the same industry? Were others of his countrymen employed with or over him? How long did he keep this job and what were his reasons for leaving it? Was his next job an advance over his first?

33. If work was of a different nature from that to which he was accustomed, what effort was made to procure work of his own kind? Has he ever procured such work since? When and how? What were the difficulties in keeping it?

34. Was he a member of a trade union in the old country, and if so, why has he not joined one in America? Is he eligible for membership here?

35. How many places has he had in this country? Has he been frequently out of work? Because of illness, hard times, lack of knowledge of English, or for what other cause? How long idle? How did he secure work again? Has his work been seasonal? Irregular? Either of these by his own choice? Has it been casual? Regular? What changes in nature of work? Has his work necessitated changes in habits of living and in his recreations?

36. Has he ever been exploited by any employment agency, broker, padrone? Compelled to pay lump sums to secure a job, or to share earnings with foremen or others? Sent to jobs which proved to be non-existent? Discharged after brief periods of employment to make way for new employes? Has there been exploitation of this family and of the colony of which it is a part by a ring composed of the employment agent, a banker, grocer, steamship agent, or the like?

37. If debts were contracted, either before or after arrival, did he pay them off? How long did this take? Did he or does he send money to the old country? In payment of debts, as an investment, or to support members of his family? How much? How frequently? Through whom?

38. Has he ever returned to the old country? If so, how was the money procured?

39. Has the wife ever worked outside the home? At what? Has she done home work? Of what nature? Has she worked whenever she could find work to do, or has she resorted to such work only in times of special emergency? What provision was made for the children during her absence?

40. If there are children of working age, at what age did they leave school, and what has been the industrial history of each? Have they frequently shifted from one job to another? Have they been shunted into "dead-end" occupations? Have they shown any ambition? Any special abilities?

VI Social Adjustment in This Country

41. Has the family lived here in a colony (or colonies) of its own nationality? Is this colony large enough to have business and interests of its own which are independent of the rest of the community? Does the colony maintain a newspaper (daily or weekly) in its own language? What characteristics does the colony ascribe to Americans in general and to American women in particular? Has there been any friction between this colony and the rest of the community? What contact has there been, by the man and the woman, with Americans or with those of any nationality other than their own?

42. In what way has the family's home life in this country differed from that in Europe? What customs had to be changed?

43. Has there been evidenced a persistent clinging to the old, or a willingness to try the new? What is the general community feeling in this respect? Has this family been particularly slow in making this adjustment?

44. How far have the husband and wife progressed in learning the English language? Has either attended night school?

45. Has it been the plan of the family to return to Europe for final settlement or to remain permanently in this country?

46. What steps, if any, has the husband taken toward naturalization?* What preparation, if any, has he had for naturalization? If he has taken no steps, what is his reason? If he has been denied his certificate of naturalization, on what ground did the court base its action?*

47. Has he shown any interest in politics? Frequented any club where public matters are discussed? Shown enthusiasm for democratic ideals?

48. Have there been changes in standard of living, in food, in number of rooms, etc., during the period of residence in this country? What and why? Has this change been for the better or for the worse? If the mother has been accustomed to do any work for pay, what effect has it had upon the family standards?

49. Have their church affiliations been vital or merely nominal? Has the hold of the church on them been strengthened or weakened by immigration? Have they contributed regularly to the support of the church?

50. Have the children attended public* or parochial school? Or both? Have their teachers been of foreign birth? Have they been taught chiefly or entirely in a foreign language? Have they mingled with native American children or children of other nationalities? Has their school progress been normal for their ages? If not, has there been anything in the family history or home life to account for the retardation? Has it been due to lack of adjustment to American conditions? Have the children been truants? Have the parents kept them out of school to work?

51. What use, if any, have the children made of night schools, special classes or clubs, the libraries?

52. Have the children grown away from parental influence? In what way was this first noticed? How early did estrangement begin? Has it reached a serious stage? Has the tendency of some teachers and social workers to disregard the parents and deal with the family only through the children been a factor in breaking down the children's respect for their parents?

53. Have the children introduced any changes into the family customs and routine? What? Are they contemptuous of all old world customs, without discrimination? Are they extravagant in matters of dress and amusement? Is there unnecessary friction or is the family willing to make the adjustment? Does the family appreciate the danger?

54. What forms of amusement have the family been accustomed to enjoy together? What forms separately? How do the various members of the family spend their Sundays and evenings?

55. Has there been any deterioration in character, or in moral or physical stamina, in any member of the family? Have any members suffered from serious or prolonged illnesses?

56. If any of the children have died, when and from what causes?*

57. Have there been emergencies in which the family has sought or accepted aid? Have relatives or friends assisted at such times? How long after arrival in America was first application for relief (if any) made to a public* or private agency? What was the occasion? What were the results? What has been the effect on the family, on relatives and friends? Is there evidence of growing dependence?

VII Housing at Present

58. How long has the family lived in its present home? How does home compare with previous ones in this country in respect to neighborhood, number of rooms, lighting, ventilation, sanitation, and furnishings? Is the landlord one of their own nationality? Is he a fellow townsman? Does he live in the same house? Is he paying for the house and therefore unwilling to put money into repairs? Do these facts affect the rental? How does rent compare with that for similar accommodations in other parts of the city? What determined the family in its choice of this location—nearness to work, presence of compatriots, any other factors?

59. How many persons sleep in a single room? Is the number a menace to the physical or moral welfare of the family? How many rooms are there for general use (not sleeping rooms)? How do these conditions compare with those in the old world, and with their previous quarters in this country?

VIII Lodgers

60. Are there any lodgers? How many? Men or women? On what terms are they kept? Does housewife cook their food? Does food left over go to the family? Do they share a room with any members of the family? Are they relatives, fellow townsmen? Have they but recently arrived in America?

61. Is the presence of lodgers rendered necessary by the family budget? Are they kept to swell a savings account, or to make payments on property possible? Are they kept from motives of friendship? Are the lodgers kept only occasionally, or is it a custom? Is the family anxious to dispense with them?

62. Are the lodgers also boarders? On what terms? Are they an added burden to the family when out of work? Does the family ever borrow money of the lodgers? Are their habits or physical condition such as to be a menace to the family in any way?

IX Health

63. What is the physical and mental condition of each member of the family? His fitness for his work? Is a cause of ill health to be found in housing or living conditions, in hours or conditions of work, or in lack of adjustment to conditions of life in America?

64. What is the attitude of the heads of the family toward medical agencies, dispensaries, hospitals? Is this attitude, if unfriendly, accounted for by exploitation in this country or abroad, at the hands of medical quacks or fake institutions? Is it an attitude characteristic of the people in the family's home town in the old country?

X Occupations[1]

65. What is the present occupation of each member of the family? Hours of work, habitual and overtime?

XI Needs and Resources[1]

66. If the family is unable to speak English, who is the person who has been acting as interpreter? Are his general intelligence, his knowledge of English and of the foreign language he claims to know, and his disinterestedness such as to make the information about needs, resources, and other matters obtained through him quite reliable?

67. If the family is in need, what circumstances are responsible? How does the present emergency, if there is one, differ from any that have previously arisen? Have relatives, friends, fellow townsmen assisted? Is their aid less than on previous occasions? Why?

68. Does either the husband or wife belong to any lodge or benefit society? If so, what are the dues? If they do not, what is their reason? If they have dropped out, when was it and why? What are the chances of reinstatement? Who are the officers, the doctor? Are some of the members fellow townsmen? Is it a religious organization?

69. Has the organization aided them by the payment of sickness or of death benefits? When? To what extent? What are the rulings as to this? Do they ever make voluntary collections in addition to the regular aid? Through whom is the money paid? Do they carry members on their books who are temporarily unable to pay dues?

70. What are the death benefits of the organization? Is it a fixed amount, or proportional to membership? How long after death is the amount paid to beneficiaries? Is the undertaker paid first? Does the society itself make the arrangements with the undertaker?

71. Has the family within recent years received any inheritance,* damages,* or insurance money? Has it, or did it recently have, savings? Does it, or did it recently, own any property?*

72. What prospect does there seem to be that this family will retain or regain economic independence? That they will make a satisfactory social adjustment in this country? If these prospects are slight, would it be possible and desirable to deport them? Are they deportable on any of the grounds specified in the Immigration Law?[2]—for example, as mentally deficient, insane, or epileptic; as

[1] For Income and Outgo and further questions relating to Occupations, see questionnaire regarding Any Family, questions 26 and 27 and 21 to 25.

[2] It should be borne in mind that an alien, to be deportable, must (with certain exceptions) have been "at the time of entry . . . a member of one or more of the classes excluded by law," or must have become "within five years after entry . . . a public charge from causes not affirmatively shown to have arisen subsequent to landing." The Immigration Law of 1917, especially in sections 3 and 19, together with the Immigration Act of 1924, especially section 14, and the Act approved June 24, 1929, amending subdivision (a) of section 1 of the Act approved March 4, 1929 (Public Law Numbered 1018, Seventieth Congress), contain a number of important departures from previous laws—as, for example, in regard to the period after landing during which deportation is possible, and inability ever to return to the United States after deportation. Consult immigration authorities as to interpretation and conditions of the enforcement of these acts.

paupers, beggars, or vagrants; as chronic alcoholics; as tuberculous or afflicted with any loathsome or dangerous contagious disease; as criminals; as prostitutes or persons who profit by prostitution; as anarchists or persons who advocate or teach the unlawful destruction of property; as contract laborers; as illiterates? If they are not deportable, would it be possible to arrange for their return to the old country by consular ticket? Are there relatives there who would assume responsibility?

CHAPTER XXII

DESERTION AND WIDOWHOOD

THE situation of the mother whose children have been deserted by their father and that of the widowed mother with children present some superficial resemblances. An early stage in the development of social treatment—one dominated by emergencies and by surface symptoms—usually leaves the two situations undifferentiated. That they present different problems is shown by the two questionnaires which follow.

State laws relating to the apprehension and punishment of deserters are so varied that no questions are included with regard to extradition, trial, suspension of sentence, probation, reimbursement of family during imprisonment, etc. It is assumed here that the social worker knows the state law or city ordinance bearing upon desertion and intends to confer with the public officials or private agencies most interested in its enforcement.

For re-enforcement of the position frequently taken in these pages that single disabilities cannot be treated as ultimate causes, and that they cannot be understood even in one case without reference to the factors behind and those entering into their manifestations, attention may be called to the desertion case summarized on page 140. Even the finding of a deserter, which is the first step in his treatment, of course, can be expedited by the attempt, from such data as are at hand, to understand him.

DESERTED FAMILY QUESTIONNAIRE

This is not a schedule to be filled out nor a set of queries to be answered by a social agency's client or clients. For an explanation of the purpose of these questionnaires see p. 373 sq.

A star (*) indicates that the answer to the question may be found in, or confirmed by, public records.

The questionnaire regarding Any Family (p. 378) precedes this one. Its more general questions are repeated here only in rare instances, when it has seemed necessary to give them special emphasis.

1. What steps, if any, have been taken to make sure that the husband is not in the immediate neighborhood and in communication with his family? That he is not in some hospital unidentified? That he has not been arrested and sent to

the house of correction or some other institution? Or that he has not gone away to seek work with the knowledge and approval of his wife? What is the wife's reputation for trustworthiness?

2. If it is clear that the desertion is genuine, what steps have been taken to trace him? Has his picture been obtained for purposes of identification? Have out-of-town and in-town relatives and friends been consulted? Or his last foreman, his fellow workmen, etc., or his neighborhood cronies, and the keeper of the saloon, if he frequented one? Or any benefit societies and trade union to which he may have belonged? Have army and navy enlistments been consulted, or the police?

I Circumstances of Present Desertion

3. When did the husband last desert? What steps on her own initiative has his wife taken to find him? What steps with the help of others, and of whom?

4. What is the wife's statement as to the immediate cause of his departure? As to her knowledge or inference with regard to his intention? As to his present whereabouts?

5. Has he ever been in other cities? Which? Has he ever expressed a desire to visit any special place? Is it likely that forwarding of mail to him has been arranged for at the post office?* Does he speak so little English that he would probably be found in the foreign colony in whatever city he went to? What languages does he speak?

6. If husband's whereabouts is known, what is his statement of the cause of his desertion?

7. What do relatives on each side, friends, fellow employes, and other references give as probable causes of his desertion? What bias have these different witnesses?

8. Was wife pregnant at time of desertion?

9. What was husband's employment at time of desertion? If none, causes of unemployment? How long had he been out of work?

10. Have any facts that explain the desertion come to light? Was there a special burden of debt, including installment purchases? Or was husband in danger of arrest for some dishonesty? Are any earlier criminal acts on record?* Is there any evidence that he is mentally abnormal or nervously unstable?

11. Did he take money (if so, how much) or clothing with him? Did he have savings? Where did he get the money to go with? Did he leave any personal or real property or money in bank? Has the wife any property?

12. Since he left, has he sent money or other supplies to his family? How much? Date of last remittance? Date and postmark of last letter?

13. If his whereabouts is known, is he at work? What are his earnings? Is he living with another woman?

14. Has the wife sworn out a warrant for his arrest?* (In some places a warrant cannot be had until the husband's whereabouts is known.) What is her attitude

toward jail sentence, probation, separate support, or reconciliation, and is this attitude likely to be a stable one? What other plans has she for the immediate future?

II Past Desertions

15. How many times has husband deserted his present wife before? How long after marriage did he first desert? Length of each period of desertion? Intervals between desertions? What events led up to each? Is there any long interval between births of the children next to each other in age that may be due to prolonged separation of parents?

16. Where did he go on previous desertions? How did he go—by freight, tramping, or paying his way? Did he get work elsewhere? Did he send money home? How much?

17. In each desertion, what action, if any, was taken by the wife, by the courts,* by public* or private charity, and with what results? How was the wife supported in his absence? What effort was made to develop his sense of responsibility for his family after his return?

18. Have there been any arrests for non-support?* If so, with what results?*

19. What were the circumstances of each return? When persuaded to take her husband back, what outside influences, if any, led to the wife's action?

III The Husband's Early Life

20. What were the general conditions of the husband's early home life? What was his home training? Was he indulged or unduly repressed? Did his father and mother fulfill their responsibilities? Did either show evidence of physical or mental defect? Did his father ever desert or fail to provide for his family?

21. Did the husband have any institutional training as a boy? Of what nature? For how long?

22. Did he earn before leaving school, either by selling papers, doing errands, or otherwise? Any truancy or other signs of a roving disposition during school life?

23. What was his age and in what grade was he when he left school? Did he go to work immediately and work regularly? If not, was it because he preferred to loaf? How often did these loafing periods come and how long did they last? Did he show a tendency to wander from home then?

24. What were his amusements in childhood and youth?

25. What employment or employments did he choose? What opportunity for development did they offer?

26. Did he, before marriage, turn over his wages to the family?

27. When did he leave his parents' home? Why?

28. Did he ever serve in army or navy?*

29. Was he ever married before? Was it a legal marriage?* Was he then a deserter or arrested for non-support?* Has he children by another marriage? What are the relations between these children and their stepmother?

IV The Wife's Early Life

30. What were the wife's early home life, education, and training? (For details that apply, see The Husband's Early Life, 20 to 29.) On what terms is she now with her own people?

31. Did she have any training at home or school to prepare her for making a home?

32. Did she work before marriage? If so, at what and under what conditions?

33. Had she been previously married?* If so, what children had she by that marriage and what have been the relations between them and their stepfather?

V Their Married Life

34. How did husband and wife meet? What was age of each at present marriage?*

35. When (exact date), where, and under what circumstances were couple married?*

36. Is marriage legal? If married by religious ceremony in the old country, is it legal here? Has either a husband or wife living from whom no divorce has been obtained? (In the treatment of desertion cases it is especially important to have some legal proof of the marriage.)

37. Did marriage take place because wife was pregnant? If so, was marriage forced upon husband? Were there any other unusual circumstances?

38. At time of marriage, did either husband or wife have any money saved? How was it spent? Did they buy furniture on the installment plan? What was their income when first married? Rent? Character of neighborhood in which they began married life? Was the home better or worse than either had been accustomed to before marriage?

39. Have they ever lived in furnished rooms?

40. Have they ever lived with their relatives? Have any of their relatives ever lived with them? Have they interfered in the home? What are the characteristics of the relatives who have been most closely associated with the family?

41. Have the family taken lodgers or have any other outsiders lived with them? Men or women? What have been their relations with the husband? With the wife?

42. If foreign born, did man precede his family in coming to this country? How long? Have differences in degree of Americanization influenced the home life? (See Immigrant Family Questionnaire, p. 387.)

43. What striking differences, if any, between husband and wife in age, race, nationality, religion, education, or personal habits? Have these differences led to disagreements and family dissension?

44. What was husband's occupation when living with his family, and his average wage? Was it enough to maintain a decent standard of living? How did his wage in the last position held compare with his maximum wage? If lower, what was reason? How did work done compare with that done at his best?

45. Was his work seasonal or otherwise irregular? Did he always work when he could get work?

46. What proportion of his wages did he give family when working full time? When working part time?

47. Has wife worked since marriage? At what and for what wage? What has been effect on her health, effect on man as a wage-earner, on home and children? What arrangement was made for the care of the children in her absence? Did she consider work a hardship, or prefer it to confinement to home duties? What are her capabilities as a possible wage-earner?

48. What is the health record of husband? Of wife? Has either any physical or mental defects? Has either deteriorated markedly since marriage? Has either been intemperate or given to the use of drugs? (See Inebriety Questionnaire, p. 430.)

49. Has either husband or wife been immoral? Given to gambling, betting, or any form of dishonesty?

50. What are husband's personal characteristics? Has he seemed fond of home? Of children? Or has he, for example, been lazy, sullen, penurious, jealous, or cruel to family? What is his employer's estimate of him? What were his relations with his fellow employes? If there were marked signs of bad temper at home or in his relations with shop mates, has the possibility of mental disease ever been considered?

51. What are wife's personal characteristics? Has she, for instance, a difficult or nagging disposition? Is she a good housekeeper? A good mother?

52. What signs are there that there has been or still is any real affection on the part of either husband or wife? How have they influenced one another? Or is estrangement due in large part to external things and not to their own dispositions?

53. What active affiliation with church, with clubs, etc., has either had? What usual recreations? Did family ever go on trips or enjoy other recreations together?

54. Are the children attractive and generally well cared for and well behaved?

55. What is the attitude of the older children toward their father? Toward their mother? Toward assuming support of family?

56. What is the attitude of any and all relatives toward husband? Toward wife? Toward helping in support of family or other solution? Do his brothers or sisters or his parents condone his desertion? Are any of them harboring him?

57. Is the present home detached, or is it a tenement? Are the rooms pleasant and well furnished? Well cared for? Are any lodgers or other outsiders now living with family?

58. What is the character of the neighborhood? How long have the family lived in this neighborhood? If they have recently come here, what was the character of their former home and neighborhood?

VI Financial Situation

59. What is the financial standing of husband's father? Has he contributed to support of his grandchildren? Has he been prosecuted for failure to do so?

60. Had family been dependent before husband's desertion? To what extent, how long, and for what causes?

61. Was relief given from public sources,* from private charities, or from relatives? Or had they received free transportation? What had been effect of aid on the husband? On the wife?

62. Is family now dependent? On whom? To what extent? What is the attitude toward the present situation of those who have assumed any part of the financial burden?

63. What is the total family income? Family expenditures? (See questionnaire regarding Any Family, Financial Situation, 26, 27, p. 380.)

64. Are the wage-earning members of family all employed at maximum earning capacity?

QUESTIONNAIRE REGARDING A WIDOW WITH CHILDREN

This is not a schedule to be filled out nor a set of queries to be answered by a social agency's client or clients. For an explanation of the purpose of these questionnaires see p. 373 sq.

A star (*) indicates that the answer to the question may be found in, or confirmed by, public records.

The questionnaire regarding Any Family (p. 378) precedes this one. Its more general questions are repeated here only in rare instances, when it has seemed necessary to give them special emphasis.

I Circumstances of Husband's Death

1. When (exact date) and where did husband die?* Who was the undertaker?

2. What was the cause of his death?* (Give exact medical diagnosis.)

3. Were the conditions of his work responsible for it? If so, what action has been taken to secure compensation? What state law is applicable to the situation?

4. Had he been physically weakened by overwork? By excessive drinking, bad living conditions, or other causes?

5. How long was he ill? What medical care did he receive? Name and address of physician who attended him?

6. Is there anything important to be noted in the inheritance—physical, mental, or moral—of the husband? Was there in his family tuberculosis, inebriety, insanity, feeble-mindedness, or epilepsy?

7. How was family supported during his illness? Were wages continued in full or in part by his employers? What were the sources of support—relatives, savings, sick benefits, wages of woman, of children, relief, other sources? Approximate amount from each source?

8. What was the amount of insurance, legal compensation, or death benefits? Amount collected by fellow workmen, contributed by employer, etc.? Cost of funeral? Amount of debts? Balance left for widow? What disposition was made of this money, and how long did it last?

II Early Life of Widow

9. What of the family inheritance of the mother (see question 6)?

10. What was the occupation of her father? Did he work steadily and fulfill his obligations to his family? Was her home a normally constituted one? If not, in what particulars abnormal?

11. Did she before her marriage live in the city or country? Did she ever have institutional care? Where? For how long? How far did she go in school? Why and at what age did she leave?

12. Did she work before marriage? Nature of occupation? Wages? Length of time employed in each place? Wages at time of marriage?

13. If before marriage she lived in another country, has she worked since coming to America? Nature of occupation? Wages?

III Married Life

14. When (exact date), where, and under what circumstances did marriage take place?*

15. At time of marriage, did either husband or wife have any money saved? How was it spent? What was income when first married? Character of neighborhood in which they began married life? Was the home better or worse than either had been accustomed to before marriage? Were they near to relatives?

16. Did they ever live with relatives? In furnished rooms? Were they separated at any time? If so, how long and for what reason?

17. Did the wife work between the time of her marriage and her husband's death? Occupation? Length of time employed? Occasion for her going to work?

18. What was the husband's occupation? Maximum wage? Was he regularly, seasonally, or occasionally employed? What were his weekly earnings just before he was taken ill? Did he pay a regular amount weekly to his wife, or turn over his pay envelope to her untouched? Was he industrially efficient? Who was his last employer? How long was he employed there? Is employer interested in the family?

19. Did the family or any member of it have relief or institutional care before husband's last illness? When? Source, occasion, kind, and approximate amount?

20. Did the character of husband or of wife change materially after marriage? Was he intemperate, vicious, or lazy? When did these characteristics begin to be manifested? Do any events explain them? What was his influence on the children?

21. Did he ever desert, or had he a court record?*

22. When did the family reach its high-water mark? What was the standard of living at that time?

23. Was this standard lowered before husband's last illness? Why? In what particulars?

IV The Transition Period

24. Have any changes in standard been made since the husband's death? Removal to cheaper rent? Children taken from school? Children put in institutions? Supply of food or clothing reduced? Lodgers or boarders taken? Have these changes been a menace to the home life and to the future of the children?

25. How long after husband's death was the first application, if any, for relief made? To what agency? Treatment by that agency and by any others that may have been called on to aid this family? Total (approximate) amount of relief given by all agencies to date?

26. How was the family supported in the interval preceding application? Insurance, relatives, savings, sick benefits, wages of widow, of children, other sources?

V Present Surroundings

27. What is the character of the neighborhood? The house? The apartment? (For detailed questions, see questionnaire regarding Any Family, 34-38, p. 381.)

28. How near are they to schools, settlements, libraries, parks, other opportunities for recreation? Where do the children play? Does the family have any recreation in common?

VI Present Family Problems in General

29. What is the widow's general health? Has she any physical or mental disabilities or defects? What is the physical and mental condition of each member of the household? If the husband died of tuberculosis, have all members of the family been examined?

30. Have any of them had, in the past, treatment by physician, hospital, or dispensary? With what results? What was the attitude of the patient, willingness to follow advice, etc.?

31. If the mother or any of the children need medical care, what is the diagnosis of physician, hospital, dispensary? What treatment or special care is recommended?

32. Is it likely that any members of the family would be benefited by removal to the country? Is there anything to indicate that the family would be adapted to country life?

33. What is the widow's character and ability? Is she moral? Temperate? Is there indication of strength of character? What resourcefulness, if any? What is her attitude toward relief, both public and private?

34. In what condition is her home and the children's clothing? Is she a thrifty housekeeper? Does she know how to select and prepare nourishing food? Is she an affectionate mother? Does she maintain discipline, especially over her boys?

35. Are the children obedient, well behaved, helpful, of good habits? Have they attended school regularly? What is the teacher's report concerning them? Are they up to the normal grade in school? What arrangement has been made

for receiving reports regarding attendance, etc., from week to week? Have they ever been under the care of a truant officer?* Have any of them been before the children's court?* If so, under what circumstances and with what results?

36. Do any of the family take advantage of clubs or social activities in schools, settlements, etc.? What is the testimony of the directors of such activities in regard to them?

37. If the family is foreign, what is the degree of Americanization? Does the mother speak English? What influence have differences in custom on her relations with the children? (See also Immigrant Family Questionnaire, p. 387.)

38. Are there other members of the household? Boarders and lodgers? What is the effect of their presence on the family life? Are any of these male adults? Are they related to the widow?

39. Does the mother plan to put any of the children in institutions? If so, what are her reasons? Or what other plans has she in detail for herself and for each of her children?

VII Present Work Problems

40. If the widow is not working, is her constant presence with the children needed? Is it good for them, or would they both gain by periods of absence? How does she spend her time? What are the work standards of women in the neighborhood who have working husbands? How much and what kind of work, if any, should she be expected to do? Would she be helped in ways other than financial by further training?

41. If employed, what is the nature of her occupation? What are her weekly earnings? Working hours, and total hours per day? Does she go out to work? If so, how many days per week and for what specific hours of the day (A. M. and P. M.) is she away from home? If she is working early and late hours, how much sleep does she get?

42. If the mother works away from home, where is each of the children under working age in her absence? Who cooks their meals? Do they get food enough and of the right kind? Who cares for them? If a neighbor does, what is her character and influence? What provision is made for care of school children out of school hours?

43. Do the children of school age help their mother at home? Do they sell papers, run errands, or do any work outside the home? If so, what are the days and hours of work and amount earned? Is the child labor law being violated?

44. What are the conditions, moral and physical, under which widow and children work? If she works at home, do conditions comply with regulations of factory inspectors?

45. Are the children of working age at work and earning maximum possible wages? Will their present occupation lead to advancement? Have they special talents to be cultivated? What are their earnings?

46. What is their attitude toward assuming family responsibility? Do they give mother full wage? Does she allow them money for clothes and spending money?

47. Is any effort being made, as younger children approach working age, to secure for them work suited to their preferences or abilities that will train them for future efficiency? What is the mother's attitude toward their further education?

VIII Income and Outgo

48. What, in detail, is the present income of the family? The present outgo? (See questionnaire regarding Any Family, 26, 27, p. 380.)

49. What does careful analysis show to be the necessary expenditure for food, rent, fuel, clothing, insurance, carfare, lunches, other items?

IX Possible Sources of Advice and Help

50. Are there relatives near at hand? Are they friendly? What plan for the widow's future do they advise? What material help can they give in carrying it out? What helps that are not material? What is their moral standing? Is their influence desirable? If they live in another community in the United States or in the old country, could the family go to live with them? Are any of them known to any social agency? If the husband was a member of a lodge or benefit society, is the man who stood sponsor for him an old friend whose advice might prove valuable?

51. Has the family attended church or Sunday school regularly? Is there any religious instruction at home? What help can the church give, either material or by supervision, encouragement, etc.?

52. Are any charities or other social agencies interested? If so, what plan do they advise?

53. Are there any other sources of information and advice as to future plans? Any other sources of material help? Friends? Previous employers? Trade unions?

CHAPTER XXIII

THE NEGLECTED CHILD

IT SEEMED best to Dr. Catherine Brannick, who prepared the questionnaire regarding a Neglected Child which follows, to classify nearly half of her material on the basis of the particular forms of neglect recognized in many of our states as statutory offenses. This was done to facilitate reference, but it has involved repeating under each form listed questions that apply to several forms. The court side is only one aspect of this important problem, but it is a side with which social workers have to make themselves familiar.

QUESTIONNAIRE REGARDING A NEGLECTED CHILD[1]

This is not a schedule to be filled out nor a set of queries to be answered by a social agency's client or clients. For an explanation of the purpose of these questionnaires see p. 373 sq.

A star (*) indicates that the answer to the question may be found in, or confirmed by, public records.

The questionnaire regarding Any Family (p. 378) precedes this one. Its more general questions are repeated here only in rare instances, when it has seemed necessary to give them special emphasis.

I The Child's Father

1. Is there any criminal tendency in his family? Any record of drunkenness, chronic dependence, unusual degree of immorality, physical degeneracy?
2. Were any members of his family insane, feeble-minded, or epileptic?
3. Was he born out of wedlock?
4. Were there elements of neglect or cruelty in his own childhood? Was he a spoiled or unrestrained child?
5. Was he country or city bred? What was the character of the community in which he was reared?
6. Was he brought up to attend any church? What was his religious education?
7. What was his school training? His record at school? Was he considered in any degree mentally defective? Did he show signs of unusual temper, inherent cruelty, moral degeneracy? Age and grade on leaving school? Reason for leaving school? Did he have any special training?

[1] Prepared for this volume by Dr. Catherine Brannick.

8. Did he have any record of juvenile delinquency?* What, in detail?

9. Was he ever an inmate of a children's home or institution? If so, under what circumstances? For how long? If he was in an institution or otherwise a public charge, at what age did supervision cease?* What was his reputation?

10. If foreign born, at what age and under what circumstances did he begin life in the United States?

11. At what age did he begin work? What kind of work was it? Was it of such nature as to have a bad effect on him physically or otherwise? (i. e., was it a dangerous trade, a seasonal trade, irregular work, etc.?)

12. What was his attitude toward his parents? Did he show neglect of filial duties in withholding wages, etc.? Was he actively abusive?

13. Did he work whenever possible, or did he show a tendency to loaf?

14. What in general were his habits? What were his recreations?

15. Is there record in lower or superior court of any charge or conviction? For what offense?*

II The Child's Mother

16. What were the characteristics and standing of the mother's parents and of her immediate family? The circumstances of her early home life? Was she herself a neglected child? What was her schooling? Was she regarded as a dull or difficult child? What work did she take up after leaving school? Did she ever have any training in her home or elsewhere to fit her for domestic life? What kind of associates did she choose? Was she ever committed to an industrial or reform school?* Was she known as a girl of "loose habits"? (For details that apply, see The Child's Father, 1 to 15.)

III The Family Life

17. Has either the father or the mother ever been married before?* If so, is former wife or husband living? If divorced, where and on what ground was divorce obtained?*

18. Has either parent any children by a former marriage or any illegitimate children? If so, how many are there, what are their ages and sexes, where are they, and what are their relations with their parents and stepparents? If any such children have died, what was the cause of death?* If any are living with the family, is marked partiality shown by stepparent to his or her own children?

19. Are the father and mother legally married? When, where, and by whom was the ceremony performed?* What were the circumstances of the marriage? Was it a forced one? How old were the parents at the time? How long had they known each other?

20. Are there any mental or physical defects in either parent that should have barred marriage?

21. Are there family difficulties between husband and wife due to racial or religious differences? To unwise interference by relatives? Are differences so serious that they are not likely ever to be overcome?

22. How many children have been born of this marriage? How many have died, and from what causes?*

23. What was the father's occupation at the time of marriage? Since? Was he then and has he since been earning enough to support a family? Has he given his family normal support? When did family reach its high-water mark and what were the conditions?

24. If the father is now working, what are his wages? What proportion of his total income does he give to his family? What is his employer's estimate of him? What is his attitude toward his fellow employes?

25. How does his present wage compare with that which he is capable of earning—his maximum wage? What is reason for lower wage? How does present type of work compare with work done at his best?

26. How does the home now provided by him compare with that which he is able to provide?

27. If he is not working, what is the reason? How long has he been out of work?

28. Is he a member of a trade union? What is his reputation in the union? Is he a member of any fraternal organization? Affiliated with any anti-social organization?

29. Is he, or has he ever been, a satisfactory husband and father? Fond of home life? Of his children? Or does he regard children as merely a means of support for himself, now or later?

30. If satisfactory at one time and now given to abuse or neglect, when did change take place? Was it apparently due to development of inherent bad qualities? To "easy disposition," bad companionship and surroundings? To discouragement over lack of work, long illness in family, debt, characteristics of wife as a homemaker?

31. What is the attitude of the children toward their father and mother? Have they real affection for them? Are they afraid of either of them? Are they controlled by either or both? How? By fear or otherwise?

32. Is the wife, or has she ever been, a good mother or satisfactory housekeeper? If her home standards were fair at one time and have since become low, what causes have contributed to lower them? Her own or her husband's habits? Her own illness or other illness in the family? Overwork? Too many children? Extreme poverty?

33. Is she obliged, or has she in the past been obliged, to contribute to the family support? To what extent? Has she had the burden of regular work away from home? Is this responsible for much of the neglect?

34. Is or has either parent ever been affiliated with any church? What is present relation to the church and clergy?

35. What are the habits of father and mother as affecting their family life? Does either drink to excess? (See Inebriety Questionnaire, p. 430.) In the home, or away from it? Does drinking bring dissolute companions into the home? Has either parent ever signed the pledge or has either any respect for it? Does

either use drugs? Is either immoral? Obscene in language or action before the children? Is father a loafer? Does mother neglect her household duties, spend much time away from home or in association with criminal or immoral persons? Has either an ugly or dangerous temper? Does either beat or otherwise abuse the children? Is either given to gambling? Dishonest? Quarrelsome?

36. Is either parent suffering from a disease that constitutes a menace to the family? Is there reliable evidence of this condition in hospital records or with a competent private physician? What is the date of this record?

37. Does the bad example of either parent show in the conduct of any of the children? Do they imitate parental vices?

38. Is either parent known to the police of the district, and what is his or her reputation with them?

39. Has either a court record?* Has the father been accused or convicted of offenses against his family—of desertion, non-support, assault, cruelty, criminal abuse?* Has the mother?*

40. Is either parent by reason of mental or physical defects, disposition, or habits unfit to have the care of children? On what grounds? Is there medical authority for this? Has either ever been pronounced mentally irresponsible? Would mental examination now be likely to result in such a decision?

IV Particular Form of the "Neglect"

(a) *Desertion or failure to provide for home*

41. Have the parents, or either of them, deserted? How long ago? Under what circumstances? Is this the first desertion? If not, what is history of previous desertions? (For other questions on desertion, see Deserted Family Questionnaire, p. 395.)

42. How many rooms in the home? Is there overcrowding beyond that which the law or decency allows?

43. Is the home furnished sufficiently for decent living and privacy?

44. What are the sleeping arrangements? Is there a decent supply of bedding? How many sleep in each bed? Are children forced to sleep with parents, adult members of family, or lodgers? Do children sleep in a dark room?

45. Are the children decently clothed? How does their clothing compare with that of other children of the neighborhood?

46. Have the children sufficient food? How is it prepared and served? What did the children actually have to eat at certain meals? If there is an infant, how is it fed?

47. What is the testimony of the teacher or school nurse in regard to these facts?

48. How long has this condition of neglect existed?

(b) *Neglect to provide medical care*

49. Are any of the children suffering from physical defects or diseases—such as deformities, rickets, persistent cough, chorea or other nervous affection, anemia,

malnutrition, adenoids, skin disease, carious teeth, pediculosis, defective eyesight—which can be remedied by proper medical care which the parents have been able but have failed to provide?

50. Has any one of the children syphilis or gonorrhea? What was the probable source of infection? Is he receiving treatment for this? Is his condition a menace to other children? Is there past history of these diseases?

51. Is either parent or any frequenter of the home suffering from venereal or other contagious disease? Is there medical authority for this? Of what date? Are conditions such that the children are inevitably exposed to contagion from this?

52. Is there record of the physical ills of the children with the school nurse or doctor, district nurse or physician, hospital or competent private physician? With the board of health?*

53. What efforts have been made through other agencies to persuade the parents to secure proper medical care for the children? With what results?

54. What is the testimony of these agencies? Is further effort by them likely to be successful?

55. Has the school physician power to act in the matter?

56. Is the neglect of such nature that the board of health has power to act?

57. Was the diagnosis of the neglected condition specified in the complaint made by a recognized medical authority whose word would be taken in court?

58. Is it likely that any other recognized medical authority would disagree with the first?

59. Have any children of the family died? When and from what causes?* Do the deaths show probable medical neglect? Were such children insured?

(c) *Lack of control*

60. Is there lack of ordinary parental guidance? Are the parents able or do they try to control the children?

61. Do the difficulties of a new country press upon the parents? Do the children take advantage of this?

62. What is the school record of the children, especially as to attendance and behavior? Are they truant? In their language or habits at school do they show the lack of salutary control?

63. Are the children constantly on the streets and late at night? Do they frequent low picture shows, visit saloons or other places likely to lead to an idle and dissolute life?

64. Has the lack of salutary control reached the point where wrong-doing is a habit and the child is delinquent? Is there record of habitual truancy? Theft? Immoral conduct or association with immoral persons? Frequenting houses of ill repute? Street walking? Begging or vagrancy? Use of vile language? Relative incorrigibility?

65. Have any of the children any juvenile or other court record?*

66. Have any of the delinquent children been pronounced defective? If so, has custodial care been refused by the parents or not been provided by the community?

(d) *Exploitation*

67. Are the children overworked in home duties?

68. Are they illegally employed? Before the legal age or at illegal hours?

69. Are they made to contribute to the family support by sweatshop work in the home? By unreasonable help in the business of their parents?

70. Are they sent upon the streets to beg? Are they sent out ostensibly to sell articles on the street, but really to use this as a means of begging?

71. Is there deliberate exploitation of the children for immoral purposes?

(e) *Cruelty, physical injury, or abuse*

72. Is parental discipline rigid to the point of cruelty? Is punishment given by parent when in anger, or is self-control exercised? Is punishment frequent, oversevere, of unnatural or cruel form, dictated by perverted religious ideas, etc.? Is there abusive treatment not associated with the idea of punishment?

73. Are the older children permitted to punish or abuse the younger?

74. Do the children show evidence of such abuse or punishments?

(f) *Moral neglect*

75. Is the neighborhood of bad reputation? Are there people of bad reputation in the same house? Are the sleeping arrangements of the home such that decent privacy is impossible?

76. Are the children exposed to lead an idle and dissolute life by the drinking of the parents? By liquor selling in the home? Have the police knowledge of liquor selling? Are the children exposed to moral contagion by the immorality of the parents? By obscene acts and language of the parents in presence of the children? By the presence of lodgers or others admitted to the home?

77. Are the children known as "young street walkers"? Have the parents been aware of such practice or have they deliberately encouraged it?

78. Are the children of bad moral reputation in the neighborhood? In the school? Is there evidence of unnatural relations between parents and children? Between the children?

79. Is there reliable record of physical examination of any of the children showing venereal disease or evidence of immoral relations?

(g) *Inducement of chronic dependence*

80. Are the parents now or have they been frequently in receipt of charitable aid either public or private for which their neglect is responsible?

81. Have the parents or children ever been inmates of public institutions?* Under what circumstances?

82. Is there record of dependency in the case of grandparents, uncles, aunts?

83. What is the testimony of public relief-giving agencies regarding family?

84. What is the attitude of parents and children toward relief?

85. Has family been aided by many private relief agencies? Have parents "worked" these agencies? What is testimony of these private agencies in regard to the effect on the children?

86. Are parents known to beg?

87. Are the children permitted or compelled by parents to ask for relief at offices of public or private relief agencies?

88. Do children show tendency to dependency in their habits? Are they known to beg with or without knowledge of their parents? What is the testimony of the school in regard to this?

V General Aspects of the "Neglect"

89. Is the neglect more truly destitution? Is it the direct result of half orphanage, illness of the parents, lack of work, or other unfortunate circumstances for which the parents are not responsible? Are the children more truly dependent than neglected?

90. If present condition has elements of dependency rather than neglect, is it the result of neglect and vice at an earlier period of the family life?

91. Is condition due in any part to racial habits or characteristics? Does the standard of the family compare favorably enough with the standards of the particular race or social group?

92. Is the condition one of all-round neglect which has reached the point where it is not sufficiently bad for court interference and yet too bad for any hope from constructive work? Is the only possible thing to wait (though with continued close supervision) for conditions to become worse?

93. Is neglect of such degree or character that remedy may be reached by prosecution of parents leading to probation?

94. Is the father so nearly wholly responsible for the neglect that action against him would be more just than the more general charge of neglect, which involves the mother? Is non-support the main factor? Frequent desertion? Can the mother be persuaded to testify to this or to bring the charge herself?

95. Has the home ever before been broken up? By reason of the (temporary) inability of the parents to provide a home? By court action?* How was the home re-established? Have the children ever been inmates of a home or institution and under what circumstances?

96. Are the conditions of neglect recent or of long standing? What is the critical point in the neglect which led to the complaint?

97. Is the complainant a reliable person? Is the complainant possibly irresponsible, biased, or vindictive? Is he willing to testify if necessary to the conditions of which he has made complaint?

98. Is there first-hand evidence of the conditions of neglect? By the complainant? By the police? By reliable neighbors? By unbiased relatives? By the worker himself? Can specific instances be cited? Have night visits been made to ascertain exact sleeping conditions or presence of undesirables in the household?

99. Is any of the evidence likely to be attacked as prejudiced?

100. Can the parents themselves be persuaded to admit the charges of neglect?

101. If evidence of any one of the children seems necessary or desirable, has the reliability of the child been investigated through the school, Sunday school, or other responsible source?

102. What is the attitude of the police toward the specific form of neglect? Of the court? Of the community?

103. Are there responsible relatives? Have these relatives in the past made any attempt to build up the family life? Can they be depended upon to take charge of the family without appeal to the court?

104. Is it best to make the appeal to the court first, for the purpose of working out plans with relatives under the court's direction or with its co-operation?

105. Is more satisfactory disposition possible without court action? If warrant for neglect is not advisable or possible, is informal summons and warning by court possible?

106. If the state laws are such that the charge of neglect is made against the child, and the law provides for prosecution of the parent by an independent action, have plans been made for such action?

VI Work of Other Agencies

107. Has family been known to other social agencies? If so, what is the testimony of these agencies regarding it, what has been their experience in attempts at constructive work, and what do they advise?

108. Has probation been tried in the case of either parent? With what success?

109. Is constructive work of any one of these or other agencies likely to succeed if strengthened by action on the part of the social agency charged with responsibility of protecting children from neglect? Is any one agency, by reason of prestige or standing with family, more peculiarly fitted to undertake such work?

110. Is the consensus of opinion of these agencies that further effort at constructive work with the family is useless?

CHAPTER XXIV

THE UNMARRIED MOTHER

WE HAVE seen earlier that the affixing of a label—even of a correct label—has no practical bearing upon prognosis and treatment, and that a classification of this sort is not a social diagnosis. This truth has been illustrated in the dealings of social agencies with the mother of an illegitimate child. There are few tasks requiring more individualization, and there are few in which there has been so little.

Mrs. Sheffield, in the questionnaire regarding an Unmarried Mother which follows, aims to bring out first, under the captions The Mother and The Father, certain facts of environment and early influence together with the outstanding traits of these two people which may throw light on their standards of conduct and habits of thought. Although, in our treatment of an unmarried woman or girl in this situation, we are liable to overlook her father, it is obvious that his characteristics and what went to mould them are quite as significant socially as those of her mother. The information may point the way not only to effective treatment in the particular case, but also to measures for mass betterment in the community.

The last part of the questionnaire calls for the more immediate explanation of the girl's or woman's situation and for facts bearing on the identity and responsibility of the man. For various reasons the child's father only too frequently escapes responsibility. Evidence of paternity may not be convincing, the man may disappear, or the social agency—occupied with many other tasks—may feel that the small amount which the mother would be likely to receive does not warrant the labor of establishing the man's whereabouts and of bringing him to trial. The question has other aspects, however. Even small sums, if required whenever paternity can be established, will have an influence in modifying public opinion, will lead it to hold a man as well as a woman answerable for the support of offspring.

In making final arrangements for mother and child, their physical welfare, including the mother's fitness for giving the baby proper care, is of course of primary concern. The need of facts that bear on the choice of work and surroundings for the mother herself is indicated by earlier questions. And it should not be necessary to emphasize an unmarried mother's need for wise supervision—whether she keeps her infant with her or not.

QUESTIONNAIRE REGARDING AN UNMARRIED MOTHER[1]

This is not a schedule to be filled out nor a set of queries to be answered by a social agency's client or clients. For an explanation of the purpose of these questionnaires see p. 373 sq.

A star (*) indicates that the answer to the question may be found in, or confirmed by, public records.

The preliminary social questions regarding the husband and wife contained in the questionnaire regarding Any Family, p. 378—those regarding names, ages, nationality, religion, language spoken, length of residence in city, state, and country—may be assumed to apply to the Unmarried Mother, and (in cases in which she is sure who he is) to the father of her child.

I The Mother

Her family and home

1. Did or does she live with her own parents? Is she legitimate? Adopted? Did she ever live in an institution, and if so, when, how long, and why? What is the standing of parents in the community? Are they self-supporting, self-respecting people? Is the home clean and respectable looking? Was her parents' marriage forced? Did her mother or sisters have illegitimate children? Were these children kept with their mothers, or what became of them?

2. Are (or were) parents fond of children? Even-tempered or irritable? Faithful to church? Earnest or indifferent as to moral standards? Lax or firm in control (for instance, are they conscientious in overseeing their daughters' recreations; did the mother teach her daughters housework, instruct them in sex hygiene)? Or oversevere (for instance, are they reasonable in allowing pleasures and part of earnings)?

Her community

3. What is the character of the city quarter or town in which the girl or woman grew up—in size, race, religion, general moral standards, faithfulness to church, predominating occupation, if any, recreations and social life? Is it a factory town, farming region, or what is its industrial character? Has it distinct foreign colonies?

[1] Prepared for this volume by Mrs. Ada Eliot Sheffield.

4. If she came from a small town or village is it within easy distance of a large city? Do her companions have local amusements or do they go to the city for them? Are their pleasures supervised?

5. Are the schools good from academic, vocational, and social standpoints?

6. Are the local police alert towards loose behavior on the streets? Are saloons, dance halls, etc., regulated well? Are they numerous in proportion to the population? Is the judge in the local police court interested in the welfare of boys and girls?

7. What is the proportion of illegitimate births in the girl's or woman's native town or country?* Does custom there treat the offense as a slight one, or is ostracism relentless? Do pregnant girls frequently leave to hide their condition and dispose of the child elsewhere? Is this region equipped to care for such girls? If not, why? If it is, what co-operative understanding has been established with local agencies?

8. Are the local doctors and clergymen (if a small community) awake to the problem? What attitude do they take in regard to young unmarried mothers keeping their babies?

The mother herself

9. What was her health as a child? At what age did she mature? Has she any physical peculiarity or deformity? Is there any evidence that she is mentally deficient or abnormal?

10. Did her parents say that she was troublesome as a child? If so, how? Did she disobey her parents, fail to heed their advice, was she disrespectful to them? Did she frequent candy, ice cream, or fruit stores for diversion? What sort of associates did she have while she was growing up? How have they turned out? Can her parents throw light on the reasons for her behavior, if loose? Of what sort are her present girl or women friends?

11. When her parents learned she was pregnant, what, if any, plans did they make for her?

12. What grade in school did she reach? What do the teachers who knew her best think of her? In what studies did she excel? What vocational training, if any, did she receive?

13. What do her employers say of her work? How long has she held her positions? If she was employed in a factory, how much judgment did her work call for? Was it mechanical? If as a domestic, what are the things that she does well, what ill? For instance, can she make good bread, season vegetables? Is she neat and clean about her person and her work? Can she wash and iron? Does she wait on table smoothly and quietly? Has she done ordering for her mistress? How much did she know when her mistress took her? Does she improve—rapidly or slowly? Does she remember directions, or do they have to be repeated? What does she do best, heavy work or light? Is she good with children? Is she capable enough to hold a place with her child?

14. What do her employers say of her character? Is she honest, of a good disposition, industrious? If a domestic, has she been discreet with tradesmen who come to the house? Has she had men callers, one or many? Have they been accustomed to go at a proper hour? Has she been given to staying out very late? Does she dress conspicuously?

15. When did girl's or woman's sexual experience begin? Under what circumstances—was it with a relative, an employer, an older man, a school boy? Has she accepted money from any man or men for unchastity, or has she received only a good time—theaters, dinners, etc.—or board? Has she lived for any period as the wife of any man or men? Has she supplemented her income through men, or has she made her whole livelihood in this way? If so, for how long and when? Has she been a common prostitute, has she had a succession of "friends," or has she been intimate with but the one man? Has she a court record?* From what she, her relatives, friends, and employers say, does she seem to seek wrongdoing, or does she merely yield when evil approaches her?

16. Has she had another child or other children by a different man or men? When were the children born and where? How long did she nurse them? If they did not live, at what age and of what disease did they die? If they are alive, where are they—with her, with her family, with the man's family, boarded out, or adopted? If the latter, through whom was the adoption brought about? What does she know of the character and circumstances of the adoptive parents of her child or children? Has she any child in charge of a society or institution? Was it placed out in a family? How often has its mother seen it? Is it under supervision? If she separated from her child, what has seemed to be the effect upon her character? If she kept it with her, what?

17. Has she ever been under treatment for syphilis or gonorrhea? When and by whom?

II The Father[1]

His family

18. What is or was the standing of the man's parents in the community? Did the father instruct his sons in sex hygiene? Did his influence in this direction tend towards high-mindedness, towards cautiousness in pleasure, or towards unabashed laxity in morals? Did the mother and sisters take a double standard for granted? (See in addition same topic under The Mother for questions that apply.)

His community

19. What is the character of the community in which the man grew up? (See same topic under The Mother for questions that apply.)

The man himself

20. Was he troublesome to his parents as a boy? Respectful and obedient, or the reverse? What sort of associates did he have while he was growing up? How have they turned out morally? Have any of them got girls into trouble? If so,

[1] To be used only in cases where the mother is sure who is the father of her child.

do they boast of it, or have they the average moral scruples? Where do they draw the line as to the things "a fellow can't do"?

21. Did he spend any part of his childhood in an institution? If so, how long was he there, at what age, and why? What was his record while there?

22. What grade in school did he reach? Why did he leave, and at what age? What have his teachers to say of his character and ability? In what studies did he excel? Has he attended a trade school or a night school?

23. Is he single or married? Is he still living at home? If not, at what age and for what reason did he leave? How has he lived since? What type of associates has he chosen?

24. At what age did he first go to work? With what employer and at what occupation has he worked longest? Where is he now working and how long has he held this place? What do his employers say of the quality of his work? How much judgment does it call for?

25. Does he drink to the point of intemperance? Use drugs? Gamble? Is there any evidence that he has been dishonest?

26. What is his record as to sexual morality? Has he been known as a loose liver? Involved in scandals? Or has he, on the other hand, borne a good reputation, and is this the first affair with a woman in which he has been involved?

27. Has he ever been arrested? At what age and for what offense? If imprisoned, for how long? What was his record at reform school or prison?*

28. Is he of the same social status as the mother of his child?

III The Situation, Past and Present

Man and woman

29. What is the girl's or woman's explanation of her going wrong? Was she engaged to the man? Was she in love with him? If not, was it loneliness, drink, ignorance, force, that led to her shame? Where and when did she meet the man? Was she living at home at the time? With relatives, friends, in a lodging house, or at service? Had she known the man steadily or was he a passing acquaintance? Did she live with him for any time as his wife? Did he promise marriage? Do her family or friends know of his seeing her often at about the time of conception? Had they been expecting that he would marry her? Has she letters from him that go to show his probable paternity? Has the man known her family, called at her home? Does she know his family?

30. Does the man acknowledge paternity? Does he acknowledge having had relations with her? Does he claim that others had also? If so, who? Did she live in a lodging house, or were there men lodgers in the same house or tenement? Is there any evidence that she was intimate with any other man at about the time of conception? Any evidence (such as that of the physician who confined her, regarding earlier abortions, miscarriages, or births) to prove her previous unchastity?

31. What is the man's opinion of the girl's character? What suggestions, if any, has he made to her regarding her plans? Did he suggest her consulting any illegal practitioner? Did she follow his advice? Name of the practitioner?

32. Do the man and the girl wish to marry? If so, why have they not done it before? Are they both such human material as to make marriage advisable? What are the man's health and habits? Has he had a medical examination? By whom? Was it clinical only or with laboratory tests? Does marriage in the mother's home state legitimize a child, or must its parents adopt it?

33. Have the couple lived together for several years and had more than one child? (Consult, as circumstances of the case demand, the questionnaires regarding Any Family, a Deserted Family, or a Neglected Child, pp. 378, 395, and 405.)

34. If the man is married, does his wife know of his relations with the girl or woman? Has he legitimate children to support? If unmarried, has he relatives whom he must help?

35. Has the man property? Has he a steady place? What is his income? Would his employers bring pressure on him to help his baby, or would they abet him in eluding his responsibility? Is he a man who would readily leave for another state if prosecuted? (See Deserted Family Questionnaire, p. 395.) How much should he pay?

36. Is there evidence beyond a reasonable doubt as to man's paternity? Has he a lawyer? If so, who? Will the man settle out of court? Is it desirable that he do so? Why? Can he get bonds? If not, is he likely to keep up weekly payments, or is he so unreliable that a lump sum is wiser? Would his family do anything for the baby? Has his father property?

37. Has the mother a lawyer? If so, who? Has she taken out a warrant, started or completed proceedings? If the latter, what was the settlement?* Has the man paid her anything towards the expenses of confinement, etc.? Did she sign a release paper? Is it legally valid? If she has taken no steps against the man, does she wish to prosecute? If not, is this a case in which it is advisable for an outside party to bring suit, supposing state law permits?

38. Is it better that the man pay the money to the girl, or to a trustee who would hold it for the child? In your opinion, is the purpose of payment in this case to punish the man, to help the girl, or to provide for the baby's future?

Mother and child

39. If this is the girl's or woman's first child, does she appreciate the seriousness of her act and of its consequences? Did she leave her home to hide her shame? To give her baby to strangers so that her misconduct might remain unsuspected at home? Does she love her baby? Does she want to keep it?

40. What preparations did she make for the child? How long before confinement did she stop work? What sort of work was she doing during the previous months? What was her physical condition at this time? Did she have instruction in prenatal care and did she follow it?

41. Was she confined in a hospital? How long did she stay? Did she receive after-care? If not confined in a hospital, where? Was she attended by a physician or by a midwife? (Name and address of either.) How soon after confinement did she go to work?

42. Is the child's birth correctly recorded?* Has the child been baptized?

43. Have the mother and her baby been examined by a physician? What is his name and address? How soon after confinement did the examination take place? Was it clinical only or was it accompanied by laboratory tests? Is the mother or her child under treatment? What is the physician's report of her health and of the child's, and what is his advice?

44. Does she nurse the baby? If not, is it by a doctor's advice? Can she get pure milk? Does she understand the preparation of food? Has she had instruction in the general care of an infant? Is she capable of profiting by such instruction? Can she easily get a nurse's visits, or take the baby to a clinic?

45. Do her parents know of her situation? Are they so circumstanced that they can help her by taking her home with the baby, by tending the baby while she goes to work, by adopting the child, or by showing their sense of responsibility in any other way? Do they feel that their younger children should be kept in ignorance of her story?

46. What are the unmarried mother's plans for herself and child?

CHAPTER XXV

THE BLIND

THE social worker may happen upon cases in which blindness is the dominant cause of the present situation, or he may happen upon any of the forms of disability outlined in other questionnaires, complicated by the factor of blindness. In the latter case, sets of questions like that regarding a Neglected Child, or a Child Possibly Feeble-minded, may be even more helpful than one on blindness. There are, however, five captions under which special consideration of the causes and results of blindness may be of service. In making the questionnaire regarding a Blind Person given in this chapter, Miss Lucy Wright has arranged her material under these heads—prevention of blindness and conservation of eyesight, special education, special employment, special relief, and recreation.

Failure to be of practical service to the individual in cases of blindness is usually due to one of two dangers—the Scylla and Charybdis of work for the blind. The one is the danger of overestimating the chances for an individual by considering the factor of blindness alone. Other handicaps—mental, moral, physical—are of even greater significance in the struggle of the blind individual than in the case of the sighted. On the other hand, the failure may be due to underestimating the chances for the individual because, through inexperience, insufficient trust is placed in the truly great possibilities of practical accomplishment, manual and intellectual, through the use of other senses. In some instances mental and moral force seems to gain strength under what appears the great disadvantage of working in physical darkness. As Norman Duncan makes Tom Tulk, the blind skipper, say, "A man, with the best of a bad job to make . . . will learn many surprisin' things . . . by means of all the little voices in the world, says he, which speak to a man without eyes."

QUESTIONNAIRE REGARDING A BLIND PERSON[1]

This is not a schedule to be filled out nor a set of queries to be answered by a social agency's client or clients. For an explanation of the purpose of these questionnaires see p. 373 sq.

A star (*) indicates that the answer to the question may be found in, or confirmed by, public records.

I Prevention of Blindness and Conservation of Eyesight

1. Has a physician, expert in eye diseases, been consulted?
2. Has the vision of each eye been recorded separately, with degree of vision, cause of blindness, and age at occurrence of blindness for each eye?
3. Does your case record distinguish clearly between patient's understanding of cause and physician's statement of cause of blindness?
4. Was the cause of blindness congenital disease or defect, acquired disease, or accident?
5. If a local eye defect, can it be helped by eye glasses, operation, or continuous treatment?
6. If congenital or acquired disease, is it due to general disintegrating trouble which may need continuous treatment or result in other complications? Are there chances of improvement in sight if general treatment is followed?
7. If accident, was the accident the fault of the individual, the occupation, or the community? Is there anything to be done about it for the future safety of others? If industrial accident, has compensation been allowed the individual?
8. Are there chances of retaining the remaining degree of vision if the right occupation is followed? If anxiety about support of self or family is relieved? If healthful life is made possible?
9. Are there other cases of blindness or eye defect in family?
10. Is the disease of a kind which may in active stages menace other members of family or fellow workers?
11. Although not blind, has the patient seriously defective eyesight, even with the aid of the best glasses obtainable? When was he first given glasses, and where? Subsequent glasses given by whom, and where? Which glasses, if any, is he wearing now? Of what value have glasses proved? How recently has he had a physician's advice about his eyes?

II Appearance and Amount of Useful Vision

12. Does the patient need to wear smoked glasses for appearance's sake? Would this make a difference about his getting work?
13. Is the patient totally blind—or at most, does he see light only?
14. Has he sufficient sight to avoid running into objects?

[1] Prepared for this volume by Miss Lucy Wright, General Superintendent of the Massachusetts Commission for the Blind.

15. Is he able to distinguish color and see to play cards but not able to read?

16. Is he able to see to read, but forbidden to use his sight long enough for that purpose?

17. Is his limitation of vision or of use to which it can be put sufficient to interfere with ordinary schooling or occupation?

III Special Education—Children

18. What is the developmental history of the child? (See questionnaire regarding a Child Possibly Feeble-minded, p. 441.)

19. Does the child appear to be mentally deficient? May this appearance be due to neglect superadded to the physical defect? Because of the effect of such neglect, should not the child's special education, whether at home, at a nursery, or at school, begin at once or at an earlier age than that at which it would be necessary to begin the education of a normal child? If the child has not learned to walk, do his parents realize that, while he may walk as early as a sighted child, he probably needs special incentives because he cannot see and imitate? If he has "habit motions," putting fingers in eyes or the like, do the parents realize that he may be cured of them if taken in hand early enough? Do they realize that his future depends upon good use of hands, and that it will help him to learn early to dress and feed himself?

20. If his parents refuse at first to let him go away from home to school and there is no compulsory education law which is effective in the case of the physically handicapped, can they be persuaded to visit the special school themselves to see its advantages? Can a blind graduate be found to persuade them? If there is no special school, can public school training with sighted children be supplemented by special teaching from some trained blind person in the neighborhood? Is there a kindergarten (worthy of being attended) which can be made use of for him?

21. If the child is at a special school, is every effort being made to keep the family and friends in touch with the child and the school in order that a recognized place of usefulness may be ready for him when he leaves school?

22. If the blind child is at home, is he being spoiled with kindness by family, neighbors, and sighted school mates, or is he having his chance to find out about life as it is? Does he do his share of errands, fill the wood-box, etc.?

23. Does the blind child have his share of play and contribute to pleasure of others, read aloud (from some form of Braille) as well as be read to?

IV Special Education—Adults

24. If there are no travelling home teachers for adults nor any special school, can some teacher (preferably blind) be found who will instruct and encourage the newly blind person, so that he may gain confidence in other senses—learn to move about freely, be independent by use of some one of the forms of Braille, the typewriter, etc.?

25. Has he established his own confidence in the sense of touch and hearing by following normal activities? If an able-bodied man dependent on his wife's earnings, do he and she realize that he can help with housework, saw wood, etc., while he is waiting for the chance to learn a new trade?

26. Can he recall any part of his occupation as a sighted man which he came instinctively to do by touch or in which his hearing aided him? Is there any part of the process which he could still do?

27. Has he sufficient executive ability to carry out a small venture of his own, like a news-stand, or does he need to work for someone else?

28. Could he compete without further aid if his chances with sighted workers are equalized by his learning a new trade, such as broom-making; if adequate provision is made for a guide; if provision is made for transcribing his music into Braille; if he has aid in marketing products; if any other extra expenses incident to his blindness are provided for?

29. If he cannot work in competition with the sighted, either in a shop or in an independent enterprise, is he strong enough nervously for a full day's work in a subsidized shop? For a heavy day's work such as broom-making or other occupation entails?

30. Had he any important hobbies, such as chicken raising, cabinet work, or basketry, before loss of sight? Does he know this hobby well enough to pursue it under handicap, effectively and with courage? Can he be given supplementary training in this direction? Can you consult some blind person who has worked out an occupation for himself under similar circumstances?

31. If home industry is possible, can adequate supervision be provided?

32. Have you, before trying to market products, considered that great as is sympathy for the blind, when it comes to business, their goods must be not only "as good as" but "better than" like products of the sighted? Does the blind worker realize that poor work means a forced, temporary market, good work a steady, permanent market?

V Special Relief for Blind as Such

33. Is the blindness in any way the fault of the community, i. e., industrial accident, industrial disease? Or is it, as with many other troubles, the fault of nature, disease, or accident not preventable with knowledge as it stands today? Or the fault of the individual, needlessly acquired disease, or accident through carelessness?

34. Has the blind individual contributed to his family and to society in proportion to his ability? Before his blindness? How? Since his blindness? How?

35. If the blind individual is dependent, in what proportion is his dependence due to lack of natural endowments other than sight? To lack of preparation for competition; that is, no special education, or lack of other resources for blind? To presence of social and industrial obstacles common to others than the blind?

36. If institutional care is asked, is it for the protection of the blind individual, for the protection of the community, or for the convenience or saving of expense to relatives?

37. Should the blind individual's economic situation be considered alone or in relation to that of his near relatives? How near are these relatives? What is their ability, financial or other, to care for him?

38. If special forms of relief are sought or needed differing from or in excess of relief received by citizens otherwise handicapped, what shall be required of him in return for such relief? Work? Reasonable standards of living and conduct?

39. Did the individual become blind after sixty? Had he been successful or had he failed while in possession of his sight? Is his problem really a problem of blindness?

VI Recreation

40. Are there not resources for recreation for sighted persons that this blind person could make use of? If he is not using them, what stands in the way and how may the difficulty be overcome? Is it lack of a guide? Is it inability to provide for double expense of carfares, etc.? Or lack of encouragement from family? Or needless sensitiveness?

41. Can the family or friends be led to encourage him to all possible normal activities, walks, church, music, theater?

42. If he minds being done *for*, can you not arrange for him to do something for somebody else, read aloud from Braille, etc., at least do things *with* others?

43. Does he realize that bowling, dancing, swimming, football, and gardening are parts of the training and play at schools for the blind? Can any opportunity for him to practice any of these exercises or games, or others that will take their place, be developed?

44. Can a friendly visitor (sighted) be found who will call and converse (be talked to as well as talk)? Does this visitor realize that automobile rides, carriage rides, street car rides, or a walk will give respite to the family of a blind invalid as well as prove a tonic to the invalid himself?

CHAPTER XXVI

THE HOMELESS MAN—THE INEBRIATE

THOUGH these two subjects overlap at one point, their juxtaposition here is entirely arbitrary. The inebriate is a patient of the physician, or should be; the homeless man is a client of the social agency—often in need of medical care, it is true, but presenting no one medical problem. Inebriety is an important topic for the case worker because the inebriate is often in need not only of medical but of social treatment, and for the further reason that he is often given a type of social treatment which ignores altogether the obvious need of medical co-operation.

I. THE HOMELESS MAN

The fact of homelessness brings under this one caption many different sorts of men and boys, from the lad seeking adventure and the seasonal laborer to the homeless aged and the confirmed wanderer or tramp. Mrs. Alice Willard Solenberger has described them all in One Thousand Homeless Men, so that it is unnecessary to do more here than to refer case workers to that book, by which some of the questions that follow were suggested.

HOMELESS MAN QUESTIONNAIRE

This is not a schedule to be filled out nor a set of queries to be answered by a social agency's client or clients For an explanation of the purpose of these questionnaires see p. 373 sq.

A star (*) indicates that the answer to the question may be found in, or confirmed by, public records.

I Present Situation

1. How long has the man been in this country, state, city? If foreign born, is he thoroughly Americanized? Is he a citizen?
2. Why did he come to this city? From what place did he last come? What was his address there? How did he get here? Did he "beat" his way? Was transportation furnished by a charitable society, an individual, an employer, or employment agency?

3. If a foreigner, has he been exploited by any employment agent, foreign banker, or padrone? Sent to this city or state on false promises of work, or discharged after brief service contrary to contract or oral agreement? Do the ascertainable facts in the case furnish a basis for prosecution under any state or federal law?

4. Where and under what conditions is he now living—with friends, in a common lodging house, a furnished room, or how? How has he maintained himself since coming to the city? What is his present income, if any? Has he money in his possession or due him? Does he receive money periodically: if so, how much and from what sources? Or is he entirely without resources?

5. Has he had a home? Where? Has he been away from it long? What have been his wanderings? In what places has he stayed? Length of stay, address, manner of life in each? Has he a legal residence anywhere?

II Home Life

6. What were the conditions of his early home life? Were his parents physically and mentally normal? Did they fulfill their responsibilities? What was his home training? Was he indulged or unduly repressed?

7. Until what age did he go to school? Did he make normal progress? If not, why? In what grade was he when he left? Why did he leave? Did he play truant or show signs of a roving disposition while at school? Did he like school? What studies, if any, did he enjoy or excel in? What was his religious education?

8. Did he spend any part of his childhood in an institution? What institution? Between what dates was he there? Why was he placed in the institution and what led to his discharge? What sort of record had he there?

9. What were his amusements in childhood and youth? What sort of associates had he?

10. After he began to work did he turn over his wages to his family? What allowance or spending money did he receive?

11. If he is married, what are the facts about his wife and children? How old was he when he married? How old was his wife? What was he earning at time of marriage? What at the time of leaving home? What sort of home had he? Were he and his wife happy? Was he fond of the children? What reason does he give for having left home? If he has deserted, is this the first time? Has he apparently broken away for good or is this a temporary desertion? What is the date of his last letter from his family? (See Deserted Family Questionnaire, p. 395.)

12. If he is widowed, when did his wife die?* How have the children been provided for since? When did he last see them? Did he begin his wanderings at time of wife's death?

13. If separated or divorced, when and for what reasons?* What provision was made for the children?

14. If single, what kind of home had he? In city or country? Were its conditions good or bad? Were both parents still living? Were they living together?

How old was he when he left home? Why did he leave? How has he lived since leaving home? What is his attitude toward his parents and other members of his immediate family? (If a runaway boy, a frank story of his home conditions and of the incidents which led to his running away should be sought.)

15. Has your agency or any other communicated with parents, other relatives, or friends in his home town? What do they give as his reason for leaving home?

III Work History

16. At what age did he begin work? Was he ever a newsboy or messenger? What was the nature and wage of first occupation?

17. Did he learn a trade? If so, why did he give it up?

18. Does he, or did he ever, belong to a trade union? If his membership has lapsed how did this happen? Does he attribute later failure to such a lapse, or feel that to become a union member would put him on his feet? Have any union officials been consulted in regard to his past record or possible reinstatement, or in regard to obtaining membership?

19. Did he ever serve in the army or navy? Between what dates? What were the circumstances of his discharge and his record in the service?*

20. What have been his various occupations, the length of time each was held, the wage, reasons for giving it up? Have his former employers been communicated with to verify these statements and to learn their view of the reasons for his industrial failure?

21. What occupation did he like best, and why? What one of his employers did he like best, and why?

22. What was the longest time he ever held a job? Which job was it? What was the highest wage he ever received?

23. What was his last occupation? How long ago? Wage? How did he lose it? Is his work casual, irregular, or seasonal by nature? How has he previously lived between jobs?

24. Was his chief occupation too strenuous? Did he have to work too long hours? What proof is there that he was not physically equal to it?

25. Has he ever been in business? What was it? Did he ever succeed? Reason for failure?

26. Could he now go back to any of his old jobs?

27. What effort has he made to get work where he is? With what success?

28. If prevented by physical handicaps from doing the work that he is accustomed to do, what else is he, or can he be, fitted to do?

IV Physical and Mental Condition

29. What is his present physical and mental condition? Has this been verified by medical examination?

30. If physically handicapped, what is the nature of handicap? Its cause? Is recovery possible? Will any special treatment, appliance, or course of training help to put him on his feet?

31. If the handicap is due to accident, when did accident occur? Where? Under what circumstances? If it was an industrial accident, who was his employer? What settlement, if any, was made?

32. If he is ill, what are causes of illness? What medical care is necessary? Is he in a condition that is a menace to those with whom he works, lives, or associates?

33. If epileptic, feeble-minded, or insane, has he ever had any institutional care? Where? When? Has the institution been asked for an account of him? Is he eligible for any institution?

34. If aged, or feeble, what is his attitude toward almshouse care? Or (if his case is suitable) toward care in a private institution?

V Moral and Intellectual Status

35. What vices, if any, has he? Is he a gambler or given to betting? Does he drink moderately or to excess? When did he begin to drink, while very young or after reaching manhood? Does he use tobacco in any form to excess? Drugs? Has he ever taken any drug or liquor cure? Has he ever been in any institution for the care of inebriates? (See Inebriety Questionnaire, p. 430.)

36. Has he ever been arrested? For what offense?* What was the sentence?* If imprisoned, what were the dates of commitment and release?* Has the prison or reform school been asked for an account of him?

37. Has he, or has he ever had, any religious affiliation? Has his family? What is his attitude toward religion?

38. Is he discouraged? What is the thing that especially discourages him?

39. Is there anything in his temperament which explains his past failures?

40. Does he really desire a chance to get on his own feet and turn his back on his present way of living?

41. Does he read much and what does he prefer to read?

42. What are his ideas about education, about politics, about capital and labor, about social conditions? Does he believe in a democracy, and under what form of government would he prefer to live?

VI Plans for the Future

43. What relatives has he? What is their ability to help or advise?

44. What other possible sources of assistance—former employers, charities interested, etc.—are there?

45. What are his own plans for the future? What is his attitude toward work? Toward institutional care?

46. If he has a home town with normal environment and influences, is he willing to return to it? If so, would anyone there take an interest in him?

47. What does he look back upon as his best period? What marks of it still remain, such as personal cleanliness, for example? Can its conditions be won back?

II. THE INEBRIATE

This word has come to have a more definite meaning than formerly. It has never applied to all who drink, nor does it apply now to all who get drunk; it does apply, however, to all who, owing to a constitutional peculiarity or defect, are habitually *overcome* by alcohol and unable to take it at all without taking it to excess. Inebriety is a disease. It requires skilful medical diagnosis—a diagnosis which includes both a general physical examination and a mental examination of the patient. The disease is not curable in the sense that one who has once suffered from it can ever trust himself even to taste alcohol without danger of a relapse. An important further fact for the social worker to know is that both the medical and the social treatment of the disease achieve a far larger measure of success if the malady is dealt with when its manifestations first appear. "Other things being equal," says R. W. Branthwaite, "the success or failure of treatment depends largely upon the early application of remedial measures."[1] If possible, prompt resort should be had to a physician specially skilled in dealing with this particular disability, and in distinguishing it from the alcoholic excess of those who still have the power of will to remain sober if they choose to exercise it. Alcoholic excess may be due, moreover, to some removable physical cause, or it may be an outcropping of mental disease or of mental defect.

We now say the "patient" and not the culprit, be it noted. The earliest draft of this questionnaire referred to the inebriate as desiring to reform, as having reformed, or as possibly being helped to do so by a "reformed drunkard." This is not the language that we can use or the position that we can take in the light of recent scientific discovery. It is true that no improvement in the inebriate's condition is possible until some personal influence or some new set of circumstances has made a sufficient impression upon his mind to give him a strong desire to win the necessary self-control. In varying degree, success in the treatment of tuberculosis and of a dozen other diseases depends upon the patient's co-operation, but individualization and long continued personal interest seem to be peculiarly needed with this

[1] Report of the Inspector under the Inebriates Act, 1909.

disability. Hence social work has an important part to play, first in gathering the pertinent social data, and later in rallying to the patient's aid every tonic influence which can supplement the medical means employed. Social work must be continued too during the long period of after-care which is usually necessary.

The writer is indebted for valuable suggestions in the preparation of the following questionnaire to Dr. Irwin H. Neff, of the Norfolk State Hospital in Massachusetts, and for the point of view expressed in these introductory paragraphs to Dr. Neff and to the remarkable report of Inspector Branthwaite already quoted.

INEBRIETY QUESTIONNAIRE

This is not a schedule to be filled out nor a set of queries to be answered by a social agency's client or clients. For an explanation of the purpose of these questionnaires see p. 373 sq.

A star (*) indicates that the answer to the question may be found in, or confirmed by, public records.

The questionnaire regarding Any Family (p. 378) precedes this one. Its more general questions are repeated here only in rare instances when it has seemed necessary to give them special emphasis.

I Heredity

1. What were the habits of the parents, grandparents, and great-grandparents in respect to alcohol and habit-forming drugs (opium, morphine, cocaine, ether, chloral, patent medicines, headache powders, etc.)? What are the habits, in these respects, of uncles and aunts, of brothers and sisters? Wherever any relative mentioned used alcohol, (1) Was his use of it strictly moderate? (2) Was he a free drinker who occasionally got drunk? Or (3) was he unable to take alcohol at all without being overcome by it? If either parent of the present patient was an alcoholic (2) or an inebriate (3), did these habits develop before the birth of the patient?

2. Is there any history of mental or of nervous trouble in the family? Were any of the ancestors and relatives mentioned above insane? Did any commit suicide? Were any feeble-minded? Epileptic? Did any have "nervous prostration," or "fits"? Did any have marked eccentricities, violent temper, periods of extreme depression?

II Duration

3. How long has patient been addicted to the excessive use of alcohol? How long has he noticed that he has been unable to use alcohol socially or drink in moderation?

4. Longest period of abstinence previous to two years ago? Longest period of abstinence during last two years?

III Causal Factors

5. What is the patient's own analysis of the cause or causes of his drinking? What are his reasons for relapses or for the continuance of drinking periods?

6. Is he nervously unstable? What evidence does he give of such nervous instability? Has this condition developed recently or has it been present since childhood? Is there reason to suspect that he is mentally deficient? (See questionnaire regarding a Child Possibly Feeble-minded, p. 441.)

7. Are the home conditions such as to incline him to seek the saloon as more cheerful? Is the home situated in the vicinity of saloons? Is it squalid and in disorder? Does he take his meals at home? If so, are they well cooked?

8. Has he been unfortunate in business or family affairs? Has he suffered from any painful disease or been in ill health? Has he suffered any severe shock or loss which unsettled him and caused him to turn to drink? Is he happily married? Is his wife of a nagging disposition, or has she any bad habits that make trouble between them? Has he children, and if so are they of good health and habits?

9. Is his employment such as to expose him unduly to the temptation to drink (brewery worker, teamster, hack-driver, bartender, butler, waiter, longshoreman, etc.)? Does he work long hours in extremes of temperature? Under trying conditions of dust, humidity, or bad ventilation? Does he get drunk only when unemployed?

10. (For a woman) Has she been in the habit of using alcoholic liquors every month when unwell? Has she had frequent pregnancies? Has she used alcohol to give her an increased supply of milk for nursing?

IV Drinking Habits

11. Does the patient have something to drink every day or every week? Are there periods of weeks or months during which he will not touch alcohol, which alternate with periods of complete intoxication?

12. Does he do most of his drinking in the saloon? In the home? With other members of the family? Does he take alcohol in the morning before taking food? Is he a solitary drinker; that is, does he drink only when off by himself? If in the saloon, does he buy his drinks or is he treated?

13. Has he any drug habit in addition to his alcoholism? Was the alcohol habit acquired as a substitute for any drug habit? Have drugs been used to promote or encourage "sobering up" from drinking?

14. Does he desire to be rid of his alcohol habit? Is he indifferent about it? Is his attitude antagonistic on this subject? If the first, is his desire due to a mental antagonism to his habit, of which he is ashamed, or is it dependent upon the need of treatment for some physical disease which may or may not be due directly to alcoholic poisoning?

V Physical Condition and Medical Treatment

15. Has he ever been under medical treatment for the alcohol habit? If so, what was the nature of the treatment? Was he treated at a hospital? How long?

Did he leave on the advice and with the consent of the physician? Did he co-operate after leaving in any medical after-care? Did he undergo treatment at home?

16. With regard to the present, has patient lost weight? Does he crave food regularly and is his appetite good? Does he sleep well? Has he any physical infirmity?

17. Has he been examined recently by a physician? If so, what was his report?

18. If no physician has been consulted about patient's habit, are not medical advice and treatment needed either before or at the same time that social treatment begins? Is it possible to secure these from a physician who is especially interested in the diagnosis and treatment of inebriety on both the physical and the mental side? Does this physician advise a general medical examination also?

VI Social Conditions

19. Patient's exact statement in detail as to feeling of inefficiency due to alcohol? Has the drink habit led to loss of work? Has unemployment from this cause been occasional? Frequent? Habitual? Time lost from work during last year? Financial loss to patient and family during this period? During his last three drinking bouts?

20. Is the patient and are his family reduced to poverty because of his drink habit?

21. Does his wife have to work to help support the family? Are the children obliged to work also?

22. If his work is steady, is he paid off regularly on Saturday? Does he, as a rule, turn over part of his wages to his wife or family? If so, what proportion of his wages?

23. Does he obtain money from his wife or children to buy drink? Does he ever pawn household articles with this object in view?

24. Does he abuse other members of the family when drunk? When sober?

25. Is there any evidence that he has criminal tendencies? Do these criminal tendencies antedate his drunkenness or do they occur only during the periods of intoxication?

VII Social Treatment

26. Has there ever been an attempt, apparently successful, to make the patient a total abstainer, and under what circumstances?

27. Has he ever been arrested for drunkenness?* If so, was he fined?* Imprisoned?* Released on probation?* Has he been repeatedly arrested for this offense?* Was he ever sent to a hospital for treatment as a condition of probation or suspended sentence?*

28. Can any new adjustment be made in the home which will help him to recovery? What will win the co-operation of his family and make his surroundings more livable?

29. Is complete change of environment desirable and possible, either as a temporary measure for a period of special treatment or permanently? Has he formed harmful associations with which his connection should be broken? Are there helpful associations which could be formed—as with a church or settlement club or with an individual volunteer? Could anyone formerly a drunkard but now an abstainer be brought to take an active personal interest in him?

30. Has he, or has he ever had, any religious affiliations? Has he shown himself susceptible to religious influences? Has he had contact with churches, missions, etc.? What is his attitude toward religion?

CHAPTER XXVII

THE INSANE—THE FEEBLE-MINDED

THESE two disabilities, of insanity and of feeble-mindedness, carry us still farther than that of inebriety into the territory where medical and social data are not easily separated. It cannot be too emphatically stated, however, that the questionnaires here given can in no sense enable a social worker to make a medical diagnosis; the diagnosis of mental disease and of mental defect must be regarded always as primarily medical, though social data of the right kind can suggest the need of a physician in the first place and may be serviceable to him later in making an inclusive examination of his patient.

Insanity is a term describing a legal rather than a medical concept. It is loosely applied to mental disorders differing widely in their origins and in their manifestations. Obviously no one questionnaire would be equally applicable to persons suffering from senile mental reduction, those exhibiting undue pressure of mental and physical activity, and those in whom slow distortions of mental life are taking place. From the alienist's point of view, the present outline merely suggests general lines of inquiry; for the social worker, however, its questions are not routine questions and must not be so understood.

The social worker without medical training is sometimes ill fitted to face the ugly facts of defect and disease. To keep his sense of values keen and true, his must be a spirit of sane helpfulness. No one has described the right attitude better than Dr. Adolf Meyer, who, five years ago, sent the writer the following comments, among others, in criticising a discouraging record of social work with a family of defective mentality.

> We meet here a very difficult problem. As far as I can see, the social worker like the physician must learn to accept human nature and human doings as they are before rushing in with the superior knowledge of how they *ought* to be. The first need is to know *what* they are. . . . The motto of every social worker and in-

vestigator must be that of Terence's Heauton Timorumenos: *Homo sum, humani nihil a me alienum puto. . . .* One who investigates must be . . . ready to accept . . . anything human beings think, feel, or do as not altogether strange in human nature: "I am but human and I do not consider anything human foreign to me"; it is at least worthy of human consideration.

He was convinced that there was no way of stating the facts effectively "except by stating them directly and concisely in terms of actions and perhaps also in terms of motives and prevailing desires and tendencies taken from the person's point of view rather than from that of the critic or helper." Such general terms in the record submitted to him as "incorrigible," "immoral," "serious trouble," "not very well," "troublesome"—all containing a judgment—were unfortunate, in his opinion, because they did not give the facts which would have enabled anyone else to judge for himself.

The questionnaire given later in this chapter on the Child Possibly Feeble-minded (the possibly defective adult must be understood to be included in this title) was prepared by Mrs. Hilbert F. Day. Mrs. Day also made the first draft of the questionnaire here given on the Patient Possibly Insane. This has been revised and added to by Dr. Thomas W. Salmon, Medical Director of the National Committee for Mental Hygiene, to whom the writer is also indebted for the following suggestions to be observed in using it:

Great stress must be laid upon *changes* in mood, mental processes, activities, and social reactions. It must be remembered too that the apparent mental status of the patient varies, in its external manifestations, at different times of the same day—for example, the nocturnal restlessness and cloudiness of toxic and of senile cases. Special effort should be made to ascertain whether abnormal manifestations are *increasing* or *diminishing* in number and in intensity, as this often has a practical bearing upon the management of the case. It might be suggested, as a good general guide, that weight be given to the apparent *reasonableness* of all activities. There could be unfavorable answers to many of the following questions when the social worker's client was a normal subject; nevertheless, the *reasonableness* of this or that activity or this or that reaction *under the circumstances which actually existed* is the significant point.

QUESTIONNAIRE REGARDING A PATIENT POSSIBLY INSANE

It should be repeated here that nothing in the following questionnaire must be interpreted to mean that a social worker is ever able to make a medical diagnosis. This is not a schedule to be filled out nor a set of queries to be answered by a social agency's client or clients. For an explanation of the purpose of these questionnaires see p. 373 sq.

A star (*) indicates that the answer to the question may be found in, or confirmed by, public records.

I History of Parents

Social

1. Were parents of patient related? In what degree?
2. Are both parents living? If dead, what was the cause of death?* Age at death?*
3. What has been their general standing in the community? Have they been self-supporting, self-respecting people?
4. Has either parent been wholly or partially dependent? Had institutional care? Which one? What institutional or other care? When?
5. What have been their occupations? Have they been successful in them? If not, to what cause was lack of success due?

Physical, mental, and moral characteristics or disabilities

6. Is (or was) either parent deaf, dumb, blind, or deformed?
7. Have they been considered normal mentally? If not, in what way abnormal?
8. Did either show sexual perversions? Did either lead a dissolute life?
9. Did either have extraordinary gifts? One-sided talents? Vacillating interests? Eccentricities? Was either absorbed in "causes" (for example, anti-Catholic, litigious)? Was either irritable?
10. Were quarrels frequent in the family? Did parents "take sides" regarding the discipline of the children? Was either parent too lenient or too severe and to what extent?
11. *Nervous and mental disorders.* Was either excessively nervous? How was nervousness shown?
12. Did either parent have epilepsy?
13. Did either have periodical headaches? Attacks of nervous prostration? Of what nature?
14. Was either ever insane? When? For how long? At what age? How long before or after patient was born? To what causes were the attacks attributed? Were they cared for in a hospital?
15. Did either have any other disorders? St. Vitus's dance? Paralysis? Apoplexy?
16. Did either have constitutional diseases? Syphilis? Tuberculosis?
17. *Alcohol.* Was either addicted to the use of alcohol or habit-forming drugs? If they used alcohol, was its use moderate, excessive? Occasional, habitual? How long was it taken? Years? With what results? Delirium tremens?

Crime and suicide

18. Did either attempt or commit suicide? Under what circumstances?

19. Has either a criminal record? What?*

(The same points of history should be considered, where the situation warrants it, for children of patient, brothers and sisters of patient, maternal and paternal grandparents, uncles, aunts, and cousins.)

II Patient's Early History

20. *Prenatal.* Within the year before this patient was born, was either parent (which parent) under great worry or strain? Was patient legitimate? Was either parent using alcohol or drugs excessively? Engaged in particularly exhausting occupations? Ill? With what disease?

21. *Gestation.* What was the condition of the mother during pregnancy, with regard to her general physical condition? Conditions of work? Nourishment? Mental condition?

22. *Birth.* Was patient born at full term? If not, at what month? Was patient born after prolonged labor? With instrumental delivery? Was more than one child born at this time? What was patient's weight at birth?

Physical history of infancy and early childhood

23. Did patient have convulsions? How old was patient when these began? How many years did they continue? How frequently did they occur? How long was each seizure? What was their character, in detail? (For example, was there loss of consciousness, local or general, and if so, how brought on?)

24. Did patient have rickets?

25. What other diseases did patient have? When and with what results?

26. When did patient learn to walk? To talk? To control urine day and night?

27. At what age did patient reach puberty? By what symptoms was it accompanied? Were there any abnormal changes noticed in the disposition, character, or instincts at this time? What, in detail?

Schooling

28. When did patient first go to school? Until what age did he remain in school?

29. Did patient like school? Why did he leave? Grade on leaving?

30. What special difficulties did patient have with lessons? Pupils? Teachers? Was he a truant?

31. What special abilities did patient manifest?

III Injuries, Diseases, and Habits of Later Life

32. *Injuries and diseases.* Has patient had any injuries, especially head injuries? How was patient affected? By loss of consciousness? With convulsions?

33. Has patient had gonorrhea? Syphilis? When? What treatment for the latter and with what result?

34. What other diseases has patient had? What were the after-effects?

35. *Alcohol.* Has patient taken alcohol in any form? Beer? Wine? Whiskey? Tonic? Medicine? How long has he been taking alcohol? Has its use been moderate, excessive, occasional, habitual? Has he ever had delirium tremens?

36. What is the effect on his disposition? Does the alcohol make him pleasant or disagreeable?

37. *Other habits.* Has the patient taken drugs—cocaine, morphine, opium, or any others—for long periods of time?

38. *Occupations.* What is patient's present occupation? How long has he been engaged in it?

39. Does he like it? Is he doing well in it? What difficulty has patient had with employes or employers?

40. What previous occupations has patient had? Highest earnings? Average during last five years? How long did he retain each position, how successful was he in each, and why did he leave each?

41. Has patient worked by fits or with regularity?

42. *Sex life.* What were earliest sex experiences? With same or opposite sex? Did patient make advances or vice versa? Any sexual attacks in childhood by older relatives (father, uncles, cousins)?

43. To what extent has patient masturbated? Before puberty? Afterwards? Has he sought advice on this subject?

44. What suggestions have there been of perverted tendencies (homosexuality, exhibitionism, "peeping," etc.)?

IV Marriage and Children

45. Is or has the patient been married? When was he married? Is the wife (husband) still living? How many times has he been married? What judgment has been shown in marriage? Has the married life been happy? If not, why not?

46. Has the patient (or wife) had any gynecological or menstrual difficulties? When did catamenia begin? Has it been regular? When did catamenia end?

47. Has the patient (or wife) had abortions or miscarriages? Still-births? (Give the details.) How often? When? How were they brought about?

48. Does husband (or wife) complain of patient's making perverse sexual demands? What ones?

49. How many children has patient had? What is the sex and age of each? From what nervous and mental diseases, if any, have they suffered?

V Character, Temperament, Disposition, and Social Instincts

50. Was patient thought peculiar in childhood? In maturity? In what way?

51. Does patient indulge in uncontrolled fits of temper? Has patient ever done so?

52. Is patient excitable? Active? Happy? Does patient belong to the "shut-in" type, being unduly quiet, sad, and moody? Given to day-dreaming?

53. Is patient free and confiding or reticent and seclusive?

54. Is patient self-confident? Diffident? Any difference in this respect when with opposite sex?

55. Is patient introspective? Does patient indulge in self-reproach? Brood over disappointments and incapacity?

56. As a child, did patient show any markedly lazy traits? Refuse to do errands? Want to sleep a great deal? Stay in bed for long periods? Was patient easily frightened and subject to bad dreams?

57. Is religion a vital part of patient's life? Is patient over-religious? Has patient shown special interest in revivalism? Clairvoyancy? Spiritualism? Hypnotism?

58. Did patient play normally with other children as a child, getting on well with them and entering fully into their games and good times? Was he inclined to assume an air of superiority?

59. What is patient's attitude toward people? Friendly and responsive or the reverse?

60. Does patient enjoy companionship or prefer being alone in his work? In his recreation? At home?

61. Is patient prone to passionate attachments?

62. Is patient attached to home, friends, and family, or indifferent to the natural bonds of affection? Attitude toward father? Mother? Marked preference? Any change at puberty?

63. *Previous attacks.* Has the patient had similar attacks before? What were the symptoms? How long did the condition last? Did he go to a hospital for nervous and mental diseases? When? Where? For how long? Why discharged?

64. If he has not had any similar attacks, has he ever had periods of depression or of exaltation? How long have these lasted? What was done during these attacks?

VI History and Description of the Present Illness

Cause and onset

65. Did the present illness seem to come on as the result of an accident or disease? What, in detail?

66. Did the patient have a physical or mental shock? What, in detail?

67. Has he been under extraordinary strain for some time?

68. Is the present attack thought to be due to excess of any sort? Nature of excess?

69. Did the attack come on gradually or suddenly? Its history in detail?

Characteristics of attacks

70. *General physical and mental changes.* Has there been a change of character in the patient mentally? Morally? Socially? Has he been agreeable or disagreeable to his wife (husband) and children? To friends and neighbors? Have they considered his conduct peculiar or remarkable? In what respects?

71. Has he appeared to be dazed, or quiet, or restless? Has he been excited? Has he temporary attacks of these conditions? Day or night?

72. Has he been tidy in eating and in his other habits, or has there been a distinct change in his personal habits of cleanliness and order?

73. Has he slept well? How many hours has he slept each night? Has he slept regularly?

74. Has he eaten well, or little? Has he had a perverse or abnormal appetite? Has he taken his meals regularly? Does he give any explanation for his poor appetite or his refusal to eat?

75. What was the patient's weight before the illness began? Has there been any change in his weight? What other changes in the physical condition of the patient have been noted since the beginning of the illness? Any change in sex life? Perversions (see questions 42 to 44)? Has he been tremulous in hands or in speech? Slurring in speech? Has he become bald or has his hair whitened?

76. *Movements.* Are there abnormal movements of the body? Of the head? Of the face? Are there rhythmic quiverings of the mouth? Are there wrinklings of the forehead? Are there stereotyped movements? Are his movements stiff and constrained?

77. *Emotional condition, especially changes.* Has the patient been depressed, or unduly joyful, or apathetic?

78. Has he been passionate, or inclined to anger, or threatening? Has he become specially sensitive and suspicious?

79. *Hallucinations and delusions.* Has he heard imaginary voices? What have they said? Have they been abusive? Accusatory? Has he had visions? Dreams so realistic that they seemed reality? Are they pleasant or unpleasant?

80. Did he go through the house looking under the beds and the furniture and in the cupboards? Did he listen in corners or at the walls? Did he look at definite points for some time?

81. Has he had ideas of persecution or of grandeur? Does he think he is being unduly influenced, watched, or poisoned? Do things seem unreal to him? Does he see indirect references to himself in newspapers, casual allusions, literature, the Bible? Are there "undercurrents" against him? Has he any special terms? What—murder, poisoning, insanity, abduction? Has he ideas of sin, unworthiness, impending punishment?

82. *Suicide and homicide.* Has he made attempts at suicide? At homicide? What were the exciting causes? Were the attempts serious?

83. *Intellectual and memory defects.* (Note especially beginning and duration of changes in these.) Has he shown any intellectual defect? Has he been able to carry on his business in the proper manner? Has he made peculiar or ill advised purchases? Other errors in judgment? Has he lost his way in familiar places? Does he remember his telephone number? Children's birthdays and birthplaces? Is there a marked difference between memory for recent and for remote events?

84. Has he shown any other defect in memory? Has he remembered his business engagements? Resorted to memoranda and devices for reminding?

85. Does he recognize his friends or relatives? Does he mistake persons?

86. Has he kept track of the days of the week and of the month?

87. Has he known where he has been?

88. *Moral and legal laxness.* Has the patient offended against the law? Against morality? How did he so offend and with what result? Has he made threats? Written to prominent persons? Has he become immodest in dress and attitude? Garrulous as to family and personal affairs?

89. *Insight.* Has he understood that he has been mentally different from what he is normally? Does he appreciate the nature of his disorder?

Description of patient

90. Does the patient look sad? Apprehensive? Furtive? Gay? Hostile? Suspicious? Visionary? Expressionless? Intent? Arrogant? Sleepy?

91. How does he carry his hands? Is his hair tidy or unkempt? Nails? Teeth? How about bathing? Is his clothing well kept? Does he show that he has been untidy in eating and in drinking? Any attempts at unusual dress or decoration? Is he fully dressed, half dressed, or naked?

92. Does the patient walk straight and to some purpose? Does he walk irregularly or go from one thing to another? Does he go slowly or quickly?

93. Does he voluntarily complain of ill-being, or ill treatment, or speak of his delusions, or his feelings?

94. Is he coherent? Has he flight of ideas?

95. What spontaneous account does he give of the whole situation?

QUESTIONNAIRE REGARDING A CHILD POSSIBLY FEEBLE-MINDED[1]

Many of the following questions apply also to an adult in years who is not an adult in mind. It should be repeated that nothing in the following questionnaire must be interpreted to mean that a social worker is ever able to make a medical diagnosis. This is not a schedule to be filled out nor a set of queries to be answered by a social agency's client or clients. For an explanation of the purpose of these questionnaires see p. 373 sq.

A star (*) indicates that the answer to the question may be found in, or confirmed by, public records.

Corrective Defects, Physical and Environmental[2]

1. Is child well nourished? If not, to what cause is under-nourishment due? To poor appetite? Abnormal appetite? Insufficient food? Condition of the teeth?

2. Has he been pulled down by rheumatism or any of the childhood infectious diseases?

[1] Prepared for this volume by Mrs. Hilbert F. Day.

[2] Before anyone can decide that the child is feeble-minded, due consideration must be given to defects needing correction.

3. Has he grown rapidly? At the appearance of permanent teeth? At puberty?
4. Has he had a general physical examination? When? By whom and with what results? Have nose and throat been examined? With what result? Were tonsils enlarged? Were adenoids found? Were they removed? By whom? When? Has vision been tested? By whom? With what result? Does child wear glasses? When was last examination? Has hearing been examined? By whom? When? With what result? What is the condition of the teeth?
5. Is there a history of lack of proper sleep?
6. Have there been too many or too few outside interests? Has child had any emotional distress due to death or illness of loved ones? Has his home been unhappy? Neglected? How? From what causes?
7. Is there any marked lack of sympathy between the school teacher and child? Does the position of his desk admit of good light and opportunity for observation?

I Etiology

Heredity

8. What was the age of each parent when this child was born? Were the parents related before marriage? In what degree? Were the grandparents on either side related before marriage? Which ones? In what degree?
9. Are both parents living? If either is dead, what was the cause of death? At what age did it occur?* Place of death?* Date?* If the grandparents are deceased, of what disease and at what age did each die?*
10. Are there deceased brothers and sisters? If so, what was the order of their birth, their sex, age, and the cause, place, and date of their death?* Were their mental and physical powers normal?
11. What have been the father's occupations? The mother's? At what age did each begin work?
12. Did father or mother or any of their relatives show signs of or tendency towards the following:

Feeble-mindedness	Tuberculosis	Intemperance
Imbecility	Insanity	Use of drugs
Idiocy	Epilepsy	Criminality
Deafness	Syphilis	Sexual immorality
Blindness	Convulsive disorders	Truancy
Being dwarfed	Scrofula	Vagrancy
Being crippled	Great nervousness	
Being deformed	Paralysis	
	Neuralgia	
	Hysteria	
	Sick headache	
	St. Vitus's dance	

In which, if in any, member of child's immediate family have any of these signs or tendencies appeared?

13. What members of the immediate family and what relatives, if any, on either side, have been wholly or partially dependent? What institutional or other care have they received? When?

14. Has child's mother had any still-births? How many and when? Any miscarriages? How many and when? Due to what causes? At what month of pregnancy did they occur? What is the order of child's birth—is he first-born? second-born?

15. Within the year before this child was conceived, was either parent (which parent) seriously ill? Under great worry or strain? Under mental excitement? Using alcohol excessively? Using drugs, such as opium, etc.?

Gestation

16. Was there anything peculiar to be noted at time of conception? Were there any abnormal conditions of the mother during pregnancy? Any attempts at abortion? Did mother work during pregnancy? How steadily? To what period? At what occupations? Did mother have sufficient nourishment? Did she retain it?

17. While child was being carried, was there on the part of the mother any disease that had begun before this time? Any disease begun during this time? What disease? Was there any abuse of alcohol or drugs? Any worry or anxiety? Any fright or shock? Any peculiar symptoms? Anything special to make an impression on her mind?

18. Was this child born at full term? If not, at what month? Was more than one child born at this time?

At time of birth

19. How long was the labor? Was it hard? Were anesthetics used? How long? Were instruments used? What was the child's weight? Did child suffer from difficult animation, breathing, or crying? Cyanosis, injury, deformity, paralysis, inability to suckle?

II Physical History

Pathological

20. Was child nursed by his mother? How long? How was he fed when weaned?

21. Was he poorly developed in any way? How did he show it? Was he a strong or sickly baby? If sickly, how did he show it?

22. Has he ever had any severe shock, fall, or fright? Any injury to the head? When? What were the circumstances and apparent results?

23. Has child ever had convulsions, fits, or spells? At what age did they begin? To what cause did they appear to be due? What was their character? How often did they occur? When was the last one? What treatment had been given and with what results?

24. Has child ever had epilepsy? Rickets? Paralysis? Character and history of attacks?

25. Has he ever had measles, whooping cough, scarlet fever, diphtheria, cerebro-spinal meningitis, varioloid, or small-pox? At what age and how severely?
26. Has child ever had sore eyes, or any skin or scalp disease? Character and history of trouble?
27. Has he ever had any disease of lungs or bowels? What?
28. Has he ever been pronounced insane? By whom? When? Character and history of attacks that led to this diagnosis?
29. Has he ever had St. Vitus's dance? When?
30. What other diseases, if any, has he had? When?

Development

31. When did child teeth? Recognize persons? Sit alone? Use spoon? Walk? Talk? How did he advance in weight and height? How did he compare in these respects with other children in family? Is he of average height and weight for his age?
32. At what age did child reach puberty?
33. When were first signs of abnormal development noticed? Nature?

Peculiarities

34. How is child's circulation? Are his hands and feet often cold? Has he been known to blush?
35. How does he sleep? Well? Restless? Noisy? Dream? Any night terrors?
36. Is he sensitive or callous to cold? Heat? Pain? Thunder storms?
37. Is appetite quick or abnormal in any way? What is the state of his taste? Is he particular about what he eats? Does he swallow things without regard to taste? Is he gluttonous? Will he eat garbage?

Appearance

38. What is the general balance of child's body? Are shoulders equal? Is back bent? Is there asymmetry of posture? Are there any abnormalities in the size and shape of the head? Does head loll to one side or droop forward?
39. Are there any variations from the normal in the size, shape, and relative position of the features? Is there any marked coarseness of features? Do the eyes roll? Shift? Are they wanting in changefulness? Is child cross-eyed? Are ears large, outstanding, or dissimilar? Is the lower jaw protruding? Is mouth usually open? Are there any abnormalities in the form, structure, and situation of the teeth?
40. What is the expression of the face? Vacant? Gaze fixed? Has the child the normal comeliness of youth? Does the skin show extreme pallor? Any other peculiarities?
41. Are there any peculiarities of speech? What, in detail?
42. Does the child show any signs of nervousness? Automatic motions of the features, hands, fingers, or limbs? Chronic frowning? Repeated grinning?

III Character

Temperament and disposition

43. Is child dull, listless, restless, or excitable? Is he active and vigorous? Does he run about and notice things, or is he indolent?

44. Is he affectionate? Reclusive? Vindictive? Passionate? Conceited? Boastful? Ungenerous? Ungrateful?

45. Is he often wilful, disobedient, and liable to attacks of stubbornness and bad temper? Has he shown himself responsive to discipline or is he ready to risk punishment for slight objects? Is he easily managed? Docile? Incorrigible?

46. Is child quarrelsome? Does he organize rebellion? Is he fond of stirring up trouble and tale bearing? Cunning in attaining his own ends? Easily influenced?

47. Does he learn by experience? Is he heedless of danger?

48. Has he sympathy with distress or suffering? Is he dangerous to himself or others during temper? Does he show embarrassment or shame when detected in wrong-doing? Does he show remorse after wrong-doing?

Morality

49. Does child know the difference between right and wrong? Is he truthful? Does he tell senseless lies? Is he trustworthy? Wantonly dishonest? Does he indulge in purposeless and needless offenses? Will he pilfer?

50. Is child sexually precocious? Does he show any sexual perversion in practice? By telling vulgar stories?

51. Does he drink or use drugs or tobacco? To what extent?

52. Has he a court record?*

Social relationships

53. What is child's attitude toward parents? Brothers? Sisters? Strangers? Playthings? Is he violent toward playmates or an "easy mark"? Is he cruel or kind to animals? To children?

54. What sort of associates does he select? Are they below him socially? Intellectually? Are they younger, weaker physically? Is he fond of other children? Does he help in the care of other children?

55. Does he show any excitement when in the presence of the opposite sex? At what age was this first noticed?

56. How does he bear himself in public places?

Habits

57. What are child's habits in regard to personal appearance? Is he tidy? Unclean? Careless? Vain in dress? Is there a marked difference in these respects between this child and the other members of the family? Does he wet or soil clothing? Bedding?

58. Is he given to self-abuse? Has he ever been?

59. Will he hide, break, or destroy things? Clothing? Furniture?

60. Is he dangerous with fire?

61. Does child show tendency to run away from home? From school? From work?

62. Has he any unfortunate habits not mentioned?

Peculiarities

63. Does child laugh or cry without cause? Quarrel without cause? Talk over-intimately about himself? Is he prejudiced against anyone without reason? Is he liable to uncontrollable anger for trifling cause?

64. Is the character subject to abrupt change or alternation? Are there any striking contradictions in character? Is child tender and cruel? Ingenuous and crafty? Phlegmatic and nervous? Unfeeling and affectionate? Frank and secretive? Artless and shy? Deceitful and truthful?

65. Are there periods of uncontrollable fear, of being impelled to violence, intoxication, or to immoral or criminal action? Have there been any periods of religious enthusiasm?

IV Capacity

Intellectual

66. What schools has child attended? How old was he when he left? Why did he leave? What grade did he reach in school? What is his history as to promotion? Has he been held in one grade more than two years with regular attendance? Has he ever attended a special class, been regarded as subnormal, or been studied by a child-study department?

67. In school is child attentive? Easily fatigued by mental effort? Can he hold his interest in one subject continuously? Does he lose interest quickly? Does he need careful and close supervision? In what does he do his best work? His poorest?

68. Does he recognize form? Which by name? Does he recognize color? Which by name? Can he count? How many? Can he read? How much? Can he add? Subtract? Multiply? Divide? Is he fond of music? What is his musical capacity? Does he delight in acting? What is his power of memory? Does he commit to memory easily? How long does it take him to learn, say, four lines? Does he soon forget what he has learned? Can he speak a piece?

Recreational

69. How does child amuse himself? Can he entertain himself while alone? Does he show any initiative or spontaneity in games? Does he show any imagination in play?

70. In what stories is he interested? Vulgar? Blood and thunder? Gruesome? How long will child play at any one thing? What, for example?

Co-ordination of faculties

71. What is child's power of imitation?

72. How does he respond to a command? Is he slow? Will he respond incorrectly though trying to obey? Can he do an errand?

73. Is he right-handed? Left-handed? Ambidextrous? Is the left hand more dextrous and stronger than the right? Is his grip weak?

74. Can child use knife and fork? Does he masticate properly?

75. Can he throw a ball? Catch a ball? Can he button clothes? Tie a knot? Lace shoes? Put on overshoes?

76. Can child write, draw, sew? In drawing, writing, sewing, and manual training, is co-ordination of hands and fingers labored? How does he write, from right to left? In writing, is there a conspicuous number of i's undotted or t's uncrossed, a lack of capitals? Can he take a simple dictation?

77. Can he handle tools? What can he make?

Industrial

78. Can child do any kind of work? What work has he done? When did he begin work? Is he thorough in it? Can he work without supervision? Does he keep his positions? Can he support himself?

V Home

79. Is home in a crowded or a suburban district? Any grounds? What is the character of the neighborhood, physical and moral? Single house or flat? Number and size of rooms? Number used for sleeping? Ventilation? Light or dark? Orderly or disorderly? Clean or dirty? Character of furnishings? Condition and location of toilets?

80. What is the size of family? Are parents living together, or are they divorced or separated? Of what members is immediate family group composed? Sex, ages, and occupations? Are there any other members of the household? What is their relation to the family?

Attitude of household toward child

81. Do family consider child abnormal? To what cause do they assign his condition? Inheritance? Accident? Acute sickness? Any other reason?

82. Do the parents have patience with child? Have they a strong attachment for him?

83. What is his relation with other children in the household? Do they abuse or tease him? Is he repulsive, and does his appearance have a bad effect on the other children? Is he a source of terror, or is he the butt of the household?

84. Who is responsible for the child's care? How continuous is the supervision? How often is he left alone or with an irresponsible member of the household? What degree of watchfulness and intelligent care can be expected for him at home?

85. What is the nature of the home training? Is he neglected? Unduly repressed, abused, or overindulged? Do parents or guardian control child? How? By fear of corporal punishment? By affection and reason?

Personal hygiene

86. Is his bedroom large or small? How many windows has it? Are the windows kept open? Does he sleep alone? With whom? In a single or double bed? What time does he go to bed and get up? Does he drink tea, coffee, milk, or cocoa? How much? Usual food, breakfast, dinner, supper? Bathing, how often? What kind? Does he use a toothbrush? Are his bowels regular?

VI Plan

87. Would parents be willing to have child placed in an institution? What is the opinion of teachers, relatives, and physicians as to the wisdom of such a step?

CHAPTER XXVIII

SUPERVISION AND REVIEW

THE foregoing analyses of the diagnostic side of a few social disabilities are only a beginning. Should the plan followed prove helpful in actual practice, other disabilities can be analyzed in the same way.

The questionnaire of this closing chapter turns from disabilities, which are not always the most important consideration in social work, to the other diagnostic topics likely to be of service to a case work supervisor. When inquiry into a client's situation has reached the stage of evidence gathered but not yet compared or interpreted, and the record comes to a supervisor, or when, in the absence of supervision, the case worker must review the evidence without assistance, what are the things to look for? This final list of questions is an attempt to answer the query. Needless to say, it does not indicate a routine to be followed; some questions will apply to the given case but many will not.

The writer has had helpful suggestions for this list of queries from former students, especially from members of the 1916 Charity Organization Institute. Page numbers after questions indicate where fuller discussion of the subject may be found in this book.

SUPERVISION AND REVIEW QUESTIONNAIRE

I Relations with Client

1. Does the record of the first interview indicate that the client has had a fair and patient hearing, and that a sympathetic understanding, or at least a good basis for further intercourse, was established at this early stage? (p. 114)[1]
2. Are there indications that advice has been given prematurely, or that promises have? (p. 129) Or has the client been put off with such artificial reasons for delay or inaction as "my committee," "we never pay rent," "this is contrary to the rules of the institution," etc.? Have there been too many ultimatums? Have "no-thoroughfare" situations developed between case worker and client due to these, due to failure to sift contradictions, etc.? Are there signs that the worker's lack of grasp of the situation has developed the scolding habit?

[1] All page references are to other parts of this volume.

3. Were good clues to outside sources of insight and co-operation procured in the first interview? (p. 120) What clues, indicated as possible by the story, seem to have been neglected? Do these belong to a group which this case worker often finds it difficult to get, or usually overlooks?

4. Were the possible signs of physical or mental disease or breakdown noted early, and were medical examination and care procured immediately thereafter? (p. 211) If the assumption that the client was lazy, indifferent, or incorrigible was made, was it possibly due to neglect of these precautions?

5. Has the worker who has conducted the first interview and seen the client's family also seen the important outside sources, or were these parts of the inquiry entrusted to someone else? (p. 176) Does the information procured from outside sources suggest that the inquirer had a sense of the relation of the part to the whole?

6. Were any confessions, especially those that were damaging to the client who made them, accepted as necessarily true? (p. 71) Has the client been protected from misrepresentation of any kind?

II Relations with Client's Family

7. Does the record give its reader a sense of the main current of the lives of the people recorded, or does it detail unrelated episodes and incidents only? (p. 138)

8. Have the relations of the members of the family to one another been noted? Have any crises been noted that tested the family power of cohesion? (p. 139)

9. Does the record reveal whether the family has or has not shown good judgment, on the whole, in its economic choices? Have expenditures been the expression of an innate craving, have they been due to imitation, or are they indicative of little judgment?

10. Are characteristic disabilities belonging to the racial or economic group all charged against the individual family?

11. Have the children of the family, especially the growing children, been individualized? (p. 153) Is there any clear picture of both their home and school life? If the problem is a family one, have the older children, those who are grown and at work, been consulted? (p. 155)

12. Has the man of the family been seen? Were he and his wife seen separately? (p. 143)

III Use of Outside Sources

13. Was the confidential exchange consulted promptly? (p. 303) Was the identifying information there procured promptly followed by consultations with the agencies named? (p. 308) Were any inquiries that had already been made by these agencies unnecessarily duplicated? (p. 311) Were the different agencies each consulted about the kind of fact that each was best able to give? (p. 297) Has any transfer of the case to another agency for treatment been preceded by sufficient inquiry to justify the reference? (p. 313)

14. If not all the clues to outside sources were followed up, does an intelligent choice seem to have been made? For example, were *some* relatives on both sides of the house seen, some former employers, etc.? (p. 175) Was the order in which the sources were consulted wisely chosen? (p. 170) Were any of the sources consulted found through supplementary clues—clues revealed casually, that is? (p. 174)

15. Have statements been sought, as far as possible, at first hand and not through intermediaries—from doctors, for example, rather than from patients, where medical facts were in question, etc.? (p. 172) Or has hearsay evidence been accepted without challenge? (p. 58) In evaluating the testimony of witnesses, has their personal bias been allowed for? (p. 73)

16. Has the worker expressed opinions, in the letters attached to the record or elsewhere, on matters about which he is not informed? Have the outside sources been consulted about possible plans of action, or have they merely been persuaded to agree to plans proposed by the case worker? (p. 293)

17. In first contacts with relatives, have questions of the material assistance procurable from them obscured more important matters? (p. 195)

18. Are the medical diagnoses from which social inferences have been drawn up-to-date? (p. 216) Has discrimination been shown in seeking medical advice, and has the needless multiplication of medical advisers been avoided? (p. 213)

19. Are the school reports quoted merely formal ones, or have the individualized observations of teachers been sought? (p. 223)

20. Have the work records been entered perfunctorily, or do they cover the points that would be of value in procuring new work, reinstatement, or advancement? (See list of suggestions on page 239.) Has underpaid or unwholesome work that tended to disintegrate the family life (such as the twelve hour shift, supplementary earning by the homemaker away from home, sweatshop work, or premature withdrawal of children from school) been noted?

21. Is any inexactness in the data at hand due to failure to consult original documents of birth, marriage, baptism, death, property, immigration, or court proceedings? (p. 255) Or to failure to consult out-of-town directories? (p. 265) Or newspaper files? (p. 269)

22. Were interviews with present neighbors limited quite strictly to procuring needed court evidence? (p. 274) Have the characteristics of the neighborhood been kept in mind, and have experienced neighborhood social workers been consulted about them? (p. 299)

IV Conduct of the Inquiry as a Whole

23. Have all the assets for reconstruction revealed by the client's history been carefully and sympathetically noted? Have they been summed up in black and white? Or are there signs, on the other hand, of a tendency to overemphasize the discouraging things? (pp. 157, 357, and 360)

24. What indications are there of the case worker's habits as a questioner? Have leading questions been asked with full knowledge of their danger, and with good

reason for taking the risk? (p. 71) Have any marked personal prejudices of the case worker's been allowed to warp the account? (pp. 94 and 97)

25. Is there evidence of a tendency to substitute such formulæ as "maladjustment," "underfeeding," "chronic laziness," "hopelessly shiftless," "drink the sole cause," "large family," "insufficient wages," for the specific fact or facts? Are there indications that the worker is hampered by some professional habit useful under other conditions but not here? (p. 96) Are there signs of automatism, of following a routine unthinkingly?

26. Has the worker been careful to clear up unfavorable items of evidence instead of leaving them neither proved nor disproved?

27. Has the worker been hurried into hasty and ill considered action by a tendency to cross bridges before they are reached, to regard situations as "emergent" that are not really so? Has some picturesque minor incident of the story demoralized the inquiry? (p. 139)

28. Is there a tendency to "make out a case" at all hazards by overemphasizing one side? Has the worker "held a brief" for or against or has he dealt even? Are first theories promptly abandoned when the facts tend to disprove them? (p. 98)

29. What hypotheses and inferences of the worker and of others have been accepted without the necessary testing? (p. 87) Have any popular explanations of things been accepted without challenge?

30. With regard to the record itself, does it develop an individual and colorful picture, or are the main issues obscured by repetition and by unverified impressions? Does it show skill in what is omitted? Is the present situation, for example, described in such detail as to throw the more permanent aspects of the story out of perspective? Are the words used as specific as they might be? (p. 349) Are general terms avoided? Are acts described instead of qualities? (p. 435) Are the statements of the record merely added or are they weighed? Are there brief entries that help the supervisor to understand the relation of an unknown witness to the matter about which he is quoted and to measure, in some degree, his disinterestedness and his personal characteristics? (p. 278)

31. Are there signs of wasting time, of doing relatively unimportant things under the impression that there is no time for the important ones? Does the investigation center round and round some one point in the story, or does it lose itself in aimless visits, many times repeated, to the client or his family? Are there, on the other hand, signs of "economy of means," of achieving results, that is, with the fewest possible motions and the smallest possible friction?

32. Has the inquiry, as it has developed, supplied a reasonable explanation for the present situation? Does the investigation, that is, lay bare the personalities of the chief actors plus the factors external to themselves that have brought them to their present pass? Does it look back to their highest achievement in the past, and give any sense of their possible resources in the joint task of reinstatement or development which is still ahead? How far does the inquiry suggest not only the diagnosis of the difficulty, but plans for its constructive treatment? (p. 360)

33. If needed evidence has not been procurable, and only partial or temporary diagnosis can be made, what modifications in treatment could be devised in order that a part of its necessary services might become also a means of pushing the investigation forward? (pp. 86 and 236)

V Wider Aspects of the Inquiry

34. Is the record one in which this case worker has tried to make an especially thorough and skilful inquiry? If not, are there any such records? (p. 362)

35. Does it contain an instance of effort to push further into an unsolved problem by presenting it, in this concrete form, to specialists in the national social reform associations or elsewhere who might be able to suggest a solution? (Examples: the possible relations between occupation and disease in a given case; the problem of the energetic boy who wishes to sell papers out of school hours; the chances of recovery for tuberculous patients returned to their own country—when, for instance, a case committee suggests sending back such a one to Messina, etc.)

36. If there is no adequate provision for the feeble-minded, or no legal redress when housing conditions threaten health (to give only two instances), what attitude does the record reveal toward these evils? Is the situation accepted, or is a disposition manifest to push hard in some helpful direction? Is the evidence bearing upon the matter accurately enough stated in the record to make it part of the data needed for community action?

37. Are there any hopeful signs of breaking through routine, of getting a result by new or unusual methods? What new outside sources, for example, have been brought to light? (See list of outside sources in Appendix II, Table A, p. 467.) Have any such new methods been noted and placed at the service of other case workers?

38. If anyone has made an inquiry, supplied information, or aided at this stage of the case in any way—if a teacher has shown interest, for example—will that interest be remembered and will it be strengthened? Has any note been made, looking to that end, to report later upon the further developments of the case, especially upon any really significant ones?

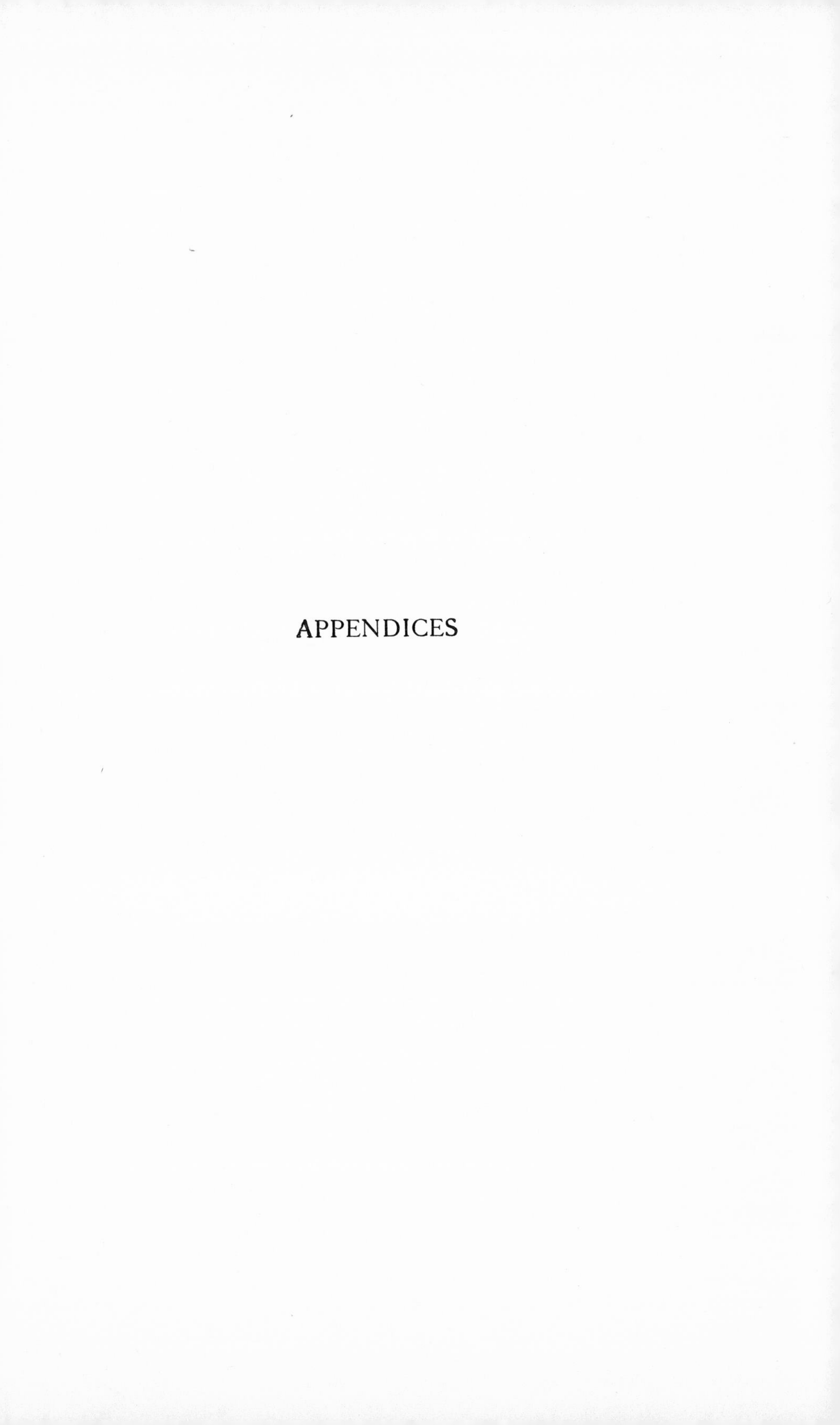

APPENDICES

APPENDIX I

FIRST INTERVIEWS

THE three analyses of First Interviews which follow have been selected from a larger number submitted in response to the questions given on p. 120. The first is with a patient in a medical-social department, the second with a deserted wife in the office of an associated charities, and the third was held in the home of a young wife, a colored woman, who had just lost a child. Care has been taken to change these interviews in minor details, which leave unchanged their value as interviews but perhaps make the identification of the persons interviewed less possible.

1. ANALYSIS OF INITIAL INTERVIEWS WITH A PSYCHONEUROTIC PATIENT

Patient is brought into Social Service Department by doctor from Male Medical Clinic, who tells worker that the case is clearly one of apprehension. Boy, sixteen years old, is physically sound. He lost his mother when very young, is unhappy, and has given up his work, because he became afraid he was sick. What he needs is a friend, somebody who will care and who will get him started.

During this conversation patient is sitting on the bench. He is a handsome boy, with a very attractive smile, looks a little embarrassed, but gets up with a friendly smile when doctor introduces worker to him. Is greeted cordially, worker shakes hands and asks him to wait a few moments while she finishes a conversation with another patient. Boy has evidently a real admiration for the doctor.

It is very helpful to have doctor introduce patient to worker. He thus shows patient that he trusts worker and that he believes in her power to help patient.

Worker can inspire confidence in patient by her manner, which should always be cheerful and at ease.

In a short time patient is invited to sit by worker's desk. Worker explains to him that the doctor has not time enough to go into all the details of his case, but wishes a study of it made, and that she and he will study it together. Patient assents.

This puts the emphasis upon the objective point of view and makes patient a little less self-conscious.

It is then explained to patient that he must be prepared to answer a great many questions and to tell everything he can think of about himself and his family. Is told that if worker had known him all his life she would know how many brothers and sisters he had, and where he had been to school, but that now he has come to her out of clear sky. He is like a figure standing in front of a white screen. He has no background. As nobody in real life stands in front of a white screen, patient must paint in the details. He understands and says he will be glad to help and will answer every question.

Again manner plays an important part. This is said as if worker and patient were about to begin an interesting game. This relieves patient's embarrassment if he feels any.

As it is late in the morning patient is invited to come in again next day and is told that the necessary study may take several interviews.

Patient is evidently amused and interested and says he will be glad to come again.

When patient comes in again record is begun by asking him where he has been previously treated. He had never had a doctor until the year before when his brother's doctor saw him a few times.

Worker helps patient to concentrate his attention upon this "study" by the businesslike way of writing down his answers to questions, or the narrative he gives unassisted. This places social record on same plane as medical record in his mind (a part of his treatment), since it is taken in same manner, and shows him that doctor considers it *all* important. This rule is broken only when in a more confidential part of the story patient needs the help of an encouraging look, or undivided attention from worker.

After initial record is made, taking notes is usually unnecessary, though worker never hesitates to take them if anything important is told. It keeps in patient's mind the fact that doctor is in touch with case.

It is then explained to patient that the study of his case necessitates his telling all he can remember about his family. He is asked about his grandparents. The only one he knows anything about (the others having died in Austria) is his father's father, who is alive and in this country. Patient has apparently no affection for him, and says he is "cross and quick-tempered" and hard to get along with; does not stay long with any of his children. Is pretty well physically.

While at first puzzled to know what is wanted, patient is very responsive. Fatigue in attention is avoided by the many interruptions which come to worker. Though these interrupt narrative they have their uses.

Patient shows little interest in ancestry.

His father is a teacher. Does not seem to know how to describe him until worker asks several questions. Then says, "He is a good-natured man, sometimes gets his temper up," but is good to his children. Came to the U. S. eighteen years ago; has lived in D—— ever since; was married when he was seventeen. Is honest; much thought of among his fellow-countrymen, but earns a very small salary. In Austria his position was very different. Is unable to help his sons much.

Great care is taken to ask questions which describe opposing traits so that patient may not have answers to questions suggested to him.

Mother died when patient was only three. He can remember nothing about her. This fact seems to have taken a certain hold upon his imagination.

Patient unconsciously finds in this loss excuse for many of his weaknesses.

Patient has three brothers and a sister and there is evidently much affection among them. They are all older than he and while his sister was at home she looked out for him. He tells of their education, occupations, and marriage with very little questioning.

After patient understood what sort of description was necessary in his father's case he described the others quite easily.

About five years ago his father married again and patient has not been happy with his stepmother. Just at present he is living with a sister of his mother.

As patient complains of pain in his side, he is told what a habit pain is—a vicious circle, "attention creates sensation, sensation causes fear, fear increases attention," which must be broken through at the point of fear, because patient is afraid the pain means something serious. As the doctor has pronounced him physically sound, patient is urged to rest his faith in this statement. He is reminded of his relations to other people and the possible effect of his discouraged attitude upon them. He is going out of town to visit one of his brothers for a few days, but will come again on his return. He is asked to write down anything he can remember of his life.

His responsibility toward others is suggested to him from the beginning.

This is intended to keep his interest in the study alive. This leisurely way of taking the record is designed to suggest to patient that he must not expect to overcome his bad habits at once. Thoroughness is much more important than speed.

Immediate effect is seen in a postal received from patient the next day in which he writes, "I am feeling fine."

A patient is very apt to respond quickly, but when he feels his old sensations come again, discouragement follows.

Five days later patient comes again. Had felt perfectly well till "yesterday when the old pain had appeared again," and he is feeling a bit discouraged. He brings a written statement of some facts in his life—his proneness to stay by himself, his industry at school, his lack of all intellectual interests outside of his school work. Family are very poor and patient does not get on well with his stepmother, though he stayed at home after all the others went away, because he wanted to get an education.

Document is read and patient is encouraged to write more, and more fully and freely. This is to increase his personal interest in study and gives him opportunity to express his own views without chance of suggestion from worker.

Record is taken up again and family history is continued. Patient tells of his father's and mother's relatives; then of what he had done since school; his habits—how he spends his time, what he eats, etc. His not having earned anything for four months is not a real source of worry to him, as his family are all good to him.

These facts make rough sketch of patient's background.

He is evidently of a retiring disposition, though not unfriendly.

Question of finances not taken up, unless pressing, until later.

Record is here interrupted by a long talk on habit and patient's future plans. His former ambitions seem to be suspended by his fears about his health. Worker suggests that she will visit patient's oldest brother.

Patient's interest is still further aroused by this personal interest. Brother lives 30 miles away.

On the following day patient comes to continue record. This part of record is the most intimate as it relates to his earliest recollections, the people and things which have most affected him. He tells of his school life, of the principles which govern his conduct, of his troubles and of his chief difficulty, which has been deciding things.

Worker tries in words and manner to impress patient with her interest. This part is the test of her power to convince patient of her real sympathy. She also learns almost as much from what he does not say as from what he tells. His manner is illuminating.

The next step is to visit the patient's brother. He is devoted to patient and is a kind and sensible man. Future plans for patient are discussed and brother's co-operation fully won.

This not only helps worker very much in her knowledge of patient's surroundings and family, but gives patient a common interest with worker.

The following day patient comes in with a longer written statement than the first. The initial interview is completed with his account of the cause and duration of his illness. He is much interested to hear about worker's visit to brother. It is decided he is to go to this brother very soon. He is encouraged to read ten minutes every day and to think about his reading. He is asked to report about it to worker. He is also advised to learn some good poetry. He is promised a list of books to read; is urged to decide some little thing every day and to stick to his decision.

It is impressed upon patient that this is only the opening wedge in his recovery. Care is taken not to urge future plans upon patient as it is deemed wiser to encourage more healthful habits of thought and let his ambitions come to life slowly. He is so young.

It is best to avoid permitting patient to depend too much upon worker's will power.

2. AN OFFICE INTERVIEW WITH A DESERTED WIFE

On the first of May, a woman aged twenty-two and two children, two and a half and one year old, are brought to the office by an officer who gives this information:

The woman was deserted by her husband three weeks before. She has since been living with her parents, but was turned out two days ago because she made slighting remarks about her sister's fiancé. The sister and mother whipped her. The officer had hoped that her family would take her back, but her father was seen this morning and refused. Both the mother and this daughter have violent tempers.

The interview begins with questions regarding the name and age of husband and wife. When was she married?

"Three years ago by a Lutheran minister."

"Are you Scandinavian then?"

"No, mostly mixed, I guess."

These are direct questions, the idea being to find whether the husband ran away because he was too young for his responsibilities.

"Tell me about your married life, have you had trouble like this before?"

This gives a chance for a rambling story which follows.

She launches into her story, saying that they were getting along very nicely in Millbank. Her husband was not drinking much and was supporting her. Then he sent her here on a visit and came himself and now he has left.

"When were you in Millbank?"

"Since last August."

"What was his work there?"

"Switching. That is what he was doing here. He showed me a pass just before he left but I have forgotten where it was to."

Maybe by returning to Millbank, if man is found, life could be made happier.

"Had you just quarrelled or had you any trouble that would make him go away?"

Trying to find the cause.

In reply to this she tells of a previous time when he deserted after selling some things which did not belong to him while working for an installment house. Her people did not like this any more than they liked his getting her in trouble before her marriage.

She is asked, "Was he willing to marry you or did he do it against his will?"

She says he was not unwilling, though not anxious. He made no objection, however, when her father insisted. But ten days after their marriage he was arrested for trying to steal a bicycle while he was intoxicated. Another time he spent two months in the Parktown workhouse for defrauding grocers.

A forced marriage might explain his dishonesty, recklessness, and desertion.

She is asked, Did she know he drank and was dishonest before marriage.

She says not, but that his responsibilities seemed to him too heavy as a man of family. He was good only while in Millbank.

"Did he like the children?"

"While in Millbank he seemed to like them all right."

The woman is then asked about her own health and what work she did before marriage.

With a view to solving the question of how she is to live till he is found, or perhaps permanently.

Her health is good. She was a mangle girl in a laundry.

Did she begin work early?

When she was sixteen years old. Her father did not wish any of his girls to work, but they all did because they wanted more clothes than he could furnish them.

A day nursery is suggested.

She does not like this idea as she says the baby keeps her up a good deal at night. She would rather put the children in a home and work in a laundry.

She is shown that thus she would have to leave the children to the care of others and is urged to consider the nursery plan.

Meanwhile, has she anywhere to go?

She mentions two relatives of hers, one of whom is telephoned to. This relative will not have her and does not wish to become involved.

The possession of a telephone suggests that her people are better able to help than are many.

The client then remembers her husband's half-sister, who is telephoned to. The sister says she will give temporary shelter but

A note is made to look up this sister-in-law and hold a private conversation with her face to face.

regrets that the client did not take her advice before marriage. The nursery plan is explained to her and she thinks it good.

The woman is then told that an effort will be made to find her husband and to call later to talk over plans. She is sent to her sister-in-law's.

It is not thought wise to insist on day's work or any plan until she begins to recover her courage.

3. A FIRST INTERVIEW IN THE HOME

A young colored couple was referred on account of the death of one of their children, for whom they wished burial clothing and assistance toward the funeral expenses, because the man was unemployed. The secretary had been warned that Mrs. Reynolds (to give her another name) was in a very hysterical state, and that it would probably be impossible to get any information at all.

On approaching the old wooden shanty, where Mrs. Reynolds lived, the writer heard a series of moans and groans. She found the mother sitting on a tumbled bed, rocking her body to and fro. Her eyes were tearless, but the moaning continued. The visitor laid her hand on the woman's shoulder and the latter, quiet for an instant, looked up inquiringly.

"How do you do, Mrs. Reynolds? I am so glad I found you in, because Mrs. Miller would have been so disappointed if I had not."

"Oh, do you know Mrs. Miller?" asked the woman, immediately brightening, "Ain't she a fine woman?"

"Indeed she is," answered the visitor, and allowed the colored woman to run on for a few moments eulogizing Mrs. Miller, for whom she worked two days a week, as it seemed to take her mind off of her loss and to calm her. She explained that Mrs. Miller had known her husband and herself when they were first married, and had been very friendly to them ever since. By immediately following this lead, it was possible to learn where they were married, what her husband did for a living at that time, and the kind of employment he now wanted. In this way were also learned some of the places at which he had worked and the addresses at which the family had lived at the time.

"Did you have two children when you were down on North Street?" asked the secretary, knowing that a direct question about the names and ages of the children would probably start a fresh outbreak of grief.

"No, I just had Willie. He was two then, and after we moved up here in 1910, Jessie came and poor Margaret would be two next month if she ——." Here the visitor interrupted quickly, "I imagine the children are very bright in school, aren't they, Mrs. Reynolds? Do they go to public school No. 2?"

"Yes," answered the mother, "and they bring home such fine grades."

"Of course you send them to Sunday school, probably to the Colored Mission around the corner," continued the visitor.

"Yes, we all go there," answered Mrs. Reynolds. "The funeral is going to be from there tomorrow afternoon."

"Is the church going to help toward the expenses?"

"No, but Dobson is very reasonable. He is only going to charge $38."

"Well, perhaps the relatives will all contribute a little."

"I haven't any relatives," was the conventional reply.

"Won't you get a little insurance perhaps?" was the next suggestion.

"No, the Metropolitan lapsed three weeks ago."

"Do you get two carriages for the amount you are paying the undertaker, or just one?" inquired the visitor further.

"Oh, we get two."

"That's good," said the visitor, "because your own little family can go in one carriage, and then you can fill the other with just your nearest relatives, not people who come out of curiosity, but your own kin."

"Yes, we have asked my sister and her husband to go and also Amos' brother John, with his wife and child," continued Mrs. Reynolds.

"You are fortunate to have your own people living right near you. All of us are not that lucky."

"I reckon we are, and they are pretty good to us. Of course we see more of my sister, Judy, for she lives just two doors from the corner. But Amos' brother lives down on East St., so he does not get up so often."

In another two minutes the secretary was able to get not only the names and addresses of these relatives, but a general idea of the status of their families.

Finally the question of burial clothes for the child had to be approached and, sobbing hysterically, Mrs. Reynolds showed the child's ragged little wardrobe, so that her visitor might judge what was needed. The office card was left in the mother's hands, and she promised to come there the next morning at nine o'clock, when the secretary was to accompany her to the department store where they could buy the necessary articles. After a few last words of warm sympathy and encouragement, the visit was over.

The chief point in this case (continues its reporter) is the importance of the first contact. It shows that, when one finds an applicant in an abnormal state of mind, the key to the situation is to introduce upon entrance a topic that will be of immediate and real personal interest, and at the same time to touch lightly upon the subject preying upon his mind.

The real problem is to keep the client from gravitating to the source of his trouble until one is ready to have him do so; this is achieved by keeping up a rapid interchange of firm but kind questions and answers, allowing no time for lapses of attention on the part of the person interviewed. One would find it difficult to get a good first statement in a case like the foregoing, if the order were reversed; if the client were encouraged to speak of his trouble first in the interview, that is, before the background had been secured.

Then another important thing illustrated is the necessity of having a legitimate introduction. In this case it was through a mutual acquaintance, Mrs. Miller. If the visitor had come in some mysterious, undefined way, she would have found it difficult to gain Mrs. Reynolds' confidence. In this type of case, moreover, it is especially important that the client get it firmly established in his mind that the visitor's attitude is one of sympathy and of determination to help in every way possible. With this impression left from the interview, the next contact will be frank and friendly.

APPENDIX II

STATISTICS OF OUTSIDE SOURCES

FORM USED

1. AGENCY

2. CITY

SOURCES OF INFORMATION USED AS A BASIS OF TREATMENT

3. RECORD No. .... 4. FORM of service asked for .... 5. DATE home first visited 19

6. SOCIAL STATUS (Put check opposite right one)	(Indicate sex by check)	Female	Male	
	b. Widowed			7. Number of children ....
	c. Deserted			8. Age of each child:
	d. Divorced or legally separated			
a. Man and wife	*e.* Single			

PERSONAL VISITS WERE MADE TO OR BY, OR LETTERS, TELEGRAMS OR TELEPHONE MESSAGES WERE EXCHANGED WITH THE FOLLOWING SOURCES

NOTE 1: Count all of the same kind of sources, *i.e.*, all clergymen, all physicians, etc., and enter the total of each in town and out of town in the appropriate column, not checking as above.

NOTE 2: If any of the information secured before the first important decision as to treatment of this case was made, came not directly but through a responsible agency, write name of agency after the original source printed below.

		Total of each: In town	Out of town
9. **Church Connections**	Clergymen		
	Fellow Church Members		
	Sunday School Teachers		
10. **Employers**	Former		
	Present		
11. **Friends**			
12. **Landlords**	Former		
	Present		
13. **Lawyers**			
14. **Medical Agencies**	Physicians		
	Dentists		
	Hospitals and Sanatoria		
	Dispensaries		
	Nurses		
	Midwives		
	Social Service Departments		
15. **Neighborhood References**	Former Neighbors		
	Present "		
	Former Tradesmen		
	Present "		
16. **Pawnbrokers**			
17. **Private Social Agencies**	C. O. S. or Associated Charities		
	Foreign Relief Societies		
	Other " "		
	Homes for Adults		
	" " Children		
	Children's Aid, etc.		
	S. P. C. C. or Humane Soc.		
	Day Nurseries		
	Settlements		
	(Specify other sources)		
	....		
	....		
	....		
18. **Public Officials**	Almshouse		
	Charities Departments		
	Health "		
	Police "		
	Court "		

		Total of each: In town	Out of town
Public Officials (*Continued*)	Juvenile Probation		
	Adult "		
	Municipal Lodging House		
	Prison or Reformatory		
	U. S. Consuls		
	Foreign Consuls		
	(Specify other sources)		
	....		
	....		
19. **Public Records of**	Birth		
	Baptism		
	Death		
	Contagious Disease		
	Marriage		
	Divorce or Legal Separation		
	Property		
	Guardianship		
	Insurance		
	(Specify other sources)		
	....		
	....		
	....		
20. **Relatives**			
21. **School Officials**	Teachers		
	Truant Officers		
	Medical Inspectors and Nurses		
	School Visitors		
	Fellow Pupils		
22. **Social, Trade and Benefit Societies**	Trade Unions		
	Fellow Workmen		
	Political Clubs		
	Benefit Societies		
	Other Clubs		
23. **Unclassified**	(Specify each source)		
	....		
	....		
	....		
	....		

TABLE A.—SOURCES OF INFORMATION CONSULTED IN THREE CITIES, AS SHOWN BY THE RECORDS EXAMINED

Source	Consultations[a] in			All consultations[a]
	First city	Second city	Third city	
Social agencies, private and public				
C. O. S. or associated charities	480	68	97	645
Public charities departments	212	57	6	275
Foreign relief societies	46	37	9	92
Other relief societies	167	48	4	219
Almshouses	23	6	2	31
Private homes for adults	32	12	4	48
Private homes for children	116	12	15	143
Municipal lodging houses	3	..	3	6
Children's aid societies, etc.	111	3	4	118
S. P. C. C. or humane societies	111	11	..	122
Juvenile probation	61	..	11	72
Day nurseries	44	1	2	47
Settlements	83	13	23	119
Organizations to provide for mothers with infants	12	11	..	23
St. Vincent de Paul Society	17	1	..	18
Adult probation	65	11	5	81
Legal aid societies	7	..	6	13
Y. W. C. A.	4	2	3	9
Y. M. C. A.	6	1	1	8
Others[b]	94	29	31	154
Total	1,694	323	226	2,243
Medical agencies				
Physicians	564	65	171	800
Dentists	6	..	..	6
Hospitals and sanatoria	357	67	34	458
Dispensaries	124	28	24	176
Nurses	103	12	16	131
Midwives	..	..	1	1
Social service departments	122	24	1	147
Total	1,276	196	247	1,719

[a] Counting, in any one case, only the first consultation with each source used.

[b] Under the headings "Others" and "Miscellaneous" are grouped: (1) sources very infrequently consulted, (2) sources somewhat more frequently consulted but only by a single agency in one city. On the other hand, a few sources very infrequently consulted are specified (see, for example, dentists, midwives, municipal lodging houses, U. S. consuls, passports, employment offices) because they are known to have proved useful in other social agency records not included in this review or are believed to offer possibilities of usefulness.

TABLE A.—SOURCES OF INFORMATION CONSULTED IN THREE CITIES, AS SHOWN BY THE RECORDS EXAMINED.—(*Continued*)

Source	Consultations[a] in			All consultations[a]
	First city	Second city	Third city	
Neighborhood sources				
Former neighbors	132	31	19	182
Present neighbors	182	139	210	531
Former landlords, agents, janitors	118	120	18	256
Present landlords, agents, janitors	106	131	78	315
Former tradesmen	22	2	6	30
Present tradesmen	31	9	15	55
Lodgers, former and present	1	7	9	17
Total	592	439	355	1,386
Relatives	769	297	121	1,187
Public officials[b]				
Health departments	81	22	6	109
Police departments	358	18	16	392
Courts	107	31	22	160
Prisons or reformatories	36	1	50	87
U. S. consuls	1	1	..	2
Foreign consuls	5	..	6	11
Immigration departments	3	..	10	13
Postmasters	5	2	2	9
District or county attorneys	..	4	15	19
Others[c]	15	11	8	34
Total	611	90	135	836
Employers and other work sources				
Former employers	330	71	69	470
Present employers	147	50	35	232
Trade unions	11	..	2	13
Fellow workmen	16	..	5	21
Employment offices	4	3	..	7
Total	508	124	111	743
School officials				
Teachers and principals	280	189	16	485
Truant officers	63	12	2	77
Medical inspectors and nurses	75	11	1	87
School visitors	34	4	..	38
Total	452	216	19	687

[a] Counting, in any one case, only the first consultation with each source used.

[b] With the exception of those connected with almshouses, public charities departments, municipal lodging houses, juvenile and adult probation, and a small number of miscellaneous public social activities.

[c] Under the headings "Others" and "Miscellaneous" are grouped: (1) sources very infrequently consulted, (2) sources somewhat more frequently consulted but only by a single agency in one city. On the other hand, a few sources very infrequently consulted are specified (see, for example, dentists, midwives, municipal lodging houses, U. S. consuls, passports, employment offices) because they are known to have proved useful in other social agency records not included in this review or are believed to offer possibilities of usefulness.

TABLE A.—SOURCES OF INFORMATION CONSULTED IN THREE CITIES, AS SHOWN BY THE RECORDS EXAMINED.—(*Continued*)

Source	Consultations[a] in			All consultations[a]
	First city	Second city	Third city	
Friends	302	106	183	591
Public records of				
Birth	139	14	..	153
Baptism	36	6	..	42
Death	28	..	..	28
Contagious disease	19	..	..	19
Marriage	143	..	..	143
Divorce or legal separation	16	..	..	16
Property	36	1	4	41
Guardianship	7	..	..	7
Insurance	15	..	..	15
Court	21	1	28	50
Immigration	4	6	..	10
Passport	..	3	..	3
Insanity commitment papers	30	..	..	30
Others[b]	7	1	10	18
Total	501	32	42	575
Church sources				
Clergymen	264	42	39	345
Church visitors or missionaries	20	13	2	35
Fellow church members	76	2	23	101
Sunday school teachers	21	2	1	24
Total	381	59	65	505
Lawyers	76	7	14	97
Benefit societies and other clubs				
Benefit societies	16	4	7	27
Other clubs	3	..	2	5
Total	19	4	9	32
Boarding homes for children	14	13	..	27
Fellow pupils	25	1	..	26
Detectives	16	1	1	18
Foster parents	10	..	..	10
Pawnbrokers	3	..	4	7
Miscellaneous[b]	46	48	88	182
Grand total	7,295	1,956	1,620	10,871

[a] Counting, in any one case, only the first consultation with each source used.

[b] Under the headings "Others" and "Miscellaneous" are grouped (1) sources very infrequently consulted, (2) sources somewhat more frequently consulted but only by a single agency in one city. On the other hand, a few sources very infrequently consulted are specified (see, for example, dentists, midwives, municipal lodging houses, U. S. consuls, passports, employment offices) because they are known to have proved useful in other social agency records not included in this review or are believed to offer possibilities of usefulness.

TABLE B.—SOURCES OF INFORMATION CONSULTED IN THE FIRST

Source	Agencies engaged in work with children									
	Juvenile court	Reform school for girls	S. P. C. C.	State department for the care of children	City department for the care of children	Placing-out agencies			Children's institution	Day nursery
						First agency	Second agency	Third agency		
Relatives	5	26	51	44	68	89	44	48	20	29
Physicians	2	11	22	23	38	33	7	20	16	17
Police	54	41	47	16	25	14	2	20	3	7
Hospitals	2	1	6	13	31	7	5	9	5	8
Former employers	17	16	12	6	11	37	3	24	4	6
Friends	6	12	9	13	19	18	4	13	15	15
Teachers	41	10	15	2	9	17	4	42	5	5
Clergymen	5	6	16	14	31	11	2	15	27	3
Present neighbors	3	5	25	3	15	..	3	27	2	6
Present employers	2	4	6	6	21	5	6	8	4	2
Marriage records	..	3	3	4	40	11	7	2	9	4
Birth records	2	36	8	3	48	8	1	3	5	2
Former neighbors	1	8	12	7	30	1	5	12	..	4
Dispensaries	..	1	..	3	10	2	3	1	..	..
Medical-social work	..	..	1	5	16	..	8	1	1	3
Former landlords	1	3	7	9	13	19	4	7	5	3
Courts	1	40	12	5	17	..	..	9	3	2
Present landlords	2	2	5	3	17	3	1	3	1	1
Nurses	..	..	..	3	22	..	2	3	2	6
Health departments	..	..	3	..	42	..	..	..	..	1
Lawyers	2	1	6	3	7	3	4	8	3	3
Fellow church members	..	2	2	..	7	1	1	1	8	1
Medical inspectors and nurses	..	..	7	..	11	..	..	..	..	..
Truant officers	1	..	6	..	3	1	..	11	..	..
Records of baptism	..	1	..	1	32	..	..	..	..	..
Prisons or reformatories	..	2	..	4	7	1	..	..	..	..
Property records	..	..	..	..	22	..	..	..	..	..
School visitors	..	..	2	..	2	..	..	1	..	4
Present tradesmen	..	..	1	..	5	1	..	..	..	..
Death records	..	..	2	..	9	6	..	..	..	1
Fellow pupils	..	..	1	..	1	..	..	2	..	..
Social agencies	30	74	83	139	129	115	52	81	60	57
Other sources	3	9	24	9	43	40	19	4	5	2
Total	180	314	394	338	801	443	187	375	203	192

CITY, BY AGENCIES ENGAGED IN SPECIFIED TYPES OF WORK

Agencies engaged in: Family work					Medical-social work			Settlement work[a]		Miscellaneous work				
Public outdoor relief	Private relief society	Relief fund	C. O. S. suburban	C. O. S. city	First department	Second department	Third department	First settlement	Second settlement	Adult probation work	State board of insanity	State commission for the blind	Bureau for the handicapped	All 24 agencies
42	39	44	35	36	11	6	23	5	41	19	18	2	24	769
9	32	14	26	22	72	65	22	22	34	1	21	25	10	564
5	11	..	4	4	2	..	1	5	8	89	..	..	..	358
13	78	2	8	16	16	6	58	12	17	..	22	18	4	357
2	13	16	31	31	8	..	8	14	24	1	..	12	34	330
2	18	38	1	8	3	1	6	17	32	4	8	9	31	302
..	38	2	7	1	4	5	4	15	33	..	..	14	7	280
17	34	15	16	8	5	2	4	6	10	1	..	3	13	264
9	18	2	1	5	2	6	7	14	19	10	..	..	..	182
5	14	..	8	11	3	1	2	1	8	6	..	..	24	147
14	17	1	..	16	..	2	2	..	6	1	..	..	1	143
6	11	..	1	..	1	..	1	1	1	1	..	..	..	139
9	18	..	1	..	..	..	4	..	17	..	..	2	1	132
..	46	1	5	2	3	2	..	18	23	..	..	1	3	124
..	12	9	5	8	..	..	3	10	29	..	..	9	2	122
5	12	3	2	10	..	..	..	1	7	..	..	..	7	118
..	7	..	1	..	2	..	..	..	7	1	..	..	..	107
13	11	4	5	4	3	5	1	2	6	7	1	2	4	106
6	13	..	..	8	2	8	4	3	18	..	..	3	..	103
..	8	..	6	..	2	2	2	..	12	2	..	1	..	81
..	1	2	..	4	2	..	2	1	4	10	2	..	8	76
1	35	6	..	1	1	1	..	..	7	..	..	..	1	76
..	5	2	3	1	3	2	3	18	20	..	..	..	..	75
..	18	..	1	..	..	1	..	..	21	..	..	..	..	63
2	..	..	..	..	..	..	..	..	..	..	..	..	..	36
2	16	..	..	1	..	..	2	..	1	..	..	..	..	36
..	..	1	3	..	1	..	1	..	2	..	2	..	4	36
..	4	..	..	..	..	..	..	1	20	..	..	..	..	34
2	17	..	1	..	..	..	..	2	2	..	..	..	..	31
1	9	..	..	..	..	..	..	..	..	..	..	..	..	28
..	2	..	..	..	..	..	..	..	19	..	..	..	..	25
121	178	38	51	74	35	64	30	27	140	13	5	41	57	1,694
12	30	13	5	9	5	5	3	7	33	19	42	3	13	357
298	765	213	227	280	186	184	193	202	621	185	121	145	248	7,295

[a] Special work chiefly for children in co-operation with the schools, juvenile court, etc.

APPENDIX III

SPECIMEN VARIABLE SPELLINGS[1]

RECORDED IN THE SOCIAL SERVICE EXCHANGE, NEW YORK. (SEE REFERENCE TO THEIR USE ON P. 270 SQ.)

Abbott
Abad
Abbette
Abbot
Abbotte

Adams
Aadam
Adam
Addams
McAdam
McAdams

Aiello
Aeillo
Aello
Ahello
Aillo
Ailo
Aiola
Aiullo
Ajello
D'Aiello

Allen
Alan
Allan
Allyn

Anderson
Andersen
Andresen
Andreson

Bailey
Bailie
Bailly
Baillie
Baily
Baley
Bayley
Baylie

Bain
Baine
Bane
Bayen
Bayne
Bean
Beane

Baldwin
Baldwyn
Balwin
Boldwin

Barber
Barbour

Barry
Barrie
Bary
Berry
De Barry

Bauer
Baier
Bauers
Baur
Bour
Bower
Bowers

Berger
Barger
Bergher
Bergor
Borger
Burger

Bisella
See also *Pisella, Basile, Bushell, Buccolo*
Barsila
Basila
Basili
Basilia

[1] It should be understood that the exchange in any city, however small, would include (1) a vastly greater number of real names than are given here, and (2) a very large number of misspellings (among foreign names especially) due to unfamiliarity with the clients' language on the part of the social workers, clerks, or others, who interview and enquire about them. Those responsible for developing an exchange will find that an important part of their work is the recording of such misspellings, since it is never safe to assume that any variation from the real spelling, however wild, may not be repeated.

Bisella (Continued)
Basilio
Basilla
Basilo
Basola
Bassalla
Bassili
Bassilla
Bassilo
Basulli
Bazalo
Becella
Besola
Biasillo
Biasoli
Biselli
Bissella
Bissellee
Bissilo
Bocelli
Borsella
Bozella
Bozzelli
Bozzola
Bucella

Borofsky
Barofsky
Barowsky
Berofesky
Borodowsky
Boroski
Borosky
Borovsky
Borowsky
Borufsky

Boyle
Boile
Boyles
O'Boil
O'Boyle

Brown
Braun
Broun
Browne
Browns

Bryan
Brian
Brion
Bryans
Bryant
Bryne
Bryon

Burke
Berke
Birke
Burkes

Burns
Beirne
Bern
Berns
Biern
Birne
Burn
Burnes
Byrne
Byrnes
Byrns

Callahan
Calahan
Calihan
Calligan
Callihan
Collihan

Carl
Carle
Carll
Carls
Karl
Karle

Cavanagh
Cavanaugh
Kavanagh
Kavanaugh

Cohen
Cohan
Cohn
Kohan
Kohen
Kohn

Connell
O'Connell

Connelly
Conley
Connolly
O'Connelly

Connor
Conner
Conners
Connors
O'Connor
O'Connors

Cook
Cooke
Koch
Kuch

Cramer
Kramer

Daly
Dailey
Daily
Daley

Davidson
Davidsen
Davieson
Davison

Davis
Davies

Dixon
Dickenson
Dickerson
Dickinson
Dickson
Dixson

Dombrofsky
Dambrosky
Dandrosky
Dembofsky
Dombofsky
Dombrodsky
Dombroski

Donegan
Doneghan
Donigan
Donnegan
Donnigan
Donogan
Dunigan
Dunnigan

Donohue
Donaghue
Donahue
Donnahue
Donoghue
O'Donahue

Donnelly
Donelly
Donley
Donnally
Donnely
Donnolly

Dougherty
Daugherty
Docherty
Doherty
Dorrity

Duffy
Duffee
Duffey
Duffie

Eckardt
Echardt
Eckert
Eckhart
Ehhardt

Evans
Evan
Evens
Evins
Ivans

Fisher
Fischer

Fitzsimmons
Fitzimmons
Fitzimons
Fitzsimons

Flannigan
Flanagan
Flanigan
Flannagan
Flannegan
O'Flanagan

Flynn
Flinn

Fox
Fuchs

Frank
Franc
Franck
Francke
Franke
Franks

Fraser
Fraiser
Frasier
Frazer
Frazier
Freizer

Gablinsky
Gabelisky
Gablonsky
Gabolensky
Galinsky
Galiski
Galitzky
Galizky
Gallinski
Gapalinsky
Gobilinski
Goliensky
Golinsky
Golitzky
Kabalinsky
Kalensky
Kalinsky
Kaliski
Kalisky
Kelinski
Koblinsky
Kolinski
Kolinsky
Kolisky

Gardner
Gardener
Gardiner
Gartner
Gertner

Gerrity
Garaty
Garety
Garity
Garrety
Garrity
Gearity
Geraghty
Gereghty
Gerraghty
Gerraty
Gerrighty

Giorlando
Gerlando
Giolando

Gordon
Gordan
Gorden
Gorton

Gould
Gold
Golde
Goldt
Goold

Gray
Graye
Grey

Green
Greene
Grun
Grunn

Griffin
Greffin
Griffen
Griffins

Guarantano
Garantano
Garatano
Garetano
Garetona
Garratano

Guarnera
Guamero
Guaneri
Guarmieri
Guarnaro
Guarneri

Haggerty
Hagarty
Hagerty
Haggarty
Hegarty
Heggerty
Hogarty

Hart
Hardt
Harte
Hartt
Hartz
Harz
Heart
Herz
Hertz

Hayes
Hay
Haye
Hays

Healy
Healey
Heally

Hines
Heins
Heinse
Heinz
Heinze
Hynes

Hoffman
Haufman
Hoffmann
Hofmann
Huffman

Hogopian
Agopian
Der Hagopian
Hagasian
Hagopian
Hagopin
Hajopian
Hayopian
Hoogosian

Hughes
Hewes
Hughs
Huse

Irvin
Ervin
Ervine
Erving
Irvine
Irving
Irwin

Johnson
Jansen
Janson
Jensen
Johansen
Johnston
Johnstone

Jordan
Jordain
Jorden
Jordon

Kane
Cain
Caine
Cane
Canes
Kain
Kaine
Kanes

Kearney
Carney
Karney
Kearny

Kearns
Kearn
Kearnes
Keirns
Kern
Kernes
Kerns
Kierns
Kirn
Kurns

Kelly
Kelley

Kenny
Kenney
Kinney
McKenney
McKinney

Klein
Cline
Clines
Clyne
Clynes
Klien
Kline

Kruger
Cruger
Krager
Kreiger
Kreuger
Krugar
Krugor

Kurz
Kertz
Kirtz
Kortz
Kurtz

Lane
Laine
Lanes
Layne
Lehn

Laughlin
Loughlin
O'Laughlin

Lawlor
Laulor
Lawlar
Lawler

Lawrence
Laurance
Laurence
Laurens
Laurents
Lorence
Lorens
Lorentz
Lorenz

Lee
Lea
Leigh

Lenahan
Lanahan
Lenehan
Lenihan
Linahan
Linehan

Leonard
Leighnard
Lenart
Lenhart
Leonhard
Leonhardt
Lienhart
Linhard
Linhardt
Linhart

Levy
Leavey
Leavy
Levey
Levi

Lewis
Louis
Luis

Lowery
Laurie
Lawery
Loughry
Lowerie
Lowrie
Lowry

Lynn
Lenne
Linn
Linne

McCarthy
MacCarthy
McCarthey
McCartey
McCartie
McCarty

McCormick
MacCormick
McCormack
McCormic

McCue
MacCue
McHugh

McDonald
MacDonald
McDonell
McDonnell
McDonnold

McEvoy
McAvoy
McVoy

McGuire
MacGuire
Maguire

McKay
Mackay
Mackey
Mackie
McCay
McKee
McKey

McKeon
McKean
McKeen
McKeown

Madison
See also *Matthewson*
Maddison
Madsen
Matheson
Matison
Matsen
Matsin
Matson
Mattison
Mattson

Maher
See also *Meyer*
Mahar
Mahr
Marr
Meagher

Mahoney
Mahony
Mohoney
Mohony
O'Mahoney

Malloy
Melloy
Molloy

Maloney
Malaney
Malony
Malloney
Moloney
Mulaney
Mullaney

Meehan
Mahon
Meehen
Mehan

Meyer
See also *Maher*
Maier
Mayer
Mayers
Meier
Meyers
Mier
Miers
Myer
Myers

Michael
Mical
Michaels
Michel
Michels
Mickel

Miller
Meuller
Millar
Mollar
Moller
Moeller
Mueller
Muller

Monahan
Mannehan
Monehan
Monohan
Moynihan

Morrisey
Morissey
Morrissey
Morrisy

Mullen
Millin
Mullane
Mullens
Mullien
Mullin
Mullins

Nelson
Neilson
Nielsen
Nielson
Nilson
Nilsson

Newman
Neuman
Neumann
Numan

Notafrancisco
See also *Francesco*
Notafrancesca
Notarfrancesco
Notrefrancesco

O'Brien
O'Brian
O'Bryan
O'Bryen

Olsen
Ohlson
Oleson
Olson
Olssen

O'Neil
O'Neal
O'Neill
O'Niel
O'Niell

Owens
Owen

Patterson
Paterson
Pattison

Payne
Pain
Paine
Pane
Penn

Petrasek
Petracek
Petresek
Pietraseck
Potucek
Potuchek
Ptracek

Pollock
See also *Bullock*
Palak
Palleck
Pallick
Pallock
Pallok
Paluch
Paluck
Parlik
Paulick
Paulik
Pavelec
Pavlick
Pavlik
Pawlek
Pawlyk
Peleck
Polach
Polack
Polak
Polich
Pollack
Pollak
Polloch
Pollok
Polock
Polyak
Povlek
Pulec

Quinn
Quann
Queen
Quin
Quinne

Reagan
O'Regan
Reegan
Regan

Reed
Read
Reade
Reeds
Reid
Wrede

Reilly
O'Reilley
O'Reilly
Reilley
Reily
Rielly
Riley

Robinson
Roberson
Robertson
Robeson
Robison
Robson

Rogers
Rodger
Rodgers

Schaefer
Schaeffer
Schafer
Schaffer
Scheaffer
Schiefer
Schiffer
Shaefer
Shaffer

Schneider
Schnider
Schnyder
Sneider
Snyder

Shea
Schey
Shay
Sheay

Smith
Schmidt
Schmitt
Schmitz
Smyth

Sprovieri
Sprofera
Sprovira
Sproviro
Sprufera

Stevens
Stefan
Steffens
Stephan
Stephen
Stephens

Stewart
Stuart

Thompson
Thomsen
Thomson

Tierney
Tarney
Tearney
Teirney
Terney
Tirney

Trainor
Traynor
Treanor

Ulrich
Uhlrich
Uhrich
Ulrick

Vano
Vaina
Vanna
Vanni
Vanyi
Vena
Viamio
Viana
Viane
Viani
Viania
Viano
Vierno

Vaughan
Vaughn

Vogel
Fogel
Van Vogel
Vogele
Vogle

Walsh
Walsch
Welch
Welsch
Welsh

Webber
Weber
Weiber

Wilson
Willison
Willson
Wilsen

Wolf
Wolfe
Wolff
Woolf
Wulff

Worth
Werth
Wierth
Wirth
Wuerth

Wishnofsky
Wasnicky
Wasnisky
Wischnefsky
Wischnewsky
Wishnefsky
Wishnewsky
Wishnosky
Wisneskey
Wisnewska
Wisnowski
Wiszhnefsky

Wynn
Whyne
Winn
Wynne

Young
Younge
Youngs
Yung

Zack
Zach
Zacks
Zaich
Zak
Zeak
Zsak

Ziegler
Seigler
Siegler
Zeigler
Ziegeler
Zigler

BIBLIOGRAPHY

BIBLIOGRAPHY

I. SOURCES

As explained in the Preface (p. 7), there have been two main sources of this study: First, a large number of social case histories have been examined. Second, individual case workers in different social agencies and different cities have been interviewed.

II. REFERENCES

There is no bibliography of the subject of investigation. The following titles are selected from the references made throughout this book, as being the ones most closely related to its theme:

Balch, Emily Greene (Associate Professor of Economics in Wellesley College). Our Slavic Fellow Citizens. 536 p. New York, Charities Publication Committee, 1910.

Baldwin, James Mark, Ph.D., D. Sc. Oxon., LL.D. Glasgow (Professor in Princeton University, Co-editor of *The Psychological Review*). Social and Ethical Interpretations in Mental Development; a study in social psychology. 606 p. New York, The Macmillan Company, 1902.

Baldwin, Roger N., joint author, see Flexner, Bernard, and Baldwin, R. N.

Birtwell, Mary L. Investigation. Pamphlet published by the Boston Associated Charities (No. 61), 1895.

Bosanquet, Helen. The Family. 344 p. London, Macmillan and Company 1906.

Bosanquet, Helen. The Standard of Life and Other Studies. 219 p. London, Macmillan and Company, 1898.

Branthwaite, R. W. Report of the Inspector under the Inebriates Acts, 1879–1900, for the Year 1909. Introduction, Habitual Drunkenness and its Treatment, p. 4–10. London, The Home Office, 1911.

Byington, Margaret F. The Confidential Exchange; a form of social co-operation. 30 p. New York, Charity Organization Department Publication (No. 28), Russell Sage Foundation, 1912.

Cabot, Richard C., M.D. Case Teaching in Medicine. 214 p. Boston, D. C. Heath and Company, 1906.

Cabot, Richard C., M.D. Differential Diagnosis; presented through an analysis of 383 cases. 753 p. Philadelphia, W. B. Saunders Company, 1911.

Cabot, Richard C., M.D. Report of the Chairman of the Committee on Health. In Proceedings of the National Conference of Charities and Correction for 1915 (Baltimore), p. 224.

Cannon, Ida M., R.N. Social Work in Hospitals; a contribution to progressive medicine. 257 p. New York, Russell Sage Foundation Publication, Survey Associates, 1913.

Chalmers, Thomas. Chalmers on Charity; a selection of passages and scenes to illustrate the social teaching and practical work of Thomas Chalmers, D.D., arranged and edited by N. Masterman, M.A. 414 p. Westminster, Archibald Constable and Company, 1900.

Charity Organization Society, London. Occasional Papers of the, 1896. "How to Take Down a Case," by W. G. Martley, p. 209–220.

Dubois, Paul, M.D. (Professor of Neuropathology in the University of Berne). The Psychic Treatment of Nervous Disorders (The Psychoneuroses and their Moral Treatment). 466 p. Translated and edited by S. E. Jelliffe, M.D., Ph.D., and W. A. White, M.D. New York, Funk and Wagnalls Company, 1907.

Flexner, Bernard, and Baldwin, Roger N. Juvenile Courts and Probation. 308 p. New York, The Century Company, 1914.

Greenleaf, Simon, LL.D. Treatise on the Law of Evidence. Sixteenth edition, revised, enlarged, and annotated by John Henry Wigmore, Professor of the Law of Evidence in the Law School of Northwestern University. 993 p. Boston, Little. Brown, and Company, 1899.

Gross, Hans, J.U.D. (Professor of Criminal Law in the University of Graz, Austria. Formerly Magistrate of the Criminal Court of Czernovitz, Austria). Criminal Psychology; a manual for judges, practitioners, and students. Translated from the fourth German edition by Horace M. Kallen, Ph.D. 514 p. Boston, Little, Brown, and Company, 1911.

Healy, Mary Tenney, B.L., joint author, see Healy, William, and Healy, M. T.

Healy, William, M.D. Honesty; a study of the causes and treatment of dishonesty among children. 220 p. Indianapolis, The Bobbs-Merrill Company, 1915

Healy, William, M.D. The Individual Delinquent; a text-book of diagnosis and prognosis for all concerned in understanding offenders. 830 p. Boston, Little, Brown, and Company, 1915.

Healy, William, M.D., and Healy, Mary Tenney, B.L. Pathological Lying, Accusation, and Swindling; a study in forensic psychology. 286 p. Boston, Little, Brown, and Company, 1915.

Hill, Octavia. Life of Octavia Hill; as told in her letters. Edited by C. Edmund Maurice. 591 p. London, Macmillan and Company, 1913.

Langlois, Charles V., and Seignobos, Charles (of the Sorbonne). Introduction to the Study of History. Translated by G. G. Berry. 349 p. London, Duckworth and Company, 1898.

Lattimore, Florence L. "Pittsburgh as a Foster Mother." In The Pittsburgh District, Civic Frontage, p. 337–449. New York, Russell Sage Foundation Publication, Survey Associates, 1914.

Lawton, Ruth W., and Murphy, J. Prentice. "A Study of Results of a Child-placing Society." In Proceedings of the National Conference of Charities and Correction for 1915 (Baltimore), p. 164–174.

Lee, Porter R. "The Culture of Family Life." In Proceedings of the National Conference of Charities and Correction for 1914 (Memphis), p. 92–98.

Martley, W. G., see Charity Organization Society, London.

Masterman, N., M.A., see Chalmers, Thomas.

Maurice, C. E., see Hill, Octavia.

McLean, Francis H. The Charities of Springfield, Illinois; a survey under the direction of the American Association of Societies for Organizing Charity. 185 p. The Springfield Survey, Charities Section. New York, Department of Surveys and Exhibits, Russell Sage Foundation, December, 1915.

Meltzer, S. J., M.D., LL.D. "Ideas and Ideals in Medicine." *Journal of the American Medical Association,* L: 1577–83, May 16, 1908.

Meyer, Adolf, M.D. "What Do Histories of Cases of Insanity Teach Us concerning Preventive Mental Hygiene during the Years of School Life?" *The Psychological Clinic,* II: 89–101, June 15, 1908.

Mitchell, S. Weir, M.D., LL.D. Doctor and Patient. Third edition, 177 p. Philadelphia, J. B. Lippincott Company, 1898.

Murphy, J. Prentice, joint author, see Lawton, Ruth W., and Murphy, J. P.

Putnam, James Jackson, M.D. "The Treatment of Psychasthenia from the Standpoint of the Social Consciousness." *American Journal of the Medical Sciences,* CXXX: 77–94, January, 1908.

Sears, Amelia. The Charity Visitor; a handbook for beginners. 76 p. Department of Social Investigation, Chicago School of Civics and Philanthropy, 1913.

Seignobos, Charles (of the Sorbonne), joint author, see Langlois, Charles V., and Seignobos, C.

Sidgwick, Alfred. The Application of Logic. 321 p. London, Macmillan and Company, 1910.

Solenberger, Alice Willard. One Thousand Homeless Men; a study of original records. 374 p. New York, Russell Sage Foundation Publication, Charities Publication Committee, 1911.

Summary of State Laws relating to the Dependent Classes. 1913. Department of Commerce, Bureau of the Census, Washington, Government Printing Office, 1914.

Thayer, James Bradley, LL.D. (Weld Professor of Law in Harvard University). A Preliminary Treatise on Evidence at the Common Law. 636 p. Boston, Little, Brown, and Company, 1898.

Thorndike, Edward L. Individuality. 55 p. Boston, Houghton, Mifflin, and Company, 1911.

Turner, C. J. Ribton-. Suggestions for Systematic Inquiry into the Cases of Applicants for Relief. 120 p. London, Knight and Company, 1872.

Wigmore, John Henry (Professor of the Law of Evidence in Northwestern University). The Principles of Judicial Proof as Given by Logic, Psychology, and General Experience, and Illustrated by Judicial Trials. 1179 p. Boston, Little, Brown, and Company, 1913.

INDEX

INDEX

INDEX

INDEX

INDEX

INDEX

INDEX

INDEX

INDEX

INDEX

INDEX